19.35

THE JEWS OF TORONTO

STEPHEN A. SPEISMAN

THE JEWS OF TORONTO

A History to 1937

McClelland and Stewart

Copyright © 1979 Stephen A. Speisman

ISBN: 0-7710-8217-7

McClelland and Stewart Limited
The Canadian Publishers
25 Hollinger Road
Toronto, Ontario
M4B 3G2

Printed and bound in Canada

This book has been published with the help
of a grant from the Social Science Federation
of Canada, using funds provided by the
Social Sciences and Humanities Research
Council of Canada.

Canadian Cataloguing in Publication Data

Speisman, Stephen A., 1943-
  The Jews of Toronto

Bibliography: p.
Includes index.

ISBN 0-7710-8217-7

1. Jews in Toronto, Ont.—History. I. Title.

FC3097.9.J5S64   971.3'541'004924   C79-094047-7
F1059.5.T689J58

CONTENTS

לזכור אבי מורי
ר׳ טוביה ב״ר אברהם שלמה ע״ה

A MEMORIAL FOR MY FATHER
TOMMY SPEISMAN
WHO LOVED HISTORY

PREFACE

This is the story of Toronto Jewry's first century. Its principal theme is the adjustment of the Jew to a new land and his effort to build a community which would serve his needs and in which he might feel comfortable. It represents perhaps the first attempt of this scope at analysing an urban Jewish community in Canada.

In examining the evolution of local Jewish institutions, I sought to answer a number of perplexing questions. How, for example, did a community develop in a city often the immigrant's second choice for settlement? How did Toronto Jews fashion a relatively unified communal structure despite their heterogeneity? To what extent was this development influenced by local events or external factors?

Some aspects of community life have been treated in detail; others, such as social mobility, the entry of Jews into the professions, and the development of the Jewish labour movement, had, because of limitations of space, to be considered only incidentally as they bear directly on the major theme. Like Samuel Johnson, I ask that "when it shall be found that much is omitted, let it not be forgotten that much is likewise performed."

One of the major obstacles I encountered was the absence of a comprehensive body of documentary evidence. Some organizations kept no records; others were careless with them, leaving long-time secretaries to take minute books home, where heirs often discarded them; still others simply allowed them to be lost in the course of relocation. The movement of the Jews to the northern part in the city in recent decades aggravated this problem.

Moreover, the very nature of the local Jewish community precluded, to a degree, that historical awareness which existed in many American cities and which might have generated an interest in the preservation of material. Toronto had no long-established Sephardic community, nor did large numbers of German Jews settle here in the mid-19th century. These groups elsewhere had the leisure to produce diaries and the self-esteem to undertake at least genealogical and filiopietistic works. Toronto was basically a working-class community, too preoccupied with earning a living to be concerned with the recent past and perhaps preferring to consign those difficult times to oblivion. Even Holy Blossom's membership was not wealthy compared to its American counterparts and seemed to have little historical interest. Only in 1973, with the establishment of the Canadian Jewish Congress Central Region Archives, was systematic collection of Jewish archival material in this city begun in earnest.

These circumstances necessitated the use of considerable oral material, representing a broad spectrum of the community. I was, however, cognizant of its limitations. Whenever possible, I used documents and unrelated interviews for corroboration, or employed the interviews themselves merely to substantiate or amplify documentary evidence. In every case, I attempted to achieve maximum accuracy by using widely accepted oral history control techniques. Especially valuable in this regard were Gould P. Coleman (ed.) "Interdisciplinary Views on Oral History" in Coleman (ed.) *The Third International Colloquium on Oral History* (New York: Oral History Association, 1968); Gould P. Coleman, Amelia Fry and Albert Lyons, "The Art of Interviewing," *ibid.*; and Donald J. Schippers "The Literature of Oral History" in Louis M. Starr (ed.) *The Second National Colloquium on Oral History 1967* (New York: Oral History Association, 1968).

My work would have been considerably more difficult had it not been for the assistance of the staff at the Baldwin Room of the Metropolitan Toronto Central Library (Edith Firth); the City of Toronto Archives (Scott James, Glenna Tisshaw); the Public Archives of Canada (Walter Neutel); the Jewish Public Library, Montreal (Evelyn Miller); the Canadian Jewish Congress Archives, Montreal (David Rome); the National Library of Canada; the University of Toronto Library; the United Church Archives; the American Jewish Historical Society; and the American Jewish Archives. To them I am truly thankful.

A list of the individuals to whom I have incurred a debt of gratitude in the course of preparing this study would fill a volume. Nevertheless, a few merit special acknowledgment. Julius Hayman unwittingly sparked my interest in local Jewish history almost twenty years ago, and I welcome the opportunity of thanking him now. Dr. David Eisen, dean of the historians of Jewish Toronto, nurtured my enthusiasm, sharing with me his intimate knowledge of its earliest years and making available to me the records of Holy Blossom. I am grateful to Professor Gerald Craig, under whom I was privileged to study at the University of Toronto and from whose patient and meticulous scholarship I was able to benefit and take example; to my colleagues at Canadian Jewish Congress, Ben Kayfetz and Nachman Shemen, who often served as my sounding boards and saved me from many errors; to Ben Libman, whose modesty precludes my detailing the help he provided me in a difficult time; to Archie and Sophie Bennett, for opening their personal library to me; to Victor Sefton, for his many acts of encouragement; to Susan Cohen, Bess Shockett, and Cyrel Troster, who permitted me to listen to the interviews they collected during their Jewish Oral History Project in 1973; to all those institutions and individuals who shared their documents and their memories with me, but especially to Ida Siegel, whose contribution to the development of this community the reader will soon discover and whose friendship I consider the most treasured product of my research.

I owe thanks also to the Canada Council and the Canadian Foundation for Jewish Culture, whose financial assistance enabled me to devote additional time to research; to Professor John S. Moir, who helped direct my work to publication; to Diane Mew, who edited the manuscript with rare skill and sensitivity and whose determination and unfailing good judgement are in large measure responsible for its realization; and to Linda McKnight and the staff of McClelland and Stewart, who guided the book to its final form.

I leave the greatest debt to last. My accomplishment is also my family's: my parents and my sister, whose sacrifices during my student days were innumerable, and my wife Leila, who not only helped polish the final work and prepared the index, but also suffered with me and was my constant source of strength in its writing, typing the original drafts, sharing my sleepless nights, listening to my chapter revisions beyond the point of endurance, yet always ready with the right turn of phrase for the text and word of encouragement for me. My gratitude is boundless.

S.A.S.
Toronto

3 Kislev 5739
December 3, 1978.

PART I

THE
OLD
COMMUNITY

CHAPTER 1

SHALLOW ROOTS:
THE EARLIEST SETTLERS

It would be gratifying indeed to be able to maintain that the
founders of the Jewish community of Toronto had arrived in
North America on the *Mayflower* or had been among the heroes
of the Loyalist migration. But although many American Jews took
the side of the crown in the Revolutionary conflict, and scattered
bits of information would seem to indicate that one or two such
families settled for a time in what was to become Upper Canada,
there is no conclusive evidence that any ever found their way to
York. If they did, their presence remains unrecorded.

The earliest documentary suggestion of Jewish settlement at
York is an 1817 communication from D'Arcy Boulton, Attorney
General of Upper Canada, to the Colonial Office in London.
Responding to an inquiry regarding the celebration of marriages
in the province, Boulton lists those residents whose marriages
were permitted to be performed according to British rather than
colonial law, and he includes Quakers and Jews among these
categories.[1] Unfortunately, the letter gives no detail which would
indicate whether actual cases had arisen or whether the Attorney
General was merely speculating.

The privilege, therefore, of being the first Jew whose presence
can be irrefutably established falls on the rather ignominious
personage of Emanuel Judah, an American actor who appeared at
least for one evening in October 1826 to perform Shakespeare in
York's only theatre, the ballroom of Frank's Hotel on Colborne
Street.[2]

Continuous Jewish settlement did not begin, however, until
1832, with the arrival of Arthur Wellington Hart. A grandson of
Aaron Hart of Three Rivers, and thus a scion of one of the oldest
Jewish families in British North America, Hart had probably come
to establish a branch of his father's Montreal wholesale mercantile
house, because York, with a population of about nine thousand

by that year, was no longer a frontier village. He also became agent for the Eagle Life Assurance Company of London. Hart obviously possessed some capital when he arrived, for he immediately occupied a two-storey merchant shop on King Street, then the principal commercial thoroughfare of the town.[3]

Unlike the majority of Toronto's early Jewish settlers, who were Europeans, Hart was born in Montreal. However, he was characteristic of at least the pre-1880 phase of Jewish settlement in that he had come via the United States and remained only a few years. In 1836, perhaps dislodged by the political disturbances of the period and certainly by the financial panic, Hart left Toronto, finding his way first to England, then to Scranton, Pennsylvania, where he became a newspaper editor and clerk for the Internal Revenue Service during the Civil War, and finally to Montreal where he died in 1894.[4]

It is impossible to determine the exact number of Jews who followed Hart to Toronto in the 1830s. Several surnames often held by English and German Jews – Joseph and Myers for instance – appear in the directories of the period, but their origins are obscure. Of the religion of a few others, however, there can be little doubt, although information even about these is inconclusive. Two brothers, Goodman and Samuel Benjamin, arrived from Montreal about 1835 and set up a wholesale dry-goods establishment on King Street. Two others, the Levies, whose origin is unknown, sold cloth and suits in Market Square about the same period. But whereas the Levies apparently did not do well and dissolved their business in 1840, the Benjamins seem to have enjoyed the confidence of government officials and certainly had good business connections outside the city, since they were contracted to supply the local troops with greatcoats during the rebellions of 1837-38. These they imported from Montreal by sleigh. The Benjamins, however, did not remain in York either, despite this relative windfall of patronage. Samuel left late in the 1830s and Goodman followed in 1835.[5]

These earliest Jewish inhabitants provided little basis for the founding of a permanent community. However, the late 1830s and the 1840s brought a new type of Jewish settler, one more consciously Jewish, prepared to strike roots in the growing metropolis and provide a foundation upon which a later Jewish community could build.

The first of these was Judah George Joseph. A native of Exeter, England, Joseph was already forty years old when he appeared in Toronto in 1838. Admittedly rather old to be starting afresh in a new city, Joseph was a man of wide experience and pioneering spirit. Much of his early life had been spent in the Channel Islands; he had emigrated to the United States in 1820 and set himself up as a jeweller and optician in Cincinnati. In the 1830s, having apparently been swindled in some business transaction, he removed to Hamilton, Upper Canada, and with his family eventually found his way to Toronto.[6] He was accompanied, or followed shortly afterward, by Henry A. Joseph, possibly a distant relative, a fur trader from Sorel, Quebec, who promptly opened a retail fur shop on Yonge Street, married out of the faith and thereafter had nothing to do with the local Jews.[7]

About four years later, the minute community was reinforced by two arrivals from England, Alfred Braham and Samuel Caspar, a clothier and a jeweller, respectively. Both were in their mid-twenties and both, like Judah Joseph, set up shop in prime commercial territory on King Street.

Beginning early in the 1840s, these were followed by a German element, somewhat predictably, since even before the failure of the liberal revolutions of 1848 forced large numbers of central Europeans to emigrate, conditions for Jews had been deteriorating rapidly. German Jews of the period were primarily artisans and petty tradesmen, and increasingly in those decades in their own countries they were forced to pay special taxes and to labour under discriminatory restrictions which ruined many economically.[8]

Most German Jewish emigrants of this period chose the United States, especially New York and Ohio. Although some came to Montreal, and in the 1850s to Fort Victoria on Vancouver Island and to Hamilton in Canada West, Toronto would never have the large influential German-Jewish population characteristic of many cities in the United States. However, in the 1840s, the arrival of only a few was significant.

Marcus and Samuel Rossin, who arrived in 1842, dealt in watches, jewellery and fancy goods,[9] and were soon perceptive enough to realize that a major lack in the city was good hotel accommodation. Consequently, in 1857, they opened the sumptuous Rossin House at the corner of King and York streets, erected at a cost of $55,000. With over two hundred rooms, it was the largest hotel in the city and compared favourably with establishments in New York. The prospectus for the 1858 Provincial Exhibition described the hostelry as being "among the chief architectural ornaments of the city," accommodating its guests "in the most perfect style of modern hotel-keeping."

13

Another contemporary observer commented enthusiastically that:

> Within its walls is congregated every appliance which affluence can desire, every pleasure which luxury can crave. Here are alluring condiments to tempt the most fastidious taste, vinous acidities to lubricate, and gastronomic ponderosities to tintillate [sic]the palate! The prandial morceau here ceases from troubling and the sated stomach is at rest. What magical transformations here await human deglutition.[10]

So excellent was the reputation of the Rossin House that the Prince of Wales (later King Edward VII) stayed there when he visited Toronto in 1860. Moreover, General Stisted lived in the hotel for a year while he was acting Lieutenant-Governor.

A catastrophic fire destroyed the Rossin House in November 1862, and since there was insufficient insurance to cover the loss, the Rossins were ruined. Yet the hotel was considered so important to the city that a public meeting was held following the fire "to express sympathy with Messrs. Rossin, and to consider the best means to be taken to rebuild the hotel."[11]

The Rossins attempted unsuccessfully to continue their jewellery business and also to operate a wholesale tobacco firm. Samuel left for the United States the year after the fire, while Marcus, probably waiting until his son Julius completed his course at University College, returned to Germany in 1864.[12]

Abraham and Samuel Nordheimer had emigrated to New York from Bavaria in 1839. Abraham, the eldest at twenty-three became a popular pianist and piano-maker. In New York, he was noticed by a friend of Sir Charles Bagot, then Governor General of British North America, who was looking for a music teacher for his daughter. Nordheimer accepted the offered position and moved to Kingston, only to be left jobless by the Governor's death in 1843. Probably having decided to devote himself to the manufacture and sale of pianos, and seeing the commercial opportunities offered by Toronto, Abraham Nordheimer joined his co-religionists on King Street in 1844. But while Abraham was to be active in Jewish communal life before his return to Germany shortly after 1860, Samuel, who had accompanied his brother and had become a partner in the firm, became a member of the Church of England when he married Edith Boulton in 1874. His marriage placed him among the elite of Toronto's Christian establishment and although he associated little with Jews in his lifetime, he did

14

leave a nominal sum to the benevolent society of the Toronto Hebrew Congregation when he died in 1912.[13]

Aside from the Rossins and the Nordheimers, the only other identified German-Jewish Toronto resident in the 1840s was Jacob Maier Hirschfelder, tutor in Hebrew at King's College. Hirschfelder's name leaves little doubt as to his religious background, and yet prior to the secularization of King's College in 1850 only professing Christians could teach there. Hirschfelder died an Anglican (he is buried in St. James' Cemetery) but whether he converted upon his appointment in 1844, or whether he left Judaism while still in Germany remains a mystery. In any case, he was highly respected in his position, which he held until his retirement in 1888, and he moved socially in the upper stratum of Toronto Christian society.[14]

The remainder of the arrivals during the forties were chiefly Englishmen, although these tended to have spent some time in the United States. Charles Kahn, a dentist, and Morris and Isaac Lumley, clothiers, are three who can be noted with certainty.[15]

A census in 1846 recorded twelve Jews in Toronto; two years later it was estimated that the community numbered twenty-seven.[16] Both these figures are probably underestimates resulting from the failure to include all of the wives and children, and from the omission of those who did not state their religion.[17] But if their number cannot be confirmed with certainty, at least several assumptions about them can be made. First, it will be noticed that, unlike many other immigrant groups, the Jews who arrived in Toronto at mid-century (and indeed during the entire period prior to the 1880s), emigrated as family groups rather than as individuals. This would not be true of many of the East Europeans who would arrive in the last decades of the century, although even among these the ratio of men to women would never be as great as among other immigrant elements.

Secondly, most early Jewish arrivals in Toronto were merchants rather than artisans, as their Russian successors would be. Moreover, they apparently came with some capital, for without the assistance of Jews already here, they occupied business quarters in prestigious commercial areas. That they often lived above or behind their places of business does not indicate relative poverty as it might in the twentieth century. These early Jews, at least the ones who remained in Toronto long enough to be recorded, seem to have done well. Henry Joseph, Abraham Nordheimer, Alfred Braham and the Rossins owned property in the city, often within a decade of their arrival. The latter even held lots for speculation.[18]

15

A third factor which should be noted is that these Jews were by no means treated like pariahs. The majority were British and were accepted as Englishmen. Judah Joseph, a strictly orthodox individual who closed his shop on the Sabbath, likely at significant financial sacrifice since Saturday was a popular shopping day in Toronto, was given a glowing obituary when he died in 1857 and was described as having been "highly respectably connected."[19] Morris Lumley must have been in the good graces of the municipal authorities, since a street was named for him in a new subdivision west of the city.[20]

As for the German-Jewish element, the Rossins' position as the principal innkeepers of the city brought them into contact with influential non-Jews, whereas the Nordheimers possibly had entry into the Tory establishment from their relationship with Bagot. Even before this relationship was cemented by Samuel's marriage (an event in itself indicative of the Nordheimers' acceptability in Toronto society), the brothers appear to have had wide connections with non-Jews. Both belonged to the Toronto Philharmonic Society and the local Masonic lodge, while in 1855 Abraham was one of the four directors of the Canada Permanent Building and Savings Society.

In the late 1840s, Judah Joseph, by virtue of his age and religious convictions, and Abraham Nordheimer, because of his social connections, were the natural leaders of the embryonic community. It was they who took the initiative toward Jewish communal organization by purchasing land for a cemetery in September 1849. The reason for the purchase at this particular date is unclear, since it had long been legal for dissenters to appoint trustees for this purpose.[21] Perhaps earlier there had been too few to support the venture; yet even in 1849 the total Jewish population numbered just thirty-five, and most of these were young people. Furthermore, one can infer that since no burials took place immediately, the sudden death of an individual by accident or disease did not prompt the purchase. The local Jews may merely have been prudent, since the nearest Jewish cemetery was in Buffalo, a day's journey away.

It is probable that Judah Joseph initiated the purchase of the land. Since his young son was one of the first to be buried there, albeit a good year after the purchase, it is plausible to believe that the child was terminally ill and that his father was preparing for the worst. For an orthodox Jew to set up a private burial ground when there were other Jews in his locality and no other Jewish cemetery would have been contrary to Jewish tradition. It is also possible that Joseph did not have sufficient capital himself; the assessment rolls indicate that all his property in Toronto was rented rather than owned. These factors likely determined Nordheimer's participation in the transaction. In any event, Joseph and Nordheimer purchased half an acre on the outskirts of the village of Leslieville, just east of Toronto. Located on Centre Road (now Pape Avenue), the lot was acquired from John Beverley Robinson, Chief Justice of the province, Nordheimer's Tory contacts probably having been in some measure responsible for this connection.

The deed specified that the land was to be held in trust for "the Hebrew Congregation of the...City of Toronto." The fact that the successors to the trustees were to be elected by "the majority of Male voters of the said Congregation above the age of Twenty-one years" suggests that Joseph and Nordheimer were backed by at least a rudimentary organization.[22] Regrettably, no records of the Hebrew Congregation survive, if indeed they ever existed. Consequently, it is impossible to determine who comprised the congregation, whether it was established merely to operate the burial ground, or whether its members undertook or planned other religious functions. They certainly established no synagogue, but probably assembled for prayer from time to time. Any effort to hold regular Sabbath services would have been unsuccessful, since most Jewish residents were merchants who would be unwilling to close on Saturday. The fact that Joseph's observance of the Sabbath was considered remarkable suggests that other Jews did not follow his example. Active Jewish communal life, therefore, would wait until the next decade.

NOTES

1 Public Archives of Canada: Colonial Office Records, Series Q, 322, Part 1, p. 216, D'Arcy Boulton to Lieut.-Colonel Cameron, July 8, 1817.

2 *Upper Canada Gazette*, Oct. 21, 1826, cited in Hye Bossin, *Stars of David* (Toronto: Canadian Jewish Congress, 1957), p. 12.

3 *Courier of Upper Canada*, October 21, 1832, quoted by David Eisen, *Holy Blossom Temple Bulletin*, Oct. 25, 1971, p. 6; *York Commercial Directory Street Guide and Register 1833-4*, George Walton, comp. (York, U.C.: Thomas Dalton [1833]), pp. 86, 145; *Assessment Roll for the City of Toronto 1834*.

4 David Eisen, "Toronto's First Jewish Resident," *Holy Blossom Temple Bulletin*, Nov. 14, 1967, p. 7. In Toronto, Hart had apparently found acceptance among the local gentry, especially with those of Reformist leanings. In a letter to Robert Baldwin written from Liverpool in 1836, he spoke of "my kind friends your parents" (Dr. and Mrs. William Warren Baldwin) who had shown him benevolence while he had lived in the city. Hart also extended regards to other prominent members of the community, including Robert Sullivan and Captain and Mrs. Baldwin of Russell Hill. The same letter suggests that Hart had at first been accompanied by a brother who probably remained in Toronto only a brief time (Robert Baldwin Correspondence, Metropolitan Toronto Central Library, Arthur W. Hart to Robert Baldwin, March 28, 1836.) Hart made no effort to disguise his Jewishness. In a second letter to Baldwin some years later, he used the phrase "our blessed religions teach us . . ." (*ibid.*, Hart to Baldwin, Apr. 3, 1844).

5 Toronto *Patriot*, June 9, 1840; F.G. Griffith in Toronto *Star Weekly*, Jan. 17, 1925.

6 Toronto *Mirror*, May 29, 1857.

7 As late as 1912, his descendants were still living in Toronto. They were, however, members of the Anglican Church. (See S.J. Birnbaum in *The Canadian Jewish Times*, Nov. 29, 1912, pp. 6-7).

8 Henrich Graetz, *History of the Jews*, ed. B. Löwy, 6 vols. (Philadelphia: Jewish Publication Society of America, 1956), V, pp. 510-35; Ismar Elbogen, *A Century of Jewish Life*, trans. M. Hadas (Philadelphia: Jewish Publication Society of America, 1966), pp. xxxi-xxxii.

9 *Brown's Toronto City and Home District Directory 1846-7* (Toronto: George Brown, 1846), advertisement section (pages not numbered); *Brown's Toronto General Directory* (Toronto: W.R. Brown, 1856), p. x.

10 *Descriptive Catalogue of the Provincial Exhibition 1858*, p. 77, quoted in Edwin C. Guillet, *Toronto, From Trading Post to Great City* (Toronto: Ontario Publishing Co., 1934), pp. 314-15; Alfred Sylvester, *Sketches of Toronto*, 1858, pp. 18-19, quoted in Guillet, *op. cit.*, p. 315.

11 *Illustrated London News*, Jan. 3, 1863.

12 S.J. Birnbaum in *The Canadian Jewish Times*, Dec. 6, 1912, p. 8; Dr. David Eisen, personal conversation, Nov. 2, 1973. Julius Rossin was the first Jew to graduate from what would become the University of Toronto. He later endowed a scholarship in his own name at University College. It is still awarded.

The Rossin House was rebuilt in the mid-1860s by a corporation in which the Rossins were not involved. However, the reputation of the original hotel had been such that the old name was retained until 1910 when the hotel was renamed the Prince George.

13 He became president of the Philharmonic Society of Toronto, vice-president of the Canada Permanent Loan Co. and, in 1887, German Consul for Ontario. Arthur D. Hart, comp., *The Jew in Canada* (Toronto: Jewish Publications Ltd., 1926), p. 52; S.J. Birnbaum in *The Canadian Jewish Times*, Dec. 6, 1912, p. 7.

14 Diary of Dr. Henry Scadding, cited in E.J. Hathaway, *Jesse Ketchum and his Times* (Toronto: McClelland and Stewart, 1929), p. 286 n. While one can be relatively certain of Hirschfelder's Jewish antecedents, it is probably wise not to take seriously the claims of "An Israelite" who published a pamphlet entitled "Review of the Teachings and the prophetic chronology of Mr. William Miller" in Toronto in 1844. (The work is cited in B.G. Sack, "Jews in Transition," *The Jewish Standard*, Aug. 15-Sept. 1, 1960, p. 5.)

15 *Rowsell's City of Toronto and County of York Directory for 1850-1* (Toronto: Henry Rowsell, 1850), p. 165.

16 *Brown's Toronto and Home District Directory 1846-7*, p. 22; Canada, Department of Agriculture, *Census of Canada 1870-71*, IV, p. 165.

17 There must have been many English Jews who cannot be identified because of their Anglo-Saxon names, and because the absence of organized Jewish communal life gave them no opportunity to appear as Jews. For example, the family of Elizabeth Driscoll, who was born in Toronto in 1838, was not identified as Jewish until her name was discovered in the marriage register of Holy Blossom.

18 *Assessment Roll for the Ward of St. George, City of Toronto 1856, 1859, 1861; Assessment Roll for the Ward of St. Lawrence, City of Toronto 1856, 1859, 1861; Assessment Roll*

for the Ward of St. James, City of Toronto 1856, 1859, 1861; *Assessment Roll for the Ward of St. John, City of Toronto,* 1856, 1859, 1861.

19 Toronto *Mirror,* May 29, 1857, quoting the *Colonist.* The article observes that "The late J.G. Joseph, Esq., was so well known and so highly esteemed in Toronto, that we cannot allow this opportunity to pass without a tribute to his memory . . .."

20 Eric Arthur, *Toronto: No Mean City* (Toronto: University of Toronto Press, 1964), p. 261. Lumley returned to England in 1862. In 1888, in order to provide an appropriate designation to the avenue leading to the new Harbord Collegiate, Lumley Street became Euclid Avenue.

21 See M.E. Gordon, *Political and Legal Aspects of Jewish History in Canada* (Montreal: Canadian Jewish Congress, 1959; mimeographed).

22 "Deed to the Pape Ave. Burial Ground," City of Toronto Registry Office, Instrument No. 69381.

CHAPTER 2

THE OLD COMMUNITY, 1849–1875

During the years following the purchase of the burial ground and the establishment of the Hebrew Congregation, Jews continued to arrive in Toronto in increasing numbers. The 1850 directory lists thirty-nine; the 1851 census notes fifty-seven in the city proper and seventy-seven in the "vicinity" of Toronto. By 1856, there were approximately sixty-five adult male Jews in the city. Like their predecessors, these men were small merchants, tobacconists, clothiers, grocers, and the overwhelming majority were Englishmen. But the fact that they rented rather than purchased their premises and usually avoided King Street addresses indicates that they came with less capital than did the early group.[1]

The newcomers, however, apparently included a greater number concerned with practical Jewish observance. Kosher food to satisfy the dietary laws, regular worship and the education of children required an organized Jewish community centred around a synagogue. By the early 1850s, there was a *shochet* (ritual slaughterer) in Toronto, and although it is unclear whether the new settlers or the Hebrew Congregation had brought him, he must have had enough clientele to make his stay in the city worthwhile.[2] In any case, the haphazard attempts to organize Sabbath services in the early 1850s had emphasized both the concern for tradition and the need for structure.[3]

That this structure became reality in 1856 was due largely to the efforts of Lewis Samuel.[4] Staunchly orthodox and finding it impossible to practise his faith without a house of worship, Samuel, together with Joseph Lyons, a local tobacconist, suggested the establishment of a synagogue. The result was a meeting at the Yonge Street home of one local Jew, Albert Ascher, in September, at which it was resolved "that from the increase of persons of the Jewish Cre[e]d becoming Inhabitants of the City of Toronto it is most proper that a Congregation be now formed."

Several facts can be deduced from the minutes of this assembly. For one thing, it is obvious that the new group did not consider the Hebrew Congregation, represented by Joseph and Nord-heimer, to be in fact a "congregation." It performed no functions of a synagogue, with the exception of operating the cemetery. Secondly, the Samuel group apparently had little contact with the older settlers. Not one appeared among the eighteen who met at Ascher's.

The initial meeting, however, was encouraging. Thirty-one Jews offered various subscriptions ranging from £1.5s. to £10, so that the synagogue began with total assets of £127.5s. It is significant that over £100 of this was donated by the eighteen at the meeting. As was to be expected, leadership came from the relatively affluent, but they evidently had no desire to make the institution exclusive. In an effort to broaden the base of the membership, a committee was appointed "to wait on all persons of the Jewish Faith residing in Toronto to ascertain their views with regard to the...proposal, and likewise to ask their aid."[5] The response must have been satisfactory, since another com-mittee was appointed to find suitable quarters for the synagogue, and a house for the *shochet*, who would become a functionary of the new congregation as well as its *hazan* (cantor). Within the week, the third floor over Coombe's drugstore at the southeast corner of Yonge and Richmond streets had been rented and plans were under way to prepare it as a place of worship for the ap-proaching High Holy Days. A scroll of the Torah was borrowed from the Spanish and Portuguese Synagogue in Montreal, and one hundred people attended the services, some undoubtedly attracted from outlying communities.[6]

It has long been implied that the Hebrew Congregation, founded in 1849, and the new synagogue, Toronto Hebrew Congregation (Sons of Israel), founded in 1856 and now called Holy Blossom, were in fact the same organization, and that the establishment of the synagogue was simply the fulfilment of a plan by the 1849 group, made possible by an increase in the Jewish population.[7] This contention is understandable since the two names are so similar (the title "Sons of Israel" was almost never used) that they could easily have been interchanged. Moreover, with the former in possession of a cemetery, and the latter having only a synagogue, the assumption appears logical. However, the minutes of the Toronto Hebrew Congregation leave little doubt that, at least until 1858, there were two distinct congregations. Not one founding member of the synagogue had been living in Toronto in 1849. Furthermore, members of the Hebrew

Congregation (that is, subscribers to the burial ground) consistently refused to join the new institution. Judah Joseph and Morris Lumley agreed to turn over to the synagogue the money they had previously paid to the *shochet* for his services, since he had entered the employ of the synagogue, but they declined membership. The same was true of Samuel Caspar, who made a sufficiently generous contribution to the congregation to secure him the full privileges of membership. The Rossins and Nordheimers did not even answer the congregation's correspondence and were conveniently absent whenever the membership committee came to call.

One can merely infer the reason for these refusals. Considering the attempts made to hold services prior to 1856, one would expect the older group to have welcomed the opportunity to affiliate. Granted, most of them were not particularly religious, but even Joseph, whose piety is indisputable, made it clear in a letter to the Toronto Hebrew Congregation "that he had no wish to become a member."[8] Moreover, there seems to have been neither ethnic nor economic barriers involved.

There are two likely explanations. First, there was a social gulf between the two factions. The Nordheimers and Rossins undoubtedly had friends in prominent non-Jewish circles. Judah Joseph's obituary speaks for itself, as do the fashionable business locations of the rest of the early group. These individuals by their purchase of property displayed a sense of security in Toronto, whereas the more recent arrivals tended to rent their premises long after they could have afforded to buy them.[9]

Secondly, the autocratic manner in which the new synagogue functioned must surely have deterred many from affiliating. For instance, the president had complete control over the distribution of the *mitzvos* at the services.* Fines were levied for being absent from general meetings, for smoking in the synagogue during prayers, and for various other infractions. Even officers were assessed for not sending an apology when they could not attend services. The members of the older group were probably unaccustomed to such strict congregational discipline, which was not universal either in Europe or in the United States. Those who had been familiar with the system in England, where it was common practice, probably resented it. Not surprisingly, the method of

* During every service, and especially when Scripture is read, certain ceremonial duties, the performance of which is considered a signal honour, are distributed among the adult males present. In this connection, the duties are called *mitzvos* (or *mitzvot*), although the term applies also to all divine commandments.

governing the synagogue followed English custom very closely.[10]

Those who arrived prior to 1850 were not the only ones who refused to affiliate with the Toronto Hebrew Congregation. There are a number of people who appear for the first time in the directories after that date who were undoubtedly English or German Jews and who, considering their occupations, may be said to fall into the same social class as the members of the synagogue. The admission fee and dues were apparently not the deterrent, for the minutes suggest that these were graduated according to the financial means of the applicant. It is possible that those who remained aloof were either unmarried or childless, and so had no fear that their offspring, lacking religious instruction, would assimilate.

The synagogue was soon beset by several major problems, the first being the acquisition of a cemetery. Considering the small number of Jews in Toronto, it seemed foolish to establish a second cemetery. It is unlikely that the holders of the original cemetery were refusing additional subscribers, as this would have been contrary to religious practice. Any member of the synagogue could have subscribed independently. Traditionally, however, a congregation without a burial ground is considered negligent of one of its principal functions. Moreover, this feature would attract members who might not otherwise join the synagogue. Consequently, in December 1856 a letter was sent to "the Trustees of the Jewish Burial Ground of this City asking of them what arrangements could be made by which the [Toronto Hebrew] Congregation could have an equal Privilege as themselves, and likewise stating that this Congregation would do all in their power to make the affair a mutual Benefit."[11] Since most subscribers to the cemetery had left the city by this time, it had apparently become the private burial plot of a small number of families. For this reason, other members of the community had probably hesitated to apply.

The congregation and the trustees differed as to what arrangement would be of "mutual Benefit." The latter were willing to sell a portion of the property to the synagogue, leaving the rest as the exclusive preserve of the old families. The money was to be used for improvements to the cemetery, including the draining of a marshy section and the erection of a cabin where the deceased could be prepared for burial. The congregation, however, objected on the grounds that the amount of land reserved was too large considering the number of people remaining in the group represented by the trustees. Wrangling over the terms of the transfer dragged on well into 1858. Several

24

times during this period negotiations evidently broke down altogether, the synagogue having been forced to appoint a committee to purchase land for a second cemetery. Finally, through the efforts of a mediator, an agreement was reached, providing for the administration of the cemetery by the Toronto Hebrew Congregation. The old Hebrew Congregation continued to exist until 1859, since John Beverley Robinson, whose presence was required for the final transfer, was out of the city. When he did return, the 1849 group was not absorbed into the synagogue; it merely dissolved.

Between the founding of the Toronto Hebrew Congregation and the transfer of the cemetery, only one member of the early community, Alfred Braham, had joined the synagogue. But with the completion of the transaction, others soon followed suit: Abraham Nordheimer in 1858, Morris Lumley in 1859, and his sons and brother early in the 1860s. Judah Joseph had died in 1857, but the affiliation of his son, George, in 1861, completed the link between the two communities.

A second, more serious, difficulty which plagued the congregation was the securing of qualified religious functionaries. The problem was aggravated by the serious financial straits in which the synagogue found itself in the 1850s and 1860s, but this was not the principal cause. Admittedly, the congregation could afford to employ only one person to perform all the official religious duties for the community, an awesome task for any individual, but Toronto was not unique in this regard. Almost every Jewish community of this size was in the same position, and each sought a man who could at once be *shochet, shammes* (sexton), *mohel* (circumcisor), *hazan, melamed* (teacher) and *gabbai* (charity collector). The real problem was that in this period there was not a single institution for the training of Jewish religious leaders of any sort, let alone rabbis, in all of the western hemisphere.[12] Those available for the position usually had no formal training beyond a brief apprenticeship in Europe. Well-educated individuals were too much in demand overseas to emigrate. It was thus virtually impossible to find a single person who would be equally proficient in all the necessary skills, or who would tolerate the countless demands made upon him. For example, a few months after the establishment of the synagogue, the ability of the *shochet*, Mr. Sharmant, was brought into question. When the congregation requested that he travel to New York, at their expense, to be examined as to his qualifications, he refused, whereupon he was dismissed and replaced by a Mr. Goldberg, who had been invited from Buffalo, and who had the necessary certification. The new *shochet* was also to act as cantor and *mohel*.

Goldberg's term of office was by no means an easy one. The congregation repeatedly refused to increase his salary, and his abilities were constantly being challenged. At one point he was "grossly insulted...in the public market," and even though he was repeatedly exonerated, the abuse continued until the trustees threatened his critics with legal prosecution.[13]

As if things were not bad enough for the poor *shochet*, it had been decided that he should devote a number of hours each week "to teaching the Hebrew language gratis to such children as the Committee [the trustees] may select," besides having to take over the duties of "lighting and firing" the synagogue from the caretaker, who had been discharged. In light of such circumstances, one cannot but wonder that Goldberg stayed as long as he did. But in the summer of 1862, he finally submitted his resignation and left for Montreal.

Friends of the Toronto Hebrew Congregation in Buffalo and Montreal were notified of the vacancy, and an advertisement was placed in the *Jewish Messenger*, an English weekly published at New York, detailing a long list of duties and stipulating that "all the qualities" required must be "combined in one person."[14] There were more applicants than one would expect considering the duties and the wages, but none seemed acceptable. The eventual choice, a Mr. Heilbrohn, appeared at first to get on better with the members than had his predecessor, but within two years a clash of personalities and doubts about his ability resulted in his dismissal. Heilbrohn had performed four circumcisions incompetently, a transgression not to be tolerated, despite the scarcity of personnel.

After six months without a minister, during which time they made temporary use of the *shochtim* of Hamilton and Buffalo,[15] the Toronto Hebrew Congregation acquired the services of the Reverend E. Marcusson, of Cleveland. Although employed as "Lecturer" (i.e. preacher) in addition to his other duties as *shochet*, reader and teacher, he was not an ordained rabbi. Despite his apparently excellent qualifications, Marcusson proved an unfortunate choice. Several times during his tenure he was reprimanded for behaving in a manner unbecoming a minister, and was instructed to "deport himself in future in every way consistant with his duties . . . ." The exact nature of the misconduct is revealed in his being "requested to take an oath before the Sepher Torah...stating that while he was engaged to this Congregation . . . he will never imbibe spirituous or fermented liquors except when prescribed by his physician for medical relief."[16] The difficulty in obtaining religious officials is emphasized by the fact that although Marcusson violated his oath, a motion to dismiss him was defeated, and he was even voted a raise in salary.[17] He resigned of his own accord in October 1865, to the relief of many.

The congregation's luck did not improve with Marcusson's departure. There followed in quick succession a series of individuals little more suited to the position than he. One was dismissed for neglect of duty, after having been rehired on probation several times; another left the congregation without notice, while yet another had to be discharged because deafness prevented his teaching the children. This situation lasted until 1880 when the synagogue was able to elect its first trained cantor.

The third major problem with which the congregation had to contend was brought on by the depression which began in 1857. A financial panic had resulted in tight credit, a series of crop failures reduced the buying power of the farmer, while unemployment increased alarmingly once the Grand Trunk Railway was completed. The resulting shortage of cash was disastrous for the urban merchant. This crisis, which affected Toronto Jews severely well into the 1860s, forced many to leave the city and aggravated the synagogue's already serious difficulties. Congregational minutes concern themselves with financial problems throughout the late fifties and sixties, almost to the point of obsession. From 1859 onward, committees were constantly being appointed "to wait upon members in arrears," and these continually complained of their inability to collect.[18] By 1863, conditions had worsened to the extent that an emergency meeting had to be called, and Lewis Samuel, who was now president, warned that "if the majority of the Members did not show more interest in keeping a Kehila [congregation] in Toronto, said Kehila must be dissolved." The congregation was, he continued, "at present several pounds in debt...and [had] not a shilling in hand to defray current expenses. He thought that a congregation in the chief city of Upper Canada ought not to be in this position."[19] Samuel's tone, and the fact that at this meeting he tried to resign as president, suggests that indifference among the members, as well as financial trouble, plagued the synagogue.

The response to the appeal could not nearly cover the congregation's debts. A plan to charter the organization on the model of the newly incorporated Hamilton synagogue had constantly to be postponed because the necessary $18 could not be raised.[20] The congregation had to ask Coombe for a reduction in rent, and a collection had to be taken up among the nonaffiliated

Jews in the city for repair of the cemetery. Not until the mid-1870s did the congregation's economic situation improve substantially.

Membership in the Toronto Hebrew Congregation brought with it a variety of advantages, including admission to the burial ground, the services of the minister without charge, and seats in the synagogue close to the pulpit, a somewhat dubious privilege considering the calibre of some of the early ministers. Understandably, members received religious honours during the services more frequently than did non-members, but they had by no means a monopoly.

However, the most desirable privilege of membership was the ability to purchase kosher meat at a saving. Non-members had to pay the *shochet,* an employee of the synagogue, one or two pence extra for his services, and the butcher an additional penny for his. Because there was still no Jewish butcher, the Toronto Hebrew Congregation contracted with one of the local non-Jewish butchers, whose shop was supervised by the minister to ensure separation of kosher and forbidden meat and utensils. The *shochet* would perform his duties only in this shop. For this monopoly on the sale of kosher meat, the butcher paid a fee to the congregation. The business must have been very lucrative, an indication of the orthodoxy of the local Jews, since other butchers were always after the concession. Members of the synagogue had the choice of the best cuts of meat, for under the terms of his contract the butcher could not sell kosher meat to non-members before 10 a.m. The congregation reserved the right to return all fees if the purchaser could not afford them, and it did so very often.[21]

According to Jewish religious law, a vigil must be kept over the body of a deceased person from the moment of death until burial. The congregation, therefore, also provided a "watching" service for the families of its members, both in Toronto and in the surrounding communities. Virtually from its inception, the Toronto Hebrew Congregation, for almost a decade the only synagogue in Canada West, had a number of non-resident members scattered as far apart as Kingston, Goderich, Stratford, Port Hope, Barrie and Markham. When one of these died and no other Jews besides his family were available for the vigil, someone was sent from Toronto for the purpose, usually the minister's wife.

Despite its continuing financial predicament, the synagogue assisted even non-members too poor to provide for themselves. For example, in September 1863, when a Mr. Abrahams took ill, the congregation voted to pay his travelling expenses to the Jewish hospital at Cincinnati and, when he refused to go, paid for his treatment in the local hospital. Moreover, since there were no facilities in Toronto for the baking of unleavened bread (*matzoth*) for Passover until 1879, this vital commodity had to be imported from New York. Although the congregation invariably lost money on the venture, it always ensured that every Jew in the city was supplied. Those unable to purchase their own were given portions of the members' share. The congregation was also concerned for unfortunate Jews elsewhere in the world. In 1859, for instance, they sent a contribution to assist their persecuted brethren in Morocco.

It is interesting to note that the Toronto Hebrew Congregation admitted widows and unmarried women to full membership with no opposition whatever. This practice was undoubtedly due to American influences, since the admission of single women was virtually unknown in Europe. Married women in the congregation had no such privileges; they could not vote even in the absence of their husbands.

The Toronto Hebrew Congregation did not secure an ordained minister until 1890. It would have been natural, therefore, for the synagogue in its early years to seek religious guidance from one of the three closest Jewish communities of significant size. Buffalo, the most convenient, was having the same difficulty in obtaining religious officials, and would not have a rabbi until 1866. Chicago and Detroit, on the other hand, with synagogues dating from 1847 and 1851 respectively, were communities with an overwhelming majority of German Jews. By the late 1850s, both had obtained rabbis from Germany, and were coming increasingly under the influence of the German reform movement, with its introduction of radical changes in the ritual.[22] It is not surprising, therefore, that Toronto Jews, staunchly traditional in the manner of English Jewry, at least in their synagogue practices if not in private life, should have turned to Rabbi Abraham de Sola of Montreal, the unofficial but universally recognized leader of Canadian Jews.

All religious controversies were submitted to de Sola in the early years, and he visited Toronto at least twice. Despite the fact that he was minister of the Sephardic (Spanish) congregation, and members of the Toronto Hebrew Congregation were Ashkenazim (followers of the German and East European tradition), de Sola, the only rabbi in British North America, was the sole source of indisputable authority.*

* Both the Sephardic and the Ashkenazic rites are recognized as legitimate forms of orthodoxy and do not differ in law. However, adherents of each are usually particular about the observance of their own customs (*minhagim*).

During its first decade, the Toronto Hebrew Congregation also corresponded frequently with Dr. Marcus Adler, Chief Rabbi of England, and for a few years paid an annual fee to the London Board of Trustees, an organization of synagogues whose most important feature was a rabbinical court to settle religious problems for its affiliates. The desire of the Toronto community to have a close connection with some authoritative body illustrates its peculiarly English tone. Jewish congregations in the United States at the same period, influenced by the congregationalism of many Protestant denominations and by the voluntarist tendency in American life generally, shunned any links which might diminish the independence of the individual synagogue.

After about 1863, however, the congregation began to be drawn closer to rabbinical authorities in the United States. As Ashkenazim, Toronto Jews had probably felt somewhat uncomfortable under the surveillance of de Sola. Although the rabbi was an Englishman, he was also a strong proponent of Sephardic custom. As early as 1856, there had been hesitation about accepting de Sola's advice. Rabbi Adler, on the other hand, although an Ashkenazi, was too far away to be of any real assistance. Moreover, by the 1860s, the Ashkenazic community in the United States had matured considerably; New York City alone had several Ashkenazic congregations and rabbis.[23]

Among these, Samuel Myer Isaacs of Congregation Shaarey Tefila, a German-Polish synagogue, was the logical mentor for the Toronto community. An Englishman by birth, Isaacs was the first American rabbi to preach regularly in English.[24] Furthermore, he was opposed to reform, as were the most influential members in Toronto. In addition, the Toronto Hebrew Congregation had probably had dealings with him as far back as the 1850s, when he had organized a certification board for religious functionaries, and he was editor of the *Jewish Messenger*, in which the congregation had advertised for its ministers.

Once the connection had been made, one would have expected the congregation to affiliate with the Board of Delegates of American Israelites, since Isaacs was its prime mover. This was to be a union of all Jewish congregations in North America, probably modelled on the London organization. However, Toronto Jews chose to remain independent. In fact, even the distant affiliation with the London Board was apparently dropped; this may have been a sign of increasing Americanization. Yet in 1890, when the congregation chose its first ordained preacher, he was an Englishman. Indeed, until 1920, when the synagogue affiliated officially with the Reform movement in the United States, its rabbis continued, with the exception of one brief interlude, to be graduates of English institutions.

The Toronto Hebrew Congregation, now known as Holy Blossom, has the probably unique distinction of having been named by someone who was never a member. Albert Ascher's father, Gottschalk Ascher of Montreal, had donated the synagogue's first scroll of the Torah in 1857, together with a silver pointer inscribed in Hebrew "Given to the Holy Congregation 'Holy Blossoms' in the city of Toronto." One can only surmise the reason for Ascher's choice of name. The expression "Holy Blossoms" (*Pirchei Kodesh*) appears nowhere in the Bible, although blossoms sometimes metaphorically connote righteousness and were a prominent component of the seven-branched candelabrum which stood in the Temple at Jerusalem. In addition, the Talmud describes young priests in training as "Blossoms of the Priesthood" (*Pirchei Kehuna*).[25] Perhaps Ascher looked upon the Toronto synagogue, then the only one in the province, as being in training to carry on the divine service in the wilds of Canada West. The new name, however, does not seem to have been popular with the congregation. It was not officially adopted until 1871, and "Blossoms" became "Blossom" shortly afterward.

The 1860s and 1870s were a period of phenomenal growth for the Jewish Reform movement in the United States, and Canada was not immune. By the latter decade, the more orthodox members of Holy Blossom had begun to worry about a tendency toward religious liberalism within the congregation. Whereas relative unanimity seems to have prevailed regarding the observance of the dietary laws, the ideological split on other issues had become apparent as early as 1857. When Ascher donated the Torah scroll, he did so on condition that the congregation always remain orthodox, but the trustees had hesitated to accept these "Restrictions," and Lewis Samuel's arguments in favour of acquiescence were successful only after a heated discussion. Even so, the motion passed by a very small majority.[26]

In 1864, the women had objected to the height of the partition which separated them from the men in the hall of worship, the sexes being segregated during services in orthodox synagogues. Traditionally, a gallery is provided for the women, but when this is not architecturally feasible, as was the case in the Holy Blossom premises, a latticed wooden screen was generally used. Eventually, a compromise was reached and part of the screen was

31

replaced by a gauze curtain. However, the division between the traditional and liberal wings of the congregation appears to have been minor at this time. Even the partition incident seems to have arisen as much from the women's desire to see what was going on in the service as from liberal religious principle. There were no major departures from orthodoxy while the congregation remained at Richmond and Yonge, and a pattern of compromise was established which for decades would prevent the alienation of either faction within the congregation.[27]

The early 1870s saw a rapid increase in the Jewish population of Toronto. Large numbers arrived from the United States, no doubt seeking relief from the economic difficulties of the recent panic. By 1875 the Jewish population of the city was estimated at about 350, and many of these appear to have joined the synagogue. Consequently, the quarters over the drugstore were no longer adequate, and after several attempts to purchase vacated churches in the area, Holy Blossom decided to build its own house of worship. This venture provided the occasion for yet another clash between traditionalists and reformers. Fortunately for the traditionalists, the building committee was headed by Lewis Samuel, who had once again become president. He and his wife, Kate, were responsible for the collection of funds, and since the congregation would not be incorporated until 1894, Samuel took personal charge of the synagogue site, merely lending it in trust to the congregation. The conditions he attached to this transfer demonstrate his concern for the preservation of traditional practice, which must once again have come under attack from some quarter within the synagogue. The land, on the south side of Richmond Street just east of Victoria, was to be held in trust,

for the congregation of Jews worshipping in the said City of Toronto called the Holy Blossom so long as such congregation continue to worship according to the doctrines rules forms and Ceremonies known and recognized as Orthodox Minhag [custom]. And if the said congregation or any other congregation hereinafter referred to do cease to worship according to such doctrines...or do introduce hereinto – or...adopt or use any doctrine rule form or ceremony contrary to such Orthodox Minhag or not professed adopted or used under due authority recognized in the Jewish Religion competent to permit the same, then upon the occurring of such event . . ., [the land shall be] in trust for any congregation of Jews to be found in the City of Toronto which shall conform to the said Orthodox Minhag and which shall require to make use of the said lands and the buildings thereon for the purposes of carrying on . . . such worship . . .[28]

The acceptance of Samuel's conditions was indicative of the ascendancy of the orthodox group in this period, as was the maintenance of traditional architectural forms in the interior of the new building. A gallery ensured separation of the sexes, while the platform from which the Torah was read was placed in the centre of the hall, rather than next to the ark as advocated by reformers. A ritual bath (mikva) was also provided. Only the fact that the hall of worship faced south rather than east represented a departure from orthodoxy, this having been dictated by the shape of the lot.

The erection of the Richmond Street synagogue was an ambitious project considering the financial position of the congregation. In fact, the members of Holy Blossom, themselves, contributed comparatively little toward the down payment on the land and to the fund initially required for construction. One quarter of the necessary $6,000 was donated by Christians, and most of the rest by Jews in New York and New England. The German-Polish congregation of Montreal also contributed a large sum, as did a number of non-Jews in that city. The congregation, once embarked upon the erection of a synagogue, spared no pains, employing a prominent architectural firm, Stewart and Strickland, to design the building. Walter R. Strickland, who probably had charge of the commission, was well regarded in the city; in 1879 he would be asked to participate in the laying out of the original Toronto Industrial Exhibition.[29]

The synagogue was not a very imposing structure. It had a thirty-three-foot frontage and extended to a depth of only sixty-three feet; but, with a seating capacity for four hundred people, it was nonetheless considered large enough to meet the requirements of the congregation, who now numbered 250. The building was constructed of red brick trimmed with white, and sat upon a foundation of stone. Since it is unlikely that Strickland had ever designed a synagogue before, the congregation probably made a number of suggestions to him. It is more than coincidental, therefore, that there is a remarkable similarity in some of the features of the Richmond Street façade to those of the Wooster Street synagogue in New York, Rabbi Isaacs' congregation. The interior of the hall of worship was plain, except for a painting of the Decalogue over the ark. A schoolroom, meeting room and vault were located in the basement. The mortgage was $4,500, an enormous sum in those days.[30]

The dedication service in January 1876 augured well for the congregation. Christians as well as Jews attended, and a large number had to be turned away. The scrolls of the Torah, protected by a canopy, were carried in procession from Yonge Street to the new synagogue, where Rabbi Meldola de Sola, Abraham's son and his successor at the Spanish synagogue in Montreal, conducted the consecration, assisted by Rabbi E. M. Myers of the German-Polish synagogue and the Reverend Mr. Landau of Anshe Sholom in Hamilton. That evening, the young people of the congregation held a festive ball at Albert Hall, where "Dancing was kept up to an early hour of the morning." The consecration of the synagogue was a sign of security and optimism on the part of the Jewish community of Toronto. The handsome financial contributions by Christians, the large number at the opening, and the favourable comment in the local press indicated acceptance by the community at large. The Jews, for their part, were not self-conscious about carrying their scrolls through the streets nor about conducting their dedication service almost entirely in Hebrew despite the presence of Christian guests. Only the sermon and the prayer for the royal family were in English.

However, beneath the apparent unity and gaiety, tension was brewing. The *Daily Mail*, which provided the most complete coverage of the events surrounding the dedication, was astute enough to observe at the service "the presence of lady singers and an organ, neither of which is allowed in Jewish worship."[31] The choir was a voluntary one, comprising wives and daughters of members, while the organ was a portable instrument rented for the occasion.* The traditionalists had apparently agreed to these aberrations for this one instance in return for more orthodox practice at regular services. The ladies did not sing regularly and no organ was used, but the very necessity for compromise illustrates that Lewis Samuel's fears for tradition had not been groundless.

---

* Orthodox practice forbids female participation in synagogue choirs. Instrumental music during worship is prohibited by all except the reform branch as a sign of mourning for the destruction of the Temple. The organ, especially, was avoided because of its association with the church.

NOTES

1 Information regarding the arrivals between 1849 and 1856 is based upon those individuals whose names appear in the minutes of Holy Blossom Congregation, and upon the City of Toronto Assessment Rolls. See *Minutes of the Toronto Hebrew Congregation* (hereafter *HBM*), Sept. 7, 1856.

Eisen finds that in the 1850s there were at least eleven Jewish clothing establishments in Toronto. This includes furriers, capmakers and dry-goods dealers, as well as haberdashers. Next in size as an occupational group were those engaged in the jewellery and related trades (opticians, watchmakers, fancy goods merchants). D. Eisen, "Jewish Settlers of Old Toronto," *The Jewish Standard*, Jan. 1, 1966, p. 5.

2 *HBM*, Sept. 14, 1856. The *shochet* was Solomon Sharmant. Since he does not appear in the directories, it cannot be determined either how long he had been in the city or if he engaged in an occupation other than his religious one.

3 Sigmund Samuel mentions these early futile efforts in his autobiography. Since Samuel was born in 1867, his information is based upon his father's (Lewis Samuel's) recollections. Sigmund Samuel, *In Return* (Toronto: University of Toronto Press, 1963), p. 11.

4 Samuel had been born in England, but had emigrated to New York City at sixteen. He later became a dry-goods peddler in the western part of the state, and eventually set up a successful dry-goods shop in Syracuse. In 1855 he was persuaded to move to Montreal where his brother Marcus was engaged in the fur trade. Lewis disliked the business and the French atmosphere of the city, and after two of his children had died of cholera, departed the next year for Toronto. Within a few years he was a successful dealer in wholesale hardware.

5 *HBM*, Sept. 7, 1856.

6 *Ibid.*, Oct. 4, 1857.

7 See for example, A.D. Hart, *op.cit.*, and Abraham Rhinewine, *Der Yid in Kanada*, 2 vols. (Toronto: Farlag "Kanada," 1925, 1927), I.

8 *HBM*, Dec. 21, 1856. Lumley sent a similar communication; *ibid.*, Jan. 11, 1857.

9 For substantiation of this hypothesis and contrary views, see

S.A. Speisman, "The Jews of Toronto: A History to 1937," (Ph.D. dissertation, University of Toronto, 1975), ch. 2, notes 12-15.

10 *HBM*, Dec. 14, 1856; Oct. 22, 1856; Dec. 21, 1856. Attempts to enforce desirable behaviour by coercion were on the increase in Ashkenazic synagogues in the United States by the time of the Civil War. However, the synagogue was far from being as authoritarian as were American churches of the period. Joseph H. Lookstein, "Traditional Judaism in America," *Jewish Quarterly Review*, New Series, XLV (Apr. 1955), p. 330.

11 *HBM*, Dec. 21, 1856.

12 An attempt would be made to establish a seminary called Maimonides College at Philadelphia in the 1860s, but it would prove unsuccessful. No higher religious training would, therefore, be available in North America until the founding of Hebrew Union College (Reform) at Cincinnati in 1875 and the Jewish Theological Seminary of America (originally orthodox and now Conservative) at New York in 1886. Even when European-trained rabbis were available, these served only as teachers, as was the case in Europe, and occasionally also as cantors.

13 *HBM*, Oct. 9, 1859; Feb. 5, 1860; June 10, 1860; Special Meeting, June 10, 1860. The members of the congregation apparently trusted the secular courts. The Russian immigrants of the 1880s, on the other hand, would never take a case to court if they could avoid it.

14 *HBM*, Sept. 5, 1862.

15 Competition to obtain *shochtim* was fierce. Each community attempted to offer the most attractive terms of employment in its advertisements. For example, the Hamilton congregation announced in *The Jewish Messenger* that "House rent and provisions [were]fully 75% cheaper than in the U.S." *Jewish Messenger*, July 14, 1865, quoted in Jeremiah J. Berman, "The Trend in Jewish Religious Observance in Mid-Nineteenth-Century America," *Publications of the American Jewish Historical Society*, XXXVII (1947), p. 34.

16 The trustees later relented and allowed him to drink beer and ale "in moderation [and] in private houses only." *HBM*, March 12, 1865. The minister had apparently made every

36

effort to ingratiate himself to the congregation; at the same meeting he is thanked for his "kindness and untiring exertions... which have raised you to a degree of popularity which cannot fail to win for you the good-will not only of this Congregation but of the entire public."

17 *HBM*, Apr. 30, 1865.

18 *Ibid.*, Nov. 6, 1859; Dec. 18, 1859.

19 *Ibid.*, July 12, 1863.

20 *Ibid.*, July 19, 1863.

21 *Ibid.*, Aug. 31, 1862. A Mr. Hutty of the St. Lawrence Market held the concession from the inception of the congregation until 1865, when he was dismissed for having used the same tools and cutting blocks for the kosher meat as he did for "chazar [pork]." *HBM*, Sept. 11, 1864. The butcher could not abuse his monopoly since the trustees of the synagogue set the price of meat.

22 Louis Wirth, *The Ghetto* (Chicago: University of Chicago Press, 1964), pp. 180-181; Robert A. Rockaway, *"From Americanization to Jewish Americanism. The Jews of Detroit 1850-1914"* (Ph.D. dissertation, University of Michigan, 1970), pp. 12, 15.

23 *HBM*, Dec. 21, 1856. Hyman B. Grinstein, *The Rise of the Jewish Community of New York 1654-1860* (Philadelphia: Jewish Publication Society of American, 1947), pp. 49-50.

24 Moshe Davis, *The Emergence of Conservative Judaism* (Philadelphia: Jewish Publication Society of America, 1965), p. 298.

25 See for example, *Mishna*, Tractate Yoma 1:7; Tractate Middoth 3:8.

26 *HBM*, April 8, 1857. Holy Blossom, now a reform synagogue, is still in possession of the scroll.

27 Advertisements for religious officials emphasize the orthodoxy of the congregation. See, for example, *HBM*, Aug. 12, 1864; Feb. 1867, *passim*. There is no evidence to support Warschauer's contention that the curtain was later removed. See Heinz Warschauer, *The Story of Holy Blossom*, lst edition (Toronto: Holy Blossom, 1956), p. 128.

28 City of Toronto Registry Office, Instrument No. 11512A,

Conveyance of Land on Richmond St. Toronto in trust for a Jewish Congregation.

29 Sigmund Samuel, *op.cit.*, p. 41; B.G. Sack, *History of the Jews in Canada*, trans. R. Novek (Montreal: Harvest House, 1965), p. 161; Toronto *Daily Mail*, Jan. 21, 1876; and *Mail and Empire*, Feb. 8, 1915.

30 Jan. 21, 1876. See Rachel Wischnitzer, *Synagogue Architecture in the United States* (Philadelphia: Jewish Publication Society of America, 1955), p. 44; *Leader*, Jan. 20, 1876. The Wooster Street building, constructed in 1846, was one of the earliest synagogues to be built as such in America and one of the first to be designed by a Jewish architect. Although Shaarey Tefila had erected a new and larger building in 1869, Toronto Jews were likely most familiar with the older structure.

31 *Mail*, Jan. 21, 1876.

CHAPTER 3

RELIGIOUS DEVELOPMENTS AT HOLY BLOSSOM, 1876 – 1900

Despite Holy Blossom's financial hardships in the decade following completion of the Richmond Street synagogue, the congregation was able to divide communal functions among a larger number of more specialized and better-trained employees – a trend evident in its advertisements as early as 1871.[1] Once the synagogue had been erected, caretaking duties could no longer be handled by the minister. Being now in the public eye, the congregation had to maintain the dignity of its pastor. Furthermore, since membership increased as a result of the merger with a second short-lived synagogue, B'nai Sholom, and from the non-affiliated being attracted by the new edifice, one person could not serve the community properly.

B'nai Sholom (Children of Peace) remains somewhat a mystery. The congregation probably organized in 1874 and held services in rented quarters on Richmond Street across the road from Holy Blossom. Little else is known about them except that they were well enough established to employ their own *shochet* and that the few of their membership who can be traced through the records of Holy Blossom appear to have been of Russian origin. Perhaps that explains the initial separation.

At the time of the amalgamation in 1878, Holy Blossom was again without a minister. The Reverend Louis Harfield, who had been serving at the time of the dedication of the new synagogue, had left Toronto. B'nai Sholom, on the other hand, had employed the Reverend Nathan Robinson, a capable and learned *shochet*, now probably the only one in the city. It is likely, therefore, that Holy Blossom instigated union in order to obtain his services. Robinson became *shochet*, *mohel*, *hazan*, and *baal koreh* (scripture reader) at Holy Blossom.[2]

In 1880, however, the congregation engaged its first professionally trained cantor, Reverend Joseph Glück, of Trenton, New Jersey. Glück, who was also a *shochet*, at first shared this function with Robinson. He was also to have a share with the *shammes*, in a house adjacent to the synagogue owned by the congregation and was to receive, in addition to his salary, 5 per cent of all synagogue dues he collected from the membership.[3]

Glück soon ran into difficulty. Robinson evidently had refused to slaughter exclusively for the butcher appointed by Holy Blossom. As the availability of kosher meat elsewhere would reduce the influence of the synagogue, the trustees attempted to coerce Robinson by denying him synagogue honours, and probably also by reducing his salary. The *shochet* thereupon either refused to submit and was dismissed, or else left of his own accord. Consequently, Glück was forced to undertake the whole function of *shochet* in addition to his other duties, and when he found this too difficult, the congregation required him to employ a *shochet* at his own expense. The minister, displeased with this arrangement, was discharged in 1883.

The congregation now advertised only for a *hazan*; a reconciliation was achieved with Robinson, who returned to perform the remaining functions. The Reverend Herman Phillips, attracted from Shaarey Tefila, Samuel Isaacs' congregation in New York, was the first polished cantor to be employed by the congregation, having studied in Berlin under the renowned cantor-composer Louis Lewandowski and served for twenty years in the United States. His advent must have done much for the quality of the services at Holy Blossom.

In the eighties, the synagogue was beginning to have trouble maintaining its authority over its members and its influence with the non-affiliated Jewish community. The congregation attempted to impose sanctions on members and seat-holders who did not patronize their authorized *shochet* and butcher. The system of fines levied in the early years of the congregation and suspended during the depression of the 1850s and 1860s was reintroduced in an effort to promote better attendance at services. Even officers were difficult to control. Disagreements over synagogue policy at trustee meetings made necessary the by-law that any officer insulting another was to be heavily fined.

An attempt was also made to associate membership and office-holding in the congregation with prestige. Seat-holders were now prohibited from attending congregational meetings, while officers were expected to pay extra dues. The practice of renting seats, the more expensive being closer to the ark, had been instituted at least as early as the opening of the Richmond Street building; however, by the mid-1880s members desiring a prestigious grade of pew had to be considered worthy of the position by the officers.

The 1880s saw also an effort to make the services at Holy Blossom more palatable to a congregation that was feeling increasingly at home in North America and was seeking to endow its worship with a standard of dignity acceptable to the community at large. The changes developed on two levels, one concerned with decorum and the other with areas specifically governed by Jewish law.

Jews in the ghettos of Europe had come to interpret liberally the rabbinic dictum that one should be as comfortable in the synagogue as in one's father's house. The result was a condition of apparent chaos which would have shocked the average churchgoer. Worshippers often walked about in the synagogue as they prayed; the congregation rarely stood or was seated in unison; congregants would pray aloud, making the cantor inaudible. The reading of the Torah was constantly being interrupted by worshippers requesting a *mi sheberach* (prayer for the sick) or an *el molei rachamim* (memorial prayer). Worst of all, in order to raise additional money for the synagogue, various duties to be performed during the services were put up for sale, the honours often being auctioned off during the actual service.

This situation was common in most orthodox synagogues in the nineteenth century. The German reformers had succeeded in introducing ecclesiastical decorum, as had many English orthodox synagogues. Samuel Myer Isaacs had insisted upon it in his New York congregation. But at Holy Blossom, the traditional marketplace atmosphere prevailed. One Jew visiting in 1885 from Hamilton, where the local congregation had been influenced by German practice, was horrified by the noise and disorder at the Richmond Street synagogue. However, the trend toward greater decorum was already under way. As early as 1882, the sale of honours had been abolished, despite the congregation's serious shortage of funds. The proposal, moreover, originated with the traditionalists rather than with the reformers in the congregation. In 1888 when the sale of *mitzvos* (ceremonial duties) was of necessity reintroduced, the auction was restricted to the annual meeting. The same year those wishing a prayer for the sick or a memorial prayer during the scriptural reading were required to notify the cantor in advance. Finally, in 1889 the congregation was required to rise and to sit in unison, following the lead of the *parnas* (president).[4]

But if traditionalists as well as reformers were agreed upon increased decorum in the synagogue, there was a simultaneous movement afoot which the orthodox would be unable to countenance. In January 1883 the liberals proposed that the reader's platform be removed from the centre of the hall to a position immediately in front of the ark, and that "Pews be built so that Ladies and Gentlemen [may] be seated together." Mixed seating, a peculiarly American phenomenon, had been introduced some years before for the first time in any synagogue by Isaac Mayer Wise in his congregation at Albany, New York, and had been accepted by some other liberal congregations in the United States. During the previous decade, a number of Jews amenable to German reform and influenced by the innovations of Wise, had arrived in Hamilton, with the result that a battle over this very issue was now raging in the synagogue there. Indeed, it must have already been apparent that the liberals would prevail. The suggestion of these changes, therefore, brought vigorous protest from the traditionalists in Holy Blossom who marshalled their forces. Alfred D. Benjamin, president of the congregation, business partner of Lewis Samuel and his co-worker as leader of the traditional wing, produced the deed to the Richmond Street building "showing that [it] is utterly impossible to receive the motion." Benjamin insisted that a committee could not even be appointed to consider the matter since "in the trust Deed it is distinctly stated that services shall be conducted in accordance with the orthodox minig [*minhag*] and no material change [can] be made without the sanction of some competent authority."

Coupled with the seating issue was that of the women's choir. Although the one formed for the opening of the Richmond Street building was not to sing regularly, Cantor Glück had agreed to tolerate a group of ladies assisting him from afar in the gallery. How frequently the women sang cannot be determined, but the practice must have galled the orthodox, who took a stand on the issue when the problem of mixed seating arose. The traditionalists wanted both questions submitted to Dr. Adler in London, as well as to two other orthodox rabbis, thus ensuring a prohibition. However, they were persuaded to compromise; only Adler, in his capacity as Chief Rabbi, was consulted and in the meantime, the ladies were forbidden to sing.[5] There is no record of Adler's reply, but the lawyers whom Holy Blossom consulted agreed that no changes contrary to orthodoxy could legally be undertaken, except if the synagogue were incorporated and the conditions of trusteeship thereby altered. This they maintained, "would be both difficult and expensive." Consequently, another compromise was arrived at. The ladies' gallery was enlarged, eliminating some of the thrust of the reformers' argument that mixed seating would alleviate the shortage of seats in the womens' section. On the other hand, the womens' choir was maintained at Sabbath services, but was secluded in the balcony, and it would remain appropriately silent in the increased sanctity of the Day of Atonement.

The presence of female choristers already disqualified Holy Blossom as an orthodox synagogue in the opinion of the East Europeans who were already beginning to arrive in Toronto, but within the congregation the departure was not considered a violation of the terms of the deed. The practice brought no significant secession. If Lewis Samuel was displeased, he was reticent about his opinion; he was perhaps not prepared at this point in his life to sacrifice his burial rights by leading a movement out of the congregation. Besides, Holy Blossom remained, in all other respects, adamantly traditional. Conformity with the dietary laws continued among the members, and the debate over changes in the ritual suggests that the orthodox element was still both numerous and powerful. Indeed, in 1885 even a minute departure from tradition like the reading rather than the chanting of the *Haftarah* (prophetic portion which follows the reading from the Pentateuch) by a reform-minded guest would cause a number of worshippers to storm out of the synagogue in protest.

That guest, however, would soon arrive permanently in Toronto, take up the leadership of the reform faction within Holy Blossom, and tip the already precarious balance to the detriment of the orthodox. Edmund Scheuer had come under the influence of German reform as a young man in his native Alsace. When the Franco-Prussian War interfered with his jewellery trade, he entered into partnership with a Jew in Hamilton, Ontario, and emigrated. Joining Anshe Sholom upon his arrival, he promptly made himself a force in that congregation by organizing, under its auspices, the first Jewish Sabbath school in Ontario. Scheuer believed that Jews should become as much like their neighbours as was feasible without rejecting the ethical elements of Judaism. He became, therefore, an outspoken antagonist of traditional ritual and of any other practices which might interfere with Jewish acculturation. To this end, he was responsible for the introduction of English prayers and the English sermon at Anshe Sholom, and promoted the adoption of reform practices. Mixed seating was adopted in 1883, and the Hamilton congregation was then leaning toward the introduction of instrumental music as well.

For the traditionalists at Holy Blossom, Scheuer's arrival

among them in 1886 could not have come at a worse time. The congregation was in the midst of a heated debate over ritual, and the traditional wing was vulnerable. Lewis Samuel, acknowledged leader of the orthodox element, was ageing; Alfred Benjamin, uncompromisingly orthodox in his personal life, tended to vacillate when it came to the synagogue, while increased numbers of Jews were arriving from the United States where they had belonged to congregations sympathetic to reform. By 1889 Scheuer wielded considerable influence in the congregation. He had taken charge of Holy Blossom's educational facilities, and his criticism of the ritual was gaining increased audience among recent arrivals. Just before the High Holy Days of that year, the reformers felt strong enough to launch a direct attack by demanding "several changes in the Order of Worship," as well as an English-speaking minister. When the trustees refused, Scheuer organized rival services in the reform manner in a nearby rented hall, with lecturers imported from New York.

Although those who left Holy Blossom for the High Holy Days did not resign from the congregation, the fact that a large number of the young people who had been studying under Scheuer followed him made it evident to the orthodox that yet another compromise was necessary to avert a split in the synagogue. Thus far, only one concession had been permitted the reformers: at the High Holy Day services of 1888, the women's choir had been permitted to sing, but the change had been passed by a very small majority. The question of engaging a "First Class" English-speaking preacher had been under discussion for a year before Scheuer's protest. This trend had been led by the orthodox, ostensibly to attract new members, but probably to dislodge the radical Scheuer as school superintendent. The new minister would be required to occupy that post. Indeed, Rabbi Adler had already been asked to suggest someone for the position, an indication that a traditionally-oriented minister was desired. Then, several weeks prior to the protest service, the traditionalists had attempted to placate the dissidents by abolishing offerings in the synagogue and agreeing to secure an organ and an "able" and presumably professional choir. The motion, surprisingly, was introduced by Benjamin himself. It was apparently their inability to bring these approved reforms to immediate fruition and their failure to secure any real modification of the order of prayers that prompted the reformers to set up their own services.[6]

Unable to delay any longer, the moderate traditionalists, who were in control of the board of trustees, permitted a small pump organ to be installed prior to Passover in 1890. This action had

44

not been taken arbitrarily, however. Rabbi Adler had nominated Reverend Barnett A. Elzas, a recent graduate of the orthodox Jews' College, London, to minister to Holy Blossom, and the congregation had sought the latter's opinion on the issue prior to his arrival in the city, thus supposedly satisfying the terms of the 1875 deed that a competent authority be consulted before changes were made. Elzas, to the consternation of the orthodox, approved the instrument; but before he could arrive to calm the situation, an open split emerged for the first time within the congregation. Cantor Phillips, who had reluctantly put up with the ladies' choir, would have no part of the organ and resigned. Then, one evening shortly before the holiday, a group of orthodox dissidents who, not surprisingly, comprised some of the East European minority in the congregation and some who had formerly been members of the old B'nai Sholom, carried the instrument into the yard. When the trustees ordered it replaced and a Christian woman was employed to play it, a number of these resigned and joined Goel Tzedec, a congregation of Lithuanian Jews which had been formed in 1883 and which, by this time, occupied a small church on University Avenue.

It is debatable whether Elzas' permission to use the organ in fact fulfilled the terms stipulated in the deed. Contrary to the belief held even by usually authoritative sources,[7] Elzas was not a rabbi in the traditional sense as the term would have been understood prior to the twentieth century. To hold the title "rabbi" in that period meant that the individual had received *semicha*, the traditional form of ordination by other rabbis in recognition of the completion of a prescribed course of biblical and talmudic study. Elzas, rather, was a minister-preacher, a Jewish religious functionary unique to England. Jews' College, London, had been founded in 1855 to deal with a shortage of Jewish religious leaders in Great Britain. Since the immediate concern was the training of teachers and readers, it was not until 1902 that a rabbinical department was established.[8] Prior to that date, it produced only minister-preachers, whose functions were pastoral and educational. They did not obtain *semicha*, their course of study being less intensive than that required of prospective rabbis. Therefore, they could not make decisions dealing with the intricacies of Jewish law.

Consequently, the orthodox might well have argued that Elzas did not qualify as a competent authority, and one can assume that Samuel had meant "rabbi" by the phrase in the deed. The minutes of the congregation, surprisingly, make no mention of this argument against the organ being used; in fact, they ignore the

45

carrying out of the instrument altogether and provide a minimal amount of detail about the dispute generally. Perhaps Elzas' decision was attacked only by those who left the congregation. The rest, even the traditionalists, seemed to have accepted him as if he were a rabbi. However, they appear to have been aware that he was not; he is seldom accorded that title in the minutes.

From 1890 onward, Holy Blossom became a curious mixture of orthodox and reform elements and the minister had to walk the thin line between the two. Only a minority among the orthodox had resigned over the organ issue and the remainder continued to insist upon strict observance in many aspects of synagogue life. The ritual bath continued to be maintained, as did the traditional custom of purification prior to burial. Moreover, the actual service remained much the same; neither the prayers nor the scriptural reading were abridged and the organ, though present, was secluded in the gallery, remote enough to be tolerated by most traditionalists. Yet Elzas must have realized that the congregation was on the verge of a major division over the question of the organ. Within a month of his arrival it was proposed that Holy Blossom offer a late Friday evening service in addition to the regular one at sunset. This practice, which had been introduced in a number of localities in the United States, was advocated by American reformers for various reasons. Since sunset in winter occurs early, the second service, though held beyond the prescribed time for it according to Jewish tradition, would give storekeepers the opportunity of attending Sabbath prayer without having to leave work before their normal closing time. Moreover, those who kept their businesses open on Saturday could not attend morning worship in the synagogue, the major Sabbath service. Therefore, it would be logical to have a major service late Friday evening.

The proposal at Holy Blossom was evidence that Sabbath observance among its members was seriously on the decline and Elzas, whatever his sympathies with the logic of the reformers, blocked the movement, agreeing to permit the late service only if a large majority of the congregation wished it. Whether the minister was refusing on principle to adapt synagogue practice to suit the needs of Sabbath violators, or whether he was merely being cautious in the hope that the majority of the members, liberal as well as traditional, would hesitate to make the change is unclear. In any case, late services were not held and Elzas succeeded in weathering the storm.

On a second issue, Elzas also took a moderate approach. While willing to condone the playing of the organ on the Sabbath, he judged that some concession must be made to the orthodox. The remnant of the group which had failed to remove the organ the year before but had stayed at Holy Blossom in the hope of stemming the tide, now demanded that the congregation eschew the sin of playing the instrument at least on Yom Kippur, the holiest day of the Jewish calendar. Scheuer, on the other hand, was pressing for its use even then. Special congregational meetings were called throughout 1891 and 1892 to discuss the matter, with the membership dividing for the first time on lines of ethnic origin. The Germans favoured use of the organ at all times, the English preferred limited use, and the East European minority was totally opposed. Elzas characteristically decided in favour of the status quo; the organ was not used on the Day of Atonement.

But Elzas was a reformer at heart and all his circumspection could not disguise it from the orthodox; they complained that he was too liberal, walking about bare-headed and not as befits an observant Jew, let alone a minister. The reformers recognized a potential ally in Elzas. As Scheuer once remarked, "The real reform started with him, and he had to bear the brunt of all the innovations we introduced gradually." Indeed, although reforms were instigated by the laity, the preacher became the central figure in the controversy over change. Traditionalists blamed him for the entire reform trend in the synagogue, while reformers deplored his failure to move more quickly. Finally, having received a call first to Sacramento, California, and then to Congregation Beth Elohim in Charleston, South Carolina, a synagogue in sympathy with American reform and so amenable to his ideological leanings, Elzas resigned late in 1892.

II

The election of an English-speaking minister in 1890 had been in response to the demands of the liberals, yet it was simultaneously an effort on the part of the traditionalists, led by Alfred Benjamin, to urge the congregation into an English rather than an American reforming direction. Indeed, the 1890s was a period of reform ascendancy in the United States. The recently arrived East European orthodox were still too few in number and too fragmented to exert any influence on the course of American Judaism. The older and more affluent English and Central European orthodox community in the United States had culturally more in common with the German-American reform Jews than with their exotic co-religionists from the east, and in the 1880s had attempted to unite with the German reformers in a national religious movement encompassing congregations of all ideological positions. A seminary, Hebrew Union College, had been set up at Cincinnati in the 1870s to train American rabbis, but by the next decade the reformers under Isaac Mayer Wise had become dominant. Then in 1885, the reformers issued a manifesto advocating changes so radical that the Americanized orthodox, and even some moderate reformers, left the movement and founded their own orthodox rabbinical school at New York, the Jewish Theological Seminary of America.[9] By 1893, however, the seminary, from which the traditionalists at Holy Blossom would like to have chosen a minister, had not yet ordained a single rabbi. Hebrew Union College, on the other hand, was far too radical for even the liberal element at Holy Blossom, with the possible exception of Scheuer. Consequently, neither institution was approached to provide a replacement for Elzas and although the congregation advertised for a minister in several Jewish publications in the United States, the tendency was again to look to England, a practice no doubt encouraged by Benjamin.

Considering the tensions which prevailed in Holy Blossom, the congregation had to exercise caution in its choice. Not only would he have to be educated for the position; the new minister would also have to present a favourable image to both factions, since the entire membership, not the trustees alone, was required to elect him. The successful candidate, Reverend Abraham Lazarus of London, also a minister-preacher, was chosen only after the rejection of numerous other applicants and after his own candidacy had been under discussion for three months. The congregation was not prepared to take any chances.

The new minister must have shocked the non-English elements in Holy Blossom when he arrived in the summer of 1893 replete with clerical collar (which even the orthodox rabbinate wore in Britain). Both sides had awaited his coming with anticipation. His credentials were outstanding; a bachelor's degree from the University of London, as well as certification from Jews' College, would impress not only the more cultured members of the congregation but also the Christian community. And more important, Holy Blossom was his first pulpit; he was only twenty-three, and likely to be easily moulded by the influence of a powerful laity. Lazarus, however, preferred not to take sides. On his arrival the changes he introduced were slight, only an English prayer at the close of the service. By 1894, he did wear a clerical gown in addition to his *tallith* (prayer shawl) and a year later he permitted the introduction of a mixed choir, but he attempted also

48

to placate the traditionalists. The female portion of the choir continued to sing from the gallery.[10]

Even before Lazarus arrived, plans were under way to replace the Richmond Street synagogue with a new and larger structure. The schoolroom was inadequate and with over one hundred member families, (which still included a significant number outside Toronto), the hall of worship had become far too small. Alfred Benjamin, the principal proponent of removal, had, together with his brother Frank, pledged $10,000 toward a new synagogue, thus practically assuring the assent of the congregation to the move. The new enterprise, however, would require the eventual sale of the Richmond Street property, an impossibility unless the trusteeship of the land were transferred from Lewis Samuel's successors to the congregation through the process of incorporation. This presented a problem for the traditionalists. By the terms of the 1875 deed, these trustees were a self-perpetuating group holding office for life and, as Samuel had envisioned, they constituted a bulwark of traditionalism. On the other hand, should title to the property be shifted to the congregation, the board of trustees of the synagogue, which was by the mid-1890s heavily weighted in favour of Scheuer's faction, would become the arbiters of religious policy. Transfer, however, was essential to a new building scheme. As a result, the property trustees agreed to transfer their rights on condition that the deed to any new synagogue stipulate that no change be made in the ritual without the consent of four-fifths of the membership voiced at a special meeting called for the purpose. Considering the slim margin by which reforms had been achieved in the past and the poor attendance at congregational meetings generally, the condition was considered sufficient to thwart the heretics. Indeed, it would prevent radical changes for almost another quarter century.

III

A visitor from Montreal, attending services at Holy Blossom in 1898, was astonished to find both orthodox and reform Jews belonging to the synagogue. In Montreal, and indeed in many other centres, the adherents of diverging ideologies had long since separated into distinct congregations. Holy Blossom was an anomaly. "I know of no city," wrote the Montrealer, "where there exists more religious harmony among the Jews than in Toronto."[11] But what he saw at Holy Blossom was, in fact, deadlock rather than harmony. The congregation had dedicated its magnificent new Moorish synagogue on Bond Street the previous autumn, and here an uneasy balance was struck between the conflicting elements. Architecturally, the building would pass for orthodox: the ark was placed properly against the eastern wall; the women's gallery remained, and although the reader's platform was no longer in its original position in the centre of the synagogue, the cantor's lecturn continued to face the ark rather than toward the congregation, as had become the practice in reform congregations. In proper orthodox manner, a *mikva* was provided in the basement of the sexton's house which stood behind the synagogue. The only apparently serious deviation from orthodoxy in the building was the installation of a pipe organ at the outset – one that could not be easily removed.[12]

The service itself had, as Benjamin remarked in his presidential dedication address, "been somewhat modified, on cautious, conservative lines, with a view of meeting the spiritual necessities of the rising generation," yet an attempt had been made to please the older members to whom any change was distasteful.[13] The traditional prayerbook continued to be used, but the ladies' portion of the choir continued to participate. It is apparent from Benjamin's speech that the younger, and likely native-born, members of the congregation were leaning increasingly toward the liberal position, and had been able to exert more influence on synagogue policy than they had at the time of the temporary secession in 1889. The traditionalists were apparently growing weaker as they aged, and fewer in number as many passed away. All the old customs that were preserved in the synagogue were, it seems, the result of Benjamin's solitary influence.[14] Lazarus perceived the reforming upsurge among the younger element as a trend toward acculturation to North American mores with which he was heartily in sympathy. At the opening of the Bond Street synagogue he urged his congregants to abandon "oriental" customs and impress upon Toronto that the Jews were "a homemade article and not a foreign production," that they were permanent residents in Canada, would defend the country if need be, and were "not liable at any moment to leave in a body."[15]

Scheuer's reformers had attempted to use the move as the opportunity to introduce more radical changes. For instance, they succeeded in reversing a decision by the trustees that men and women be seated separately at the dedication service. Once in the new building, Lazarus immediately authorized a late Friday evening service, not a traditional one, as proposed during Elzas' tenure, but rather one almost totally in English and including an organ prelude. Opposition from the orthodox led first to its discontinuation and, after much debate, to the agreement upon a traditional service with organ accompaniment. The late services, which included a sermon, were well attended by both Jews and Christians, but they doubtless generated a great deal of tension within the congregation. Although the minister gave no explanation for his resignation in 1898, the constant feuding over reform was the likely reason. He took a more liberal congregation in Houston, Texas.

The invitation to Rabbi Henry Morais of Philadelphia as Lazarus' successor can be interpreted as a traditionalist attempt to draw the younger members out of Scheuer's camp. Morais, son of the founding president of the Jewish Theological Seminary of America and an accomplished author, was an outstanding exponent of Americanized orthodoxy. His was exactly the position to satisfy the advocates of dignity in the services, while eliminating the changes which threatened orthodoxy. A modern but uncompromisingly traditional rabbi would surely take the wind out of Scheuer's reforming sails. Unfortunately, Morais refused the position. He no doubt considered Toronto a backwater and, his father having just died and the Seminary being in serious difficulty as a result, Morais probably preferred to remain close to New York where he could assist the struggling institution. The trustees settled, therefore, on Rabbi David H. Wittenberg of Congregation Beth El in Buffalo.

Wittenberg, a graduate of the Jewish Theological Seminary, and thus professing to be orthodox, was expected at least to hold the line against further reform. The reformers, on the other hand, were willing to accept him as a conciliator, since he had apparently played that role at his previous post. At Beth El he had always expressed a moderate position. By this time, the liberal element had concluded that they must compromise with the traditionalists or else form their own congregation, a step the majority were not prepared to take. "Although orthodox in his views," one reforming member wrote of Wittenberg,

he is not ultra-orthodox. Our congregation is a very mixed one; a mixture of orthodox and reform and it is no easy task to steer the middle Path. There is one thing certain, that we will never have a really progressive congregation until the sincere believers in reform have a temple of their own. So, perhaps, it is well that until that comsomation [sic], so devoutly to wished for, arrives, that we all bury our differences ....[16]

51

The rabbi himself saw his new position as one requiring conciliation. In his initial sermon, Wittenberg pledged himself to "hold fast to the letter of God's law," but at the same time exhorted his congregation to "be liberal in their interpretation of the spirit that actuated the commands of God." He urged unity, counselling members "not to come to synagogue as critics but as helpers."[17] Wittenberg's position as peacemaker was recognized even in Montreal, where the *Jewish Times,* the principal Anglo-Jewish newspaper of the period, expressed the hope that he would be successful in satisfying both the orthodox and the reform at Holy Blossom.[18]

Too little is known of events at Holy Blossom during Rabbi Wittenberg's tenure to be able to state that he was either an adamant traditionalist who was overruled by an increasingly reform laity, or a liberal in principle. For example, one of his first acts was to discontinue the late Friday services, and since these had been well attended, it would appear that he opposed them on ideological grounds. On the other hand, his Buffalo congregation had offered late Friday services, indeed with mixed seating, and Wittenberg had tolerated them there. Perhaps he had, in fact, opposed the late services at Beth El as well, but considering that that congregation had introduced them fifteen years before his arrival, he had likely found them too entrenched and the reform group too strong. At Holy Blossom late services were experimental and still under attack by the orthodox. Another step in favour of tradition was Scheuer's inability to have the Torah read on a biennial rather than on the traditional annual cycle. It is probable that Wittenberg persuaded him not to press the issue.[19]

As for the rabbi's liberalism, without too much pressure from the laity Wittenberg introduced a confirmation service for girls. This ceremony had been common usage at Beth El and had, like the late Friday service, preceded Wittenberg's arrival. That he approved the practice, which was not permitted in orthodox synagogues, and even instituted it in Toronto, would seem to suggest that he was not totally traditionalist. Admittedly, the confirmation took place on a Sunday morning and, in all likelihood, was not a part of the regular service, but the seating of the sexes together was a departure from tradition, especially in light of the pressure for the elimination of segregation at Sabbath worship. Another indication of Wittenberg's apparent permissiveness was the experimentation with a mixed choir no longer divided between gallery and ground floor.

The dominant public perception of Wittenberg, however, was

that of a traditionalist attempting to draw Holy Blossom closer to modern orthodoxy in the United States and there may have been several reasons for his failure to do so.[20] Just prior to his appointment, there had been taking place in North America what might be called a Jewish synod movement. A conference had assembled in New York in 1898 to establish the Orthodox Jewish Congregational Union, in an attempt to unite Americanized and recently arrived East European traditional elements. The purpose was to combat rampant and well-organized reform, and the Jewish Theological Seminary was expected to play an active role. As Holy Blossom stood ideologically at this period, the position of the new organization should have been eminently acceptable, and yet the congregation sent no delegate. Perhaps they were not invited; indeed, Rabbi Meldola de Sola of Montreal was the only Canadian present, certainly because of the preeminence of his congregation in Canada and perhaps also because he was a cousin to Rabbi Henry Pereira Mendes, one of the organizers of the Union. The Orthodox Union was unable, eventually, to unite all orthodox elements, but at first its prospects were very encouraging. It is, therefore, almost inconceivable that Holy Blossom, which appointed a graduate of the Seminary as its rabbi while success was still in sight, should have had so little contact with the Union and with the Seminary that no vestige appears in any of the congregation's surviving records. Perhaps the reform element found the Union distasteful, but it is unlikely, considering the traditionalist domination of congregational affairs in this period, that affiliation with the Union could have been blocked had the trustees seriously desired it. Perhaps the latter felt it better to avoid commitment and so not provoke further conflict. It is more probable, however, that despite Wittenberg's appointment, since Samuel Myer Isaacs' death in 1878 Holy Blossom had been leaning once again toward England, with which it had never ceased to identify.

In any case, when Wittenberg's contract was not renewed in 1900, it was reported that the cause was a disagreement with the officers of the congregation over the exact definition of the rabbi's duties.[21] The refusal of the trustees to look to the United States for guidance was probably the real source of the rift. Applications from the United States seem not to have been seriously considered this time, and a Montreal rabbi with German reforming tendencies was also turned away. Alfred Benjamin, the ever-present English influence and still president, made the eventual selection. The new minister, Rabbi Solomon Jacobs, would serve Holy

Blossom for almost twenty years. He was to be its most successful peacemaker, but for the moment, of prime importance was that he was an Englishman. Now Benjamin must have felt assured that tradition was secure.

NOTES

1 See, for example, *HBM*, June 16, 1871. Much of the information upon which this chapter on the early history of Holy Blossom is based is contained in the synagogue *Minutes*. More complete references are given in the author's dissertation, "The Jews in Toronto: A History to 1937," chapter 3, footnotes.

2 Robinson (1840-99) had been born in Russian Poland and had served congregations in Insterburgh, East Prussia; Cleveland, Ohio; Bay City, Michigan; and Utica, New York. He arrived in Toronto in 1877. Hart, *op.cit.*, pp. 112, 113.

3 Nineteenth-century synagogues usually required one of their employees to act as dues collector. The commission was also typical, since salaries were generally very low.

4 Moshe Davis, *The Emergence of Conservative Judaism*, (Philadelphia: Jewish Publication Society of America, 1965), p. 298; Edmund Scheuer, "Reminiscences of Canadian Jewry to be appended to Thesis of Arthur Brodey, Oct. 9, 1933." MSS, American Jewish Archives, Cincinnati.

5 Memoir on the subject by Edmund Scheuer. MSS, Holy Blossom Archives. This manuscript contains much valuable information on this period.

6 Ida Siegel, personal interview, Aug. 5, 1971: Arthur Cohen, personal interview, Dec. 15, 1971.

7 E.g., D. Eisen, "Toronto's First Rabbi," *Holy Blossom Temple Bulletin*, Feb. 16, 1970, pp. 6-7.

8 Letter to the author from Frank H. Levine, Executive Director of Jews' College, London, Nov. 29, 1973.

9 For a more detailed account of this controversy, see Davis, *op.cit.*

10 *The Jewish Times*, Sept. 15, 1899, p. 321. It seems that the motion that there be men in the choir was first proposed by

A.D. Benjamin in an effort to phase out the lady choristers. The movement, however, was not successful.

11 *Ibid.*, June 24, 1898, p. 231.

12 Toronto *World*, Sept. 15, 1897; Ida Siegel, personal interview, Aug. 5, 1971; Ben Geldsaler, personal interview, Sept. 28, 1972. A Christian organist continued to be employed.

13 *Mail and Empire*, Sept. 16, 1897.

14 *The Jewish Times*, June 24, 1898, p. 231.

15 *Mail and Empire*, Sept. 16, 1897.

16 *Jewish Times*, Jan. 20, 1899, p. 58.

17 *Ibid.*, March 17, 1899, p. 118.

18 *Ibid.*, March 3, 1899, p. 101; March 31, 1899, p. 131.

19 Heinz Warschauer's contention that the services were discontinued because they were poorly attended is not substantiated by the Holy Blossom minute books, whereas the *Jewish Times* insists that they were indeed well attended. *Jewish Times*, Sept. 15, 1899, p. 321. *HBM*, Aug. 27, 1899; Sept. 24, 1899.

20 Ida Siegel, personal interview, July 29, 1971.

21 Wittenberg apparently would have preferred to stay. The congregation was advertising for a new minister while he was still applying for re-engagement. *HBM*, Apr. 13, 1900.

CHAPTER 4

PHILANTHROPY AND EDUCATION IN THE OLD COMMUNITY, 1856 – 1900

For most of the nineteenth century, the social life of the Jewish community in Toronto centred around the single synagogue, Holy Blossom, and much of this activity prior to the 1890s had to do with philanthropy. Whereas the Victorian conception of charity emphasized the role of the individual, Judaism has always promoted communal responsibility. Consequently, the Toronto synagogue from its inception had assisted the needy – albeit in an informal and sometimes haphazard fashion – by providing transportation to hospital, remission of *shochets'* fees, distribution of unleavened bread and aid in various other forms. But the increase in the Jewish population of the city and the recurrent economic crises made necessary the establishment of more formal philanthropic machinery and, in true Victorian fashion, it was the women of the congregation who took the initiative. The Toronto Hebrew Ladies Sick and Benevolent Society (Chebre Gemilas Chesed), organized in 1868 as a mutual benefit as well as a charitable society, provided an assortment of services to its members, who included women from outlying towns as well as Toronto residents. Among these were free loans, "watchers" for the sick, funeral expenses and support for bereaved families during the week of mourning when work is forbidden.[1] As for assistance to the poor, it appears that the organization, which in 1870 was renamed the Ladies' Montefiore Hebrew Benevolent Society after the renowned Anglo-Jewish philanthropist and former mayor of London, at first concentrated on Jewish orphans and widows, and on transients who needed railway tickets or employment. Jews overseas were also assisted financially.[2] By the 1880s contributions were being offered to non-Jewish charitable institutions such as the Sick Childrens' Hospital, the Infant's Home and the Children's Aid Society. In its early years, the Society used only the funds contributed by its own members, but by the 1880s various fund-raising devices were being employed.

Male members of the synagogue were slower in organizing for charitable purposes, content to let the ladies care for the poor or have official charity dispensed by the trustees. Moreover, men had outlets for their social inclinations which were unavailable to women: business relationships, the operation of the synagogue itself and participation in fraternal organizations. By the mid-1870s there were at least two Jewish fraternal lodges in the city – the Canada Lodge of B'nai B'rith (founded in 1875) and a chapter of the Kesher Shel Barzel (Chain of Iron), both branches of American societies. Both were closely associated with Holy Blossom; in fact, the meeting room in the Richmond Street synagogue was included specifically for their use. These lodges undoubtedly engaged in some philanthropic activity, but fraternity and mutual aid were their principal aims. Consequently, in the summer of 1877, a charitable society "for the assistance of their coreligionists" was organized at Holy Blossom. Originally envisioned as both a men's and women's organization, the group developed into an exclusively male society under the name of the Toronto Hebrew Benevolent Association and, unlike the lodges, its function was purely philanthropic. Possibly as early as 1882, and certainly by the 1890s, it received an annual municipal grant for relief work. Like the Ladies' Montefiore, the men's society contributed to non-Jewish causes in the city.[3]

While the trustees of the synagogue continued to dispense funds to the poor, most philanthropic work in the 1870s and 1880s was undertaken by these two specialized societies attached to Holy Blossom, and by the Toronto chapter of the Anglo-Jewish Association. Branches of this English organization had been established simultaneously in Montreal and Toronto in 1880. Its purpose was to unite North American and British Jews in the idealistic cause of working for Jewish emancipation everywhere. Its more practical goal was to assist British Jewry in settling overseas those Central and East European Jews who were flocking to England in unmanageable numbers after the promulgation of the May Laws of 1882.* The English wing of the organization

* The May Laws were repressive legislation introduced in the Russian Empire following the assassination of Tsar Alexander II in March 1881. Their purpose was to crush radicalism of all sorts, but they were especially directed at Jews, who often favoured social reform and who were unjustifiably blamed for the assassination.

would provide passage to Canada, while the Canadian branches were expected to care for the refugees until they could be established in Western Canada, where the federal government had promised them land. In Toronto, the branch comprised exclusively Holy Blossom members.

Although the Toronto branch of the Anglo-Jewish Association would be reduced in the twentieth century to raising money for Jews in Europe and Asia, it was very active on the local scene in its early years. In the summer of 1882, when the great mass of East European Jews began to reach North America, the Association leased an old hotel, the National, on Bathurst Street, and offered a night's lodging and a warm meal to the refugees before they were sent westward. On at least one occasion the basement of the Richmond Street synagogue was used as a shelter. In June 1882 alone, seventy immigrants were cared for, a mammoth task considering that there were only about five hundred Jews in the city. [4] Of the seventy, twelve remained in Toronto and, being destitute, had to be found accommodation and employment. "The members of the Jewish community here are doing all in their power to provide for the immediate wants of the people ..." the *Globe* observed, "but as the community is small, embracing only eight[y] families, they would be glad of the assistance of any who may be able to help, especially in finding immediate employment for the strangers." Interested parties were asked to apply at the immigrant sheds, where the Anglo-Jewish Association had apparently provided an interpreter, and Christians, touched by the plight of the refugees, responded generously. The public, of course, was assured that only farm labourers, or those skilled in a trade and willing to work were being sent by the Association. [5]

II

Jews had still other opportunities for social activity in Toronto. A minority of the male members of Holy Blossom, usually Englishmen, were accepted into local chapters of non-Jewish international fraternal orders. The Nordheimers, it will be recalled, had belonged to the local Masonic lodge; in the 1890s, the Reverend Lazarus was appointed chaplain of a Masonic chapter, the Zetland lodge, and as early as 1879 a number of Holy Blossom members were Oddfellows, although there was no Jewish lodge in the city. Lewis Samuel, in fact, was one of the three trustees of the Canadian Order, at the same time as he was president of the Mechanics' Institute and president of the

58

synagogue. However, by the 1890s, perhaps because the influx of East European Jews had produced some discrimination among the Gentile lodges, the tendency toward exclusively Jewish chapters of international fraternal societies increased and branches of Jewish orders based in the United States proliferated. Lazarus, during his tenure, helped found a Jewish Foresters' lodge, while in the 1890s there were at least two chapters of the Sons of Benjamin in the city.[6]

By the 1890s, also, the members of Holy Blossom had become economically secure enough to afford more leisure and to desire purely cultural activities. When this occurs in North American Jewish communities, the almost inevitable consequence is the formation of a literary society, and in this Toronto was typical. In 1892 the Toronto Jewish Literary and Social Union was formed "to promote literary tastes and cultural intercourse amongst its members."[7] There was a proliferation of literary societies in Toronto generally in this period and since the city had a strongly religious tone, these affiliated with the various churches. Naturally, as acculturated citizens, the Jews of Holy Blossom wanted to participate; their only recourse was to found a society associated with the synagogue.

The study of Jewish literature appears to have played a negligible part in the activities of the Literary and Social Union. At one meeting, a member read a "pungent [sic] paper" on the subject of prohibition, while another gathering was devoted to a study of Kipling. The Union sponsored "hops" for young people, and while its principal aim was the Victorian virtue of mutual improvement, the social meetings seem to have been better attended than the literary ones.[8]

While Jewish literary societies tended, in German-dominated communities, to become enclaves of the elite, the Literary and Social Union apparently never attempted to be exclusive; nevertheless, its membership seems to have been confined to members of Holy Blossom. Until 1904 it met in the synagogue unless the size of a function precluded use of the building, when other quarters were sought temporarily. In fact, when a trend developed in the 1890s for Jewish lodges to meet in public halls such as the Victoria or Shaftesbury, the phenomenon originated not in the search for exclusiveness but rather in the ever-increasing ease with which the Jews of Holy Blossom were coming to move in Toronto society, and in the limited space offered by the Richmond Street synagogue and even by the new edifice on Bond Street.

While the men responded to the influx of East European Jews by means of the Anglo-Jewish Association, the women of Holy Blossom acted not only through the Ladies' Montefiore but also through the Toronto branch of the National Council of Jewish Women. Founded in Chicago in 1893 the Council was organized to encourage Americanized Jewish women to study the Bible and works on scientific philanthropy, and to assist in the adjustment of immigrant girls to North American life. Mrs. Meldola de Sola of Montreal, a national vice-president, had visited Toronto in 1895 and urged members of the Ladies' Montefiore to organize a chapter. As a result, in October of the following year twenty-five Holy Blossom women, some of whom were Americans married to Torontonians and familiar with the Council in the United States, began a study of Genesis as a preliminary to their philanthropic work. The Council soon offered literary evenings and English classes to immigrant Jewish girls, endeavoured to find them jobs and placed those without relatives in "respectable homes."

By the end of the decade, in an effort to make these girls self-supporting, the Council had established a sewing school at the Bond Street synagogue. Members of the chapter volunteered as instructors, continuing to meet regularly for Bible study and for literary and musical gatherings for their own edification. Early in the twentieth century this sewing school became the Jewish Working Girls' Club, which met in the homes of various Council members until 1909, when the organization was able to rent a clubhouse on Walton Street in the immigrant residential area.[9]

III

Unlike many Jewish communities in the United States where, in the absence of professional clergy, education had been ignored in favour of ritual and cemetery administration, Holy Blossom had been concerned about religious instruction almost from the beginning. As early as 1859, ten children were being taught by the *shochet* three afternoons weekly in a room at his house, fitted up by the congregation as a schoolroom. The problem was not indifference but personnel. For twenty years, no teachers associated with Holy Blossom devoted themselves exclusively to instruction. The *shochet*, the sexton and the reader each were required to teach, and since their principal interest and training lay elsewhere, the quality of instruction must have been severely lacking. The situation was not improved by the number of incompetents employed by the congregation prior to the 1880s and by the frequent absence of a minister. In 1864 it is evident that the teacher was having difficulty communicating with his pupils purely on the basis of language; the congregation was advertising for an individual capable of teaching in English.

There were difficulties in communication on other levels as well. The employees of the synagogue were Europeans, whereas most of the children had probably been born in North America. At least one frustrated individual offered to take a reduction in salary in order to be relieved of his teaching duties.[10]

Once the Richmond Street synagogue had been built, the physical facilities improved but the quality of the teaching did not. By the early 1880s a capable teacher, Mr. Mintz, had been employed to assist the *shochet*, the Reverend Robinson, in his teaching duties and both men were apparently well educated. Mintz, however, died in 1885 and Robinson had too many other duties. Consequently, by 1886 the trustees were warned that "a great improvement is needed in teaching the children."[11]

At this point, steps were taken to ensure a more systematic approach in curriculum, the engagement of teachers and in school administration. There had been an educational committee at Holy Blossom in 1869, but apparently its sole function was to have the schoolroom properly equipped. The teachers were technically responsible to the trustees, but seem to have been left to their own devices except where salary, misconduct or incapacitation were concerned. Financial support was haphazard; parents – members and non-members alike – were obliged to pay fees according to the number of children sent. Poor children were admitted free. Tuition varied from one period to another and seems to have constantly decreased under parental pressure.

When Edmund Scheuer arrived in 1886, the trustees jumped at the opportunity of investing him with control over the school. He was already known as an educator in the province, through his activity as Anshe Sholom in Hamilton. Scheuer immediately mobilized a group of volunteers, mostly wives and older children of members, to teach without fee, in addition to the paid officials of the congregation, who were to teach on a limited basis. Scheuer himself acted as both principal and teacher. Consequently, tuition fees could be dispensed with altogether, and a greater number of students were attracted.[12]

Another attraction was the "de-Hebraizing" of the school. Children wishing instruction in the Talmud and rabbinic codes could still obtain lessons from the minister-preacher, from Robinson, from Mark Geldzaeler who was sexton and *baal koreh* after 1892, or from any number of recently arrived East Europeans. The curriculum at Holy Blossom, however, was modelled on the Sunday School, a phenomenon which had grown up in the United States in the middle of the nineteenth century and was common there, even in traditional congregations, by the time Scheuer arrived at Holy Blossom.[13] Bible was taught, as were the rudiments of prayer and some elementary Hebrew, but the emphasis was on Jewish history, ethics and etiquette rather than upon ritual. Classes were restricted primarily to Sunday mornings, an indication of the difficulty of attracting students after school during the week. Report cards and formal examinations were introduced and prizes were awarded for excellence. An effort was made, in addition, to increase discipline. About 1900, for instance, Holy Blossom sent notices to parents requesting

> your cordial co-operation in enforcing the REGULAR and PUNCTUAL attendance of your CHILDREN. We would also ask you to kindly assist in securing the due preparation by them of the lessons given them for home study. If all parents will earnestly second our efforts to promote the Hebrew and religious education of the children, the results will undoubtedly, be satisfactory to all concerned.[14]

The new system was effective in attracting large numbers of students to Holy Blossom. In fact, one reason for the erection of the Bond Street synagogue was the inadequacy of the schoolroom at Richmond Street. Indeed, commenting on the Bond Street building, the *World* stated that "The education of the young in the principles of the Hebrew faith . . .is being very successfully carried out" and the new synagogue had "probably the best-fitted schoolroom in the city." By the end of the century, not only Holy Blossom children but also a large number of East Europeans, mostly girls, were being sent to study under Scheuer.

IV

The Jews of the old community had had little difficulty in adjusting to life in Toronto. For most, language was no barrier; either English was their native tongue or they had lived in Britain or in the United States prior to their arrival. Nor had the majority ever suffered the insecurity of living in the Russian Pale of Settlement, in constant fear of pogrom. Most had emigrated in order to improve themselves economically rather than to escape persecution. Consequently, they were eager to accept ideas from the community at large.

They tended to adopt North American practices almost immediately. Although most of the members undoubtedly under-

62

stood Yiddish, the minutes of Holy Blossom were taken in English from the first, while the system of ballotting on the admission of new members and the drafting of a constitution were principally American phenomena. By the 1890s Americanisms had penetrated the actual ritual of the synagogue. For instance, the Governor General suggested in 1892 that all congregations hold a Thanksgiving service; the trustees reacted favourably and only the opposition of the Reverend Elzas prevented its taking place. However, from the following year, when Lazarus replaced him, the Thanksgiving service became an annual event. The same decade saw other signs of acculturation among Holy Blossom members, even to the extent of their minimizing specifically Jewish behaviour and encouraging adoption of Canadian customs by the East Europeans. The annual charity ball of the Ladies' Montefiore, now held complete with orchestra at the new Foresters' Temple on Bay Street became the principal social event of the year and was the occasion for debutantes to appear. At Holy Blossom Sabbath (Sunday) School, the prizes awarded for achievement were not books of Jewish content; for instance, Samuel Johnson's *History of Rasselas*, *Robinson Crusoe*, and books of ballads. Daughters of the old community acquired finesse by attending such institutions as Miss Amy Sternberg's classes in physical culture (gymnastics) and dancing held at St. George's Hall, while the Jewish Working Girls' Club attempted to divest the East European newcomers of their unacceptable alien characteristics. The Council of Jewish Women, it was reported, "watch over them," and encourage immigrant girls to spend their evenings at the club, "thus enabling them to come into touch with the best Canadian life at once . . . ."[15]

The increased formalism, the departure from tradition at Holy Blossom and the signs of what might be called Canadianization were part of a trend among the long-established sectors of Jewish communities throughout the continent. In Toronto, however, this was not merely an attempt to emulate the non-Jews in order to gain acceptance, as had been the case in many instances elsewhere. That element was not totally absent here; some members of the old community were actually ashamed to admit that they were Jewish and needed the reinforcement of Gentile approval. But the community's predominantly English composition made possible in the nineteenth century the general acceptance of the Holy Blossom group by at least the middle class, if not by the elite, of Christian society. By the mid-1870s the Richmond Street synagogue could be opened with a minimum of self-consciousness. In the 1880s non-Jews responded generously to fund-raising appeals by the Anglo-Jewish Association, while in the following decade they contributed to the building fund of the Bond Street synagogue.

At the opening of the new building, Alfred Benjamin praised the "courtesy, sympathy and liberality" displayed by Gentiles toward Jews in Toronto.[16] The *Evening Star* and the *World* accorded the dedication front page coverage; the latter described the service as "one of the most impressive ceremonies ever seen in Toronto," and quoted Lazarus' lengthy sermon verbatim. The *Mail and Empire* took notice of the large number of non-Jews present, including Mayor Shaw, the local member of Parliament, Professor Goldwin Smith and, significantly, Samuel Nordheimer. "While many present had never before taken part in a service with their Jewish fellow-citizens," the *Mail* remarked, "they could not but have been impressed with its solemn beauty."[17]

The Jews of Holy Blossom were sufficiently confident of their relationship with the Christian community in this period to speak out on matters of civic policy, even when these involved the church. In 1897, for instance, when the Anglican clergy urged the introduction of religious instruction into the public schools of Toronto, the Reverend Lazarus, Alfred Benjamin and Edmund Scheuer presented a brief to the Public School Board calling the proposal "in the last degree ill-advised, inexpedient and objectionable . . . . Though we feel confident that our interests are safe in your hands," the brief stated, and were sure that the Jews' "rights and liberties" would not be encroached upon, the congregation thought it "prudent" to insist that the state not interfere in religion. Jewish children who attended the public schools, they continued, "do not wish to be differentiated from their fellow-pupils. They have no wish to draw upon themselves unnecessary attention, nor do they like to be looked upon, or to be singled out from the general body as if they were inferior to the rest." Religion in the school would produce sectarian disputes which would harm not only the Jews but the very principle of secular schools. The congregation drew the board's attention to the system of religious education at Holy Blossom and asked "why cannot the Church follow the example of the synagogue in this respect . . . ."[18]

Jews and non-Jews met also less formally, being encouraged to do so in the 1890s by Mr. Lazarus, who was active in non-sectarian philanthropic work. He was highly regarded in the city; the *World* called him "a true friend to the helpless, forlorn and poor," and Christians regularly attended his lectures at the late Friday evening services. It was doubtless through his efforts that the Toronto Jewish Literary and Social Union began to meet with a club of Bond Street Congregational Church and came to be addressed frequently by its minister. In addition, many Holy Blossom members probably met socially with non-Jews, as evidenced by the fact that a large number of Gentiles attended the girls' confirmation ceremony at the synagogue in 1899. Presumably they had been invited by the parents of the participants. Whatever anti-semitism existed in Toronto in the nineteenth century remained latent so long as the principal Jewish image was projected by Holy Blossom. The advent of the East Europeans, however, was to change the situation radically.[19]

NOTES

1 Toronto Hebrew Ladies Sick and Benevolent Society, *Minutes*, Jan. 5, 1868; May 20, 1868; *ibid., By-Laws and Regulations 1868*.

2 For example, widows were given a weekly allowance to help them maintain their children. Toronto Hebrew Ladies Sick and Benevolent Society, *Minutes*, Jan. 4, 1874. In 1872, the Society provided $20 for the relief of Persian Jews; *Ibid.*, March 17, 1872. In 1876, eighty cases were assisted in Toronto. "The Development of the Social Services in the Toronto Jewish Community," (mimeo. *ca.* 1965. Canadian Jewish Congress Central Region Archives), p. 3.

3 "Preliminary agreement to form a 'Charitable Society'. "MSS, July 9, 1877, Holy Blossom Archives; Heinz Warschauer, *The Story of Holy Blossom Temple*, 2nd ed. (Toronto: Holy Blossom, 1959), p. 130; *Mail and Empire*, Sept. 25, 1897.

4 In 1880 there were 534 Jews in Toronto. Canada, Department of Agriculture, *Census of Canada 1880-81* (Ottawa: 1883), I, p. 174. Warschauer, *op.cit.*, 2nd ed., p. 217.

5 *Globe*, May 27, 1882. Anglo-Jewish Association, Toronto Branch, "Report for General Meeting Held Sunday, April 19, 1896" (typescript, Holy Blossom Archives). Public sympathy for the refugees is illustrated by the recounting of their tragic experiences in the press, e.g., *Globe*, May 18, 1882.

6 *Jewish Times*, Sept. 15, 1899, p. 321. *Toronto City Directory for 1890* (Toronto: Polk, 1890).

7 Toronto Jewish Literary and Social Union, *Constitution and By-Laws*, 1894. Between 1886 and 1895, an organization called the Hebrew Congregational Society or the Toronto Hebrew Congregation is listed in the directories as meeting at Holy Blossom. This was either a men's mutual benefit branch of the synagogue or the congregation itself, meeting as a corporate body to deal with non-religious matters. It was probably the former and, as suggested by the date of its apparent demise, was superseded by the fraternal lodges.

8 *Jewish Times*, Nov. 25, 1898, p. 405; March 3, 1899, pp. 101, 102.

9 Ida Siegel, personal interview, Aug. 26, 1971; National Council of Jewish Women, *Proceedings of the First Convention of the National Council of Jewish Women* (Philadelphia: Jewish Publication Society of America, 1897), pp. 142-43, 153; Bertha Draimin "Memory Open your Door," *The Canadian Council Woman*, III, 2 (Jan., 1967), p. 5.
   In 1904, the school had been expanded to include "poor children as well as working girls." *Jewish Times*, Oct. 7, 1904, p. 364.

10 *HBM*, April 15, 1860; Warschauer, *op.cit.*, 1st ed., p. 98, Toronto Hebrew Benevolent Society [Association] *Minutes*, Feb. 7, 1869; *HBM*, Aug. 12, 1864.

11 Mintz received no remuneration for his services. *HBM*, July 6, 1884; July 11, 1886.

12 Toronto *Star Weekly*, Feb. 12, 1916; Scheuer, *Reminiscences*, 1933; *HBM*, Aug. 13, 1893; Arthur Cohen, personal interview, Dec. 20, 1971.

13 Leo J. Honor, "The Impact of the American Environment and American Ideas on Jewish Elementary Education in the United States," *Jewish Quarterly Review*, New Series, XLV (1955), pp. 467-68.

14 Printed notice sent out *ca.* 1900. Fragment found in Holy Blossom Minute Book (Holy Blossom Archives); Toronto *World*, Sept. 15, 1897; *Jewish Times*, July 7, 1899, p. 251. The assembly hall in the basement of the new Bond Street edifice boasted movable partitions which could be arranged to divide the auditorium into eight classrooms. Movable partitions had already been introduced in several churches in Toronto, including St. Paul's Anglican on Bloor Street.

15 Abraham I. Willinsky, *A Doctor's Memoirs* (Toronto: Macmillan, 1960), p. 13; Ida Siegel, personal interview, Aug. 12, 1971; National Council of Jewish Women, *Proceedings of the First Convention . . .,*pp. 142-43; *Jewish Times*, Jan. 6, 1899, p. 38; April 18, 1913, p. 49.

16 Quoted in *Mail and Empire*, Sept. 16, 1897. Among the contributors to the Bond Street structure were Henry Pellatt, Timothy Eaton, Robert Simpson and one of the Masseys.

Christians in Toronto had rallied to assist Jews as early as 1859. When the Jewish quarter of Tangiers was sacked in the war between Spain and Morocco, forcing many Jews to flee destitute from their homes, Morris Lumley persuaded John Beverley Robinson to set up a committee to help the refugees. The response, Lumley reported to the congregation, was gratifying.

17 *Evening Star*, Sept. 15, 1897; *World*, Sept. 16, 1897; *Mail and Empire*, Sept. 16, 1897. While Goldwin Smith is generally regarded as having been an anti-semite because of his articles in various publications disparaging Jewish characteristics, his appearance at Holy Blossom lends credence to the contention that his position was xenophobic rather than anti-Jewish and that he was perhaps willing to accept those Jews who would adopt the customs of the general community.

Samuel Nordheimer had become so assimilated by this time that he was regarded as a Gentile. Indeed, when the Duke and Duchess of York (later King George V and Queen Mary) visited Toronto in 1901, the bouquet on behalf of the Daughters of the Empire would be presented by his daughter Phyllis. Joseph Pope, *The Tour of Their Royal Highnesses the Duke and Duchess of Cornwall and York Through the Dominion of Canada in the Year 1901* (Ottawa: King's Printer, 1903), p. 111.

18 Quoted in *Mail and Empire*, June 12, 1897. For details of the plan for the introduction of religious instruction, see *Globe*, June 4, 1897, and *World*, June 4, 1897. The Anglicans insisted that religious instruction be compulsory. When some children were excused, those who remained became restive. They also stressed that this process be begun first in St. John's Ward, the principal area of residence for immigrant Jews.

Benjamin reiterated the synagogue's position on religion in the public schools at the opening of the Bond Street building and maintained that if the proposal were approved, Jews would reluctantly be obliged to establish their own separate schools.

19 *World*, Sept. 15, 1897; *Jewish Times*, Sept. 15, 1899, p. 321. It would be interesting to know if Lazarus was invited to address the church group. One suspects that he was.

CHAPTER 5

THE NEW COMMUNITY, 1883 – 1914

The process of industrialization, slow to reach Eastern Europe, progressed steadily after the mid-nineteenth century. By the 1870s its effects were everywhere apparent. Throughout most of Russia, Lithuania and the Austro-Hungarian province of Galicia, economic dislocation became commonplace, especially for artisans and tradesmen whose livelihood depended on the time-honoured relationships between craftsman and merchant in a non-industrial society. Since it was practically the universal rule in Eastern Europe to forbid Jews to own agricultural property, it was in these vulnerable craft and mercantile occupations that most Jews made their living.

While a small number of Jews emigrated to North America from these areas in the 1860s and 1870s, most attempted to withstand the hardships of their native countries; for centuries it had been difficult but they had always managed to adjust. It was better, perhaps, to suffer in familiar surroundings than to leave their established communities for the unknown hazards of the New World. However, with the assassination of Tsar Alexander II, conditions for Jews, especially in the Pale of Settlement (the area of western Russia and Poland) became intolerable. All Jews in the Russian Empire, except for the few with permits, were forced into the large towns, aggravating the economic hardships of those already struggling there. The May Laws of 1882 prohibited Jewish movement even within the Pale, restricted Jewish assembly and worship, pushed the last Jewish farmers off the land, prevented Jews from holding public office and from entering the professions, denied them higher education and excluded them from the ever-increasing number of factories. In addition, the Slavs had, even before the assassination, given vent to their emerging nationalism in attacks upon Jewish communities. The Tsarist government, when it did not openly encourage these pogroms, at least turned a blind eye, a tendency which increased late in the nineteenth century as official attempts were being made to distract the populace from government incompetence. Few years passed without such acts of vandalism, but especially destructive were the pogroms of 1881-82, 1891 and 1905-6.[1]

There can be little doubt that some East Europeans had already, by the late 1860s and early 1870s, found refuge in Toronto. They were certainly settling in the area; Buffalo for instance, had a sizable Jewish population of East European origin by 1865.[2] Yet too little is known about the East Europeans in Toronto to offer any definitive statement about them. They appear to have remained on the margins of the established community and Holy Blossom probably had dealings with them only in the distribution of charity. Prior to the 1880s they were not numerous enough to be considered a group apart from the old community. The minutes of Holy Blossom make no mention of them as a separate entity. Orthodoxy was still strong in Eastern Europe and there was the feeling that it could not survive in America. Individuals who left in this period were, as a rule, those relatively indifferent to tradition. Holy Blossom would suffice for those who wished to pray, if they were not alienated by its English atmosphere. As with Toronto's earliest Jewish inhabitants, it would be only in the purchase of a cemetery that they would make evident their presence as a distinct group. This did not transpire until the 1880s.

By that time, however, conditions in Russia, Lithuania and Galicia had worsened to such an extent that a mass exodus of Jews had begun. In areas struck by pogroms, whole families – indeed entire villages – left for the New World. In areas less affected physically but nonetheless economically depressed and labouring under legal sanctions, heads of families and unmarried sons emigrated, and it was expected that once established in the "Golden Land" they would send for their kin.

The United States and not Canada was the goal of most, and many did achieve it, despite expensive fares and a poor reception by a country doubting its ability to assimilate them and already considering immigration restriction. Others, however, congregated in London and in other British ports, attracted in the case of Canada by government propaganda promising land grants in the West and by the cheaper fare which prevailed between Great Britain and her possessions. Elaborate organization was established in London, Montreal and Toronto to assist Jews who wished to take advantage of government offers. But all the efforts of groups such as the Anglo-Jewish Association in London and Toronto, and the Montefiore Agricultural Aid Association in Montreal failed to persuade more than a fraction of the newcomers to take up the plough. The majority, unaccustomed to the land, preferred to remain where they saw the first sign of Jewish life on this side of the ocean. For those landing at Halifax or Quebec City, Montreal became the logical place to settle. For those bound for Canada via New York, Toronto was more convenient. Some, intent on joining families in midwestern American cities such as Chicago, ran out of funds, found themselves stranded in Toronto and remained. Others stopped over on the way westward from Montreal and also remained. And once a nucleus of families from a particular area in Europe had established themselves in Toronto and began to write home, others were attracted quickly.[3] By 1900 certainly, and perhaps even before, Jews were leaving Europe bound specifically for Toronto.

When the Richmond Street synagogue opened, a building accommodating four hundred people was considered sufficient. By 1881 the Jews of Toronto numbered 534, by no means a significant increase. Within the decade, however, the Jewish population almost trebled and by 1901 it exceeded three thousand.[4] By 1911 the number of Jews in the city had increased by 401 per cent, (compared with an increase in the total population of 72 per cent), due largely to immigration. The following decade saw an increase of another 90 per cent, with the greatest periods of influx being between the end of the Russo-Japanese War and the outbreak of the First World War, and in 1919-20. Between 1911 and 1913 alone, the number of Jews jumped from just over 18,000 to about 32,000.[5]

II

The East European Jew arriving in Toronto in the last two decades of the nineteenth century was almost destitute. Consequently, he had to find accommodation and employment quickly in order merely to subsist. His choices were limited. Frequently he found his skill useless in Toronto, or discovered that he did not have the capital necessary to establish himself as an independent artisan or tradesman. Since Toronto had no established clothing manufacturing network operated by Jews, as was true in larger centres such as New York and Montreal, factory employment was at first avoided. Most Jews had not been factory workers in Europe and so in these early years found the plants strange and even frightening. But more important was the fact that one did not seek employment by Gentiles except as a last resort. Non-Jewish

71

manufacturers were unlikely to have regard for the intricacies of Jewish Sabbath observance.

The immigrant therefore sought an occupation which required little initial capital and offered some degree of independence. Peddling, rag-picking, bottle-washing, dealing in used furniture and other salvaged goods had several advantages in these circumstances. As activities low on the scale of prestige, they were avoided by the non-Jewish native. Christian immigrants either did not congregate in the cities as did the Jews or, not having been subjected to occupational restrictions in their native countries, had developed traditional skills which they were able to use in North America. Peddling and the salvage trades became occupations in which Jews found little competition. A few pennies could provide merchandise – sewing supplies, stationery, cutlery and other small housewares. A knapsack or ramshackle pushcart enabled goods to be transported to the homes of prospective customers, be they in towns surrounding Toronto or in the city itself.[6]

These were menial jobs but they offered the immigrant an opportunity to maintain the traditional Jewish values that might be endangered by the regular hours of the factory. He might, if he chose, attend services in the synagogue each morning and linger to study a page of Talmud afterwards. By not working on Jewish holy days, he might lose money, but never his job. Peddling enabled the East European immigrant to retain his dignity which depended, at least prior to 1900, on his role within the Jewish community, on piety and learning rather than on wealth or occupational status.[7]

By 1910 there had developed in Toronto a hierarchy in the Jewish salvage trades. Some of the more prosperous East Europeans were able to become rag-processors, taking stock from the rag-pickers and often dealing unscrupulously with these collectors, who had few other places to dispose of their goods. The processors, in turn, sold to Gentile salvage firms or to the Frankel brothers, German Jews and members of Holy Blossom, who then had one of the largest waste-processing establishments in the city. Others became purveyors of peddlers' supplies, enabling the peddler to obtain all his myriad items of merchandise at one location. At the top of the scale were those with enough capital to open secondhand and pawnshops, and those few clothing peddlers who had acquired experience in dealing with non-Jewish wholesale firms and were able to develop small wholesale concerns supplying Jewish tradesmen. This was the ideal, to set up a little shop of one's own.

For some, however, especially for many who arrived after 1900, peddling was not a feasible vehicle to the attainment of the independent shop. For all its advantages, it required physical stamina, a persistence and often an audacity in dealing with clients which all did not possess. Moreover, both rag-picking and peddling necessitated outdoor work in all kinds of weather, exposure often coupled with abuse from insensitive anti-semites and xenophobes. Besides, there was a great deal of competition even among the peddlers by this time, making it increasingly difficult for them to make a living. By 1916 there were six hundred Jewish rag peddlers in the city and conditions were so bad that they each offered to pay the Red Cross ten dollars to stop collecting rags to augment its funds.[8] The alternative, as in so many other North American cities, was the ready-made clothing factory.

It has been argued that the Jews gravitated to this particular branch of manufacturing because large numbers had resorted to tailoring when they were legally excluded from other occupations in Russia and Poland. Tailoring required little capital and at least a tailor's family could be clothed. Furthermore, the garment factory would employ all members of the family; it was a readily available source of employment for penniless new arrivals. But these factors do not in fact explain the flocking of East European Jews to the garment trade. Admittedly, Russian and Polish Jews had had some experience in handicraft industries in Europe and the few who had been wholesalers there had tended to deal in clothing or in textiles. But only 10 per cent had actually been tailors. Jewish women, moreover, unlike their counterparts in other immigrant groups, tended to remain at home after marriage, while Jews whenever possible preferred to send their children to school rather than to the factory. The principal attraction of the clothing industry was that in contrast to other forms of factory employment, earnings were directly related to individual effort. Experience and capital could be acquired solely by personal conscientiousness. Since the aim of the Jew was to set up shop for himself, and since the unit of industrial production was smaller in the garment industry than elsewhere, the chances of this becoming a reality were enhanced. Jews in North America, particularly the East Europeans, tended to avoid situations where discrimination might be a problem for them. Consequently they strove to establish small businesses – grocery stores, junkyards and clothing shops – rather than to seek administrative positions in larger firms owned by non-Jews.[9]

At the beginning of the twentieth century the garment manufacturing industry was dominated by non-Jewish firms. The

Lowndes Company of Front Street, Johnson Brothers (later Randall-Johnson) on Wellington Street, and the T. Eaton Company were the major establishments, but there were a host of smaller concerns on Church, Bay, Adelaide and Victoria streets. It is estimated that by 1911 there were twelve hundred Jews employed in the cloak industry alone. Although Johnson's ran a close second, the largest single employer of Jewish labour in Toronto in the decade prior to the First World War was the T. Eaton Company. Eaton's had begun manufacturing its own goods to supply its mail order customers as early as the 1890s. By 1910 it had erected a large manufacturing complex occupying most of the block bounded by Teraulay (now Bay), Albert, Louisa and James streets and was producing a variety of merchandise, ranging from underwear to ladies' cloaks. The number of Jews employed at Eaton's in this period was in the hundreds and, while working conditions in factories were generally poor in the early twentieth century, those at Eaton's were better than most. Moreover, at Eaton's the management did not object to workers taking the Sabbath off even though the factory remained open on Saturday mornings, and a qualified operator there could earn extra money by teaching boys who were sent into the factory to learn the trade.[10]

Even in the worst Toronto factories conditions were nowhere as bad as in the sweatshops of New York and Montreal, where the scale of the industry was larger. Operators in Toronto were not, as a rule, forced to take work home under tacit threat of dismissal, nor did they have to do so voluntarily in order to pay exorbitant rents. Rents in Jewish residential areas for most of the period before the First World War were not excessively high.[11]

By 1910 an increasing number of Toronto Jews had entered the garment manufacturing industry and related trades such as wholesale textiles on an independent basis. Some were expert operators who had gained experience in non-Jewish firms and ventured out for themselves, but others were able to establish themselves shortly upon their arrival from Europe. These tended to be Galicians; in Austria it had been easier for a Jew to amass capital and to emigrate with it relatively intact. Moreover, many Jews had been engaged in the wholesale woollens trade in Galicia.

The impetus for the establishment of these Jewish manufacturing firms frequently came from Montreal. That city was the centre for the importation of European cloth and the trade was almost an exclusively Jewish activity. Importers made frequent trips to Toronto to arrange contracts with local non-Jewish firms and, in the process, also made contact with local East European

Jews, encouraging some to set up for themselves by supplying them with raw materials. By the early twentieth century, a flourishing trade was in progress between Jewish wholesale firms in Montreal and independent Jewish manufacturers in Toronto. Jewish manufacturing firms, however, could by no means compare in size to even the smallest of the Gentile concerns. They operated in rented lofts and in small cottages adjacent to the central business district, often in the home of the owner. Their employees were exclusively Jewish, but were not restricted to the *landsleit** of the manufacturer. In fact, the majority were probably not Galician but Russian, Lithuanian and Polish.[12]

These Jewish establishments were not as independent as they would have liked. Their principal business came in the form of subcontracts from the large Gentile firms. Since Jews would tolerate poorer working conditions and longer hours simply to work for other Jews, and since the overhead of the small Jewish factories was low, goods could be produced there more cheaply than by the large concerns themselves. The skilled labour of the Jewish manufacturing plants did not comprise, as one might expect, large numbers of people attracted from the Gentile firms. Those who had jobs at Eaton's, for example, tended to keep them or else to set up shop for themselves. Of those resident in Toronto, the Jewish concerns attracted only the ultra-orthodox (since all Jewish firms prior to 1914 closed on the Sabbath), the most recent immigrants, or relatives of the employer and his workers. A principal source of labour was New York. While every garment industry is seasonal, the greatest seasonal dislocation hits the largest centres and those concentrating on the constantly changing fashions of women's clothing. New York fitted both categories, and as a result large numbers of New York workers had to look elsewhere for employment in the off-season. This dislocation was aggravated by the frequency of strikes as manufacturers in New York and other American cities attempted to exclude unions from their shops in the decade before 1914. For some reason those laid off, and especially those in New York, tended to flock to Toronto on an almost annual basis, and a significant number remained.[13]

Prior to the outbreak of war, Jewish manufacturers in Toronto were at the mercy of the large retail establishments, especially Eaton's. Jewish producers wanting to expand or needing money to purchase raw materials could offer no security on a bank loan. Lack of credit, therefore, forced them to offer large job lots of goods in return for ready cash to the local department

* Immigrants from one's town or district in Europe, (Singular, *landsman*).

stores, and the latter, realizing that no offer could be refused, constantly forced prices down. Consequently, expansion was a virtual impossibility for Jewish garment firms in this period, a fact which did not displease the established non-Jewish companies who resented the competition.[14]

While these conditions did not in themselves determine the location of the East European Jewish "ghetto" in Toronto, they were an essential factor in its economic life and one which for decades delayed the removal of the Jewish community from the streets adjacent to City Hall.

NOTES

1 Maldwyn A. Jones, *American Immigration*, Chicago History of American Civilization (Chicago: University of Chicago Press, 1960), p. 202. For a more complete account of the factors encouraging emigration from Eastern Europe, see Mark Wischnitzer, *To Dwell in Safety* (Philadelphia: Jewish Publication Society of America, 1948), chaps. 2-4, and Louis Greenberg, *The Jews in Russia*, 2 vols. (New Haven: Yale University Press, 1944) I, chaps. 10-12.

2 Adler and Connolly, *op.cit.*, pp. 38, 114.

3 J.B. Salsberg, personal interview, Jan. 15, 1973.

4 Canada, Department of Agriculture, *Census of Canada 1880-81* (Ottawa: 1883) I, p. 174. In 1891 the Jewish population of Toronto stood at 1425 and in 1901 at 3090; *ibid., 1890-91*, I, p. 283; Canada, Census & Statistics Office, *Fourth Census of Canada, 1901* (Ottawa: 1902) I, p. 219. These census quotations are probably slightly below the true figures. This is to be expected when confronted with a language barrier and with a people suspicious of government.

5 Louis Rosenberg, "Jewish Mutual Benefit and Friendly Societies in Toronto. The First Fifty Years 1896-1945," (typescript, 63 pp., *ca.* 1947: Canadian Jewish Congress Central Region Archives, Toronto), p. 18. In June 1907 it was estimated that there were between 8,000 and 10,000 Jews in Toronto. In the spring of 1909 there were 15,000 Jews in the city. By 1911, the number stood at 18,237, and in 1921 at 34,619.

It is interesting to compare the growth of the Jewish

76

population in Toronto with that of Detroit which was, like Toronto, a point of second instance; that is, immigrants did not land in either city directly from Europe. They were either stranded there on their way to some other destination or were attracted by relatives or countrymen already living there. Furthermore, both cities now have a Jewish population similar in size and in ethnic composition.

Whereas Detroit was an older settlement and had a larger initial Jewish population because emigrating German Jews in the mid-nineteenth century tended to choose the United States over Canada, by 1910 Toronto's Jewish community had reached almost the same number. In 1880, Detroit had 1,000 Jews, by 1900 over 10,000 and by 1910, 18,600. Between that year and 1914 the populations of the two cities seemed to keep pace with each other almost exactly. The significant difference is that while the influx to Detroit prior to 1910 had been relatively steady, that to Toronto developed rapidly and must have come as more of a shock to the established community.

6 It has been suggested as a general theory that discrimination or fear of competition led Jews into occupational fields which had somewhat of a stigma attached – peddling in the early years of immigration and the motion picture industry later on. Carey McWilliams, *A Mask for Privilege*, cited in Moshe Davis and Isidore S. Meyer, eds., *The Writing of American Jewish History* (New York: American Jewish Historical Society, 1957), p. 121. For a contemporary description of Jewish occupations in the 1890s, see *Mail and Empire*, Sept. 25, 1897.

7 See Bernard D. Weinryb, "Jewish Immigration and Accommodation to America: in Marshall Sklare, ed., *The Jews: Social Patterns of an American Group* (Glencoe, Ill.: Free Press, 1958), pp. 4-22. East European Jews who arrived after 1880 tended to be observant. It is a widely accepted fact among Toronto Jews with an intimate knowledge of the phenomenon that these religious motives, and especially the desire to observe the Sabbath, were most influential in directing Jews into the peddling trades. (E.g., J.B. Salsberg, personal interview, Jan. 15, 1973 and Harry Korolnek, personal interview, Dec. 26, 1972.)

8 Toronto *Daily Star*, May 30, 1916.

9 Maldwyn Jones, *op.cit.*, pp. 219-20.

10 Samuel Charney of the Toronto Cloak Manufacturers Association, quoted in Charles Shidlowsky, "From Rags to Riches," *Masada*, IV, 2 (Oct. 1972), p. 11. David Green, personal interview, April 9, 1973. Ida Siegel, personal interview, Dec. 23, 1971.

11 For sweatshop conditions in garment factories in Montreal, see *The Jewish Times* (1903), p. 73.

12 Ida Siegel, personal interview, Aug. 12, 1971. William Leibel, personal interview, Jan. 28, 1972.

13 Montreal, curiously, seems not to have experienced this influx.

14 Ida Siegel, personal interviews, Dec. 23, 1971; Aug. 12, 1971.

PART II

EAST
BECOMES
WEST

CHAPTER 6

RESIDENTIAL PATTERNS IN THE NEW COMMUNITY, 1880–1914

Members of Holy Blossom, like Central and West European Jews throughout North America, tended to integrate residentially with the rest of the city's population in this period.[1] They had not lived segregated in Europe and they had no reason for doing so in Toronto. Their British tone made them acceptable to the community at large, and while few were actually wealthy compared to established non-Jewish families in the city, the majority were at least what might be described as middle class; consequently, they could choose their residential location without restriction. Indeed, in the 1890s the more prominent – Edmund Scheuer, Alfred Benjamin, Frank Benjamin and Leo Frankel, for instance – were living on fashionable Sherbourne and Jarvis streets and counted such illustrious families as the Masseys among their neighbours. Almost without exception, members of the old community lived between Yonge and Parliament streets, south of Bloor.

For East Europeans, however, the choice of location was limited, if not non-existent. Arriving with little money and desiring to save as much as possible in order to bring their relatives from Europe, they gravitated to the cheapest accommodation available. Seeking work in garment factories for long and awkward hours at low pay, they wanted dwellings close enough to their places of employment to allow them to walk to work, thus avoiding the expenditure of time and cash in travelling. Moreover, the ready-made clothing industry had inherent features which encouraged its workers to live near the factory. Although one of these, daily hiring, was uncommon in Toronto, there was still considerable uncertainty in employment. With the development of the piecework system, the tasks performed came to involve a minimum of skill, while the increased influx of immigrants heightened competition for them. Tenure was therefore precarious. In addition, seasonal layoffs were common, as were strikes encouraged by the developing labour unions. One soon realized the wisdom of living where alternative employment was likely to be available. In Toronto, therefore, as in other cities on this continent, the immigrant reception area emerged immediately adjacent to the central business district.[2]

But while other immigrant groups in Toronto followed a similar residential pattern, concentration in one district was greatest among the East European Jews. Toronto in the late nineteenth century was a city divided into pockets of distinct groups segregated by religion and by social status. This was true even within immigrant groups; Italians, for instance, were distributed in a number of tiny regions throughout the city.[3] Only the East European Jews departed from this pattern by settling in one major area.

Traditional Jewish values have always emphasized the importance of community and fellowship among Jews. The East Europeans, especially, had had centuries of conditioning to the fact that spiritual survival depended upon cohesiveness; a clustering of the orthodox for better religious observance was therefore to be expected. The prohibition of travelling on the Sabbath made residence within walking distance of the synagogue imperative. There was a need, moreover, to be close to the ritual bath and to shops catering to observers of the dietary laws. But even the non-observant and those who could have afforded to live elsewhere clung tenaciously to the same area as the orthodox. Economic and emotional insecurity forced the immigrant to seek companionship with those who shared his Yiddish language and upon whom he could rely for assistance in difficult times. Cultural affinity helped cushion the blow of departure from well-organized Jewish life in Europe, and the impact of North American freedom which appeared at first as bewildering chaos. The voluntarily created ghetto, representing an attempt to transplant in Toronto the *shtetl* (Jewish village) of Russia, Galicia or Poland, gave immigrant Jews a sense of belonging. Here they created their own cultural amenities: synagogues, schools, mutual assistance and fraternal societies, a theatre and even a newspaper.

The earliest East European arrivals rented quarters along Richmond Street between Yonge and York, and on York Street itself, where by the 1890s a number had opened small retail shops. By the turn of the century, however, the centre of gravity of the ghetto had shifted north of Queen Street, to the area bounded roughly by Queen, Yonge and Gerrard streets and by University

Avenue. It thus included most of what had, prior to 1891, been designated St. John's Ward. Other immigrants had preceded the Jews here, but from the late 1890s, Jews outnumbered all other ethnic groups in the vicinity, the first time they were to constitute a majority of the population in any group of streets in Toronto.[4]

Originally called "Macaulay town," but popularly labelled "the Ward," the area had been the first speculative development on park lots in the city, having been well subdivided by 1850. Construction was dense by Toronto standards, most of the buildings dating from the 1850s and 1860s being stuccoed frame cottages of one or two stories. Rear cottages were a common feature. The streets, characteristic of developments of this sort, were numerous, close together and punctuated by alleys and laneways bearing names such as Foster Place, Price's Lane and Cuttle Place.

Already at the middle of the nineteenth century the area was considered a slum, as indicated by the placing of the House of Industry at Elm and Chestnut streets in 1848. Centre Avenue, originally Centre Street, was then thought of as a "red light" district, a reputation that persisted to the turn of the century.[5] Although physical conditions were deplorable, residential use being intermingled with light industry, they nowhere approximated those in immigrant reception areas in larger North American centres. Tenements were few, those that did exist having been erected by speculators around 1900 specifically to house immigrants.*The growth of tenements in Toronto was inhibited by a municipal by-law restricting the density of building. There was, however, no limit on the number of people who could inhabit a given structure. By 1911, there were only eight tenements in the Ward, in addition to a number of old hotels that had been converted to boarding houses. These were scrupulously avoided by Jews, probably because rents there were exorbitant. Most of their dwellings had formerly been single-family structures; the majority were rented from non-Jews.

Large families crowded into these cottages; there was always room for the relative or *landsman* from Europe, who was accommodated until he found employment and a place of his own, and for the multitude of boarders who abounded in the district. Unmarried men, or those who had emigrated without their families, sought shelter with Jewish families from their localities in

---

* Following the definition employed about 1900 by the commission on building standards in New York City, the term "tenement" in this study will signify a barracks-like structure housing more than three families.

a KENSINGTON MARKET

b THE WARD

1 SITE OF FIRST SYNAGOGUE 1856-75

2 RICHMOND ST. SYNAGOGUE 1876-97

3 BOND ST. SYNAGOGUE 1897-1938

4 UNIVERSITY AVE. SYNAGOGUE, OPENED 1907

5 McCAUL ST. SYNAGOGUE, OPENED 1905

6 SIMCOE ST. (ASSOCIATED HEBREW CHARITIES, TALMUD TORAH, ORPHANAGE, ZIONIST INSTITUTE)

7 JEWISH DISPENSARY, OPENED 1909

8 LYRIC THEATRE 1909-C. 1923

9 STANDARD THEATRE (OPENED 1922)

10 BRUNSWICK AVE. TALMUD TORAH (OPENED 1924)

11 NATIONAL RADICAL SCHOOL

12 EITZ CHAIM TALMUD TORAH

13 SCHEUER HOUSE

14 OLD FOLKS' HOME

15 MT. SINAI HOSPITAL

16 ZIONIST BUILDING

17 LABOUR LYCEUM

Plan of the City of Toronto, Copp Clark, 1903, presented with The Canadian Almanac for 1903.

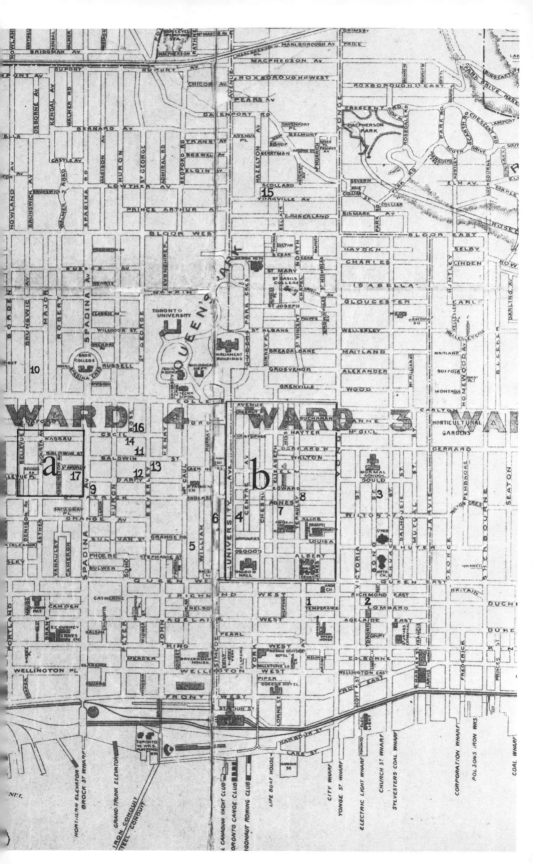

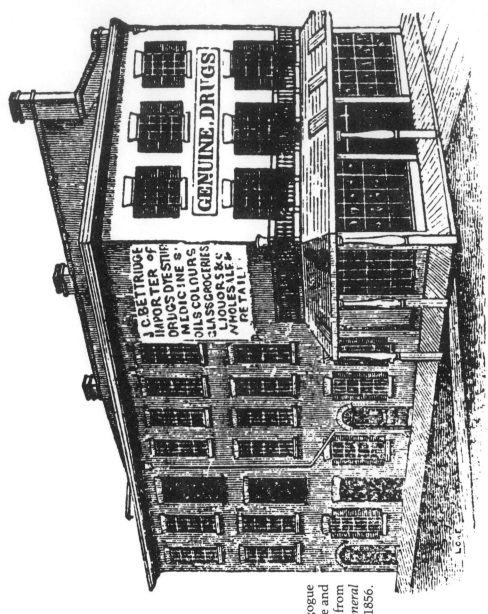

Site of the first synagogue in Toronto, Yonge and Richmond streets, from *Brown's Toronto General Directory*, 1856.

Europe. A number of women supplemented the family income by turning their residences into formal boarding houses and these tended to cater to their own *landsleit*: Mrs. Levinsky's, for example, to Russians, and Mrs. Steinwortzel's to Galicians. There also existed institutions such as the New York Kosher Temperance Hotel, on Adelaide Street at York, which served primarily as restaurants but also accommodated individuals who preferred not to sacrifice privacy by living in someone else's household. The majority, however, seemed to prefer the sense of security provided by the family; Jewish hotels were rarities in Toronto.

Although the East European Jews tended to divide by country of origin in their synagogues and in business partnerships, they did not do so in their places of residence. No section of the Ward, therefore, was occupied primarily by Russians, for example. Obviously, Jews of various nationalities found an affinity for each other through language and religion. This pattern would persist even after the area of Jewish residence had expanded beyond the Ward.

It is not surprising that the Ward had a high population density – eighty-two persons per acre according to a report of Dr. Charles Hastings, the city's Medical Officer of Health, who conducted an investigation into slum conditions in 1911. Yet, although this figure was greater than for any other part of Toronto, including the predominantly Irish "Cabbagetown" in the east end, and was therefore considered a condition of crisis, the area was not nearly as congested as immigrant districts in the larger American cities.[6] It could be contended, however, that in view of the presence of smaller buildings in Toronto in contrast to comparable areas of New York City, for example, the number of people per room, if not per acre, would be as high here as elsewhere. Some buildings housed between ten and fifteen people, although the average was between six and eight. Futhermore, higher densities did not necessarily coincide with large buildings. Most houses had from three to five rooms, but the amount of space available for purely residential purposes was substantially diminished by the sewing machines and workshops of the domestic industries. Therefore isolated buildings in the Ward were as crowded as those of the worst slums of New York. In total, however, living conditions in Toronto were far more tolerable.

By 1912 Jewish residents of the Ward had, in certain respects, succeeded in recreating the *shtetl*. The area had become virtually a self-contained community as regards services and cultural, religious and educational facilities. A rich variety of stores was available within the radius of a few blocks. The majority of the service establishments in the area were by this time operated by Jews. There were kosher restaurants which were patronized only by Jews, while some of the "comforts" of Eastern Europe had been transplanted in the form of Halpern's *seltzer* (soda water) factory on Chestnut Street.

Synagogues abounded in the Ward, each ethnic sector or group of townsmen striving to set up its own. By 1912 the majority of the synagogues in Toronto were located here, or in the three blocks between University Avenue and McCaul Street just to the west; Centre Avenue alone had at least four. Besides serving their obvious functions, the synagogues, whether grand structures built for the purpose, refurbished churches, or converted stores or cottages, were social and cultural centres for a large segment of the Jewish community, providing facilities for charitable organizations, social gatherings and religious schools. The non-religious found their recreation in the local Yiddish theatre, and intellectual stimulation and social interaction in informal meeting places such as Dworkin's news agency on Elizabeth Street, where conversation always flowed freely and where one could enjoy a soft drink and read the latest Yiddish newspapers from New York.

Prior to the First World War, most Jewish storekeepers in the area lived in the Ward itself, and a majority inhabited the buildings where they did business. Stores of a similar type located in close proximity to each other; consequently, competition was strong and profits meagre in most enterprises. It was often impossible, therefore, for a storekeeper to employ even his own children. These found work in the neighbouring factories or engaged in a trade of their own in the residential part of the family dwelling. This home industry was usually some form of tailoring. Tailors did not usually operate shops for the sale of goods to the public; they prepared piecework for nearby clothing factories. The upper floors and back rooms of some of the dwellings were in fact little sweatshops. At least one residence was discovered to have had as many as eight sewing machines.[7]

Although the moral tone of the Ward improved considerably with the arrival of the Jews, and a few attempts were made by wealthy Jewish investors to improve the physical aspect by erecting rows of modern brick houses on Chestnut and Armoury streets in the first decade of the twentieth century, living conditions continued to deteriorate, especially after large numbers of new arrivals began to appear in 1905. As the demand for housing increased, rents soared, while the maintenance of buildings fell off considerably. Landlords saw their cottages as potentially valuable commercial and industrial property and so undertook few repairs. By 1911, Dr. Hastings reported, 108 houses in the area were unfit for habitation; yet, almost all were occupied. Some buildings did not keep out the cold, while on rainy days inside walls were found to be "soaking wet." Another structure housed three families in five rooms, one of which contained two sewing machines. Still another, rented at the scandalous sum of twenty dollars a month, had four feet of water in its basement. Almost a third of the houses visited had no drainage; waste and slop water were merely thrown into the yards. This was, as Hastings observed with profound understatement, "a plan certainly not conducive to pleasant neighbourly relations or sanitary ideas."[8]

About 10 per cent of the dwellings had no water:

> '$17 a month, and I have not'in', said a poor foreign woman near City Hall, as she showed our inspector the big holes in the wall, and one water tap that had been stopped up a long time, and an outside closet that was past description.... 'Where do you get your water', said the inspector. The woman pointed up the street and across. Sixty-six paces from her door to the tap and sixty-six paces back...that woman, a mother with three children around her, carried all the water supply for the family during the entire winter.[9]

Conditions in rear houses were especially disturbing. Surrounded by stables, privies and yards full of rags, the inhabitants found the odour so offensive that windows could not be opened even in the hottest weather. As the First World War approached, congestion in the Ward increased alarmingly, a situation aggravated by the influx of new immigrants and by the encroachment of the business and administrative sector of the city on the residential portion of the area. Eaton's factories, the store itself and the City Hall occupied a large area between Yonge and Teraulay streets. The clearing of the site of the new General Hospital on College Street in 1911 and the erection two years later of a city registry office in the block bounded by Louisa, Elizabeth, Albert and Chestnut further reduced the amount of available residential space.[10]

As early as 1900, those East European Jews who could afford to do so had been moving to the streets further west. University Avenue a broad, tree-lined and prestigious boulevard leading to the provincial legislative buildings at Queen's Park, marked the western boundary of the Ward and in the one block between Centre Avenue and University Avenue the transition took place between slum and respectability in housing. At first only the relatively prosperous lived west of University Avenue – Jewish doctors and successful manufacturers, for instance, who gravitated toward Beverley Street. But by the outbreak of the war, even those of middle and lower incomes were deserting the area adjacent to the central business district in search of better accommodation. The Jewish residential district began to resemble a contiguous ribbon stretching westward from St. John's Ward, bounded on the south by Queen Street and on the north by College, with the heaviest concentration along what is now Dundas Street. "The confines of the Jewish Ghetto are always shifting," wrote a Toronto correspondent to the *Jewish Times*, "so that no definite limits can any more be assigned to it .... The Jewish population is extending in all directions but most of all towards the west." The area of Jewish residence, he observed, once reaching westward only to McCaul Street, had now traversed Bathurst and included such streets as Euclid Avenue, Markham Street and Palmerston Avenue.[11] The Ward did not lose its Jewish flavour until the early 1920s, but by 1909 only a third of Toronto's 15,000 Jews lived there, the area having become increasingly populated by non-Jewish immigrants, notably Italians. In 1912 Jewish children constituted a majority at McCaul School on the western side of University Avenue. In fact, by that date 66 per cent of the Jews in Toronto lived in the area bounded by Spadina, Palmerston, Queen and College. Certainly by 1914 the district between McCaul and Bathurst constituted a new reception area for immigrant Jews arriving from Europe.[12]

Movement had to take place in a westward direction. East of Yonge Street accommodation was either too expensive or was in worse slums than in the Ward. North of Bloor, in Rosedale and the Annex, similar economic deterrents prevailed, to which possibly could be added social exclusion by Anglo-Saxon residents. There is little doubt that restrictive covenants existed, although many of these were unwritten. Even so, it was not necessary to have any formal restriction in order to keep Jews out; as a rule, East European Jews, used to minority status, tended to accept their inferior position more readily than did other immigrant groups. They were also very sensitive to criticism by the dominant group. As a result, they avoided areas where they suspected discrimination might be encountered, no matter how slight the possibility. Security could best be assured by moving en masse.[13] Areas to the north and east, moreover, could never be contiguous with the Ward, where most synagogues were located, where Yiddish predominated, and shops and other Jewish amenities were still to be found. Blocks of retail stores separated the ghetto from the residential streets east of Yonge, while to the north lay the General Hospital, the provincial Parliament Buildings and the University of Toronto. On the other hand, a Jewish residential area west of University Avenue could be physically adjacent to the Ward; it was also connected by a single streetcar line along Dundas Street, affording easy access to the major ready-made clothing establishments which had not yet shifted to Spadina Avenue and where many Jews were still employed. Streetcar route improvements along Dundas, and to a lesser degree along College, correspond closely to increases in Jewish population west of University Avenue.[14]

If the search for security produced residential grouping among the East European Jews, it also fostered a tendency to purchase real property.

> Slowly and thoroughly the Jews are establishing themselves as citizens of Toronto [the *Mail and Empire* commented in 1913]; already several entire streets are owned by them, and it is the desire of each immigrant to as speedily as possible become the owner of his own house. This he contrives to accomplish by means of strenuous self-denial and simple living.[15]

The Central European Jews who had arrived in the 1860s and 1870s had come to better themselves economically. They were prepared, if things did not work out, to seek their livelihood in the Ontario hinterland, in the United States, or even if necessary to return to Europe. East Europeans, on the contrary, came to stay; they had no choice. To return to Russia or Galicia would be to abandon themselves to the persecution from which they had fled initially, and to hated conscription, especially as war threatened. Moreover, since often they arrived in Toronto virtually penniless, they could not leave even had they wished to do so. Besides, for the religious and for those emotionally insecure after the trauma of emigration, a substantial concentration of Jews was the only refuge. As the Jewish population grew, this attitude solidified. And grow it did, for Jews from the smaller communities flocked to Toronto prior to 1914 in search of employment, Jewish education and mates for their children, and security in general. Consequently, as soon as they were able, East European Jews sought a sense of permanence by buying their own homes.

The earliest East European arrivals on York and Richmond streets were unable to do so. Indeed, as late as 1910 most of the properties inhabited by Jews on these streets were rented from non-Jews. The few Jews who did own property in the area held the land only for investment purposes and lived in the prosperous vicinity of Beverley Street. North of Queen, however, a different pattern emerged. While Jews never owned a majority of properties in the Ward, by 1911 there was a significant degree of Jewish ownership in the area. A substantial number of Jewish residents either owned the buildings they occupied or else rented from Jews who had lived in the ghetto within the last decade and had, by this time, moved west of McCaul. A characteristic feature of Jewish ownership is that it was not restricted to storekeepers and craftsmen; a surprising number of peddlers and "operators" owned their dwellings as well.

Movement within the ghetto was frequent; the poor shifted from one dwelling to another in search of better accommodation at cheaper rents. Even property owners were not secure. The slightest economic setback might mean foreclosure of a mortgage and a move to rented premises. But removal west of University Avenue was, for the majority of the residents of the Ward, prior to the First World War, indicative of achievement, signifying both economic and social upward mobility. The farther west one travelled, the greater was the tendency to Jewish ownership, or at least to rental from other Jews. In this area especially, Jews who had left their families in Europe would make an effort at least to place a down payment on a house prior to bringing them to Toronto. A portion of the building was then rented to a less prosperous family.[16]

The movement westward gave rise to a new phenomenon within the East European Jewish community – social distinctions based on economics. Now for the first time there were Jewish landlords; some were relatively wealthy manufacturers and real estate brokers, but most were shopkeepers financially secure enough to retain their old cottages or stores in the Ward after they had moved out. Social and economic division between the East Europeans and the old Jewish community had been commonplace; but now, perhaps by 1905 and certainly by 1914, these distinctions had become evident among the East Europeans themselves. Residentially, these divisions appeared not only in the contrast between the Ward and the area west of University, but also in the streets surrounding Spadina Avenue.

The streets on either side of Spadina had developed in the 1870s and 1880s as a fashionable residential quarter. By about 1914, when the influx of Jews had gained momentum, the area had lost most of its upper-class character. The original residents had fled to Rosedale and to other localities north of Bloor, a process no doubt accelerated by the advent of the wealthier Jews. Much of the area remained a respectable middle-class residential district when the Jews began to arrive. It was not, however, homogeneous. The streets east of Spadina Avenue – for example, Huron and especially Beverley – boasted larger and more elegant houses than those to the west; it was here that the most economically favoured East European Jews chose to live. West of Spadina, housing was by no means unacceptable, but the houses were smaller and the streets narrower. Frame houses were common and disreputable rear structures, especially off Kensington Avenue, were to be found. Here the less affluent gathered and, as the influx from Europe increased prior to the war, housing deteriorated as single-family dwellings were subdivided to create more living space. By the end of the war, an outdoor market had begun to develop on the western streets – Kensington, Augusta, Baldwin, Nassau – and a *shtetl* atmosphere, perhaps closer to the European model than New York's Lower East Side or London's Whitechapel, had been created. However picturesque it may have been, the phenomenon did nothing to enhance the desirability of these streets for the wealthy, who remained east of Spadina or moved still farther west to the predominantly Anglo-Saxon enclaves of Euclid Avenue and Palmerston Boulevard.

NOTES

1 Bernard D. Weinryb, "Jewish Immigration and Accommodation to America," *loc.cit.*, p. 15.

2 For comparable patterns of ghetto formation and additional detail on the process, see David Ward, "The Emergence of Central Immigrant Ghettoes in American Cities: 1840-1920," Association of American Geographers, *Annals*, LVIII (June, 1968), pp. 343-59, esp. p. 346; and Moses Rischin, *The Promised City: New York's Jews, 1870-1914* (New York: Corinth Books, 1964).

   According to Louis Wirth, Jews tended to settle near the central business district not only because rents were low but also because European experience had taught them the value of living in close proximity to the commercial centre of a city. Louis Wirth, *The Ghetto* (Chicago: University of Chicago Press, 1964), p. 202. For a perceptive account of the amenities offered by the ghetto, see Hutchins Hapgood, *The Spirit of the Ghetto* (New York: Funk and Wagnalls, 1902).

3 See Peter G. Goheen, *Victorian Toronto 1850 to 1900: Patterns and Process of Growth* (Chicago: University of Chicago Department of Geography, Research Paper No. 127, 1970), pp. 191 ff.

4 Canada, Department of Agriculture, *Census of Canada 1890-91*, I, p. 283.

5 J.E. Middleton, *The Municipality of Toronto: A History*, 2 vols. (Toronto: Dominion Publishing Co., 1923), I, p. 402. C.S. Clark, *Of Toronto the Good* (Montreal: Toronto Publishing Co., 1898), p. 89.

6 In some parts of New York, for instance, a block of ten tenements, occupying an area of approximately 2,500 x 100 yards, might house as many as 4,000 people. C.N. Glaab and A.T. Brown, *A History of Urban America* (Toronto: Macmillan, 1967), p. 162.

7 City of Toronto, Assessment Rolls, Ward 3, 1911, 1912. City of Toronto, *Report of the Medical Health Officer Dealing with the Recent Investigation of Slum Conditions in Toronto* (Toronto: 1911), p. 5.

8 *Ibid.*, pp. 4, 8, 9, 12. Rents were increasing as the First World War approached, but they were still lower than those in cities such as New York. None of these tenements was owned by Jews.

9 *Ibid.*, pp. 10-11.

10 Canada, Bureau of Statistics, *Fifth Census of Canada, 1911* (Ottawa: 1913), esp. II, p. 158. *Globe*, June 21, 1911; *Evening Telegram*, July 17, 1913.

11 *Jewish Times*, Aug. 23, 1912, p. 16. For evidence of westward movement by middle-income families early in the century, see Toronto Hebrew Ladies Aid Society *Minutes*, July 24, Nov. 3, 1905. By 1913 East European Jews were found in isolated pockets outside this area, notably in the West Toronto Junction and in the eastern part of the city in the vicinity of Parliament Street. However, the area described was by far the major concentration.

12 James S. Woodsworth, *Strangers Within Our Gates* (Toronto: The Missionary Society of the Methodist Church, Canada, 1909), pp. 256, 258; *Globe*, June 21, 1911; Rev. S.B. Rohold, *The Jews in Canada* (Toronto: Board of Home Missions,

Presbyterian Church in Canada, 1912), p. 13. See also Louis Rosenberg, "Population Characteristics of the Jewish Community of Toronto" (Jewish Community Series #3 – Canadian Jewish Population Studies; mimeographed; Montreal: Canadian Jewish Congress, 1955). For a statistical analysis of the growth of the Jewish population in a portion of this area, see Vicki W. Graff, "A Quantitative Historical Study of the Social Geography of an Urban Community: Kensington Market 1901-1950" (unpublished paper, University of Toronto, 1972).

13 Weinryb, "Jewish Immigration and Accommodation...," p. 15. Personal interviews: Dr. M.A. Pollock, March 15, 1973; S. Rhinewine, Feb. 9, 1972; B. Hyman, Oct. 8, 1972; and A.B. Bennett, Oct. 3, 1972.

14 See Louis H. Pursley, *Street Railways of Toronto 1861-1921* (Interurbans Special #25; Los Angeles: Electric Railway Publications, 1958), p. 41.

15 *Mail and Empire*, Oct. 18, 1913.

16 J.B. Salsberg, personal interview, Jan. 15, 1973.

CHAPTER 7

A COMMUNITY OF "JOINERS": RELIGIOUS AND FRATERNAL ORGANIZATIONS IN THE NEW COMMUNITY, 1883 – 1920

As the East Europeans began to arrive in significant numbers during the 1880s, the members of Holy Blossom assumed that, as the established community, they would remain the arbiters of Jewish life in Toronto. Through the Anglo-Jewish Association and the Ladies' Montefiore Society they offered assistance to those unable to fend for themselves, and it was taken for granted that even after the East Europeans had become settled they would defer to Holy Blossom. This was not an irrational expectation, since at that period the synagogue still conformed to orthodox religious practice.

Unlike their counterparts in the United States, the old community did not try to exclude Russian and Polish Jews from Canada. The established Jewish community in the United States attempted to prevent large numbers of East European Jews from emigrating, principally because they believed their presence would cause economic difficulty and foster anti-semitism. The United Hebrew Charities in New York, reflecting the prevailing attitude, even attempted to return some of the newcomers to Europe as being unemployable or paupers.

But although the Jewish community in Toronto accepted the new arrivals and did not panic when large numbers of East Europeans refused to be shipped off to the West, they did fear that the newcomers' exotic appearance and practices might produce anti-semitic sentiment which had, thus far, been largely absent in Toronto. Consequently, while attempting to assure the public of the industriousness of the immigrants, they tried to accelerate the process of acculturation by drawing the East Europeans under their authority. This could be most easily accomplished by forcing all Jews in the city to resort solely to Holy Blossom's religious officials, specifically to the *shochet*. In 1881, therefore, the ministers of the old community were forbidden to serve non-affiliated Jews, except with the authorization of the synagogue. At this juncture, it will be recalled, Nathan Robinson balked at the restriction and temporarily severed his connection with Holy Blossom.[1]

The difficulty with Robinson had apparently arisen over the *shochet's* insistence on serving an independent group, or perhaps a number of groups, of East European Jews, while retaining his post at Holy Blossom.[2] The immigrants of the 1880s were scrupulously religious and attempted from the outset to observe traditional practices. They sought out a *shochet* to provide kosher meat and undoubtedly gathered for prayer, but they did both apart from Holy Blossom. For however well that synagogue conformed to the letter of the Law, it held little attraction for the new arrivals. The order of service may have been familiar to them, but the ceremonies surrounding it were unlike anything they had known, in Europe. The formal dress, relative affluence and "American" habits of the congregants made the East Europeans self-conscious. They felt themselves separated from the old community not only by economic status and residential location but also by a seemingly unfathomable cultural gap.

Consequently, in 1883 a group of recent immigrants, mostly Lithuanians, founded a new congregation, Goel Tzedec ("Righteous Redeemer"). As the name implies, this was probably at its roots a mutual aid and burial society,* but regular services were held in a room at Richmond and York streets, and for the High Holy Days premises were rented at nearby Temperance Hall. Within three years, the congregation had purchased a former Methodist church on University Avenue at Elm and formed a real alternative to Holy Blossom.[3]

During its first years, Goel Tzedec attracted new immigrants with a variety of ethnic backgrounds. The necessity of renting

* The term "Goel" is most frequently used in the liturgy in reference to God as the redeemer of Israel. However, the biblical and talmudic idiom uses the word to connote a person whose role it is to ransom a captive relative.

larger space for the High Holy Days suggests that even East Europeans who did not actually join the new congregation chose it for prayer over Holy Blossom.[4] But this apparent unity among the East Europeans was illusory. As soon as a group from any locality in Europe became numerous enough to establish their own congregation, where the *minhagim* (customs) of their particular region would be followed, they did so. In 1887, therefore, a group of Russians and a number of Galicians seceded from Goel Tzedec and organized their own *minyan*,* designated Chevra Tehillim ("Fellowship of Psalms"), over Broudy's grocery, again at Richmond and York.[5] The following year, the Galicians set up a synagogue of their own. Shomrai Shabboth Anshei Oistreich Minhag Sfard ("Guardians of the Sabbath, Men of Austria who pray according to the Sephardic custom") met in a room on Richmond Street.

By the time the Bond Street synagogue opened in 1897, the East European Jews far outnumbered the English and Germans of Holy Blossom and had three rooted and expanding congregations in the city. The year before, Chevra Tehillim had found enlarged quarters over a blacksmith shop farther east along Richmond Street from its original location, while the Galicians, having also expanded to larger premises on Queen Street, were considering the purchase of a church on Chestnut. The Polish element, until this time insignificant, was also in the process of organizing a synagogue.

Some at Holy Blossom still hoped to absorb and dominate the East Europeans. The *World* was told that one reason for the new edifice was to encourage all Jews in the city to worship there, including the congregation at Richmond and York and at Elm and University "where the ritual is very strict and orthodox." "There is no valid reason why all should not meet together in the new temple on Bond Street," the paper observed, probably reflecting opinion at Holy Blossom. "It is central, and though the service is somewhat modified, it is not considered so reformed as to exclude any of the race." "The erection of this synagogue," the *Evening Star* commented, "will probably result in the union of all the Hebrews in the city in one congregation."

In fact, however, that probability did not exist by 1897. Even if the old community and the new had not been culturally so divided, the fact that Holy Blossom had introduced instrumental music and a mixed choir in its services made it "deitsch,"

---

* The quorum of ten male Jews over the age of thirteen required for public worship.

assimilationist,* a place to be visited not for prayer but rather to see how "Americanized" Jews behaved. In addition, religious observance among the members of Holy Blossom had fallen off considerably by this time. So difficult was it to obtain a quorum for daily services that Alfred Benjamin was reported to have paid East European peddlers a dollar each to be present. If, therefore, as one paper reported, Sabbath services at Bond Street were attended by "all classes of the community," one can be sure that most recent arrivals were attracted only by curiosity and a desire to be entertained.[6]

If Holy Blossom was unable to dominate the East Europeans organizationally and by direct action, it probably did exert an unwitting but very real indirect influence at this period. The majority of the Russian, Galician and Polish Jews preferred their own enclaves to Holy Blossom, but a number of the more prosperous of each group did become members, providing a link between the old community and the new.

It has been suggested that these East Europeans resigned in significant numbers once reforms were introduced at Holy Blossom, that they were instrumental in the founding of Goel Tzedec, and that they provided a practical and ideological connection between the two synagogues. Once established in the new congregation, they comprised a group familiar, from their experience in Holy Blossom, with British parliamentary procedure, and shared with the old community the opinion that Jewish citizens should join with non-Jews in the common cause of civic improvement. Moreover, they were familiar with the Canadian environment and were anxious, like the old community, to have the new arrivals adapt to it. It was they, according to this view, who assured the success of Goel Tzedec by enabling it to adjust quickly to Canadian conditions.[7]

This hypothesis is intriguing but difficult to substantiate. It is not true, for example, that the dynamic in the founding of Goel Tzedec came from orthodox secessionists from Holy Blossom. By 1883 no reforms had been introduced which would have produced a major exodus from its congregation. The link was formed not in the 1880s but in the following decade, and it was the result not of secession but of dual membership. Moreover, influence was apparently exerted in the nineteenth century on the Galician and

* The Yiddish term "deitsch" (from the German "deutsch") is a pejorative expression used by East European Jews to designate Jews who attempt to imitate their non-Jewish neighbours by cultural assimilation. This practice was most common in Germany. Synagogues which adopt non-traditional forms are also referred to as being "deitsch."

Polish synagogues as well as Goel Tzedec.[8] It is probable that as Scheuer's faction increased in strength at Holy Blossom, those East Europeans who remained orthodox did eventually leave the older congregation. In the 1890s, however, dual membership was still common for the few who could afford it; there was even an increase late in the decade in the number of prosperous East Europeans seeking membership in Holy Blossom. As for the role that these East Europeans played in the acculturation of the rest, they probably did infuse new ideas into the growing immigrant congregation. As prominent entrepreneurs and budding manufacturers, and as employers of other Jews, their views undoubtedly carried considerable weight.

II

This link with Holy Blossom, however, grew more tenuous as the East European community increased in numbers and stability. As the older congregation became more liberal, those of its East European members who had maintained the connection were forced to choose between Holy Blossom and the Ward. The old community generally, the English and the Germans, expended little effort in relating to the new immigrants on an equal basis. Their goal was to Canadianize the inhabitants of the Ward as quickly as possible and to retain their influence over the entire Jewish population of the city. Alfred Benjamin, as president of Holy Blossom, shared these views to a degree; but virtually alone among the established Jews he attempted to understand the newcomers and help them organize themselves independently of the old community. For instance, he participated actively in an effort by the East Europeans to found a communal religious school; he helped Shomrai Shabboth acquire the mission church on Chestnut Street as their synagogue and spoke at its dedication in July 1899. He made himself popular among the East Europeans by his orthodox practice and by the fact that on Friday afternoons he would seek out Jewish newsboys and purchase all their papers so that they could inaugurate the Sabbath at home.

One man, however, could not overcome the justified belief of the East Europeans that they were being patronized by the old community; by the early twentieth century they were using the facilities at Holy Blossom only out of necessity. When Shomrai Shabboth dedicated their Chestnut Street building, Cantor Solomon of Holy Blossom was invited to participate, but probably only because he was the sole trained cantor then in the city. The dedication itself was conducted not by David Wittenberg, the only rabbi in Toronto, but rather by an authority of unquestionable orthodoxy, Rabbi Aaron Ashinsky of Montreal. At the turn of the century some women from the Ward still attended the ritual bath in the Bond Street synagogue, but this was certainly because it was relatively modern and was perhaps for a time the only one available. When the Roumanian congregation organized in 1902, their first services were held in the basement of Holy Blossom, but they soon found premises of their own. And while even the most orthodox East Europeans still sent their daughters to the Sabbath School at Holy Blossom, boys, whose religious education was taken seriously, were usually not entrusted to the "assimilationists." They were educated within the East European community itself. As the formal religious and fraternal organizations of the Ward multiplied, and especially after Benjamin's death in 1901, Yonge Street became increasingly a barrier between the two groups.[9]

A multiplicity of such East European organizations emerged in the early twentieth century. In 1899, the Polish element organized Toronto's fifth synagogue and, between 1904 and 1906, were able to purchase a church on Elm Street. Another Russian congregation, Shaarei Tzedec, founded about 1901,[10] was followed during the next fifteen years by a host of other *shtiblach** respectively representing Roumanians (the First Roumanian Congregation Adath Israel of Toronto, 1902); Galicians apart from Shomrai Shabboth (Machzikei HaDas, 1906; First Narayever Congregation, probably 1914); Russians who arrived after 1900 (Beth Israel Anshei Minsk, 1905; Tzemach Tzedec Anshei Libavitch Nusach Ari, *ca.* 1905; Shearith Israel Anshei Lida, 1910; First Russian Congregation Rodfei Sholom Anshei Kiev, 1912); Moldavians (First Moldaver Congregation Tifereth Israel Anshei Roumania, 1910); recently arrived English Jews together with East Europeans who had lived for a time in England (Anshei England, 1909); and groups from a variety of localities and towns in Poland (Ezras Israel Anshei Apte, 1905; Anshei Stashov, 1905; Chevra Tomchei Shabbos, 1907; Chevra Knesseth Israel Anshei Slipia, 1908; Tifereth Israel Bikur Cholim Anshei Ostrovtze, 1908-1910; Anshei Chmelnik, 1910; Anshei Lagov, 1913; Anshei Kielce, *ca.* 1913; Anshei Shidlof, 1914). There was even a *shtibl* with the unlikely name of Chevra Tifereth Israel Anshei New York (1912), which bore little relationship to the actual origins of its members.[11]

* Shtibl(e) (pl. Shtiblach), from the German "Stube," meaning apartment. The term usually refers to a small synagogue in a converted house or store.

As most of their names imply, these East European congregations comprised relatively homogeneous ethnic groups;* the Russians, Galicians and Roumanians divided by country or district of origin, whereas Polish Jews, because of their large numbers, tended to found synagogues representing towns. Like Goel Tzedec, these synagogues were more than places to pray; they were fraternities – *landsmanshaften* – where the immigrant could associate with Jews who shared his European experience, whose families he had known in the homeland, and upon whom he could rely for assistance in difficult times. Here he could depend upon being visited when he was ill; Congregation Anshei Ostrovtze even incorporated the concept of *bikur cholim*, visiting the sick, into its name. He knew also that he would be trusted with a loan, with neither interest nor collateral being demanded. Here, also, he could socialize freely and engage in cultural activities in his leisure time, always certain of a group who would share his pleasure.

The basis of the ethnic synagogue, like that of residential clustering, was the quest for security. The *landsmanshaft shul*† provided the immigrant Jew with familiar surroundings over which he felt he had some measure of control. He sought, therefore, to associate in his synagogue with those who shared his opinions and ceremonial practices. Whenever this homogeneity broke down there were secessions and new congregations formed, often leaving considerable bitterness in their wake. For instance, the division between Goel Tzedec and Chevra Tehillim in the 1880s apparently had its roots in a striving for homogeneity. Well into the twentieth century members of Goel Tzedec disdainfully called their sister congregation "the Kosatzke shul," the synagogue of the Cossacks, and had a tendency to regard Chevra Tehillim as being somewhat uncouth. Efforts to reunite the two congregations in the first years of the separation were uniformly unsuccessful.[12]

When the Galicians split in 1906, the absence of homogeneity was definitely the cause. The Jews of Galicia were divided in their synagogue customs according to their residence in either the eastern or the western part of that province. When Shomrai

---

* The Hebrew word "anshei" means "men of" and usually connotes the place of origin of its members; hence, Anshei Apte, "Men of Apte" (Opatov); Anshei Oistreich, "Men of Austria." The term can also be applied to a virtue: Anshe Sholom, "Men of Peace." In Toronto, the appearance of "anshei" always signified an ethnic congregation.

† A synagogue composed of *landsleit*.

Shabboth had been formed, the group was composed almost entirely of Jews who had originated in one section, but by 1906 they were outnumbered by more recent immigrants from the other part. The dispute originated in religious practice; that is, whether or not the *shofar* (ram's horn) should be sounded on the festival of Hoshana Rabba, a *minhag* over which there had long been a difference of opinion between the two parts of Galicia. In Shomrai Shabboth, the religious element of the dispute manifested itself politically. When the congregation was torn by a disagreement over disposition of the synagogue's finances, the members divided between easterners and westerners. The newer arrivals, having a majority, used the pretext to vote out the incumbent president and trustees who for decades had represented the original members and whom the new group considered an oligarchy. So deep had the animosity become by the time of the election, that when the new officers took their places beside the ark, as was the custom, on the eve of the Sabbath of Passover, supporters of the opposing faction, who considered the election invalid, attempted to dislodge them physically. The result was a donnybrook which overflowed into the street, was reported in detail by the public press and caused the Jewish community considerable embarrassment.

> The Austrian Jewish Synagogue on Chestnut Street was the scene of a riot last night, in which one section of the assembled congregation attacked the other, both sides engaging in a general scrimmage, in which beards were pulled, clothes torn, chairs overturned and rough house generally prevailed. Inspector Stephen and a squad of police from No. 2 Station were called in, and put an end to the row by clearing the building and ordering it locked up for the rest of the evening.[13]

The dispute was eventually settled after the minority offered to purchase all the seats of the dissidents. The latter withdrew, merged with another struggling Galician synagogue on Centre Avenue and founded a new congregation on Teraulay Street, defiantly called Machzikei HaDas, ("Upholders of the Tradition").

Similar but less violent congregational splits were commonplace in the early years of the twentieth century. In 1907, the issue of whether or not tickets were to be required for admission to the synagogue on the High Holy Days produced a division in the Polish congregation, Beth Jacob. The dissidents withdrew and established Chevra Tomchei Shabbos in a rear cottage on Chestnut Street.

The majority of the synagogues in Toronto prior to the First World War and for many years afterwards, therefore, were of the *landsmanshaft* type. Congregations founded in the early twentieth century tended to be ethnically mixed only when they were located geographically distant from the major centre of Jewish residence.[14]

Sociologist Charles Liebman maintains that this multiplicity of synagogues in American cities served only a minor religious function, and that their principal purpose was social and cultural. He cites as evidence the fact that in the United States the number of synagogues far exceeded that necessary for worship.[15] In Toronto, on the contrary, traditional religious sentiment, if not practice, remained relatively strong in the years before the First World War, and although attendance was not large throughout the year, at the High Holy Day period synagogue space was inadequate. Since the late nineteenth century auxiliary services had been necessary, while early in the twentieth, makeshift synagogues were set up for the High Holy Days in public halls and empty stores; services were conducted by immigrant self-styled cantors and tickets could be purchased by Jews unaffiliated with any of the established congregations. Moreover, in the prewar years, synagogues consistently outnumbered purely secular fraternal organizations; in 1901, for instance, only 3 per cent of the Jewish population belonged to secular societies and by 1911 the figure had climbed to only 5 per cent. In fact, it was common for a member of a fraternal organization to belong to a synagogue as well.[16] Admittedly, some secularists saw the fraternal society as a substitute for the synagogue, providing Jewish identification, social, mutual aid and cemetery benefits of the synagogue without the religious obligations. These, however, were in the minority at least until the 1920s. Most preferred the synagogue.

III

The East European Jews in Toronto, however, produced a large number of fraternal and mutual benefit societies independently of the synagogue. Many Jews who wished to join a synagogue could not afford to do so. Dues were generally high, and, except for the High Holy Days, one did not have to become a member or purchase a ticket in order to attend services. Most synagogues, in addition, had neither rabbi nor religious school, amenities which might persuade the worker to dip into his precious savings for dues. On the other hand, mutual aid was a virtual necessity for the average immigrant, be he peddler or factory operative. His earnings were small and whatever little he saved often went in passage for his family still in Europe. Even this might be obliterated by a short spell of illness or unemployment. Furthermore, if he died his family would be left destitute. Therefore, he needed an institution which could satisfy immediate needs.

Granted, there were Jewish philanthropic societies in the city which could provide assistance in an emergency: the Ladies' Montefiore at Holy Blossom and, after 1899, the Toronto Hebrew Ladies' Aid Society, operating from the Ward and loosely connected with Goel Tzedec. The Ladies' Montefiore, however, tended to dispense its aid superciliously. A complaint against the old community in the United States, published in *Yiddishe Gazetten* for April 1894, probably reflects the attitude of the East Europeans in Toronto to the charity offered by Holy Blossom:

> In the philanthropic institutions of our aristocratic German Jews you see beautiful offices, desks, all decorated, but strict and angry faces. Every poor man is questioned like a criminal, is looked down upon; every unfortunate suffers self-degradation and shivers like a leaf, just as if he were standing before a Russian official.

And if the Ladies' Aid Society offered assistance with a fuller hand and a softer heart, it remained charity nonetheless.

The mutual aid society was the ideal solution, pooling the immigrant's resources with those of his peers and freeing him from the stigma of accepting charity. When he received aid, it was merely his due since through the society he had done the same for his neighbour. The mutual benefit society, moreover, was by its nature able to offer advantages which the *landsmanshaft* synagogue could not. It provided a weekly income in case of illness and, perhaps best of all, it employed the "lodge doctor."

It was common practice for mutual benefit societies, Jewish and non-Jewish alike, to contract with local doctors to serve their members. The society paid the doctor an annual lump sum in return for which he attended members and their families, regardless of how many times he was called or how large the family. For this service, members paid a nominal annual sum to the organization, usually one dollar. While this arrangement was exceedingly advantageous to the lodge members, it was not for the doctor. He was freely called for minor disorders at all hours of the day or night. At first, when there were few Jewish doctors, non-Jews were appointed. Once Jewish doctors began to graduate, they had difficulty establishing themselves in private practice because they were Jews. Gentiles would not patronize them, nor could they rent offices in certain areas of the city. Moreover, hospitals in Toronto refused to accept Jewish interns. As a result, Jewish doctors who did not intern elsewhere were generally considered lacking in experience and were avoided even by Jews. The only means for a Jewish doctor to establish a practice was to become attached to a lodge. Not only did this give him an enormous, however bothersome, clientele, it also brought the opportunity to refer patients to eminent Gentile specialists, a valuable contact indeed. By the 1920s, Jewish physicians were actually campaigning for posts as lodge doctors.[17]

Mutual benefit societies were nothing new to the Jewish experience; they had existed for burial purposes as far back as talmudic times and had also been formed for various other functions in medieval Europe. In Toronto, however, as in other North American Jewish communities, they divided into three categories: the *landsmanshaften*; the non-ethnic societies united by ideology; and the non-partisan, ethnically mixed organizations. The latter emerged earliest. In the nineteenth century, and early in the twentieth, the community did not encompass large enough groups from each East European locality to make the purely ethnic *landsmanshaft* feasible.

The first non-partisan and non-ethnic organization to emerge was atypical; it was actually a society of young English-speaking Jews, formed partly for purposes of recreation, rather than an organization born out of necessity and composed of recently arrived Yiddish-speaking wage-earners. However, the Young Men's Hebrew Association, founded about 1894 by Joseph Harris, a local haberdasher, became the first mutual benefit society established in Toronto independently of Holy Blossom. Despite its name, the group had no connection with the American organization from which its modern namesake is indirectly descended, and it engaged in little athletic activity. It did, with the assistance of "several non-Jewish public-spirited politicians," establish a clubroom on Adelaide Street with facilities for billiards and boxing, but it remained basically a sick benefit society. Unfortunately, the Association was short-lived; although it began propitiously with a membership of thirty-eight which had increased to sixty by 1904, it seems to have depended heavily on Harris' leadership, especially in obtaining funds for operation. When he left the city in 1898, the society disintegrated, vanishing altogether by 1905.

It was revived, after several unsuccessful attempts, in 1910. An effort was made to attract members by the purchase of a cemetery, by making prominent local Jews honorary members and by importing a well-known communal worker from London, England, to address the opening meeting; but the group could not assemble enough members to obtain a provincial charter until 1912. Even after that date, it remained comparatively weak. This second YMHA, a purely fraternal organization, engaged in no athletic activities whatever.

The Toronto Hebrew Benevolent Society,* on the other hand, was more successful. Incorporated in 1899 but probably founded a few years earlier, the THBS drew together a variety of Yiddish-speaking East Europeans, and although it eventually branched out into social activities, its primary role was the provision of illness and funeral benefits. Consequently it grew rapidly. With only thirty-seven members at the time of incorporation, the society expanded from eighty-five in 1905 to over two hundred in 1916, a figure which would remain relatively constant.[18]

Similar success was evident in the Pride of Israel Benefit Society which met in a cottage on Chestnut Street in 1905 and grew to be the largest Jewish benevolent society in the city. In its first two years, Pride of Israel grew from 38 members to 110. By 1911 it had expanded to three hundred and had established a branch in Hamilton, while by 1914 it exceeded four hundred.[19] Membership increases were directly proportional to the number of services offered. When Dr. Samuel Lavine, the first Jewish physician in the city, was appointed lodge doctor in 1907, new members were attracted in droves. After the society acquired a cemetery the following year and had begun to provide financial assistance to families of deceased members – additional services which one hopes did not reflect the abilities of the doctor – expansion by leaps and bounds was assured.

An assortment of other non-ethnic Jewish benefit lodges appeared in the pre-war years and during the war itself;[20] the more acculturated members of the community gravitated to Jewish branches of national and international fraternal orders which also served an insurance function. In 1910, for instance, a branch of the Canadian Order of Chosen Friends was established in

* The Toronto Hebrew Benevolent Society should not be confused with the Toronto Hebrew Benevolent Association, which was associated exclusively with Holy Blossom. It is possible that the East European organization was modelled on the latter, but memberships do not appear to overlap and influence from the United States or from Montreal likely provided the driving force.

Toronto, to be followed in 1914 by the Sunnyside Lodge of the Oddfellows. Both, as branches of non-Jewish orders, were unique in Canada.[21]

Also remarkable was the Toronto branch of the Grand Order of Israel, established in 1905. In the prewar years it remained the only branch of an international Jewish order in the city. The local branches of the three international Jewish lodges, founded in the previous century–B'nai B'rith, Kesher Shel Barzel and the Sons of Benjamin – had all dissolved by this time. The chapter was the creation of recently arrived English Jews who wanted a fraternal and sick benefit society on the English model. Understandably, they affiliated with the Grand Order of Israel in London. Finding the overseas connection cumbersome, the group withdrew about 1906 and transformed themselves into a lodge of the Ancient Order of Foresters. This had the advantage of transferable benefits for those who might return to England. Court King David, as it was called, survived until 1917 when it again joined the Grand Order which, by this time, had established Canadian headquarters in Hamilton. Again, this did not work well and in 1919 the lodge became the independent Judaean Benevolent Society.[22]

None of the non-ethnic benevolent societies, however, approximated the success of Pride of Israel. Its activities were conducted with a *savoir faire* which made it extremely attractive. In 1909, for instance, the society endowed a bed at the Toronto General Hospital to guarantee members entry even when their doctors had no admitting privileges, as was the case with most Jewish physicians. From 1910, the calibre of the membership was kept up by accepting applicants only after investigation. Members were penalized for voting for candidates whom they did not know. The society provided informal arbitration facilities to settle disputes between members out of court.

Pride of Israel, moreover, conducted its financial affairs scrupulously, but provided widespread assistance, a practice which won it a reputation for generosity within the East European community. The society also held its annual fund-raising ball in a businesslike fashion. Consequently, Pride of Israel was one of the few mutual benefit societies in Toronto, and perhaps the only one, with sufficient resources to assist non-members who were unemployed.

This phenomenon of assisting the unemployed regardless of affiliation was doubtless due to the fact that Pride of Israel was overwhelmingly working-class in membership and sympathies. The society offered donations to assist strikers in Montreal,

Winnipeg, Rochester, New York and Chicago, as well as in Toronto itself. Indeed, once unions appeared in the city, non-union workers were refused admission if a labour organization existed in their trade. However, Pride of Israel was not concerned with working-class ideology; it was merely dealing with matters of practical consideration for its members. Furthermore, it spread its donations among such varied institutions as the Sick Children's Hospital, hospitals for respiratory diseases from Denver, Colorado, to Muskoka, the Hebrew Ladies' Aid Society, the orthodox Simcoe Street Talmud Torah and the secularist Peretz School. Another contribution went in 1912 to victims of anti-Jewish riots in Morocco. By 1918 the society had begun to sponsor cultural activities in addition to its benefit functions, and by 1924 it was toying with the idea of establishing a synagogue.[23]

This policy would have been unthinkable for the secularist and class-conscious Workmen's Circle (Arbeiter Ring). Unlike the non-partisan societies, the Workmen's Circle was part of a nationalist Jewish working-class and social democratic movement known in Europe as the Bund. Socialism, its adherents believed, could be the only solution to the so-called "Jewish problem."

Late in the nineteenth century, large numbers of Bundists emigrated to the United States and in 1900, the Workmen's Circle, its American counterpart, was established in New York City. The organization continued its ideological connection with the Bund, but it had been founded in response to the immediate need to protect the families of factory operatives, especially in the garment trades, who might be injured or killed in their work. Its principal function was to provide insurance benefits. Consequently, it attracted non-Bundist workers as well as a variety of secularist immigrants from Russia and Poland who were anxious to combine Jewish identification and social reform. The Arbeiter Ring, therefore, was explicitly proletarian in outlook and in its early years encompassed a conglomeration of ideologies, ranging from anarchism and communism to moderate social democracy. The organization became popular and widespread in the United States, establishing its own sanatorium in upstate New York and sending speakers from its headquarters to sympathetic groups in other cities where it hoped eventually to organize branches. Once formed, these were seldom at a loss either for direction or for imported rhetoric from New York. In 1908, the society was brought to Toronto by East European Jews who had lived in the United States, and it grew steadily as increased numbers of secularists and social reformers arrived following the abortive Russian revolution of 1905. The Workmen's Circle soon became a major advocate of unionization of the garment trades in the city, and demanded that its members support labour organizations.[24]

Members of the Workmen's Circle were united by a number of characteristics; they looked upon workers as a distinct class but at the same time, as a result of their European anti-semitic experience, preferred to keep their Jewish identity within that class. Therefore, they favoured specifically Jewish cultural activities and the use of Yiddish. In addition, the Arbeiter Ring was bound together by its virulent anti-Zionism and enthusiastic secularism. It was the organization's class identification and doctrinaire stance, however, which proved its greatest weakness in Toronto. When a number of workers with initiative became small manufacturers and attempted to retain their affiliation with the Workmen's Circle, they found that the issue of unionization often forced them out. Employers unwilling to unionize, or employing strike-breakers, were immediately expelled. This effort to retain the proletarian character of the organization had the effect, in the long run, of depriving the Workmen's Circle of essential leadership. Men of intelligence who were able to move up the economic ladder soon found themselves out of place, and especially after the First World War, when affluence increased, members left the organization for Masonic and Oddfellow lodges.[25]

Ideology also created difficulties. The three major constituent groups – communists, anarchists and social democrats – managed to work out their differences reasonably well prior to the First World War. In 1915, however, the political issues of the time resulted in the anarchists' establishing their own branch of the Arbeiter Ring in Toronto. Tension developed between the remaining elements of the original branch until, in the 1920s, communists held undisputed control of the organization; but the Bolshevik Revolution encouraged them to such militancy that the social democrats were alienated. Consequently, the postwar period would see a struggle for power between the two groups in the Arbeiter Ring, eventually generating yet another split. The communists would be ejected and the organization would finally achieve socialist homogeneity.

The emergence of the third category of mutual aid societies, the *landsmanshaften*, understandably coincided with the arrival of large numbers of Jews from Russia and Poland in the years immediately preceding the war. Prior to 1913, only two such organizations had existed; the Mozirer Sick Benefit Society, founded in 1905, and the Nova Radomsk Society, formed in 1909.[26] But in the war years and immediately afterwards, a great proliferation took place.[27] Vital as they were to the welfare and security of the average Jew in Toronto, however, the *landsmanshaften* do not require detailed description. Suffice it to say that they were established for much the same reasons as the *landsmanshaft* synagogues and that they performed similar but non-religious sunctions.[28]

Several factors encouraged the growth of the *landsmanshaften* after the war. For one thing, the influenza epidemic of 1918-19, in which large numbers died, made everyone feel especially insecure. Secondly, the 1920s saw the influx of large numbers of Polish Jews, displaced by the hostilities, who were not orthodox but to whom the doctrinaire proletarianism and secularism of the Arbeiter Ring did not appeal. Besides, there was greater security for the immigrant among his own townsmen "who . . .understand his thoughts and feel his heart." In addition, the *landsmanshaften* helped immigrants secure passage to Toronto and, when the newcomers arrived, found them accommodation and employment. It was natural, therefore, for those helped to join the assisting organization. Many of the Polish *landsmanshaften* had been formed specifically to help Jewish war victims from the members' towns in Europe and dissolved as soon as the crisis had passed. Those that survived to the mid-1920s retained only their insurance, free loan and cultural functions.

In contrast to societies such as the Workmen's Circle, the *landsmanshaften* attracted storekeepers as well as workers. Even young Jewish professionals in the 1920s joined, as they did Masonic and other such lodges, to secure business contacts. Indeed, some local Jews belonged to several, in addition perhaps to a synagogue and a Zionist society, a phenomenon which prompted the *Canadian Jewish Review* to comment, tongue in cheek, that "The Toronto Jewish community is composed of born 'joiners'. Not to belong to at least sixteen organizations is open confession of financial or physical disability."[29] The *landsmanshaften* were doomed, however, by their very nature since they depended for their continued existence on sentimental attachment to the European *shtetl* and on the insecurity inherent in the immigrant experience. In the 1920s, these elements were being constantly revived by the influx of new immigrants. After 1931, when the federal government curtailed immigration from Eastern Europe, this situation no longer persisted. Few new *landsmanshaften* were established after this date; as immigrant Jews came to feel less strange in Canadian culture, they gravitated increasingly to voluntary organizations such as Masonic lodges and a revived B'nai B'rith, which emphasized social activity, ritual and community service.

NOTES

1 *HBM*, Jan. 2, 1881; *supra* chap. 3.

2 When one segment of the East Europeans formalized their relationship by purchasing a cemetery in 1883, it is no coincidence that Robinson appeared among the trustees. Deed to the Jones Avenue Cemetery; "Martin McKee et ux. to Trustees Jewish Burying Ground," City of Toronto Registry Office, Instrument No. 15101 (York) May 9, 1883.

3 "Mary A. Mussen to Trustees of the Jewish Synagogue Gol. Tcadek," City of Toronto Registry Office, Instrument No. 14585 CW. The contention presented in the *Canadian Jewish Review*, and repeated by Rhinewine, that Goel Tzedec was founded in 1862 and moved to Elm and University in 1865 is incorrect. All evidence points to the 1880s as the founding date. See *Canadian Jewish Review*, Dec. 29, 1922, p.4; A. Rhinewine, *Der Yid in Kanada*, I, pp. 127-28.

4 Like Holy Blossom in its early years, Goel Tzedec had non-resident members. Storekeepers in Bancroft, Marmora, Hamilton, Brantford and Whitby affiliated with the congregation, although they were able to attend services only on the High Holy Days when they were accommodated in Toronto either by relatives who lived in the city or by other members of the congregation (Ida Siegel, personal interview, Aug. 5, 1971).

5 See S. Traub, ed., *50 Years of History of the Beth Medrosh Hagodol Chevra Tehillim* (Toronto, 1938).

6 *Canadian Jewish Review*, Jan. 30, 1925, p. 7; Arthur Cohen, personal interviews, Dec. 15, 20, 1971; *Jewish Times*, April 14, 1899, p. 150.

   There was an additional deterrent to most East Europeans joining Holy Blossom in this period. A by-law had recently been adopted which prohibited members who paid less than a prescribed amount in dues from voting on ritual and financial questions. It is evident, therefore, that Holy Blossom was becoming increasingly the preserve of the wealthy. *HBM*, July 4, 1897.

7 Sidney S. Schipper, "The Contribution of Holy Blossom to its Community," in Albert Rose, ed., *A People and its Faith* (Toronto: University of Toronto Press: 1959), p. 34.

8 A number of prominent East European Jews can be located at Holy Blossom in the 1890s. Paul Levi, for example, later became president of Goel Tzedec; Louis Gelber and Henry Greisman were prominent in Shomrai Shabboth, while Mendel Granatstein was to be one of the founders of the Polish Beth Jacob. *HBM*, Apr. 13, 1896; Feb. 8, 1897; Aug. 9, 1897.

9 *Jewish Times*, Sept. 29, 1899, p. 343; Aug. 18, 1899, p. 294; personal interviews: Arthur Cohen, Dec. 15, 20, 1971; Ben Geldsaler, Sept. 28, 1972; Milton P. Haberman, "The History of our Congregation," in Adath Israel Congregation, *Golden Jubilee Book* (Toronto: 1952).

10 Shemen erroneously gives the founding date for Shaarei Tzedec as 1910. See N. Shemen, "Orthodoxy in Toronto" (unpublished article in Yiddish prepared for the jubilee edition of the *Daily Hebrew Journal*, 1950). In fact, the synagogue was in existence as early as 1901 (Toronto Hebrew Ladies Aid Society, *Minutes*, Dec. 8, 1901). It was only in 1910 that their synagogue on Centre Avenue was acquired (Benjamin Sherman, interview, March, 1973, Jewish Oral History Project).

11 This list is of course by no means complete. For example, there existed a synagogue called Chevra Bnai Avraham (1904), the ethnic origin of which is unclear, as well as a host of other *shtible* congregations which met for short periods and then either disbanded or were absorbed without a trace by larger institutions.

12 Ida Siegel, personal interview, July 29, 1971. Rhinewine, *op.cit.*, I, p. 128. It has been contended that Chevra Tehillim was by design not exclusively ethnic. See Traub, *op.cit.*, chap. 1. This may have been true in its later years, but in the 1880s and 1890s, especially after the Galicians founded their own congregation, Russians were overwhelmingly in the majority.

13 *Mail and Empire*, April 14, 1906; Samuel A. Kurtz, personal interview, Nov. 27, 1972. Shemen ("Orthodoxy...," p. 8) maintains that the principal cause of the split in Shomrai Shabboth was the question of admission of Sabbath violators to membership. The weight of the evidence favours the explanation offered in the text. However, even if Shemen were correct, homogeneity would still remain the basic issue.

14 For example, Knesseth Israel in the West Toronto Junction, *ca.* 1907-8; Agudath Israel Anshei Sfard (Palmerston Avenue) 1914 and Chevra Bnai Israel (originally on Ossington Avenue, then on Shaw Street), 1913 in the western part of the city itself; Beth Jacob Beach Hebrew Institute and Bnai Israel Hamizrachim (Berkeley Street), both 1918, in the east.

15 Charles Liebman, "Orthodoxy in American Jewish Life," *American Jewish Year Book,* Vol. 66 (Philadelphia: Jewish Publication Society of America, 1965), pp. 27-28.

16 Another indication of the strength of traditional observance among the East European community in Toronto was the presence of the ritual bath. Not only did a number of major synagogues possess one, but *mikvaot* were also set up in commercial Turkish baths such as Mendel Reimon's notable establishment on Centre Avenue. This tended not to be the case in cities of comparable size in the United States.

17 Dr. M.A. Pollock, personal interview, March 15, 1973; A.I. Willinsky, *op.cit.,* p. 47.

18 *Y-Time*, Jan. 28, 1949; Feb., 1938; Louis Rosenberg, "Jewish Mutual Benefit Societies . . .," pp. 11, 43; *Jewish Times,* Dec. 9, 1910, p. 7; July 5, 1912; *Report of the Registrar of Friendly Societies of Ontario 1918* (Toronto: King's Printer, 1919), p. 335; John J. Glass, personal interview, Dec. 13, 1972.

19 Louis Rosenberg, *op.cit.,* pp. 12, 44, 45. Pride of Israel Sick Benefit Society, *Silver Anniversary Souvenir,* pages not numbered. In 1925, the membership stood at 435.

20 Among these were the Toronto Independent Benevolent Society (organized *ca.* 1908, chartered 1911); the Hebrew Friendly Society (1909); The Canadian Hebrew Sick and Benevolent Society (1913); the Sons of Jacob Benevolent Society, a secession from Pride of Israel (1918); and the United Hebrew Benefit Society (1918). See *Canadian Jewish Review,* Nov. 16, 1923, p. 12; L. Rosenberg, "Jewish Mutual Benefit Societies . . .," pp. 44-45; *Report of the Registrar of Friendly Societies . . .1918,* pp. 330-335.

21 *Canadian Jewish Review,* Dec. 29, 1922, p. 13. There also existed at this period two Jewish Foresters lodges, Court Israelite and Court Progress. These, however, appear to have been dominated by members of the old community rather than by East Europeans (*Jewish Times,* April 11, 1913), p. 28.

22 *Canadian Jewish Review*, Dec. 16, 1921, p. 11; Dec. 29, 1922, p. 17; A. Greenbaum, "The First Fifty Years," in Judaean Benevolent and Friendly Society, *Golden Jubilee Book* (Toronto: 1955), p. 5.

23 Pride of Israel Sick Benefit Society, *Silver Anniversary Souvenir*; L. Rosenberg, "Jewish Mutual Benefit Societies...," p. 38; Mr. Lean, interview, March 5, 1973 (Jewish Oral History Project).

24 Henry J. Tobias, *The Bund in Russia from its Origins to 1905* (Stanford: Stanford University Press, 1972), p. 241; Bernard K. Johnpoll, *The Politics of Futility: The General Workers Bund of Poland, 1917-1943* (Ithaca: Cornell University Press, 1967), pp. 15-17; *Globe* April 28, 1922; *Telegram*, May 1, 1922. See also Bernard H. Bloom "Yiddish-Speaking Socialists in America: 1892-1905," *American Jewish Archives*, XII, No. 1 (Apr., 1960), pp. 34-68.

By 1910 the Workmen's Circle branch in Toronto already had 139 members (L. Rosenberg, "Jewish Mutual Benefit Societies...," p. 44). A branch of the society was also established in Montreal. However, because the majority of Toronto Jews were wage-earners, while those in Montreal tended to be entrepreneurs, the Workmen's Circle never would achieve the size there that it did in Toronto (Julius Seltzer, personal interview, Feb. 15, 1972).

25 A few members were religious in the prewar period, but their number was minute. These often did not join synagogues because it was felt that they were dominated by the employers. Julius Seltzer, personal interview, Feb. 15, 1972; Paul Frumhartz, interview by Julius Hayman, March 17, 1957 (typescript, 6 pp., Canadian Jewish Congress Archives, Montreal).

26 A number of ethnic synagogues had formal mutual benefit societies associated with them. For instance the First Roumanian Sick and Benevolent Society Ahavas Achim (later the Roumanian Hebrew Benevolent Association) was established at Adath Israel in 1907. These, however, were restricted to synagogue members.

27 Among the *landsmanshaften* founded in this period were the Kieltzer Sick Benefit Society, the Linitzer Sick Benefit Society, the Beizetchiner Bnai Yaakov Mutual Benefit Society, the Chenstechover Aid Society (all founded 1913), the Polish

Young Men's Hebrew Society (1915), the Berditchever Brother-Love Sick Benefit Society (*ca.* 1916), the Staszower Benefit Society (*ca.* 1918), the Ostrovtzer Independent Mutual Benefit Society (1924), the Radomer Friendly Society (1925) and the Minsker Farband (1926). *Landsmanshaften* were being established as late as the 1930s; for instance, the Lagover Sick Benefit Society was founded in 1931 and the Ivansker the following year.

28 Louis Rosenberg, "Jewish Mutual Benefit Societies...," pp. 44-45; *Report of the Registrar of Friendly Societies...1918*, pp. 330-335; *Canadian Jewish Review*, March 14, 1924; N. Shemen and L.J. Zuker (eds.), *Yovel-Book, Talmud Torah "Eitz Chaim"* (Toronto: 1943), p. 470; Ben-Zion Hyman, personal interview, Oct. 8, 1972.

29 *Canadian Jewish Review*, March 24, 1922, p. 5.

CHAPTER 8

THE COMMUNITY
AT LARGE REACTS,
1880 – 1920

THE HEBREW CHURCH, known by the familiar name of synagogue (which is simply the name for a meeting-house in the bastard Greek formerly spoken in Palestine), is a massive building in Romanesque architecture, on the south side of Richmond Street, corner of Victoria Street. The pastor or rabbi is the Rev. H. Philips (rabbi is the Hebrew word for "boss").[1]

This supercilious description of Holy Blossom, from a popular handbook of Toronto published in the early 1880s, and Goldwin Smith's virulent anti-Jewish articles in various publications during that decade and the next, have been widely quoted as evidence that in the nineteenth century anti-semitism was rampant in Toronto.[2] In truth, however, such sentiments were not typical of the Gentile attitude toward the Jews in Toronto. The relationship between the old community and non-Jews was nothing less than cordial in the late nineteenth and early twentieth centuries. When the old community protested the proposed introduction of religious instruction into the public schools, a situation which might conceivably have produced hostility in piously Christian Toronto, the *World* announced that the Jews were "right in demanding that the Public schools shall not be used to disseminate this or that particular religion." Moreover, when the opening of the Bond Street synagogue elicited an anti-semitic letter to its editor, the paper responded in a paean of praise for the Jews, describing them as "a desirable element in the community" and a class "that minds its own business, that is loyal to the country, . . .asks no favors, and . . .expects nothing but fair and impartial treatment at the hands of the Government and the rest of the people."

There was good reason for members of Holy Blossom to consider themselves fully integrated into the civic, religious and social life of the city. In 1898 Miss Etta Birkenthal, a young woman active in the synagogue and the daughter of the reform rabbi in Hamilton, was appointed assistant principal at Palmerston Avenue Public School. In the same period, a member of the old community, probably an Englishman, belonged to the Caer Howell Bowling Club, while another unofficially represented Toronto at the Canadian chess championship in Montreal. Dr. and Mrs. Algernon Temple and Major Henry Pellatt attended a dinner party at Frank Benjamin's in 1899, and in 1901 several non-Jewish couples, among whom was Mayor Howland, were present at a ball hosted by the Toronto Jewish Literary and Social Union. Barnett Laurance, another Englishman and a trustee of Holy Blossom, was active in the St. George's Society, the Masonic Order, the Municipal Reform Association and the Albany Club, and when he died in 1905 large numbers of non-Jews attended his funeral.[3]

Especially popular with the community at large was Rabbi Solomon Jacobs, who succeeded Wittenberg at Holy Blossom in 1901 and whom, after the demise of Alfred Benjamin, non-Jews came to consider the official head of the Jewish community. A native of Sheffield, Jacobs never lost an opportunity to voice pride in his British heritage. Consequently, Holy Blossom came to be looked upon as a stronghold of patriotism. The rabbi also had the advantage, over any of his predecessors, of wide experience both in Jewish affairs and in communal activity generally. Forty years old when he came to Canada, he had already served as principal of a Jewish school in Manchester and as minister, prior to his ordination, at Newcastle-upon-Tyne. Before his election to Holy Blossom, he had been rabbi in Kingston, Jamaica, and had served as director of the municipal dispensary there.

Immediately upon his arrival, Jacobs was accepted by the Gentile community and invited to participate in local affairs on an equal basis with other ministers of religion and with superior status to some. He was invited, for instance, to the provincial reception for the visiting Duke of York in 1901; he was asked to address Christian congregations, as well as groups such as the Toronto Theosophical Society and the Overseas Club, and in return he invited Christian ministers to Holy Blossom. On several occasions he was invited to state dinners tendered by the Lieutenant-Governor and when King Edward VII died in 1910, he was asked to participate in the memorial ceremony at Queen's Park. Rabbi Jacobs took part in other communal affairs beyond the circle of the Jewish population. In 1910 he was elected vice-president of the Associated Charities of Toronto and soon afterward was appointed to the city's first Charities Commission. The rabbi often pleaded in court for non-Jews whom he believed had been unjustly accused or had committed crimes under extenuating circumstances. In the same period, he served as a member of the advisory board of the Toronto Ladies' Aid Society and the Association for the Care of the Feebleminded. Mrs. Jacobs, incidentally, did similar work in the Local Council of Women and in other organizations outside the Jewish community. Rabbi Jacobs' statements were taken seriously by the Gentile community; local newspapers quoted his sermons frequently.[4]

Despite this apparent integration into the civic life of Toronto by many of the English and German families at Holy Blossom, in the private, as opposed to the official, social sphere, there was probably considerable exclusion even of the most "acceptable" Jews. While the Benjamins and others invited non-Jews to their homes, there is little evidence of their having been invited in return, and although a few of the old community did belong to Gentile social clubs, the majority did not. This was regretted, but accepted as the natural order and the Holy Blossom community went about satisfying their social needs within their own circle.

If overt anti-semitism did not erupt immediately, once the presence of the East European community became apparent the public attitude toward the Jewish population became more ambivalent. Although few were as explicit as Goldwin Smith in announcing that "no invasion could be worse" than an influx of East European Jews,[5] subtle public criticism of Jews became more frequent. As early as the 1880s the *Telegram* had taken "the opportunity of bringing Jews prominently before the public when they are unfortunately associated with anything that can be viewed as derogatory to their religious belief,"[6] and while this practice was restricted only to that paper prior to 1900, it soon became more widespread. Rabbi Jacobs complained in a sermon of 1902 that local newspapers "often referred to any who were unfortunate enough to appear in the Police Court, as Jews. They did not call them by their name . . ., without emphasizing that they were Jews." On another occasion, Jacobs "remarked how frequently the Jew is lampooned and misrepresented in the local newspapers. . . .One paper in particular [probably the *Telegram*] is so badly biased on matters Jewish that one would think Goldwin Smith had in some manner influenced . . .[its] policy . . . ." In 1912 one journal declared that the "Increase of Jewish citizens [is] astounding," while another headed an article on politics with the caption "For $5 I will bring you five Jews." The *Jewish Times* observed from Montreal that such statements "are more to be expected . . . in Kishinef than in Toronto." Comments in the *Telegram* had become so viciously anti-semitic by 1913 that Edmund Scheuer asked its editor, John Ross Robertson, to put an end to the practice.[7]

This effort was largely successful, but discrimination and even open attack continued nonetheless. Madame Bella Pevsner, a Zionist lecturer from Europe who visited the city in 1912, was struck by the anti-semitism evident in Toronto. It was virtually impossible, for instance, for a Jew not of English parentage to join a Gentile social club in the early twentieth century even if he had been born in Toronto. The York Club, the Lawyers' Club and various boating clubs and golf courses remained very exclusive, resisting even prominent, affluent and educated Jews. A few were admitted to the Albany Club, the social wing of the Conservative party, but these often found themselves snubbed by those resenting their membership. In 1898, and again in 1907, the editor of the *Jewish Times* had noted with satisfaction that Jews were not being excluded from Canadian hotels as they were in the United States. They were treated rather on their personal merits, in typical British tolerance of strangers. But by 1911, it was reported that a number of Toronto Jews who had been denied admission to bathing facilities had purchased a farm in Long Branch for the purpose of establishing their own resort.[8] Indeed, even as early as the turn of the century the *Jewish Times*, which reflected the opinion of the acculturated community both in Montreal and in Toronto, had found it necessary to publish a formula to minimize discrimination at summer resorts. Its readers were instructed to "avoid loudness and assertiveness. To appear well-bred, people shun all display in dress, extravagance in expense and attempts to outshine others."[9]

In the period before the war and into the twenties, anti-semitic sentiment, while usually veiled, appeared also when Jews attempted to seek employment outside the factory. Jews were seldom hired as sales staff at the major department stores or as clerks in local banks. Jewish university graduates who wished to become teachers found acceptance in Toronto schools impossible, and frequently sought careers in law or medicine as a result. Even independent professionals found Toronto rife with discrimination. Lawyers and engineers could not find employment with Gentile firms. Moreover, Jewish medical graduates were refused as interns in local hospitals, found it difficult to locate their offices in fashionable districts and sometimes had to disguise the fact that they were Jews in order to secure desirable accommodation.[10] Admittedly, in the war years Dr. Abraham Brodey was appointed Acting Head of the Department of Pharmacology at the University of Toronto, a position he held until 1919, and during the 1920s two other practitioners held posts at the Western Hospital; but for the most part, Jewish doctors were excluded. Indeed, no Jewish doctor was to have a clinical appointment at the university or an indoor staff position at a teaching hospital in Toronto until after the Second World War.[11]

Jews encountered difficulty in some public hospitals and schools as patients and students as well. Nurses often treated immigrants with indifference. In the public schools, although in theory Christianity was not officially taught, many of the teachers were children of clergymen; religious indoctrination was often the tacit policy and Jewish children were punished for refusing to read from the New Testament. This situation was not universal, however; some schools had enlightened principals who de-emphasized Christianity in predominantly Jewish classes. As for anti-semitism on the part of elementary school children, this was rare until just before the First World War, while Rabbi Jacobs found it altogether absent at the University of Toronto. Certainly, there were no entrance restrictions, and Jews were freely admitted to the excellence clubs at University College. However, extra-mural social activities, especially when they involved the opposite sex, were difficult.

Anti-Jewish behaviour also manifested itself in less subdued forms. Outside the Ward it was not uncommon for a bearded Jew to be attacked on the street at the turn of the century and even as late as 1917. Indeed, the danger of assault was so real in some areas of the city that East European Jewish schoolboys were instructed by their parents to make themselves inconspicuous.[12] Jewish peddlers were especially in danger of being dragged from their wagons and pelted with stones and garbage. "Why are Jewish peddlers viciously assaulted on our public thoroughfares," Rabbi Jacobs inquired in a sermon of 1909, "and passersby look on smiling and often join in the savage act?" Violence against Jews was not restricted to native-born elements. In 1913, for example, a Jew was attacked by Macedonians, drenched with dirty water and thrown into a rubbish heap. Other immigrant groups, especially Italians, experienced discrimination as well, but in few cases was it as vehement as against the Jews.

The anti-semitism experienced by the Jews in Toronto was characteristic of that manifest throughout North America. It was not, as a rule, national anti-semitism like that of Russia, affecting

121

all Jews; it was, rather, rooted in traditional religious prejudice and affected individuals rather than the entire group. This prejudice, as Rabbi Jacobs perceived, was based to a considerable degree upon ignorance and stereotypes of the East European Jew. Those who ill-treat the Jewish immigrant, the *Mail and Empire* commented, "are acting on hereditary traditions and do not study the Jew's character . . . ."[13]

Most Jews experienced no direct anti-semitism, except for slights noticed in the newspapers, because most lived in self-imposed isolation and had little contact with Gentiles other than their immediate neighbours with whom, for the most part, they got on well. Only those who circulated widely outside the ghetto, the peddlers and the more prosperous, experienced real hostility. The latter, when they moved out of the predominantly Jewish neighbourhoods in the years following the First World War, were often confronted with the "spite fence."[14]

The extent of ignorance about the conditions of Jewish life in Toronto was astonishing. One "Thoroughbred Canadian" complained to the *Star* in 1913 that "these Jews live worse than dogs," while another citizen called them "uncivilized barbarians" who "have too much liberty." When a Canadian Zionist convention was held in Toronto in 1910, the *Canadian Baptist* found it remarkable that most of the speakers had "a good command of our language." Indeed, as late as 1922 a reporter who attended a service at Holy Blossom was surprised to learn that the sermons were delivered in English.[15]

Many more examples could be cited to illustrate the fact that by 1914 the image of the Jew as Englishman and solid citizen, which for many years had been projected by Holy Blossom, had been supplanted in the minds of a significant portion of the non-Jewish population of Toronto by that of the exotic, boisterous and poverty-stricken East European Jew of the Ward and by the stereotype of the Jewish peddler.

The sources of the stereotype are not difficult to see. The dilapidated Ward, adjacent to the principal shopping district, was the most obviously Jewish area in the city in the prewar years. That period also was one in which Torontonians of all classes made use of the city's extensive streetcar network. Since a large number of major routes passed through the Ward, shoppers on their way to the large department stores at Queen and Yonge or office workers travelling to the central business district would naturally come to equate Jews with slums. Secondly, for some Gentiles, their only Jewish contact was probably the rag peddler, a phenomenon which was disturbing the more self-conscious acculturated elements of the Jewish community.

> So identified have the Jews become with the peddling business in Toronto [the local reporter to the *Jewish Times* complained], that it is looked upon as a purely Jewish enterprise. The peddlers of course, who call at homes to purchase goods at the lowest possible prices, journey around the nicer residential quarters of the city, and have become extremely unpopular with the Gentile population, who at best, in Toronto, have never shown a too friendly disposition to our people . . . .
>
> The peddler has to beg the house occupants to let him buy something from them; he is often insulted, but having become hardened, he returns the next day. All this is evident, too, in the little attention he is led to take of his appearance, and the humble, melancholy, drawl of his voice, which has become trained to the awful call of "Rags," etc. So grotesque a figure indeed is he becoming in and around the city that Gentile mothers are overheard to quieten their children with the remark: – Hush, hush, or I will call the Jewish peddler. Thus the child grows up to know the Jew as something to be afraid of . . . .

The paper insisted that the presence of the peddler was a "sore that is troubling the healthy growth and development of the Jews of Toronto" and urged that the "leading Jews of Toronto who have the fair name of the Jew at heart" see that new arrivals were directed into "less degrading occupations."[16]

Although the Jews still lacked the organization to deal with this problem as a body, attempts were made in the prewar years to improve their public image. Within the Jewish circle itself this defence came principally from Rabbi Jacobs, whose sermons made popular copy and who was approached by the press for opinions supposedly representing those of the entire community. When it was charged in 1911, for example, that Jews spent Sunday in drunkenness, Jacobs issued an eloquent denial, maintaining that since Jews observed the Sabbath on Saturday, a practice involving "considerable sacrifice on their part," it was no one's concern how they occupied themselves on Sunday. When a speaker at a charities conference in the city attempted to prove that wife desertion was more common among the Jews than among other groups, the rabbi successfully countered the argument. Edmund Scheuer, one of the few socially acceptable local Jews, added to this defensive effort by sending prominent Gentile acquaintances books on Jewish subjects.[17]

The major attempt to rehabilitate the Jewish reputation came, however, not from the Jews but from enlightened sources in the non-Jewish community. It emerged not only from an understanding of the Jewish character and lifestyle in Toronto but also in humanitarian reaction against the persecution of Jews in Europe and in sympathy for the Zionist movement, which many local Christians interpreted as having religious implications for themselves. Sympathy for the East European Jew was manifest especially in response to two incidents in Russia: the massacres at Kishinev in 1905 and the blood libel of Mendel Beiliss in 1913.* Large numbers of Christians, including the Premier of Ontario and Mayor Urquhart, attended the meeting at the McCaul Street synagogue in November 1905 to protest against the pogrom. The assembly petitioned King Edward to intercede for the Jews of Russia and there was wide approval of the suggestion that the persecuted be admitted to Canada. When the Beiliss case erupted the Toronto City Council passed a resolution of protest, the synod of the Presbyterian Church publicly condemned Russia and once again Gentiles flocked to the protest meeting organized by the Jewish community at Massey Hall, there to be addressed not only by Jews but also by various Christian clergymen, a prominent labour leader and three local politicians.

The Zionist movement, which sought to re-establish a Jewish homeland in Palestine and encouraged Jewish settlement there, was looked upon favourably by at least the official and articulate element of the community at large. Sympathy was evident early in the century when Sir William Mortimer Clark, Lieutenant-Governor of Ontario, attended a reception tendered the vice-president of the international Zionist organization on a visit to Toronto in 1904, and the governor continued to be vocal in support of Jewish aspirations in this regard. Canadian Zionist conventions, which were frequently held in Toronto, offered still other occasions for expressions of Gentile sympathy and for praise of the Jews. At a 1906 gathering such prominent individuals

* The case involved the preposterous charge, revived from the medieval period, that Jews killed Christian children in order to use their blood in the preparation of unleavened bread for Passover. In 1911 the body of a murdered child was discovered in Beiliss' brickyard in Kiev. Despite overwhelming evidence that thieves had committed the crime, Beiliss was brought to trial in 1913 on a charge of ritual murder. He was acquitted, but the incident nevertheless provided numerous pretexts for the persecution of Jews.

as Professor Ramsay Wright, Alderman Vaughan, Alderman Graham and T.C. Robinette, a prominent local attorney, were among those present. Mayor Coatsworth, addressing the meeting, "found the Jew as good a citizen as can be desired." In 1910 the City Council voted a sum for the entertainment of delegates to the convention held in Toronto that year. "The warm welcome made by the Mayor, Controllers and Aldermen of the Queen City to those delegates residing in less broad-minded provinces ... [is] most flattering," the *Jewish Times* mused. "Happy Toronto to possess such tolerant, peaceful City Fathers." It was not, of course, expected that the Jews of Toronto would all emigrate to Palestine. The Zionist movement did not propose to "take away any of our Jewish citizens," one alderman remarked. He was quick to add that "We want them all here and as many more as we can get."[18]

Another outburst of civic support coincided with the visit of the renowned Hebrew author and Zionist leader Nahum Sokolow in May 1913. Mayor Hocken sent his private car to bring the visitor to City Hall and personally escorted him on a tour of Toronto. The city also tendered him a kosher luncheon at the Queen's Hotel and gave all Jewish children in the public schools a half-holiday. By the time of the Balfour Declaration in 1917, which announced the British government's sympathy with the concept of a Jewish homeland in Palestine, large numbers of local Christians were coming to see the return of Jews to the Land of Israel as the fulfilment of prophecy. The *Star*, convinced that Zionist agricultural efforts in Palestine would succeed, urged the public to support the local campaign to aid Jews in the Holy Land.

But favourable comment about Jews in this period was not confined to situations involving vague humanitarian principles or messianic yearnings. It appeared also to be based upon a real understanding of local Jewish immigrants, or at least upon a desire to know them. When the Jews of the Ward were being accused of creating slum conditions, Dr. P.H. Bryce, the chief medical health officer of the Department of the Interior, told the Empire Club in 1906 that the real causes were the grasping landlords and incompetent civic administrations. These immigrants, he maintained, "have proved themselves very good citizens, and have come up very largely to our ideals of thinking and doing." They had a right, he continued, "not to our criticism, but to our sympathy and kindly interest." Some years later, when Jews were accused of being slovenly, one Anglican clergyman told the *Star* that after having lived for two years in the Jewish area he had "never seen a drunken Jew," and that the Jews were honest, hospitable, pure and responsible in their family life and in industry. "As a Christian," he observed, "I desire to be at peace with them, I want their respect, and therefore I will not withhold the expression of mine for them .... We have sat in the seat of the scornful long enough."[19]

Other non-Jews were offended by the criticism of the Jew, and to a degree all Toronto papers except the *Telegram* published supporting editorial comment. The *Globe* considered them a "valued and respected element," while the *Daily News* offered a feature entitled "Our Debt to the Jews," outlining Jewish contributions to western civilization. "As a body," one *News* editorial remarked, "they are singularly thrifty and enterprising. No more industrious or law-abiding people come among us .... We should seek, therefore to interest him [the Jew] in all our various social and civic activities rather than exclude him from places of responsibility." In 1911, when a member of the Queen City Yacht Club proposed that Jews be excluded, one Toronto paper commented that "To label the Jewish citizens of Toronto as undesirables, ...is a gratuitous insult to a class of citizens that Toronto has reason to be proud of and to respect." The proposal was overwhelmingly rejected.

Most vocal in their support was the *Mail and Empire*, which became so incensed by the deprecation of Jews as an argument against further Jewish immigration in the immediate prewar years that it poured forth a blanket defence in October 1913. "The Jew is by nature a law-abiding individual; he is also an extremely moral individual; in the annals of crime he stands at the foot of the list, and in the records of rescue homes and missions to fallen women there are few Jewish names to be found .... Also the Jews are extremely temperate. . . ." The Jews "make a point of Canadianizing themselves and their children," the latter being imbued in their Sunday schools "with a sense of loyalty to the British Empire and to the Dominion." The Jew "is accused of meanness, of always getting the better of anyone with whom he deals . . .whereas, as a matter of fact, and those who have worked intimately with Jews or anyone of Jewish extraction will vouch for the truth of this, he is not only just, but often extremely generous, even to those outside his own race and creed .... The wealthy Jew never refuses charitable aid to worthy objects." The poor Jew always repays his loans. "Thus it will be seen," the *Mail* concluded, "that, so far from being an undesirable settler for the Dominion, the Jew is, as a matter of fact, if possible more desirable than many others who are more warmly welcomed."[20]

Numerous instances could be cited of private, official and

journalistic good relations with the Jews in this period.[21] By 1920 even the East European Jews were evidently on their way to achieving some measure of acceptance, at least in the public sphere, and they seized each opportunity for participation with enthusiasm. Latent anti-semitism and subtle discrimination continued to exist, however, despite all attempts to eradicate them. To this the Jewish community was prepared to resign itself. Jews simply would not apply for jobs where they were unlikely to obtain them, nor seek to rent cottages or establish homes at beaches or in neighbourhoods where they expected to encounter discrimination. Anti-semitism, except where it attempted to gain official and legal recognition, could be tolerated. It did not threaten Jewish survival. Missionary activity, on the contrary, did just that, and whereas the Jews offered only weak organizational resistance to discrimination, they rallied in furious opposition to attempts at conversion.

NOTES

1 C. Pelham Mulvany, *Toronto: Past and Present* (Toronto: W.E. Caiger, 1884), p. 182.

2 Smith's criticism was directed principally at the East Europeans, whom he described as "encamping in all other nations, absorbing their wealth by financial skill..." (*Weekly Sun*, quoted in *Jewish Times*, Feb. 4, 1898, p. 69) and bringing pogroms upon themselves by their exclusiveness (*Weekly Sun*, Sept. 20, 1899). "We freely admit the Polish Jews...," he complained. "The Chinaman, though he may be vicious himself, is not a corrupter of the community; the Polish Jew unhappily is" (quoted in *Jewish Times*, Aug. 3, 1900, p. 280; see also *Jewish Times*, Apr. 1, 1898, p. 139).

  For a complete account of Smith's literary activities see Elisabeth Wallace, *Goldwin Smith: Victorian Liberal* (Toronto: University of Toronto Press, 1957). Fortunately, his writings on Jewish subjects did not gain wide acceptance in Toronto (Ida Siegel, personal interview, Nov. 25, 1971).

3 *Jewish Times*, March 31, 1899, p. 134; April 14, 1899, p. 151; June 9, 1899, p. 222; March 15, 1901, p. 119; Nov. 17, 1904, p. 413.

4 Personal interviews: Arthur Cohen, Dec. 20, 1971; Mrs. M. Goodman, Jan. 12, 1972; and Bertha Draimin, Jan. 10, 1972.

5 Quoted in *Jewish Times*, Aug. 3, 1900, p. 280.

6 Lewis Samuel to John Ross Robertson, quoted in Sigmund Samuel, *In Return*, pp. 40-41.

7 *Jewish Times*, Oct. 9, 1902, pp. 362-63; Nov. 1, 1907, p. 402; Mar. 1, 1912, p. 1; Aug. 15, 1913, p. 1; Feb. 7, 1913; *Star* and *Telegram*, Feb. 1912, *passim*; Arthur Cohen, personal interview, Dec. 20, 1971. Other papers were less overtly prejudiced than the *Telegram*, but often mentioned Jews in pejorative contexts. E.g., see article entitled "Seven Hebrews and Crown Bank Are Being Sued for $10,000 Damages," *Mail and Empire*, March 11, 1909, and that headed "Jew has Disappeared," *Mail and Empire*, Feb. 15, 1909. For examples of articles on Jews appearing in court cases, see *Evening Telegram*, June 10, 1907; June 13, 1907.

   While the *Telegram* was openly anti-semitic, the *Globe* and the *Mail and Empire* merely used "Jew" as they would "Russian" or "Dane," but most frequently in mentioning events which would disparage the Jewish character. The *Star*, the *World* and the *News*, on the other hand, were, as a rule, openly sympathetic to the Jews and their problems. But even the *Star* occasionally named a person simply as "Jew" (e.g., Dec. 24, 1913; May 3, 1916). For examples of articles in the *News* which were sympathetic to Jews, see clippings in the Edmund Scheuer Scrapbook, Holy Blossom Archives.

8 In this period it was very difficult, for instance, for Jews to rent accommodations at Lake Simcoe (Dr. M.A. Pollock, personal interview, March 15, 1973). As early as 1907, when the Young Men's Zion Club wanted to establish headquarters on one of the islands in Toronto harbour, they were denied permission by the City Island Committee. They suspected, probably not without justification, that Gentile clubs on the islands had pressured city politicians to exclude them (*Jewish Times*, Apr. 19, 1907, p. 167). The Jewish club set up a committee to act on the matter, but it appears that nothing came of it.

9 *Jewish Times*, July 5, 1901, p. 249.

10 A.B. Bennett, personal interview, Oct. 3, 1972; David Eisen, "My Life in Toronto" (typescript, 1973), p. 4; personal interviews: Arthur Cohen, Dec. 20, 1971; Ben-Zion Hyman, Oct. 8, 1972; Dr. M.A. Pollock, March 15, 1973. A few young Jews did obtain sales positions in the major department stores

in this period, but only by disguising the fact that they were Jewish (Ida Siegel, personal interview, Sept. 2, 1971).

11 D. Eisen, *Toronto Jewish Doctors* (Toronto: Maimonides Medical Society and Canadian Jewish Congress, 1960), p. 14; confidential interview.

12 A.E. Willinsky, *op.cit.*, pp. 7-9; William Leibel, personal interview, Jan. 28, 1972. For an incident of Jews being insulted in the street by native youths, see *Star*, July 22, 1913. See also Ida Siegel, personal interviews, Aug. 5, Sept. 2, 1971 for similar incidents in the late nineteenth and early twentieth centuries.

13 *Mail and Empire*, Oct. 18, 1913.

14 Ida Siegel, personal interviews, Sept. 2, 1971; Aug. 26, 1971.

15 *Star*, July 28, 1913; July 11, 1913; *Canadian Baptist*, quoted in *Jewish Times*, Jan. 13, 1911, p. 8; *Canadian Jewish Review*, Dec. 22, 1922, p. 7. Holy Blossom had had English sermons since the 1890s and by the 1920s Goel Tzedec also employed an English-speaking rabbi. Indeed, Rabbi Barnett Brickner, who served Holy Blossom at that time, had been born in the United States.

16 *Jewish Times*, March 28, 1913, p. 1.

17 Newspaper clippings *ca.* 1911, in Edmund Scheuer Scrapbook, Holy Blossom Archives; *Jewish Times*, Oct. 29, 1909, p. 1007; Warschauer, *op.cit.*, 1st ed., p. 147. The paper and the City Health Department supported Jacobs' position.

18 *Jewish Times*, Nov. 25, 1910, p. 11; Ald. Heyde, quoted in *Jewish Times*, Dec. 30, 1910, p. 8. Such statements by politicians are lent credence when it is realized that in no riding did Jews constitute a majority of the voters.

19 Dr. P.H. Bryce, "Civic Responsibility and the Increase of Immigration," *Empire Club Speeches 1906-7*, pp. 188-89; Rev. A.N. McEvoy, quoted in *Star*, July 28, 1913.

20 *Mail and Empire*, Oct. 18, 1913.

21 For instance, non-Jews contributed to the building fund of the new Goel Tzedec synagogue on University Avenue and civic officials attended the dedication both of that structure and the McCaul Street synagogue. Local politicians, including the mayor, appeared at social and charitable functions sponsored

by Jewish organizations, such as the annual ball of the Roumanian Sick Benefit Society and the "at home" of the Daughters of Zion. In 1909, when Jacob Cohen became Toronto's first Jewish magistrate, the local press responded most favourably. And increasingly, papers began to take notice of Jewish holy days. It was not remarkable for the *Star* to carry a sympathetic account of Hanukkah in 1915, nor for the *Mail* and *Empire* to describe Shavuoth. Even the *Telegram* condescended occasionally to mention a Jewish holiday. Indeed, by 1917 the *Star* was carrying a regular "Jewish News" feature.

CHAPTER 9

THE MISSIONS,
1894 – 1914

As long as the projected image of the Jew remained predominantly that of Holy Blossom – English-speaking and Anglophile, cultured and middle class – the community at large was content to leave him to his own devices when it came to religion. But just as the outnumbering of the acculturated Jews by East European immigrants in the late nineteenth century produced some anti-semitic sentiment in the Christian community, so also did it give rise to efforts to "save" the newcomers by converting them to Christianity.

When the first such venture, the Toronto Jewish Mission, opened in the Ward in 1894, the Christian churches were somewhat ambivalent toward it. Most approved of Jewish conversion, but they hesitated to become involved with this type of evangelism themselves. The new mission, therefore, remained an interdenominational one, supported by wealthy individuals, but looked upon as slightly suspect by the major denominations.[1] The early efforts of the new mission were largely wasted, for it encountered bitter hostility from all Jews who were approached. By 1897 it had become apparent that if the institution were not to collapse altogether, new tactics would have to be found. The group therefore sought out the Reverend Henry Singer, a Polish Jew who had converted to Christianity and who was then proselytizing in Boston. Fluent in Yiddish and highly personable, Singer was expected to attract large numbers of local immigrants into his mission on Centre Avenue. "Singer the Meshummed" (apostate) did become a well-known figure in the East European Jewish community, but for all his amiability he was not taken seriously by more than a very few.

A Presbyterian mission to the Jews had existed in Toronto as early as 1898, but the local presbytery found it "difficult to support." Money could better be expended on foreign missions and so local activities were left to the struggling interdenominational institution. The failure encountered by Singer, however, coupled with the rapid increase in the Jewish population of Toronto after 1905 and an upsurge in support for home missions within the church, resulted in the establishment of a new Presbyterian mission. In 1907 the General Assembly of the Presbyterian Church authorized its Foreign Mission Committee "to commence a mission to the Hebrew People in Toronto, with the privilege of extending this work elsewhere in Canada as the circumstances may warrant.[2] The Foreign Mission Board appointed a prominent local pastor, the Reverend J. McPherson Scott, to head a Jewish Mission Committee. This, in turn, secured the services of the Reverend Sabeti B. Rohold of Glasgow as superintendent.

Rohold, they believed, was eminently suited to his position as missionary. His father had been a rabbi in his native Jerusalem, and he had studied at a number of rabbinical academies prior to his conversion. Upon his arrival in March 1908, he was quickly ordained by the local presbytery and immediately set about mobilizing the missionary resources of the church. Within a month, the Presbyterian Jewish Mission had been established at Teraulay and Elm streets, where Rohold, assisted by another convert, Henry Bregman, five lady missionaries and fifty volunteers, organized a multiplicity of activities to attract Jews. A reading room and a nursery were opened; a night school was established; sewing and manual training classes were offered for young people, as was a Sabbath School. Open-air services accompanied by a portable organ were held on Saturday rather than on Sunday, in order to minimize the differences between the mission and the synagogue.

The principal attraction of the mission, however, was none of these. Rohold was perceptive enough to realize that what the Jews needed was material rather than spiritual assistance. "We found them disorganized, strangers in a strange land," he later wrote, "with a feeling of despair and as it was soon after the crisis in the United States, the poor were many and sickness prevalent." The Presbyterian Mission, therefore, established a free dispensary which treated over three thousand patients in its initial year of operation and over eighteen thousand in its first decade.[3] Since immigrant Jewish women in this period could rarely be persuaded to enter hospital to give birth, the missionaries undertook also to care for maternity cases at home. By 1911 six doctors and a nurse were donating their services to the mission on a rotation basis. The missionaries also visited Jews at home and in the factories, and offered rent subsidies and supplies of coal where these were required. In 1911 alone, the mission provided outdoor relief for 756 families and its employment service secured jobs for 75 individuals. The mission also operated a fresh-air home which enabled children to be sent to the country during the summer. "We think that we have one of the most successful Jewish Missions on this continent," the Superintendent of Foreign Missions wrote in 1910, "and there is no room for any question as to the possibility of converting the Jews to Christianity. The interest in the city is quite marked and it is evidenced by the fact that the Jews amongst us are greatly excited over the success of the Mission." Reverend Scott was also optimistic. The Mission, he announced to a contributor, "have now in our hands really more than we can do. The whole work is full of encouragement."[4]

In this spirit of apparent success, the Presbyterians erected a commodious new building at Elizabeth and Elm streets and when it opened in June 1913, renamed the mission "The Christian Synagogue." All the activities carried on at the Teraulay Street premises were continued at the new building on an expanded scale. The number of full-time employees was increased to five and it was reported that the new edifice brought hundreds into the mission. The playground of Elizabeth Street (Hester How) School across the road now became a hotbed of attempted proselytizing. The missionaries would commonly escort Jewish children to school where they would wash them and even rinse their clothes in the drinking fountains. In addition, a Hebrew Christian congregation was organized at the mission within the Presbytery of Toronto and it was claimed that 114 Hebrew Christians attended the first communion in 1913.[5]

Not to be outdone by the Presbyterians, the Church of England had, as early as 1909, ordered its local Diocesan Mission Board to "deal with the question of 'The work among the Jews' in the City of Toronto, and to take such steps as may be thought proper to prosecute mission work among the Jews of our city, in co-operation with other religious bodies engaged in this work, or otherwise as may seem best." The location of the proposed mission was to anticipate the movement of the Jewish population west of University Avenue and, as was the case with the Anglican mission in Montreal, it was to be connected with the London Society for Promoting Christianity among the Jews. The Church of England hierarchy considered the issue of conversion of immigrants an urgent one; they equated it with acculturation and considered it essential to the defence of Anglo-Saxon society. As

Bishop Sweeney remarked in a sermon of the period, the alien was "an element of danger to the future of Canada."[6]

Funds allotted to the project, however, were diverted to foreign missions, and so it was not until 1912 that an Anglican mission to the Jews was opened in Toronto; this was sponsored not by the denomination as a whole, but rather by Holy Trinity, the parish which included St. John's Ward. Consequently, the mission was located on Edward Street in the Ward. In 1914 the Anglican diocese of Toronto took over the venture and appointed a committee to teach Yiddish to its missionaries. By the early years of the First World War the usual mission activities were under way: a night school, a dispensary, home and hospital visits, mothers' meetings, Sunday school, sewing classes and occasional open-air meetings. In 1916 the mission, now renamed Nathanael Institute, moved west of Spadina to Bellevue Avenue and embarked on a program of co-operation with Rohold's group in the spheres of outdoor relief and the finding of employment.[7]

However, despite the shift of the Jewish population to the Kensington Market area, missionary activity remained most intense in the Ward, where the most recent arrivals settled and consequently where the poorest elements of the Jewish community lived. These, especially the children, were most easily attracted to the mission. At Elizabeth Street School the teachers cooperated closely with the missions, sending their students across to Rohold for parties and taking them to revival meetings at Massey Hall with the approval of the principal. Indeed, as early as 1903 Jewish children were being encouraged to attend Anglican services in a clandestine chapel within the school building; this was removed only after one Jewish resident, A.P. Lewis, discovered it and protested to the municipal authorities. "There is the hiring of apostate Jews," Rabbi Jacobs complained, "to entrap our little children, or the ignorant, or the starving, the weakminded and the unprincipled among our poor." Children were induced to come to the mission by gifts of candy and "other trifles." On some occasions, overzealous volunteers even forced some into the building against their will.[8]

The Ward was also the centre for street preaching, a practice generally eschewed by the Anglicans but popular with both Singer and Rohold. The latter used a wagon from which to preach, especially on Friday evenings. At one point he made a practice of stationing himself at the corner of Elizabeth and Agnes (Dundas) streets where Rabbi Weinreb, the senior orthodox rabbi in the city, resided. Again, a protest to City Hall was necessary to persuade Rohold to change his position.

134

Throughout their existence, the three missions encountered similar setbacks. First, there was the difficulty of attracting qualified personnel. Yiddish-speaking missionaries were rare; the Presbyterians and Singer competed for the few who were available. The Anglicans could get none at all and were forced to concentrate their evangelizing efforts exclusively on English-speaking families. There was also the problem that mission work tended to attract "unbalanced" converts who wanted to assist in proselytizing. These were a nuisance, especially to the Presbyterians.

A second hindrance was the lack of enthusiasm exhibited by the denominations themselves. Anglicans and Presbyterians alike were more interested in foreign missions than in domestic ones. Despite its wealthy patrons, the Presbyterian mission was constantly short of funds, while the Anglican Committee on Jewish Work appealed continually for "a more general interest" in domestic missions to the Jews. One member of the Synod, reflecting the general apathy, insisted that "it is as futile to try and convert a Jew as to convert China in a day .... The very intellectual superiority of the Jew is not in favor of missions for his conversion."[9]

This pessimism was largely justified. Attendance at the Anglican mission was poor compared to the effort expended. Peak attendance at one function seldom exceeded forty people. By 1912 Rohold could claim only forty-two Jews who had accepted baptism, and despite the large attendance at the opening service of the Christian Synagogue, it was reported that only thirty-two people were in full communion. Rohold, especially, professed to be pleased with his accomplishment in this regard, but he repeatedly maintained that greater numbers would have been attracted except "for fear of the Jews." "Many, yea many would thus confess Him," the missionary insisted, "were it not for the awful hardships they are called upon to face...."[10]

It is improbable that many more Jews would have been attracted to Christianity, since Jewish traditions were strong among most of the immigrants who had religious inclinations of any sort. It was true, however, that increased numbers might have sought material assistance from the mission had the East European community not exerted powerful social pressure in opposition to the practice and aroused popular sentiment against the missionaries.

Prior to the reorganization of the Presbyterian mission,

proselytism had not been considered a serious threat by the Jews. As missionary activities became more widespread, however, Jewish resentment grew. The efforts of the Presbyterians at Elizabeth Street School were especially infuriating. By 1909 public appeals to children by Rabbi Jacobs, urging them to refuse gifts and to avoid missionary gatherings, had become commonplace. In February the Jews held a public meeting to determine how missionary influence was to be counteracted and by the next spring a group called "The Alumni" were active in the effort.[11] This organization was composed primarily of teenagers, who would stand at the door of Rohold's mission to discourage Jews from entering by informing them of the philanthropic services offered by the Jewish community. Some were so persistent in keeping Jews out of the building that they were arrested, but despite these difficulties the efforts of the group had considerable success. They did not succeed, however, in eradicating the problem. Late in the year, Jewish indignation was aroused further when a local Presbyterian congregation sponsored a Christmas Eve dinner for one hundred Jewish children from Elizabeth Street School. To add insult to injury, they were taken to the church in vans provided by Marmaduke Rawlinson, chairman of the Board of Education, and were provided with toys and old clothing. English-speaking Jews denounced this action and missionary work generally in letters to the local newspapers. The Jews had indeed become "excited" and by the spring of 1910 the *Jewish Times* could report that "a fierce controvery [is] raging in the Toronto press between the local Jews, and zealous, but misguided missionary supporters."[12]

The following year, Rohold delivered a speech in Winnipeg during which he claimed that 250 Jewish children were attending the Sunday school at his Toronto mission, with the consent of their parents. The missionary's statement was not far from the truth; when a Jewish committee visited the Presbyterian mission on Teraulay Street in 1911 they found almost two hundred Jewish children ranging in age from two to fourteen. These apparently attended the mission once a week, the girls receiving instruction in sewing and the boys in Christianity.[13]

The resentment generated by these activities among the children came to a head in June 1911 when Rohold imported a Dr. Soskin from Louisville, Kentucky, to aid for several weeks in street preaching. Each day for a week, Soskin vilified Judaism from the corner of Agnes and Teraulay streets while hundreds of Jews gathered to shout vituperation. Each day the missionary became more audacious and even threatened with arrest anyone who questioned his remarks.[14]

For a number of years, it had been common, whenever a missionary held an outdoor meeting, for local Zionists, especially Bnai Zion, the oldest men's chapter, to station themselves on an opposite corner and conduct a rival gathering on the subject of Zionism. The week before Soskin's arrival, a visiting Baptist missionary had made some disparaging remarks about Jews, and the Bnai Zion, which had been planning to call a protest meeting anyway, announced the gathering for the first Sunday evening of Soskin's stay in the city. As was to be expected, it was an outdoor affair located directly across from Soskin's pulpit at Agnes and Teraulay.

Before long, the assembled crowd of hundreds became enraged by the missionary's harangues and began to pelt him with all manner of debris – stones, tin cans, pieces of chair and garbage-can lids. The fighting which then broke out between the Jews and the supporters of the missionary lasted intermittently for two and a half hours. The police eventually succeeded in quelling the disturbance and arrested eight persons, all Jews. The constabulary, however, further alienated the crowd by what the president of Bnai Zion considered indiscriminate use of the club. In fact, an innocent woman sitting in front of her store on Agnes Street was struck when she refused to retreat inside.[15]

Understandably, this incident did not enhance the popularity of the missionaries, either within the Jewish community or in the local press. Rabbi Jacobs, who was called to put up bond for those arrested, insisted that the Jews of the Ward were law-abiding and would not have resorted to violence except at profound provocation. "It is much to be deplored," he remarked, "that the city authorities give permission to any particular sect or preacher to attack any religion in this uncalled-for manner." All the Jews asked was to be "rid of the nuisance created by these over-zealous soul-grabbers."[16]

Although some charged the Jews with intolerance, the secular press was generally sympathetic to Jewish sensitivities. The *World*, referring to Rohold, warned:

Under the circumstances he would be well advised to leave his former co-religionists alone, and betake himself to the vast army of the unattached, who are much more in need of Christian training than their Jewish contemporaries.

Whatever personal prejudice may assume, the Jews in

Toronto are fairly good citizens, and in general peaceably disposed. If some of them are restive under the preaching of the Rev. S.B. Rohold, they are not any more so than a similar body of Christians would be if assailed by a Jewish proselytizer who attempted to convert them to Judaism. Just imagine the reception that would be accorded to a former Christian, converted to Judaism, who attempted to proselytize among members of his former faith!

The paper accused Rohold of being unable to distinguish between liberty and licence and maintained that the Jews had the right to "peace and quiet."[17]

To assure themselves of this luxury, the Jews held a protest meeting at the local Yiddish theatre and appointed a delegation to persuade the civic authorities to prohibit Yiddish preaching in the Ward. Unfortunately, the police commission, in whose jurisdiction the problem lay, refused to interfere with the missionaries, despite the fact that some members of City Council supported the Jewish position.[18]

Consequently, while one newspaper predicted that the riot would produce no "serious or continued conflict between Christians and Jews in Toronto," the missionaries were allowed to continue and Jewish resentment continued to grow. When it was rumoured in 1912 that the Presbyterian mission had applied to the city for a grant, the Toronto correspondent for the *Jewish Times* warned that should the municipal authorities accede to the request, "there will be an overwhelming protest by the entire Jewish community, which it will be impossible for our city fathers to overlook." Throughout that year Rabbi Jacobs wrote frequently in the local press urging the evangelists to cease, and Barnet Stone, a prominent local manufacturer and Zionist leader, wrote to the Secretary of the Presbyterian Church to protest missionary activity.[19]

These warnings were to no avail; in October placards began to appear in the Jewish neighbourhoods apprising parents of the danger of the missionaries to their children and exhorting young people "to use force in rejecting Christianity." Each time Henry Singer attempted to preach, as he often did at the corner of Agnes and Elizabeth streets, he was shouted down "by some two hundred young men." Finally, on Hallowe'en night, his mission was attacked and "in spite of the promised watch of the police, the little church was badly broken up."[20]

Missionary activity, however, continued apace. By the spring of 1913, the *Jewish Times* reported that large numbers of Jews were attending the missions and that Jewish children were even being brought by their mothers, probably to the dispensary. Moreover, the night classes in English were nowhere else "so well patronized by our co-religionists as they are in Toronto."[21]

In May 1913 one missionary group sponsored a "Palestine Exhibition" for Jewish children of the Ward at the Canadian National Exhibition grounds, without publicizing the fact that the aim was conversion. When its true purpose was discovered, "white hot rage" was evident among the Jews. "Such men as Rohold," the *Times* complained, "are a menace to the good fellowship that should exist between Jews and Christians."[22]

In the midst of this ugly mood, Singer unwisely extended his street preaching to the newer Jewish district west of Spadina Avenue, conducting regular outdoor meetings at the corner of St. Patrick Street (Dundas Street West) and Kensington Avenue. At first, he was merely heckled, but eventually Singer asked for police protection. As the harangues continued, it was reported that thousands of people gathered and the missionary was pelted with stones. The *Jewish Times* remarked that "it was a miracle that dozens were not seriously injured with missiles flying about in all directions." Extra police had to be called out to put down the disturbance and five Jews were arrested, including a nine-year-old boy.[23]

Once again the civic officials refused to take decisive action. "The question as to whether the Rev. Henry Singer has the right to create a riot on the street corners of the city by the fire of his religious utterances is not bothering the Chief of Police very much," the *Star* observed. As long as he did not obstruct traffic, the chief maintained, he had the right to speak. The Bench was little better. Judge Winchester, responding to a request for an injunction against street preachers attacking Judaism, insisted that Canada was a Christian country.[24]

Most Toronto Christians, the *Jewish Times* admitted, did not support this method of gaining converts. The *Star*, while not condoning the attack upon Singer, urged the missionaries to change their tactics. "Let Christian civilization show its worth by kindness and sympathy. These newcomers need help, guidance, education in citizenship, playgrounds for children, better housing accommodation." "Is it good citizenship to insult newcomers because they wear beards, or in other ways dress or act a little differently from the majority?...If the whole Christian population will unite in showing kindness and courtesy to Jews, Christian missionaries to the Jews will be more hospitably received." On the other side, acculturated Jews did not approve of the attack either. "If our co-religionists could, in spite of their irritation, be prevailed upon to leave these so-called Jewish Christians alone," wrote the Toronto correspondent to the *Jewish Times*, "and thus not furnish the material to their audiences, many here think that they would soon cease preaching to empty sidewalks."[25]

Neither side was perturbed by the criticism, however. Singer continued to preach at St. Patrick and Kensington, surrounded by four constables and four plainclothesmen, while the Jews responded with rival meetings up the street and a noisy gramophone in a nearby window to drown out the preaching. The selections on the machine, one paper reported, "were not chosen for their religious value."[26]

By 1914 there had arisen a good deal of pressure in the East European community in favour of a formal organization to counter the missionaries. The *Hebrew Journal*, spokesman for the Yiddish-speaking Jews, insisted upon action. "Our hands are not washed," cried one editorial, "the paper calls you to battle; the cause is yours and if you do nothing, the responsibility for the tragedy will also be yours." Referring to the new American rabbi at Goel Tzedec, the *Journal* demanded that an English-speaking spiritual leader should take the lead in the anti-missionary agitation.[27]

The Anti-Missionary League, more commonly known as the Anti-*Shmad* Organization, established in the fall of 1914, was probably not generated by the Yiddish press, but the press did reflect popular opinion, especially among the residents of the Ward and its Spadina Avenue extension. The new group was to encompass the entire Jewish community, Holy Blossom as well as the East Europeans, although leadership seems to have come from the latter. Direction emanated from a board of fourteen prominent Jews, including all the rabbis in the city. Membership was reputed to be six hundred.[28]

The aim of the organization was simply to persuade Jews to keep out of the missions and especially to avoid Rohold's premises on Elizabeth Street, which appeared to be the greatest threat. Little information survives concerning the organization from the Jewish point of view, but according to Rohold himself the group "secured premises facing our mission on the north side," where English classes and a soup kitchen were established. It had, by this time, become obvious to the Jews that the attraction of the missions was not Christianity but rather the material assistance and aids to acculturation offered there. The most effective counter-measure, therefore, was for the Jews to set up parallel

140

facilities. Indeed, if the work of the missionaries did eventually end in futility, it was largely because of Jewish efforts to establish their own philanthropic and educational institutions. These had been developing gradually since the late nineteenth century and it was their fruition which would spell disaster for the missions.[29]

NOTES

1 Rev. S.B. Rohold, *Presbyterian Church in Canada, Missions to the Jews, Historical Sketch* (Toronto: The Christian Synagogue, 1948), p. 4; Rev. J.M. Scott to Miss Martha Dickson, Peterboro, 1910 (United Church Archives); Rev. J.M. Scott to John D. Naismith, March 23, 1911 (*ibid.*).

2 Resolution of the General Assembly of the Presbyterian Church in Canada, quoted in Rohold, *Presbyterian . . . Missions to the Jews, Historical Sketch,* p. 7. This appeal was well received. Strong financial support came, especially from prosperous Erskine Church (Presbyterian Church in Canada, "Minutes of the Committee on Jewish Work [Toronto] ", April 27, 1908). For an account of Singer's early efforts, see Rabbi Jacobs' sermon quoted in *Jewish Times,* Jan. 11, 1907, p. 50.

3 Rohold, *Presbyterian . . . Missions . . .,* pp. 11-12, 19. The role of the dispensary in attracting Jews was aptly described by one missionary in 1918: "The Dispensary work is one of the chiefest means of giving us an open door into many hearts and homes. It is encouraging to see many of the patients come back bringing their friends with them. This is an excellent advertisement among the Jews of the good work done in our mission. . . . When visited one finds them very hospitable. . . ." Christian Synagogue, Toronto, "Miss Elizabeth Brown's report for the Year 1918" (typescript, United Church Archives).

4 Rev. R.P. Mackay to Thomas Clive, May 28, 1910, United Church Archives; Rev. J.M. Scott to Miss Martha Dickson, 1910, *ibid.* In the same year, a Bible Society agent reported that the organization was selling ten times as many Hebrew and Yiddish bibles in Toronto as they did prior to the establishment of the mission. (R.P. Mackay to Rev. Dr. Taylor, Jan. 5, 1910, *ibid.*.

5 United Church of Canada, Committee on Archives, "Finding Aid Relating to the Presbyterian Church in Canada. Mission to the Jews in Canada 1907-1925 (typescript, United Church Archives), p. i; Rohold, *Presbyterian . . . Missions . . .*, pp. 14-15. The wealth backing the venture is indicated by the list of subscribers, which included Sir W. Mortimer Clark, Hamilton Cassels and Joseph Pickering. Rohold's marriage into a prominent Christian family in the city assured him social standing and doubtless enhanced the financial resources of his mission. Although Presbyterian missions were established in Winnipeg in 1911 and Montreal in 1915, none attained the size of the Toronto institution, especially in its charitable work, and Toronto remained the acknowledged headquarters of Presbyterian mission work among the Jews.

6 *Journal of the Incorporated Synod of the Church of England in Canada in the Diocese of Toronto 1909* (Toronto: Parker, 1909), p. 77; *ibid., 1910,* p. 158.

7 *Ibid., 1913,* p. 69; *ibid., 1914,* pp. 227, 228; *ibid., 1916,* pp. 250 ff.

8 *Jewish Times,* Jan. 8, 1909. When one Jewish schoolgirl was asked why she liked Jesus better than God, she replied, "From Je[sus] you get more" (A.P. Lewis to *Jewish Times,* March 19, 1909, p. 315).

9 Quoted in *Telegram,* June 12, 1914. This sentiment was reflected in some of the local newspapers, especially the *World* which condemned the missionaries, urged "mutual forbearance" and declared that "no Jew wishes to be so Christianized . . . . Nobody looks after its poor and the stranger within its gates better than the Jewish" (quoted in *Jewish Times,* June 24, 1910, p. 14).

10 Rohold, *Presbyterian . . . Missions . . .*, p. 20. For an account of the difficulty in converting Jews despite large attendance at the Presbyterian mission, see R.P. Mackay to Rev. Dr. Taylor, Jan. 5, 1910 (United Church Archives). In the same year, Rohold reported that he had been able to convert only six women and two men *(Mail and Empire,* May 14, 1910).

11 HBM, Feb. 7, 1909. It has been impossible to determine whether the impetus for this gathering came from Holy Blossom or from East European sources; one suspects that the former took the lead in this regard.

12 *Jewish Times*, May 13, 1910, p. 9. See also Mackay to Clive, May 28, 1910.

13 *Jewish Times*, March 31, 1911, p. 8; June 30, 1911, p. 13. Indeed, a major reason for the removal to Elizabeth Street was that the Teraulay Street mission was seriously overcrowded (Presbyterian Church in Canada, Toronto Mission to the Jews, *Minutes*, Feb. 12, 1912).

14 *Mail and Empire*, June 19, 1911.

15 *Globe*, June 19, 1911; *Jewish Times*, June 23, 1911, p. 11.

16 Quoted in *Mail and Empire*. In a sermon on the riot, Rabbi Jacobs declared that "The Jews of the ward look upon the missionary as a pest . . . They object to his methods of enticing little children to attend his classes unknown to their parents, and offering them baits and rewards; visiting the sick in hospitals in spite of the protests of patients and nurses" (clipping in Edmund Scheuer Scrapbook, Holy Blossom Archives).

17 Quoted in *Jewish Times*, July 28, 1911, p. 2.

18 *Mail and Empire*, June 21, 1911.

19 *Jewish Times*, Nov. 1, 1912, p. 23; Rev. R.P. Mackay to Barnet Stone, June 13, 1912 (United Church Archives).

20 *Star*, Nov. 1, 1912. Singer later claimed that the attack was incited by the Zionists (*Mail and Empire*, Nov. 2, 1912). The charge was probably justified.

21 *Jewish Times*, Apr. 4, 1913, p. 3. Rohold wrote several years later that in 1913 "all threatening and boycotting proved of no avail to get the Jews away from the Mission. . ." (Rohold, *Presbyterian . . .Missions to the Jews . . .*, p. 21).

22 *Jewish Times*, June 13, 1913, p. 4.

23 *Jewish Times*, July 18, 1913, p. 26; *Mail and Empire*, July 15, 1913. Violent attacks on missionaries by Jews occurred nowhere else in Canada, even though attempts at conversion were made in Montreal, Winnipeg and in other centres of Jewish population. Only in Toronto, however, did apostate Jews undertake to lead the movement; this is what particularly incensed the local population (*Jewish Times*, July 25, 1913, p. 1). There might have been additional violence in 1913 had Jacob Cohen not used his influence as magistrate to postpone

the hearings of those arrested for a week in order to allow matters to cool off. They were later fined and released (*Telegram*, July 15, 1913).

24 *Jewish Times*, July 25, 1913, p. 1.

25 *Ibid; Star*, July 21, 1913; *Star*, editorial, July 22, 1913; *Jewish Times*, Aug. 22, 1913, p. 13.

26 *Star*, July 29, 1913. Singer also opened a branch mission in the West Toronto Junction, which had a sizable Jewish population, but before long disturbances put an end to outdoor meetings there (*Mail and Empire*, Oct. 13, 1913; Jan. 26, 1915).

27 *Hebrew Journal*, July 24, 1914.

28 N. Shemen "Orthodoxy in Toronto," p. 14; Rohold, *Presbyterian...Missions to the Jews...*, p. 21.

29 In fairness to the missionaries, it should be noted that they did perform a valuable service for the Jewish community in their public statements to non-Jews. Despite the fact that Dr. Mackay, the Superintendent of Foreign Missions of the Presbyterian Church, considered the Jews a heathen people (quoted in Toronto *News*, 1911, clipping in Edmund Scheuer Scrapbook), a publication of the Women's Missionary Society of that church described them as industrious, law-abiding and eager for education (Presbyterian Church in Canada, Women's Missionary Society, *The Story of Our Missions* [Toronto: 1915], p. 242). Rohold was important in arousing sympathy for immigrant Jews by publicizing their plight in Russia and local newspapers usually sought him out for information on Jewish holidays. Singer also stood up for his former co-religionists. He denied the charge that Jews were drunkards and that they created slums, and insisted on municipal repairs to streets in the Ward and the introduction of efficient medical inspection. For a similar defence by Rohold, see his pamphlet, *The Jews in Canada*, p. 15.

CHAPTER 10

PHILANTHROPY IN THE NEW COMMUNITY, 1899 – 1915

For practical purposes, systematic distribution of charity was non-existent in the East European Jewish community of Toronto when Samuel Lewis and his family arrived in 1893. As long as the community remained small and intimately acquainted, the three East European congregations then in existence – Chevra Tehillim, Shomrai Shabboth and especially Goel Tzedec, the largest – could offer some assistance in an informal manner, much as Holy Blossom had done twenty years earlier. But by the mid-1890s, increased population, recurrent depressions and precarious employment made the system inadequate. Admittedly, Holy Blossom provided some relief through the Ladies' Montefiore Society, but residents of the Ward were loath to suffer the condescending interrogation, implied criticism and humiliating investigation which accompanied it. The few men's benevolent societies which existed in this period rarely offered assistance outside their own memberships.

The Lewises, having lived in Pittsburgh after their arrival from Lithuania, were appalled at the absence in Toronto of East European relief organizations such as existed in that city and, as active members of Goel Tzedec and residents of the Ward, they were aware of the poverty that surrounded them. The necessity for taking action was brought home dramatically to Mrs. Lewis just prior to Passover in 1897, when one of their neighbours on Elizabeth Street was killed as he was carrying down a barrel of wine from the loft where it had been stored. His widow and large family were left without means of support and Mrs. Lewis was prompted to propose to her acquaintances that a weekly collection be undertaken to sustain them. Other indigent families, she believed, could be cared for in the same manner.

At first the group lacked permanence. Whenever a case in need was discovered, an ad hoc committee would be formed to deal with it, each woman enlisting as many of her friends as she could. Before long, however, the increasing Jewish population gave rise to numerous such cases and the group began to be approached more frequently as its existence became known. By 1899 there was a pressing need for a more formal organization.

For East European women who had been used to having their philanthropic organizations in Europe under male direction, the idea of establishing an independent women's charity society must have been strange indeed. It is significant that leadership in this instance came from Mrs. Lewis, who had experienced such phenomena in Pittsburgh. At her instigation, sixty women from the Ward assembled ambitiously at Shaftesbury Hall to form the Toronto Hebrew Ladies' Aid Society.[1]

Officers were duly elected, including Mrs. Lewis as secretary, but the organization was not seen as being by any means a blow for women's independence. Unlike the more acculturated Montefiore, Ladies' Aid lacked the confidence to elect a female president. Since such an official would be required to act as an intermediary between the society and the Jewish community, whose assistance must surely be enlisted, it was considered improper for a woman to hold the position. Consequently Louis Levinsky, president of Goel Tzedec and a respected and prosperous member of the East European community, was asked to take the office. Indeed, as long as the organization existed, it had a male president and seemed generally to seek his advice before attempting any major project.[2]

The Hebrew Ladies' Aid Society at first included women from all ethnic groups, but the majority were Russian or Lithuanian and increasingly the organization came to be associated with Goel Tzedec. Monthly dues of not less than 25 cents were demanded from every member, with regular meetings taking place monthly, or more frequently as circumstances required. In true North American fashion, a constitution was approved, doubtless modelled on that of a Pittsburgh organization. Although Ladies' Aid adopted a policy of not limiting their activities to Toronto, and dealt with a number of external cases, their work was concentrated primarily in the metropolis itself. Funds were raised by means of a team of volunteer door-to-door canvassers, an annual charity ball after the pattern of the Ladies' Montefiore and, occasionally, by a concert or a picnic.[3]

Because Ladies' Aid grew up partially in reaction against the patronizing approach of the Ladies' Montefiore, its explicit policy was to offer relief on the basis of those talmudic principles which

146

had been practised in the *shtetl*; that is, one who asked for assistance was entitled to relief with no questions asked. Moreover, if the poor had been accustomed to luxuries in better times, the charitable organization had the responsibility to provide them. The Ladies' Montefiore, on the other hand, followed the contemporary trend of scientific philanthropy which demanded thorough investigation to establish need. Indeed, one of their investigators insisted that if luxuries such as candlesticks were found in an applicant's home, they must be pawned before relief would be offered. This approach was perhaps indicative of the acculturation of the members of the old community to their Canadian environment; it did nothing to endear them to their East European co-religionists.[4]

In line with their open-handed policy, Ladies' Aid appointed a committee to distribute relief "to whomever they think worthy, without limit." Before long, however, it became apparent that unless some controls were exercised on expenditure, the organization's limited funds would soon evaporate. Consequently, on the suggestion of Mr. Levinsky, who probably had more practical experience in financial matters than any of the women, a more cautious system had been adopted by the fall of 1899. A standing committee of three was empowered to give freely up to two dollars, but larger disbursements had to be approved by a second committee comprising ten members. The society, however, seldom refused assistance; even applicants who were unknown to the women were usually assisted without much discussion.[5]

The Toronto Hebrew Ladies' Aid Society offered a panoply of relief services for the penurious Ward, including supplies of coal, cash for groceries and even curtains and cooking utensils. Weekly grants were offered to various applicants for several months at a time, and in extraordinary cases, long-term support was apparently undertaken. Recent arrivals were assisted financially, brides were dowered and funeral expenses covered. Those unable to find a livelihood in Toronto were frequently assisted in travelling to the United States or back to Europe. Hospital expenses were paid in part where necessary, and those with tuberculosis were assisted with transportation to the Jewish respiratory hospital in Denver, Colorado. Recuperating patients were accommodated in private homes at the expense of the Ladies' Aid. And in order to ensure reasonable treatment of Jews in hospitals and counter the accusation that Jews sought public assistance for nothing, the Society donated substantially to many local institutions. The sick were also visited in their homes and

147

assisted with preparation of food and with housecleaning.

After 1903, the Ladies' Aid Society appointed a committee of investigation, not, as in the Montefiore, to determine whether relief was really needed, but actually to seek out destitute families who may have been ignorant of the philanthropic facilities available in the Jewish community or were too proud to ask for help. In cases where pride was a factor, the Society arranged for a grocer to leave food packages on the doorstep of the indigent family and then disappear.[6]

Ladies' Aid was not exclusively a society of the wealthy, or even of the middle class. Some members had to be assisted themselves. The affluent, however, were expected to offer more of their substance and they appear to have done so readily. Each Passover, a wealthy woman was assigned a poor family whose needs for the holiday she was to supply at her own expense. This was to include not only food but also new clothes for the children and some household furnishings. The size of the family assigned was proportional to the prosperity of the patron.

Personal hardship on the part of poorer members in order to contribute to the Society was to be expected, but occasionally even the wealthy found themselves in difficulty. One prosperous woman, for instance, whose husband kept her on a strict allowance, was unable to afford even the small monthly dues to the Ladies' Aid. However, she did have relative freedom in the purchase of groceries. Consequently, she would buy enormous amounts of food, ostensibly for her own sizable family, and donate a part to the organization.

In accordance with the highest rabbinic principle of charity (that is, to enable a man to earn his own livelihood and thus obviate the necessity of his receiving assistance in future), Ladies' Aid allocated funds to enable Jews to set up businesses of their own, usually as peddlers. These were helped in the purchase of horses and wagons.

Despite its haphazard beginnings and the inexperience of its members, Ladies' Aid conducted its financial affairs in a businesslike manner, a barometer of its growing acculturation and perhaps also because of the influence of the male president. For instance, the funds of the organization were kept in a bank and when a rival institution raised its interest rates, the money was promptly transferred. All money was carefully accounted for and a provincial charter was sought. In addition, and commensurate with the society's personal approach to philanthropy, cases were followed up after the initial grant. If, after inquiry, it was discovered that the assistance offered was insufficient, the subsidy would be increased; where it was no longer needed, it was withdrawn. When the relief being supplied to certain families by the Montefiore was inadequate, Ladies' Aid would provide a supplement.

By 1901 other East European women's charity societies had been formed in addition to the Toronto Hebrew Ladies' Aid, one operating from Chevra Tehillim, a second – the Austrian Ladies' Society – at Shomrai Shabboth on Chestnut Street and a third associated with the Russian congregation, Shaarei Tzedec, on Centre Avenue. Ladies' Aid, with at least three hundred members by 1905, appears to have remained the mentor of the others.[7]

These societies co-operated in their efforts, while men's groups such as the YMHA benevolent society often referred cases to the women's organizations. Ladies' Aid also co-operated with the Montefiore in its early years but consistently rejected the latter's offers of amalgamation. They disliked the patronizing air of the older group and what they considered its impersonal and hard-hearted method of operation.* Moreover, the East Europeans suspected, probably with justification, that the amalgamation would in fact be merely an absorption of Ladies' Aid and that control would rest with Holy Blossom. "No amalgamation," therefore, became a slogan of independence for the East Europeans and a defiance of the complacent old community. For the time being, Holy Blossom had to be content with the status quo.

II

While these East European women's charity societies were attempting to care for Jewish poor in the Ward and to maintain their own independence from Holy Blossom, missionary activity in the neighbourhood was encouraging the establishment of Jewish facilities for the exclusive care of children, since none yet existed. In 1906, coincident with the opening of the Presbyterian Jewish Mission, a Hebrew Ladies' Sewing Circle was organized by a number of young women in the Ward led, not surprisingly, by Mrs. Lewis' daughter, Ida Siegel. The group at first intended merely to teach Jewish girls to sew and to distribute the products

* An illustrative incident of the period is that of the East European woman who joined the Ladies' Montefiore. The Society met in the basement auditorium of the Bond Street synagogue; the relief committee sat on a platform in the front of the hall and applicants were relegated to a bench at the rear. When she appeared for her first meeting, the Holy Blossom women mistook her for a candidate for charity because of her East European appearance and consequently ordered her to the back of the hall. She never returned.

of these lessons to the poor.[8] As the missionary threat became more evident, however, it was decided to adopt a more comprehensive approach. The Sewing Circle now began to organize recreational activities for children, beginning with a picnic to Centre Island, a device that Rohold had found most effective in attracting young Jews. The first Sewing Circle picnic drew two hundred Jewish children, not only students of the sewing school itself but others from throughout the Ward as well.[9]

By the following year, the name of the organization had officially been changed to the Hebrew Ladies' Maternity Aid and Child Welfare Society. As the new title implied, Maternity Aid sought to provide new mothers and their infants with medical care, domestic assistance, linen, milk and food, as well as with luxuries such as fresh fruit and sweets which might not otherwise be available. It also assured entry of the public health nurses into the homes of the Jewish poor by accompanying them and acting as interpreters.[10]

Maternity Aid supported its activities not only through its dues and collections but also by an annual ball which often yielded a surplus. This made possible the supplying of delicacies to patients at the Weston Consumptive Hospital without, it should be noted, regard to religion, as well as contributions to the three major Toronto hospitals, the General, the Western and St. Michael's. Various Jewish charities also received funds from the society. These activities by Maternity Aid and by the ladies' aid societies were not only indicative of a sense of civic responsibility on the part of East European women; they probably helped as well to break down somewhat the stereotype of the immigrant as a parasite.

It soon became apparent that if the efforts of the missionaries were to be countered effectively, welfare facilities such as they offered would have to be established under Jewish auspices. Maternity Aid had been an auspicious beginning, but especially important was the Jewish Dispensary which opened on Elizabeth Street in 1909, serving as an outpatient clinic for immigrants who feared hospitals or who could not make themselves understood there.

Unlike most of the Jewish philanthropic societies then in existence in Toronto, the dispensary was under exclusively male direction, headed by Reverend Maurice Kaplan, cantor of the McCaul Street Synagogue and the driving force behind a number of charitable ventures. The men determined policy and superintended the building, but day-to-day work was done by women, as, indeed, was a good deal of the fund-raising in the early years. Moreover, a woman was the guiding light of the institution. Miss Dorothy Goldstick, the daughter of a local family, had received a certificate in midwifery from the State Medical Board of Ohio in 1909, and had returned to Toronto to become the first nurse at the dispensary. Probably at the instigation of Maternity Aid, a milk depot was established in the building. Here the poor could obtain daily supplies free or below cost.[11] The few Jewish doctors and dentists then in the city offered their assistance, but the principal technical guidance came from a non-Jewish practitioner who had become vehemently opposed to conversion efforts after having worked in one of the missions. A local surgeon and an otolaryngologist, both non-Jews, also donated their services. Medicine was dispensed by A.B. Hashmall, who had graduated in pharmacy from the University of Toronto in 1909, the first Jew to do so.[12]

The Jewish Dispensary shared its three-storey premises with yet another anti-missionary welfare institution, the Jewish Day Nursery. This was the outgrowth of a daycare centre established by Hebrew Ladies' Aid in 1909 to prevent children of working mothers from being placed in Christian orphanages. Whenever possible, Ladies' Aid had attempted to arrange for care with Jewish families, but the increase both in the Jewish population and in missionary activity made this problem increasingly difficult. Their search for premises happily coincided with the efforts of the dispensary group to find a building for their own project. Consequently, Ladies' Aid rented the house on Elizabeth Street south of Agnes, established the day nursery in the upper floors and offered the ground level to the dispensary. The connection between the two groups was probably facilitated by the fact that Ida Siegel and her brother Abraham Lewis were intimately involved in the dispensary movement, and in no small measure responsible for its fruition. In addition, Reverend Kaplan had long been urging both organizations toward a nursery undertaking. He was to serve as president of both the dispensary and the day nursery.

III

These efforts threw into relief the necessity of reaching immigrant parents if the children were to be helped. The recent arrivals were no strangers to anti-semitism and forced conversion, but they were unprepared for the subtle and benevolent approach of the local proselytizers. Moreover, they had no solution to the problems which made the missions so attractive – the language barrier, poor physical living conditions and the absence of a sense of belonging to Canadian society. The Yiddish-speaking missionary often appeared as a comforting link between the two cultures.

Ida Siegel, president of Maternity Aid and well aware of local missionary activity, was perhaps the person in the community best equipped to deal with the situation. Early in the century, she proposed the establishment of a mothers' club at Hester How (Elizabeth Street) School, where parents and teachers could meet to discuss the welfare of the children. Highly respected for her philanthropic work, Mrs. Siegel had the confidence of the East European community. She was also acquainted with the school authorities through her founding of a Jewish girls' club which met Saturday afternoons at Hester How, ostensibly to prevent idle children from engaging in shoplifting at the nearby department stores, but actually to inculcate them with some Jewish values in an age before formal religious education for East European children was available. The principal, moreover, was encouraged to co-operate by the fact that the Maternity Aid Society was supplying needy children at the school with clothes and milk.

The mothers' club later grew into a city-wide Home and School Association with no Jewish connections. But in its early years the organization conducted its meetings in Yiddish and in English. Ida Siegel moulded the group into an instrument of acculturation as well as a vehicle to combat the missionaries. Local doctors, often Jews, were asked to speak on techniques of hygiene and child care; a judge of the juvenile court was invited to instruct in the prevention of juvenile delinquency. In the course of such personal contact with municipal authorities the immigrants lost their fear of the state; and, perhaps most important, such contacts brought the mothers increased familiarity with the English language and an added ability to cope with their Canadian environment.[13]

Another of Mrs. Siegel's anti-missionary projects was the expansion of the sewing school and girls' club established under the auspices of the Hebrew Ladies' Sewing Circle (Maternity Aid). The group met over a store on Elizabeth Street north of Queen, in a building where early Zionist meetings were also held.

By 1912 the institution had become formalized as the Jewish Endeavor Sewing School with a library to keep young people who wished to read in English out of the missions. Classes were held after regular school hours and, in addition to sewing, girls were taught Jewish religion, history and Zionism. The effort was most successful; ten volunteer teachers were instructing two hundred girls in 1913. The teachers were themselves young women of East European background who had been born or who had grown up in North America; the sewing school, therefore, also helped immigrant girls adapt to Canadian life.[14]

While girls in the East European community were generally well served by the various ladies' societies in this period, very little existed in the way of Jewish-sponsored recreation and training in skills for boys, especially those of elementary school age. For the adolescents, the situation was not much better. An effort in their behalf, however, had been made by Abraham P. Lewis as early as 1900. Lewis believed that the most serious consequence for young people of the move across the Atlantic was dislocation in the traditional home environment. Children grew accustomed to their new surroundings more quickly than did their parents. Frequently they became the teachers in the family group and parental authority suffered as a result. Parents, on the other hand, often found their hopes for a better life frustrated, while at the same time, they sought to maintain a measure of security in strange surroundings by insisting on the preservation of European customs. These they imposed upon their children with a persistence and irrationality stemming from panic, and sometimes with harshness based on frustration. Tragically, their efforts were in diametric opposition to the trend toward assimilation promoted by the public schools. Worse still, there arose a tendency for the young to see Judaism as another element among the countless restrictions insisted upon in the home, and so to reject it outright.

Rebellion against this authority and against what many young men considered archaic hindrances to survival in North America produced a large number of idle youths, potential delinquents, loitering about the billiard parlours of the Ward. Lewis provided a solution in the Young Men's Hebrew Progressive Club which he organized in a rented hall on Edward Street. Rudimentary athletic equipment was set up and regular social activities were made available. Occasionally, when actual poverty was producing problems for youths at home, cases were referred to the Ladies' Aid Society for material assistance. Although the Progressive Club certainly could not deal with the totality of the dislocation and delinquency in the Jewish community, it did provide a powerful alternative to idleness until other organizations, notably the Zionists, could come into existence and attract large numbers of young people.

One additional philanthropic organization deserves consideration at this point: the Hebrew National Association or Folks Farein. Formed in the Ward just prior to the outbreak of the First World War as a literary and cultural club of recent immigrants, mostly young men with secularist leanings, its purpose was to provide a forum for aspiring Yiddish authors and poets. Meetings in its rooms on Elm Street at Elizabeth consisted primarily of readings of new works by local talent. However, once the Presbyterian mission to the Jews began to flourish on Elizabeth, the society transformed itself into an anti-missionary organization, adopting the name "Folks Farein" (People's Association) after an anti-missionary group in England. Its relationship to the community-sponsored Anti-Missionary League is unclear, but the League apparently used the Folks Farein's premises close to the mission as their headquarters. Originally the organization proposed merely to disrupt Rohold's street meetings, but the moderates within the group won the day and a more practical plan of action was adopted.[15]

Since the economic difficulties of the immediate prewar period were forcing many to accept material aid from the mission, the Folks Farein operated a soup kitchen and an employment service. English classes were offered and a reading room opened. Following the example of the missionaries, the group sent visitors to the homes of the poor and the infirm. Furnaces were stoked, houses cleaned and food supplied. The provision of kosher food, fruit and candy to Jewish patients in the hospitals was also undertaken, and members of the Folks Farein acted as interpreters.[16] Much of this had originally been done by the Maternity Aid Society, but by the early twenties, once the missionary menace had passed, hospital work became the principal function of the Folks Farein and Maternity Aid was free to concentrate exclusively on child welfare cases.

IV

While it was true that women played the major role in the development of philanthropic services within the East European community in the early twentieth century, the men were not entirely inactive. Synagogues continued to dispense charity informally beyond their membership and, indeed, provided a base of operation for the women's organizations. On occasion, synagogues also acted in an official capacity; at least two congregations, Goel Tzedec and Anshei Ostrovtze, undertook to raise funds to support the unemployed during the economic difficulties of 1913-14.[17] There is little doubt that other synagogues engaged in philanthropic ventures as well.

However, it was in the development of charitable institutions transcending the individual synagogue or society that the male element actually took the lead. As had often been the case in Toronto, problems surrounding the death of an individual acted as a catalyst for philanthropic efforts. In 1906 a Jew was fatally injured in an accident at the outskirts of the city. Since there was no organized Jewish community in Toronto to take charge of the matter, he had been buried in a Christian cemetery. Horrified that a growing Jewish community had no facilities whereby to deal with such occurrences, Samuel Weber, a pious member of Goel Tzedec, purchased a parcel of land on what is now Roselawn Avenue and donated it for a cemetery to a Hebrew Free Burial Society (Chesed Shel Emes) which he himself organized. Through the efforts of Rabbi Gordon, spiritual head of Goel Tzedec and Chevra Tehillim, the unfortunate accident victim was disinterred and buried in the new Jewish cemetery. In addition to ensuring that all Jews received proper burial, the society established a Chevra Kadisha (Holy Society) which had the responsibility of purifying the dead prior to interment.

These efforts coincided with the financial panic of 1907 which brought with it widespread unemployment, especially among the Jews of the Ward. Initiative in dealing with the predicament came from the Reverend Kaplan, who had lived in the United States and had probably had experience with communal philanthropy prior to his arrival in Toronto. Moreover, as a *mohel* he had entry into the homes of all groups in the Jewish community and knew their problems. His first effort in response to the unemployment problem was the establishment of a soup kitchen in the Ward, a venture in which he enlisted a number of his acquaintances, mostly members of his own congregation and of Goel Tzedec, who constituted the most prosperous elements among the East Europeans. By 1908 the group had decided to organize a hostel for immigrants (Hachnosas Orchim) and a Jewish hospital.

The need for a hospital was especially great; there was as yet no organization for the provision of kosher food to Jewish patients and many of these could not be cared for properly because they could not explain their symptoms to doctors and nurses who understood no Yiddish. A Toronto Jewish Hospital Committee met frequently throughout the frustrating year of 1908, calling together delegates from virtually all East European organizations then in existence in the city, but funds were simply not to be had for a separate Jewish hospital. The group, therefore, had to be content with the Jewish Dispensary. More success was achieved with the Hachnosas Orchim, although not until 1912 when the financial crisis had passed. Samuel Weber had been drawn into the immigrant aid effort early in the project and so it was not surprising that Kaplan's Hachnosas Orchim and Weber's Burial Society acquired joint ownership of a house on Grange Avenue.[18]

The most effective sphere of male activity, however, was in Jewish philanthropy along the lines of Charity Organization theory. The Charity Organization movement, originating in England in the late 1860s, rejected the equation of poverty with improvidence and embraced the theory of environmentalism. Under the Charity Organization system, a variety of societies would co-operate by establishing a central clearing-house for information on charity cases and a single depot for the distribution of relief, thus avoiding duplication of services.

By 1912, Charity Organization among Christian and non-denominational philanthropies was fairly commonplace in the larger cities of North America, including Toronto, and various centres in the United States had seen similar co-operation among Jewish charities as well. By this time the variety of unco-ordinated Jewish philanthropic societies operating in Toronto had resulted in confusion and overlapping in the distribution of relief. Their limited financial resources were being dissipated by duplication of effort, and cases of legitimate need were being neglected because communication between the societies had to wait for the chance meeting of individuals. On the other hand, the unscrupulous among the poor did not hesitate to apply to the Ladies' Montefiore and, having received assistance, approach the Hebrew Ladies' Aid, calculating, usually with justification, that none would ever be the wiser.

The need for co-operation among the Jewish charitable societies grew out of the financial difficulties of Ladies' Aid. An influx of penurious Roumanians in 1907 had brought matters to the point of crisis. Throughout the following year, the society tried every conceivable device to augment the treasury, but had constantly to draw upon its banked savings. By autumn the group had accumulated a deficit of $400. The members themselves apparently realized that the lack of co-operation between the various philanthropic organizations was the root of the problem, and in November 1908 they invited the ladies of the Montefiore to a meeting to discuss a solution. Nothing was achieved however; the ideological gulf was still too broad.

Active Jewish communal workers, however, remained convinced that the elimination of duplicate services would bring everyone out of the red, and throughout 1909 and 1910 agitation for the formation of some kind of Charity Organization society continued. Rabbi Gordon, Reverend Kaplan, Abe Lewis and Ida

Siegel were all urging the establishment of a United Hebrew Relief Society in this period.

In June 1911, while the process of persuasion continued, agreement was achieved on a merger between eight of the existing Jewish societies, including the Free Burial, Hachnosas Orchim, Dispensary, Day Nursery, Free Loan Society and Maternity Aid. By this time, the newly established Jewish orphanage (the Hebrew Shelter Society), the Dispensary, Day Nursery and Maternity Aid had had the foresight to acquire a large house at 218 Simcoe Street as a community charities building.* This was convenient to both Jewish areas, the Ward and Spadina Avenue, and here the Associated Hebrew Charities of Toronto, as the new united society was named, initiated its activities in January 1912.[19]

The Associated Hebrew Charities was, in several respects, an unusual phenomenon in Canadian Jewry and had few counterparts even in the United States. It was the first Jewish Charity Organization society in Canada; Winnipeg, admittedly, had had a United Hebrew Relief as early as 1909, but it had no central distribution system. Even Montreal, with a larger and more prosperous community, had nothing to compare with it. Secondly, unlike the majority of Jewish philanthropic amalgamations in the United States, the Associated Hebrew Charities did not engage in joint fund-raising campaigns; it merely provided a central depot for the collection of information and the distribution of relief. In this regard, therefore, it was closer to the model of the non-denominational Associated Charities of Toronto than to any of the American Jewish organizations. Thirdly, in contrast to the latter, Jewish Charity Organization in Toronto grew not out of the old community, but rather from the East European sector. The Associated Hebrew Charities was directed by the established Russian and Galician elements, mostly members of Goel Tzedec and the McCaul Street Synagogue, and the organization was seen by many as an assertion of East European independence and dignity in the face of the patronizing Holy Blossomites.

The new organization became the administrative hub of its various affiliated institutions, although the individual societies connected with these services continued to finance them. It also

* The Simcoe Street premises consisted of a three-storey house, the dispensary being located on the ground floor and the upper levels providing rooms for the nursery and dormitories for the orphanage. Actually, although the need for an orphanage prompted the purchase of the building, it was not until 1913 that the institution began to function as such.

operated a branch of the International Desertion Bureau to locate missing husbands.

Before long, it became evident that only an all-inclusive organization could be effective; the ladies' societies and the philanthropies based at Holy Blossom would have to be drawn in. To this end, it was agreed that each affiliated organization would retain complete autonomy in officers, volunteer visitors and means of collection, but all funds were to be channelled into a central pool for distribution by the Associated Charities. The agency responsible for the financial aspect was to be the Co-operative Relief Board (also called the United Board of Relief); this committee consisted of three representatives of each organization, who met every Monday afternoon. Anyone requiring assistance could come to the central office on Simcoe Street and would often be granted money on the spot. When investigation was felt to be necessary to determine the nature and amount of relief required, the Board would dispatch the visitor of the relevant society. Emergency relief could be dispensed outside the meeting by a standing committee of three women, who were empowered to spend up to the princely sum of three dollars without approval, but after appropriate investigation, of course. This "Immediate Relief Committee," however, was required to report to the Board in detail.[20]

The informal constitution of the Associated Hebrew Charities reflected the uneasy peace which prevailed in the organization from the outset. Each constituent group, and especially the East Europeans, was suspicious of impersonal institutions and jealous of its identity. A delicate balance was necessary. Consequently, the Board of Relief was presided over by the presidents of all the affiliated societies in rotation; each society was to have three votes on any decision, regardless of whether all of its three delegates were in attendance at a given meeting.[21]

Although the establishment of the Associated Hebrew Charities produced a significant improvement in Jewish philanthropy, the association did not live up to everyone's expectations. Complaints of indifference toward it on the part of male members of the community were commonplace, while there were claims that, despite the new organization, "There is . . .a drowsy inactivity in nearly all the benevolent and charitable societies and institutions in Toronto."[22]

In another respect, also, the Associated Hebrew Charities was only a qualified success. The East Europeans had indeed succeeded in fathering a Jewish Charity Organization society with neither instigation nor instruction from the old community. They could not, however, avoid admitting the Holy Blossom societies to the association, nor were they able to prevent the latter from exercising a powerful influence by dint of their wider experience and the sheer volume of the relief they distributed. The East Europeans had to keep Holy Blossom influence carefully in check; on the committee of three which comprised the Immediate Relief Committee, Montefiore members won two positions, but East Europeans fought for control of the investigation committee and apparently got it. If the same variety of services continued to be offered as had been by the individual ladies' societies, the Relief Board did, it seems, defer to Holy Blossom in the matter of scientific method. A printed application form suggested by the Montefiore was adopted, as was the motion "that every applicant must give a name and an address to be considered [i.e., a reference]otherwise the Chairman of the meeting must be satisfied that the case is Bona fide."

The balance, therefore, continued to be maintained and the Associated Hebrew Charities continued for nearly five years. But the tribulation of war and the arrival of an unprecedented number of destitute immigrants which accompanied its approach would make simple Charity Organization obsolete. By 1916, a more sophisticated approach had to be found.

NOTES

1 Although the official founding date of the society is 1899, its minutes suggest the existence of a cohesive group prior to that date. See Toronto Hebrew Ladies' Aid Society, *Minute Book* (MSS., Yiddish, courtesy Mrs. Ida Siegel). This chapter is based primarily on information provided in the Minute Book of the Toronto Hebrew Ladies' Aid Society, the *Jewish Times*, and in interviews which the author conducted with Mrs. Ida Siegel during 1971 and 1972. Limitations of space have precluded complete documentation here. Readers wishing specific references may consult the author's dissertation.

2 The male president was, as a result, nominated in absentia from among the prominent members of Goel Tzedec. He was then asked by formal letter to accept the position. A Mrs. Harris did hold the office for a few months in 1900, but she soon resigned, perhaps under pressure, and a man was once again appointed (Toronto Hebrew Ladies' Aid Society, *Minutes*, Aug. 5, 1900).

3 Shaftesbury Hall on Queen, the Temple Building on Bay and St. George's Hall on Elm, were popular sites for the charity balls. These functions were apparently the highlight of the social year in the East European community. For a fee of between 50 and 75 cents, one could enjoy the music of a band (Jewish musicians were not available for employment until 1907), as well as home-made refreshments donated by members. A wide variety of these was available. One could enjoy either meat or dairy, but since religious law forbids their being served together, they were available at opposite ends of the hall (Ida Siegel, personal interview, Jan. 20, 1972).

4 For an account of this attitude in the general community, see Kathleen Woodroofe, *From Charity to Social Work* (Toronto: University of Toronto Press, 1962) and R.B. Splane, *Social Welfare in Ontario 1791-1893* (Toronto: University of Toronto Press, 1965).

5 It should be noted, however, that the Society was not careless with its funds. Requests which could be proved to be un-justified were refused.

6 Mr. Weinberg, the grocer with whom the Society dealt, apparently became very adept at this practice. He also donated a good deal of these goods to the organization.

7 A similar society at the Roumanian synagogue would be formed in 1905, while the Polish ladies' aid society, the Malbish Arumim, would not emerge until 1913.

8 The *Jewish Times* reported that "The growth of the city recently is such that it urgently demands that work of this nature be taken up . . . . The work is on a large scale and is a dire necessity" (*Jewish Times*, Dec. 14, 1906, p. 22). The group also collected clothing for the poor, as well as textiles to be sewn by the girls. The local Zionist society, Bnai Zion, offered their premises for meetings.

9 *Jewish Times*, Aug. 23, 1907. Actually, outings to Centre Island were not a phenomenon new to the Jewish community. As early as 1904 A.P. Lewis and his sister Ida (later Siegel) had organized them simply to get children out of the Ward on hot summer afternoons (*Jewish Times*, Sept. 10, 1909, p. 869). The efforts of the Sewing Circle were merely their logical extension. By 1910, this picnic had become an annual event and would be sponsored jointly by a number of Jewish organizations, including the Jewish Dispensary, the Talmud

Torah and the Herzl Girls. Ferry tickets were financed by the *Star* Fresh Air Fund, while donations of food were provided by the City Dairy, Eaton's, Christie Brown & Co. and by a number of private individuals. A total of five hundred Jewish children attended the picnic in that year (*Jewish Times*, Aug. 5, 1910, p. 3).

10 The transformation of the Sewing Circle into Maternity Aid had taken place for much the same reasons that Ladies' Aid had come into existence. Mrs. Siegel had been attending a wedding at Goel Tzedec when one of the other guests happened to bring to her attention the case of a woman about to give birth who had money for neither food nor medical care.

11 At this time, Ida Siegel had become involved in the Local Council of Women in her capacity as president of Maternity Aid. The Council, a federation of women's charity societies, had recently begun to establish pasteurized milk stations throughout the working-class areas of Toronto. Mrs. Siegel and Miss Goldstick organized a women's auxiliary to the Jewish Dispensary, which then undertook to operate a milk depot in the Ward with financial assistance from the Local Council. This service had previously been provided by a number of non-Jewish groups, some of them with missionary attachments.

12 A Jewish dispensary of sorts had existed in Toronto as early as 1906 when a Dr. Kaufman had emigrated from Cleveland to Toronto and was prohibited from practising until he had passed the Ontario medical examinations. In the meantime, he opened a dispensary for Jews and attracted patients who could not speak enough English to attend the outpatient clinics at the local hospitals. This was not a free dispensary, as the communal effort was to be, but Kaufman's fee was half that of licensed practitioners. He returned to Cleveland shortly after the opening of the Elizabeth Street dispensary.

13 This discussion of the mothers' club is based largely on interviews with Mrs. Ida Siegel. Her role in this connection is generally acknowledged in Toronto and not a single item of documentary material which has survived contradicts her description of the venture. Similar activities were later begun at York Street School which also had a large Jewish student population.

14 It should be noted that while the sewing school concentrated on instructing children who were still in elementary school,

the only facility in this period for girls in their upper teens was the Jewish Working Girls' Club operated from 1909 by the Council of Jewish Women at the instigation of Rabbi and Mrs. Jacobs. Unlike the sewing school, the Working Girls' Club emphasized acculturation rather than Jewish content in its program. The English classes were especially popular, as were the social evenings each Saturday, especially after the patronizing "Working" was dropped from the title of the organization (Mrs. B. Draimin, personal interview, Feb. 15, 1972). Indeed, by 1912 over four hundred girls were in attendance, a phenomenon which made necessary the acquisition of larger quarters on McCaul Street the following year. Virtually alone among the philanthropic services offered by the old community, the Girls' Club was accepted by the East Europeans.

15 Personal interviews: J.B. Salsberg, Feb. 21, 1973; David Green, Apr. 9, 1973.

16 Personal interviews: David Green, March 28, 1973, Apr. 9, 1973; William Leibel, Jan. 28, 1972; Marvin Selicson, "The Folks Farein at Fifty" (pamphlet; Toronto: Folks Farein, 1964).

Jews were informed of the existence of these facilities by a legendary personality of the period, Chona Mosoff. A lanky, awkward-looking young man with a booming voice, Chona was an ardent Zionist and it was he who became the principal speaker at street-corner rallies organized in opposition to Rohold and Singer. Chona, a bachelor, also had the monumental task of frustrating all efforts by the ladies' societies to find him a wife. He later left Toronto for the United States and by the mid-1920s he was a prominent Zionist lecturer.

By the 1920s the Folks Farein had moved west of University Avenue and operated a shelter for recently arrived immigrants. It also developed a policy of paying hospitalization fees for those unable to do so and by the 1930s it was supplying the needy with artificial limbs, dentures and other medical appliances. Originally, its membership had been entirely male and working-class, but as its work expanded, women and more affluent men in the community were drawn in.

17 Goel Tzedec *Minutes*, Apr. 2, 1911; *Hebrew Journal*, Sept. 7, 1914; Shemen, "Orthodoxy . . .," p. 9.

18 H.N. Sivitz in *Kanader Adler*, Feb. 23, 1913; *Jewish Times,*

Dec. 13, 1912, p. 31. A morgue was established at the rear of the building and a free loan society (Gemilas Chasodim) was attached to the shelter (H.N. Sivitz to A.G. Volpe, Dec. 18, 1959, Canadian Jewish Congress Archives, Montreal).

19 Sivitz in *Kanader Adler*, Feb. 23, 1913; *Jewish Times*, June 9, 1911, p. 8; Associated Hebrew Charities "Minute Book containing the minutes of the several relief societies assembled in co-operation for the relief of the local poor and unfortunate at the Charities Building, 218 Simcoe St.," Jan. 3, 1912; *Jewish Times*, Oct. 13, 1911, p. 6; *Mail and Empire*, June 10, 1911; *Jewish Times*, May 16, 1913, p. 27.

20 The Monday afternoon meeting time suggests that while the top administrative posts in the Associated Charities were held by men, the actual operation must have been accomplished by housewives.

21 If a formal constitution ever existed, it has not been found. In all probability, the informal arrangement was considered sufficient since the organization received no government funds. See City of Toronto, *Report of the Charities Commission 1911-12* (Toronto: Carswell, 1912). By 1913, the following societies were represented on the Relief Board: Hebrew Ladies' Sewing Circle (Maternity Aid), Austrian Ladies' Aid Society, Polish Ladies' Aid Society, Jewish Benevolent Society (Holy Blossom), Associated Hebrew Charities, Hebrew Ladies' Aid Society and Ladies' Montefiore Society (*Jewish Times*, Jan. 17, 1913, p. 30).

22 *Jewish Times*, Sept. 6, 1912, p. 20.

CHAPTER 11

RELIGIOUS LEADERSHIP AND EDUCATION IN THE EAST EUROPEAN COMMUNITY, 1900 – 1917

Until the later decades of the nineteenth century, orthodox rabbis of the East European school were rare in North America. It has already been remarked that the East Europeans who ventured forth to the New World prior to the pogroms of the 1880s were relatively unconcerned with the niceties of religious law. They demanded no expert religious arbiters, and those who were the least concerned about the observance of the Commandments were content with *shochtim*, cantors and sextons. There was no orthodox rabbi in all the North American continent until 1840 and, by the end of the century, even New York City, with many thousands of Jews, had only three or four worthy of the name.[1]

In fairness to these early settlers, it should be noted that they could probably not have secured an ordained rabbi even if they had insisted upon one. Few observant Jews, let alone rabbis, would cross the ocean where, it was believed, Judaism could not survive. As late as 1900 Rabbi Jacob David Willowski of Slutzk (Russia), addressing a throng of East Europeans during a visit to New York, could castigate his audience for having emigrated to a "trefa land where even the stones are impure."[2]

If the attitudes of East European Jewish communities toward their North American counterparts were slow to change, the uprooting of large numbers of traditionalist Jews after the assassination of Tsar Alexander II in 1881 radically altered the situation in American cities. By 1900 there was a demand for rabbis, if only they could be persuaded to come. In the meantime, immigrant Jews had to be content with less qualified personnel.

Too little is known about the religious functionaries of the East European community in Toronto prior to the advent of the rabbis to be able to estimate how well the local Jews were served. Certainly those who acted as ministers in the 1890s appear to have been highly regarded. Isaac Halpern, for example, who was *shochet* for the Galician congregation, had a reputation for piety and profound intellect, and he gratified the East Europeans by speaking out against Holy Blossom whenever its members became patronizing or attempted to speak for the Jews of the Ward. Judah Breslin served capably as cantor for Chevra Tehillim in the same period, while the senior East European congregation, Goel Tzedec, had a succession of *shochtim* and readers until they secured the services of Reverend Isaac Berkowitz about 1898.[3] No matter how satisfactorily religious functions were carried out, however, the absence of an ordained rabbi meant that there was no authoritative source of religious decisions in the city, and observant immigrants from Europe would hesitate to settle in such a community. Admittedly, there were the ministers of Holy Blossom, but most East Europeans considered their learning insufficient and their piety suspect, and sought guidance, when necessary, either in Montreal or in New York. But this could not provide religious direction in the Ward, which required an authority to supervise *kashruth** and to organize more intensive Jewish education than that offered by Holy Blossom.

The Galician synagogue, Shomrai Shabboth, though neither the oldest nor the largest East European congregation in the city, took the initiative in securing an ordained spiritual leader for Toronto. Understandably, they decided upon someone of Galician birth. In 1899, coincident with the opening of their new synagogue on Chestnut Street, they invited Rabbi Joseph Weinreb to become their mentor. At 32, "Yossele" Weinreb was already a renowned scholar and rabbi of a prosperous congregation in Jasi, Roumania. Under normal circumstances he probably would not have considered the call to such a backwater, but anti-semitism had erupted in his city and consequently the invitation appeared unusually attractive.

If the Galicians expected Toronto's religious problems to be solved when Rabbi Weinreb finally arrived in 1901, they were sadly mistaken. They had invited him to be rabbi of the entire East European community, and the small Polish element did immediately place itself under his authority. But while Weinreb was personally popular and most adhered to his religious decisions, ethnic prejudice prevented his establishing anything

* The system of biblical and rabbinic law governing the criteria for pronouncing food kosher.

165

approaching universal authority. The Russians and Lithuanians could accept only a rabbi trained in the *yeshivoth* (talmudic academies) of their own homelands, and so, while they deferred to Rabbi Weinreb out of necessity, they longed for a pastor of their own.

It is not surprising, therefore, that when Jacob Gordon, a recently ordained graduate of the Yeshiva of Volozhin (Russia), arrived in Toronto in 1904 to collect funds for his school, both Goel Tzedec and Chevra Tehillim descended upon him with entreaties to remain. His acceptance the following year was to alter considerably the religious complexion of the community. One by one, each synagogue of Russian Jews elected him its rabbi, so that by the First World War his authority was accepted not only by Goel Tzedec and Chevra Tehillim (which assumed the name Beth Hamidrash Hagodol after the opening of its McCaul Street synagogue in 1905), but also by Tzemach Tzedec, Anshei Lida, Yavne Zion, Knesseth Israel in the West Toronto Junction and a number of other congregations. This fact, coupled with his tireless activity in the establishment of communal charities and a Jewish educational system, made him dean of the orthodox rabbinate in the city.[4]

Two additional orthodox rabbis served in Toronto during this period: Rabbi Meyer H. Levy and Rabbi Yehuda Leib ("Yudel") Rosenberg. Rabbi Levy, a native of Russia, had emigrated to Detroit but, having been unable to secure an acceptable rabbinic post, had become a merchant. When Shomrai Shabboth split in 1906, Rabbi Weinreb followed the dissidents to Teraulay Street and the former invited Rabbi Levy to its pulpit. Simultaneously, he served the Roumanian congregation, Adath Israel, and the Russian congregation, Shaarei Tzedec, on Centre Avenue. The latter eventually became his principal congregation, while Shomrai Shabboth, once the wounds of the dispute had healed, again accepted Rabbi Weinreb.

The arrival of Rabbi Rosenberg in 1913 reflected the growth of the Polish community. A movement to invite a Polish rabbi to Toronto had resulted about 1911 in the offering of the pulpit of Beth Jacob to a prominent European talmudist. When he arrived, however, it became apparent that his abilities were exclusively academic and that he could not cope with the problems of the rabbinate in an immigrant community. The congregation, therefore, refused to elect him and instead, in 1913, called Rabbi Rosenberg, himself a scholar and author of no mean reputation.

Rosenberg was highly respected, but so inadequately paid that he lived in virtual poverty. This was due in part to the lower economic status of the local Polish Jews compared to that of other ethnic groups, but also to the fact that the rabbi could not conceive of the necessity of actively seeking to make himself popular with his congregation. As the years passed, he became increasingly disgruntled and withdrawn, and in 1918 accepted a position in Montreal.[5]

II

Just as the rabbinate was deterred by the "impure stones" of North America, so also qualified professional teachers hesitated to leave Europe. As a result, Jewish education suffered a deplorable decline in the later years of the nineteenth century. In Toronto, a variety of misfits who could earn a livelihood in no other manner found their way into the field. Individuals lacking business acumen and having themselves only an elementary grasp of the Hebrew language and religious law became itinerant teachers, *siddur melamdim*, who attempted to eke out a living peddling their limited knowledge door-to-door in the Jewish neighbourhoods. In the 1890s, a qualified *melamed* such as Samuel Lewis would charge two dollars a month per student. He took fewer and devoted more time to each, while the *siddur melamdim* would accept as little as fifty cents. Since parents were often peddlers who needed each penny for subsistence, they contented themselves with the itinerant teacher.[6]

Although most teachers, the qualified and the charlatan alike, offered instruction in the kitchens of their students' homes, a few attempted to enlarge their operations by opening one-room schools, *chedorim*, in their own dingy residences or in rented premises. Few lasted very long or provided anything approximating an adequate religious education. Some in fact were outright frauds. One unscrupulous *melamed*, for instance, fitted up a classroom with new desks and convinced parents to enroll their children by paying large sums in advance. He even rented the local Yiddish theatre for a public examination to prove the success of his teaching. Once the money had been collected, however, he disappeared and was never heard from again. In Europe such abysmal quality of instruction would not have been tolerated, but in most North American cities the Jewish public was content. Indeed, those indifferent to Jewish education were only too pleased to use the lack of adequate facilities as an excuse to provide their children with no religious instruction at all.[7]

By the 1890s, the only formal Jewish educational institution in Toronto was still the Sabbath School at Holy Blossom and, while even a few learned East Europeans such as Isaac Halpern and Samuel Lewis enrolled their daughters, most were not prepared to see their sons fall under Scheuer's reforming aegis. Besides, the Sabbath School provided no talmudic instruction whatever and, for the East European, Talmud represented the essence of Jewish learning.

The traditional element, both at Holy Blossom and in the Ward, were aware of these educational shortcomings. In September 1899, therefore, local Jewry held a "mass meeting" at the Foresters' Temple on Bay Street "for the purpose of establishing a Talmud Torah under efficient teachers." Between two and three hundred heads of families turned out to the gathering which was chaired by traditionalist A.D. Benjamin. With due deference, the meeting elected Benjamin permanent president of the newly organized Talmud Torah Association, while the presidents of the three East European synagogues, Goel Tzedec, Chevra Tehillim and Shomrai Shabboth, were appointed vice-presidents. A committee of four from each synagogue, including Holy Blossom, was elected to oversee the details of the project. "The school," reported the *Jewish Times*, "will be established in the west end of the city [i.e., west of Yonge St.] where the greater number of our co-religionists reside. A large sum of money was subscribed and promises were obtained from the parents that their children would attend. The object in view is to perpetuate the study of the Hebrew language doing away with jargon and teaching pure Hebrew from pure English."[8]

The Talmud Torah Association demonstrated unprecedented co-operation between the East European congregations and Holy Blossom, illustrating the urgency with which the educational situation was regarded. This was undoubtedly accomplished only through the good offices of Alfred Benjamin, and marked the apex of good relations between the old community and the new at the end of the century. After Benjamin's death, it would not be reached soon again.

The proposed *talmud torah*, moreover, reflected the desires of the acculturated but traditional elements in the community; instruction was to be "pure Hebrew from pure English," rather than from the Yiddish as the most recent immigrants would have preferred. The established East Europeans insisted upon this because they planned to send their own children. The institution, therefore, was not to be a school only for the poor. In Europe, the communal *talmud torah* had originated as a means of educating the children of those unable to pay a *melamed*, a natural development since Jewish tradition assigns to the organized Jewish community the duty of seeing that all its children receive religious instruction. What ensued, however, was unexpected. The European *talmud torahs* adopted a grading system like that of the state schools and, because they were community organizations, could erect better facilities than the private *chedorim* and attract the best teachers. Consequently, even children whose parents could afford to employ a private *melamed* were drawn in and the institution soon lost its charity stigma. It is apparent that the proposed institution in Toronto was to be a product of that evolution.

The grand plan, perhaps itself a reflection of the *fin de siècle* confidence that pervaded much of the English-speaking world, did not materialize. Certainly failure was not due, as it was elsewhere, to unwillingness on the part of the East European congregations to co-operate. The *talmud torah* movement had not originated in Toronto solely with the old community, as had been the case in a number of cities in the United States. It might, of course, be contended that the demise of Alfred Benjamin in 1901 deprived the movement of leadership and that without him Holy Blossom's co-operation in a traditionalist effort would be impossible. However, prosperous East European Jews from Goel Tzedec also provided leadership in the organization and although Benjamin was the driving force in the traditionalist wing at Holy Blossom, he was not alone, especially after the arrival of Rabbi Jacobs.

Perhaps qualified teachers could not be secured. Most professionals who emigrated in this period went to the United States, since Canadian communities with comparatively small Jewish populations could not offer the competitive wages necessary to attract them. Perhaps, also, the arrival of rabbis Weinreb and Jacobs at the turn of the century produced currents away from a communal *talmud torah* movement. Jacobs probably did not support the movement because he felt that the school in his own congregation could be made to serve that purpose and his attempts to make it so forced Scheuer to withdraw. Rabbi Weinreb, on the other hand, would unquestionably have been opposed to instruction "from pure English." His mandate from Shomrai Shabboth was to recreate the atmosphere of the *shtetl*, and he would soon embark on educational efforts of his own. The *talmud torah*, therefore, did not dawn with the new century; the movement disbanded.

The communal workers of the Ward, in the meantime, were not idle. Henry Singer's missionary activities highlighted the void in local Jewish education and prompted Ida Lewis, then only eighteen, to organize a girls' sewing club as a countermeasure in 1903.* The following year, the local Zionists, having organized themselves into a mutual aid society called Bnai Zion, opened a storefront meeting hall at the southern end of Elizabeth Street and, realizing the vital nature of Miss Lewis' work, offered the sewing club their quarters. Ida Lewis now took the opportunity of extending the club into a Zionist Sunday School. Here girls studied Jewish history, presented plays on Jewish subjects and were taught Zionist songs that Miss Lewis had learned during visits to the United States and through the New York *Tageblatt*, then the most widely read Yiddish newspaper in Toronto. But while she felt strongly about the ideals of Zionism (i.e. Jewish nationalism), her principal purpose was to impart Jewish religion, and Zionism was an invaluable vehicle, for it provided the young people with a sense of identity in a strange land. Although the Zionist Jewish Free School, as it came to be called, attempted no formal Canadianization of the students, Ida Lewis effected it indirectly by emphasizing the responsibilities of citizenship as an aspect of proper Jewish observance, a lesson she had learned in her own home. Despite the skepticism of the elders of the East European community, the institution proved an important stopgap against the flow to the missions; for although attendance at classes seldom exceeded seventy-five in its early years, the school's extracurricular activities attracted girls in much larger numbers.[9]

By 1908, however, the Bnai Zion had come to the conclusion that the work of Ida Lewis (now Ida Siegel) lacked sufficient formality. Believing that an experienced male educator could better superintend these efforts and seeing that Edmund Scheuer had left Holy Blossom, they invited him to take charge, a rather incongruous choice considering that, as a reformer of the German school, Scheuer was vehemently opposed to political Zionism.[10]

Scheuer did minimize the Zionist aspect, apparently without much objection from the sponsoring society, and concentrated, as he had at Holy Blossom, on ethics, deportment and good citizenship at the expense of ritual. Despite the change in

* This should not be confused with the Hebrew Ladies' Sewing Circle founded in 1906. The sewing club was quickly transformed into a Sunday School, while the circle concentrated on recreation.

curriculum, the school grew from twenty-three students in 1908 to a registered average of about three hundred at its peak in 1916, an increase undoubtedly due to the policy of charging no tuition and because, despite Scheuer's presence, the school had the appearance of being under East European auspices. Indeed, most of the teachers were young men and women of East European origin. Pupils were primarily recently arrived immigrant girls from the age of seven upward. Scheuer's concise textbook, published in 1915 for use in the school, was perhaps the first Jewish pedagogic tool produced in Toronto.[11]

While the Zionist School was in its initial stages, progress was being made toward more comprehensive Jewish education for boys. Through the efforts of Leibush Gelber, a member of Shomrai Shabboth, and Rabbi Weinreb, the first *talmud torah* in the city was set up in 1904 in the basement of the Galician synagogue on Chestnut Street. The program, exclusively for boys, was more intensive than anything thus far attempted. The school met each afternoon except Friday; instruction, carried on by three teachers under the rabbi's direction, was in Yiddish on the model of the *shtetl*.[12] The Chestnut Street school, however, served only the relatively small Galician community. An effort of wider scope, therefore, was imperative, especially after the increased influx of immigrants following 1905.

It was perhaps the arrival of Rabbi Jacob Gordon that provided an impetus for several East European congregations led by Goel Tzedec and Beth Hamidrash Hagodol to revive the community *talmud torah* project. The enterprise culminated in 1907 in the purchase of a dilapidated eight-room house on Simcoe Street just west of the Ward and the establishment of the Toronto Hebrew Religion School (Simcoe Street Talmud Torah). It appears that organizationally the new *talmud torah* was patterned after a similar institution in Pittsburgh. Its constitution was a virtual reproduction of theirs, as was the method of attracting financial support by promoting "membership" as one would belong to a synagogue or a society. No secular subjects were taught at Simcoe Street; Toronto seems to have preferred the European model in this regard.[13]

Although Toronto had difficulty in attracting any significant number of teachers, the instruction at the school was of a superior quality. Four teachers presided, including Ben-Zion Nathanson, a Lithuanian Hebraist who headed the institution, L. Madorsky, a local teacher renowed for his learning, Mr. Steiner and Mr. Greenberg. Together with Rabbi Gordon, the spiritual force of the institution, they made the Simcoe Street Talmud Torah into one

171

of the few progressive community religious schools in North America. These men were traditionalists, but they were also *maskilim*, "enlightened ones," favouring secular as well as religious education. At the opening of the school, Rabbi Gordon announced that its purpose was not only to foster Judaism, but also to teach the children "patriotism for their adopted land."[14] In contrast to many orthodox religious leaders elsewhere, Rabbi Gordon and his teachers were staunchly Zionist and taught in Hebrew (*ivrit be'ivrit*), rather than in Yiddish. In fact, the Simcoe Street Talmud Torah was among the minute number of American Jewish schools modelled on the European Tarbut schools.[15]

The Simcoe Street Talmud Torah was unusual in the nature of its support. In a number of American cities, *talmud torahs* had been organized by the recently arrived East Europeans, while the more established and affluent orthodox remained aloof, preferring not to have their children associate with immigrant youngsters. In Toronto, on the contrary, the members of the senior East European synagogue, Goel Tzedec, supported the Talmud Torah both financially and by enrolling their children. There may have been two reasons for this: in the first place, because of the short time span separating the arrival of the various groups, a smaller social and economic cleavage existed in the Toronto community. Secondly, despite its Zionism and use of Hebrew, the Talmud Torah was uncompromisingly orthodox. Non-religious teachers, regardless of their scholarship, were refused employment and within the school no deviation from tradition was tolerated. For example, when, during the First World War, a photograph depicting the noted Yiddish author, Mendele Mocher Sforim, bareheaded, was found hanging in one of the classrooms, it was ordered removed.

Classes were offered at Simcoe Street five days a week after regular school hours. The curriculum included Bible, religion and Talmud, but with the unusual addition of Hebrew conversation and grammar. Average registration in the early years was approximately one hundred. Simcoe Street was a "free school," which signified that no particular religious or social ideology beyond traditional Judaism and Zionism was promoted and that the school was not affiliated with any other institution, rather than that no tuition was asked. Indeed, most students did pay on a graduated scale ranging from three to twenty-five dollars a year, but those unable to afford any fee were admitted without cost.[16]

Simcoe Street was intended to serve the entire East European community regardless of ethnic background and although the efforts had been instigated by the Lithuanian and Russian sector, the Galicians and the Polish at first also lent their support. In fact, the Galicians went so far as to merge their school with the Talmud Torah in 1908.

Unhappily, the symbiosis was less than successful. Rabbi Weinreb insisted on separate quarters for the Galician classes within the building, where he could superintend his own group, leaving the rest to Rabbi Gordon, with whom he disagreed over the policy of teaching in Hebrew. After six months a dispute over that issue prompted the Galicians to withdraw. Reestablishment on Chestnut Street was now impossible because Gelber, who had single-handedly administered the school there, had been killed in a construction accident. Consequently, the Galician school dissolved; the bulk of the Galician students were taken up by private tutors who taught in Yiddish, but a few, especially the children of the more affluent who had begun to drift into Goel Tzedec after the opening of their magnificent new synagogue on University Avenue the previous year, remained at Simcoe Street.[17]

As unalterably opposed to the *ivrit be'ivrit* system as the Galicians, the Polish Jews of the city were neither numerous enough nor sufficiently organized prior to the First World War to take effective action. Many had left their families in Europe and hoped eventually to return to them. Furthermore, they were the least prosperous of the local Jews in this period and they lacked a rabbi who might take the lead in an independent effort by at least providing them with one teacher. Yet they were rankled by the domination of the "Litvaks" (Lithuanians) at Simcoe Street, with their "modernist" and unemotional approach to religion. By 1912, however, large numbers of Jews were arriving from Poland with the intention of remaining in Toronto, a sentiment which the outbreak of war would strengthen for many already in the city. Forced to make peace with their new environment, the Poles set about the process of transplanting the institutions of the *shtetl*. It was this movement which resulted in the importation of Rabbi Yudel Rosenberg.

By the time of his arrival, large numbers of children, especially Jewish newsboys, were receiving no Jewish education whatever. Consequently, in the summer of 1915, a meeting of Polish Jews at Rabbi Rosenberg's house resolved to establish a second *talmud torah*. The initial participants each agreed to contribute 5 to 10 cents a week and a house-to-house collection was undertaken. By October of the following year, eighteen dollars had been scraped together and the "Polish Talmud Torah" was officially organized. Its founders were fortunate in that there had recently arrived in

Toronto from Palestine a young *melamed* (teacher) named Nachum Hyamsohn, who was then teaching several children in the *beth midrash* (chapel) of the Polish synagogue on Elm Street. This class became the nucleus of the new school set up six weeks later in a rented house on Chestnut Street.

Although the non-Polish element ridiculed the effort and charged that to establish a rival *talmud torah* would be to dilute communal educational efforts and aggravate Simcoe Street's already chronic financial difficulties, the new institution grew apace. Response from the Polish Jews was overwhelming. Larger quarters soon had to be found, also on Simcoe Street, and the school was able to employ four teachers and a collector to solicit door-to-door donations. Although the school had been unsuccessful in its original purpose of educating the Jewish newsboys, the superior standards of the institution were so evident to the average Polish parent that he enrolled his own children. Indeed, within months after the move to Simcoe Street, the number of pupils had increased to the extent that non-professionals had to be co-opted to take classes. By 1917, the premises were already inadequate and, since no fees were yet demanded, the increased enrolment had drained the resources of the school's financial supporters.

At this point, two entrepreneurs in the Polish community, Itshe Meyer Korolnek and Joseph Cooper, came up with a solution. They proposed to purchase an Italian club on D'Arcy Street, calculating that a move to the west would attract more students and that opening ceremonies would generate both enthusiasm and contributions. The refurbishing of the new building and the naming of the school Talmud Torah Eitz Chaim had the desired effect and even succeeded in drawing large numbers of Galicians away from Rabbi Gordon's facility.[18]

Eitz Chaim, in tone and curriculum, remained true to the principles upon which it was based and which had caused its founders to oppose the Lithuanian Talmud Torah: it was rigidly defensive against radical ideas. Rabbi Rosenberg, who superintended the institution, carefully scrutinized printed material brought in and ordered offending items destroyed. All instruction was to be in Yiddish; religion was emphasized at the expense of Hebrew grammar and secular authors. The avowed policy was to offer an education exactly as in Poland.

The first teachers at Eitz Chaim were Toronto residents co-opted into the teaching profession. Some worked in factories during the day. Increasingly, however, attempts were made to secure professionals, usually through advertisements in the New

York Yiddish press. But even the promise of high wages failed to eliminate the continual shortage of teachers and the school had to depend upon non-professionals. Eitz Chaim, like Simcoe Street, held its classes outside of normal school hours: 4 to 8 p.m., Monday to Thursday, and Sundays, 9 to 12 and 2 to 5.

The opening of the D'Arcy Street Talmud Torah was a significant event for the Polish Jews. With an initial enrolment of 120, it represented a successful alternative to the "modernist" Simcoe Street school. More importantly, it underlined the shift in attitude of the Polish Jews toward Toronto. The actual purchase of property and the application for a provincial charter indicated that the city was no longer a temporary stopping-point until a return to Europe could be effected. They were here to stay.

Although the Simcoe Street Talmud Torah and Eitz Chaim both offered orthodox education and could probably have complemented each other, they in fact maintained little contact, except for the occasional brawl between chauvinistic students.[19] There was neither exchange of teachers in periods of shortage nor consultation on curriculum, and while the older institution became more progressive, Eitz Chaim clung firmly to the atmosphere of the East European *yeshiva* (talmudic academy), holding Rabbi Gordon's school in contempt. Admittedly, the more prosperous Polish Jews, especially those who, like the wealthy among the Galicians, were attracted to Goel Tzedec, contributed to both institutions and a few even sent their children to Rabbi Gordon. The majority of the Poles, however, preferred Eitz Chaim.

IV

If the orthodox could not agree on common ground in education, it is not surprising that the non-religious should have sought to establish an independent system. The reaction which followed the Russian revolution of 1905 had sent thousands of secularist and socialist Jews fleeing to North America, and these arrived in increasing numbers between 1906 and 1908. In September 1911, therefore, in opposition to Rabbi Gordon's school and even before the Polish Talmud Torah had become reality, the Jewish National Radical School was opened on Simcoe Street, the first of its type in North America. Its founders were adherents to a variety of ideologies: socialist, territorialist,* communist and anarchist. They had, however, a common bond, a sympathy for the working classes, an adamant secularism and a belief in the necessity to

---

* Territorialists favoured the idea of a Jewish homeland, but unlike the Zionists they did not insist on Palestine.

perpetuate secular Jewish culture through the Yiddish language. Chief among the founders was Isaac Matenko, a Russian-Jewish intellectual who had been forced to emigrate after 1905. In Toronto, he found employment as a factory operative and worked to organize a garment workers' union in the hope of increasing literacy among the Jewish labourers and ameliorating their living conditions. The founding of the Radical School represented one aspect of this effort, an attempt to bridge the growing gap between immigrant parents and their acculturated children.*

The curriculum consisted exclusively of secular subjects, principally Jewish history and Yiddish language. Some elementary Hebrew was offered in the higher grades. Jewish nationalism was emphasized, but with Yiddish rather than Hebrew as the national language. Although socialism was suggested in class, there was no formal indoctrination.

The establishment of the National Radical School provoked a furor in the Jewish community. The school's difficulties stemmed on one side from its unpopularity with some elements and on the other from its extreme popularity with the remainder. Rabbis Gordon and Weinreb were vehement in their condemnation of this godless effort. Zionists criticized its lack of sympathy with Jewish nationalism in Palestine (most of the teachers were Socialist-Territorialists) and ousted the school from the Zionist headquarters on Simcoe Street (known as the Zionist Institute), where it had originally begun,[20] while extreme radicals attacked the institution's refusal to stress ideology. On the other hand, the poor were attracted in droves by education offered virtually free;

---

* The school was actually the outgrowth of a workers' cultural society, the Progressive Literary Dramatic Club, founded in the winter of 1907-1908 to promote Yiddish literature "among the masses." It was particularly influenced by the ideas of Dr. Chaim Zhitlowsky, a Jewish secularist and former Russian revolutionary then living in New York, who saw Yiddish language as a tool for promoting socialism among the Jewish working class. Furthermore, he condemned the internationalism of the socialist movement and insisted that Jews survive as a separate entity. Jewish culture expressed through the Yiddish language he believed was the best means to Jewish survival. Coupled with this point of view came the news that the Yiddish author, I.L. Peretz, had begun to establish Yiddish schools in Poland. The Socialist-Territorialists, of whom Matenko was a member, appear to have taken the lead in the Toronto project.

Among the founders of the Radical School were Abraham Rhinewine, later editor of the *Hebrew Journal*; Paul Frumhartz and Louis Koldofsky, staunch union advocates; a Mr. Bromberg and an English-born anarchist named Abe Goldman. Most were factory workers and all became part-time teachers in the school, over which Matenko presided as principal.

176

as the school increased in size, it also increased in respectability and even some religiously inclined parents began to enroll their children. By 1913 the school had three hundred pupils instructed by twelve teachers, and with the advent of war would open branches on Bellwoods Avenue, at Earlscourt and in the West Toronto Junction.* This expansion was a crippling strain on the resources of the school. Despite the fact that the teachers were unpaid, the financial backing of the institution was never large enough to assure its existence. Funds came from a variety of sources: the minute tuition fees, taxes on members of sympathetic organizations such as the Workmen's Circle, fund-raising events and especially house-to-house collection by the wives of supporters. By 1916, therefore, the virtually bankrupt institution was taken over by a number of secularist organizations and renamed the I.L. Peretz School.†

In theory, the Peretz School was to receive support not only from the Workmen's Circle but also from other secularist organizations, notably the Labour Zionists and the Socialist-Territorialists, and the policy of compromise on the issue of ideology was to continue. In fact, however, the stance of the Workmen's Circle was adopted. The Peretz School was dominated by the extreme Yiddishists, by opponents of Zionism and by the communists who, in this period, exercised considerable influence within the Workmen's Circle. These facts, coupled with the promulgation of the Balfour Declaration, which infused new life into the advocates of a Jewish national homeland, prompted the Socialist-Territorialists and the Labour Zionists to withdraw in 1917 and the latter to throw their support behind a rival secular institution, the Jewish Folks Shulë.[21]

The curriculum of the Folks Shulë differed little from that of the Peretz School. Although Yiddish remained the language of instruction, however, modern Hebrew literature and language were taught, Zionism was explicitly advocated and left-wing ideology

* Students who could afford to do so paid 50 cents a month at this period. The Earlscourt school was short lived, but the Junction branch lasted until 1920. That was a working-class area which attracted residents susceptible to left-wing ideology.

† Isaac Leib Peretz (1852-1915), author of some of the classics of Yiddish fiction, is considered one of the founders of the movement for a modern secular Yiddish and Hebrew literature. The Peretz School had actually originated with a Yiddish literature class run by Abraham Rhinewine in the Junction. About 1915, Rhinewine set up the Peretz Institute on Grange Road in the Beverley-Dundas area. In 1916, when the Radical School found itself in trouble, the Workmen's Circle effected a union between the two institutions and undertook to provide financial support for the combined effort.

177

minimized. By 1918, therefore, there were two secularist school systems in the city and the relationship between the two was hardly less cordial than that between the Simcoe Street Talmud Torah and Eitz Chaim. The Yiddishists at Peretz considered the Folks Shulë a bourgeois institution, little better than the religious schools, while the orthodox branded both secular schools blasphemous. Some at the McCaul Street Synagogue even went so far as to accuse them of attempting to turn the children into apostates.

Despite the criticism and the rifts within the movement, the secular schools expanded rapidly during the war years as immigrants continued to arrive. By the 1920s, however, attendance had begun to decline, for if the bulk of the newcomers were not orthodox, they were at least sympathetic to religious tradition, perhaps because it provided a degree of security in the new environment. Others had been alienated from socialism by the excesses of the Soviet regime. Indeed, so traditional was Toronto in the period of the war and for some time afterwards that the National Radical School, in defiance of the demands of some of the doctrinaire secularists, deferred to public sentiment and avoided holding its picnics on the Sabbath as did secular institutions in other cities.*

V

Even before the secular schools had begun to proliferate and prior to the establishment of Talmud Torah Eitz Chaim on a secure basis, there was a continuous battle between the religious element represented by the Simcoe Street Talmud Torah and the secularists at the National Radical School. So bitter had the struggle become by 1912 that many parents hesitated to send their children to either, for fear of being caught up in the dispute. The beneficiaries were the private *chedorim* and the incompetent *siddur melamdim*. This situation, coupled with unsatisfactory conditions at Simcoe Street and the fact that many parents, for financial reasons, were unwilling to send their children to a Jewish

---

* The only attempt to do so in this period was in 1912 and it drew an outcry even from non-orthodox Jews, causing many to withdraw their children from the school. The principal objection was that the children would have to use the streetcars to reach the site of the festivities.

This is not to say that the secularist organizations outside the schools did not purposely violate Jewish law. Some secularists openly attended the theatre on holy days and stood smoking in front of the synagogues. Indeed, after 1920 there were a few instances of school activities on the High Holy Days as well.

school five or six afternoons a week, prompted the senior East European synagogues to establish congregational Sunday Schools and Holy Blossom to reorganize its own.

The need for a change in the older congregation had been apparent as early as 1909 when, despite the enrolment of over one hundred students, there was great difficulty in persuading children over fourteen to attend. By 1912 a reorganization was considered urgent because a large number of members and seat-holders at Holy Blossom were refusing to send their own children to the Sunday School. Since no fees were charged, the Council of Jewish Woman undertook to finance the school; this permitted the engagement and remuneration of additional teachers, most of whom were undergraduates at the University of Toronto or recent graduates. The reorganization apparently succeeded in blocking the trend of declining attendance, but it produced little increase in the enrolment.

Goel Tzedec had attempted to set up a school early in the 1890s, with its reader acting as teacher. No girls were admitted and the number of students never exceeded nine. Since the split between the old community and the new had not yet developed seriously, Edmund Scheuer was invited to be examiner. This school, however, appears to have dissolved within a few years, and Goel Tzedec's participation in the Talmud Torah movement at the end of the century was an attempt to replace it.[22]

After the collapse of that effort, some in the East European community considered establishing a Jewish day school which would teach secular and religious subjects on the model of the Catholic separate schools. The movement was vehemently opposed by those in favour of integration with the community at large, particularly the congregation of Holy Blossom. "To secure a separate school for our children would be a retrograde step," Edmund Scheuer charged, "and one that no right thinking Jew in our church would consider for a moment." Holy Blossom, he insisted, was "in favor of taking immediate action against it . . . . The movers of the scheme . . . are a small minority of the Jewish community in Toronto, and more than not being in sympathy with them I would fight such a movement tooth and nail."[23]

The fight never became necessary. If the East Europeans resented Scheuer's speaking for them as a body, it was probably true that they had neither the resources nor the inclination to bring the movement to fruition. Indeed, once the Simcoe Street Talmud Torah was opened, its officials made it clear that "The Talmud Torah is in no sense a separate school . . . ."

The establishment of Simcoe Street also superseded an effort by

179

the major East European synagogues to organize a system of congregational afternoon schools in response to a large immigration in 1906. Goel Tzedec contented itself with permitting Abe Lewis to assemble the boys of the congregation during Sabbath services and to "lecture them according to his understanding."

By 1913, however, action by the individual congregations could be postponed no longer. The expansion of the Presbyterian mission and the proposed new building across from Elizabeth Street School horrified the Jewish community. "The missionary influence among Jewish children is not a mere figment of the imagination," the Toronto correspondent to the *Jewish Times* warned, "but an actual living fact, and the Jews of Toronto should awaken to it. If the children in the Ward are not to lose the faith of their fathers...Sunday Schools should be instituted in the synagogues of the Ward as soon as possible." The Simcoe Street Talmud Torah was inadequate. Although its enrolment had risen to three hundred, the number of pupils was still too few to meet the challenge. Moreover, the shortage of teachers permitted only eight classes, a circumstance hardly conducive to quality instruction. Physical arrangements were even worse; there was insufficient classroom space, poor lighting and so little ventilation that the children appeared "dull, tired and restless." In addition, the public could not be persuaded to support the institution financially, despite attempts by Rabbi Gordon and his supporters to arouse interest. The bulk of the finances came from a dwindling membership and from voluntary offerings pledged on the Sabbath at Goel Tzedec and the McCaul Street Synagogue. As a result, the building was poorly maintained. "The exterior and interior of the Talmud Torah alike leave a most unpleasant impression on the visitor."[24]

The demands for congregational schools in 1914 were not an attack upon the Talmud Torah; all admitted it to be a "good institution, conducted on modern lines," but no one could deny its limitations. Rabbi Gordon castigated the East European synagogues for spending large sums of money on cantors to the neglect of Jewish education, while Scheuer urged "every synagogue in this city" to establish a religious school.[25]

Once again, an attempt was made to organize a city-wide system of congregational Sunday schools, this time through the co-operation of Holy Blossom and the East Europeans. Impetus came from Mrs. Maurice Frankel, principal of the reorganized Holy Blossom Sabbath School, and from Barnet Stone, a Galician clothing manufacturer and Zionist, active both with the Galician community and with Goel Tzedec. In May 1913 Stone arranged a meeting between Mrs. Frankel and the presidents of the Russian and Roumanian synagogues in the Ward, at which she urged them to establish schools. The McCaul Street Synagogue, in response to missionary activity, had already opened a Sabbath School at the suggestion of the Daughters of Zion* and in the following months additional meetings persuaded other congregations to follow suit. Mrs. Frankel probably advised on curriculum, while Stone advocated a united Board of Education, after the pattern of the Associated Hebrew Charities, which would supervise the congregational schools. Such a board, however, was a chimera. The community still lacked the maturity to engage in united action, even within the East European sector itself, let alone in conjunction with Holy Blossom. Perhaps, also, as Stone predicted, enough teachers could not be found. Certainly, professionals were not available.

Fortunately, an effort was under way which would have more substantial results; as with a variety of activities in the East European community, Ida Siegel was the driving force. Goel Tzedec had decided to engage an English-speaking rabbi because younger people were being alienated from the synagogue. Mrs. Siegel felt that the congregation must make a good impression on its new Americanized pastor by presenting him with at least the embryo of a congregational school, and this she set out to do by organizing a school on the model of those she had seen on visits to her native Pittsburgh. By the time the new rabbi, Dr. Julius Price, arrived in 1914, the school was already in operation, with Ida Siegel herself in charge of the kindergarten. The venture was supported not officially by the congregation, but rather by the ladies' auxiliary, who undertook the task after much urging and with hesitation. They had been, Mrs. Siegel recalls, "only recently released from the kitchen"; they were unaccustomed to assuming responsibility and only gradually gained experience and confidence.[26]

At first, the school met only Sunday mornings, but after Price took charge, it expanded to include a weekday afternoon class as well. An attempt was made to accommodate children from kindergarten age to about 16 or 17, and it seems that most of the students were the children of those unaffiliated with any synagogue. These were attracted by the free tuition. In the ab-

* The Daughters of Zion was a group of teenaged girls formed by Ida Siegel in 1899. It was the first Zionist youth organization in Toronto. The school at McCaul Street met Saturday afternoons and apparently also on Sunday evenings.

sence of professional teachers, Goel Tzedec followed Holy Blossom in co-opting high school and university students into this role. Originally these were unpaid, and the ladies of the congregation rewarded them for their efforts by cooking and serving supper for them in the synagogue after classes.

Rabbi Price was appointed superintendent of the school but Ida Siegel had already set the pattern for the curriculum. Influenced by the Holy Blossom Sabbath School, she introduced instruction in Hebrew vocabulary, a departure from the format of the traditional *cheder* and of most *talmud torahs*, where vocabulary was only incidental to textual study. Unlike Holy Blossom, however, which stressed acculturation, Goel Tzedec taught only Hebrew songs or English ones with Jewish content.

A second influence came from New York. For a number of years before 1914, Goel Tzedec had been contemplating the engagement of an English-speaking rabbi to draw the younger generation into the synagogue. Since, for a considerable time, the trustees could not be persuaded to take the step, a compromise was reached whereby Eugene Kohn, a rabbinical student from the Jewish Theological Seminary, was invited to preach for the High Holy Days in 1911. This was the beginning of a lifelong friendship between Kohn and Mrs. Siegel, with whose family he had stayed while in Toronto. Back in New York after his ordination, Rabbi Kohn interested himself in curricula for Jewish schools and was in a position to obtain outlines, prepared for the newly established United Synagogue of America,[27] from educators at the Seminary. These he forwarded to Ida Siegel, who implemented them not only at Goel Tzedec but also at the McCaul Street Synagogue and at Adath Israel, where she had persuaded the congregation to open schools of their own.

VI

The congregational school movement in Toronto also arose from the failure to establish a community centre which would encompass educational, athletic and social activities. The early years of the twentieth century saw the emergence of a variety of organizations which might have been drawn in, beginning with the Judean Literary and Debating Society founded in 1901 largely through the efforts of Abe Lewis. Its members – high school students, young working men and a few university students – met to discuss the social issues of the day. The Judean Society provided a link between the young men of Holy Blossom and the

Ward until it disintegrated into an exclusively upper-class organization. A similar society called the "Literdram" existed at the McCaul Street Synagogue in 1906.

Purely athletic pursuits for young people were undertaken by the Judean Athletic Club which appeared about 1908 and by the Hebrew Literary and Athletic Club, organized in 1914. Both participated in baseball, rugby, basketball and hockey. Jewish newsboys organized their own rugby team in 1909 and were frequently successful in matches against their Irish competitors.

Another youthful link between the old and new communities was the Mosaic Alumni, a debating club at the University of Toronto, founded in 1911. This also included undergraduates from McMaster (which had not yet moved to Hamilton) as well as some young Jewish professionals in the city. This and several others which existed simultaneously, had no official campus recognition and met usually in the Zionist Institute, first on Simcoe Street and then on Beverley. The same was true of the Toronto Hebrew Students' Association which survived only a short while after its organization in 1916.

The Menorah Society, on the other hand, which grew out of a Yiddish club at the University of Toronto in 1917 and superseded most of the other Jewish student groups, had a sort of semi-official status. Although it seldom met on campus, it did have a faculty advisor in its early years – Professor W.R. Taylor, who taught Hebrew at University College. A branch of an intercollegiate Jewish society first formed at Harvard in 1906 for the study of Jewish history and culture, Menorah flourished in Toronto until it was undermined by the Greek-letter fraternities in the late 1920s. In 1931 it dissolved.

Most of these clubs were short-lived and those which survived left many in the Jewish community untouched, since there was little co-operation between them. By 1912 the *Jewish Times* was complaining that all across the continent Jews were forming YMHA's on the model of the YMCA, while in Toronto although "hundreds of Jewish young men are at present members of non-Jewish athletic associations" for want of Jewish facilities, no one would take the initiative in founding a Jewish Y. Many became members of the YMCA, despite reports that its membership fees partially financed proselytizing among the Jews. The *Times* maintained that a Jewish Y would not only combat delinquency and the missions, but would also attract those for whom the synagogue had no appeal. This agitation by the *Jewish Times* prompted the YMHA Benevolent Society to launch a campaign to erect an athletic centre and clubrooms, to be called the YMHA Institute.

When a call went out for public support, however, a debate arose over the utilization of the proposed building. The YMHA Society insisted that all using the new facilities would have to affiliate with them. Another group suggested the formation of a new YMHA Association, of which the Society would be only one component, while a third element saw the new communal edifice as offering the Simcoe Street Talmud Torah an opportunity to acquire new premises. They wanted the Zionists to lead in the movement by securing the co-operation of all social and educational organizations and build a multipurpose centre with classrooms, gymnasium, meeting rooms, assembly hall and even a roof garden.[28]

It was impossible to reach agreement on this multitude of proposals, even though there was great enthusiasm for the project in the city. The YMHA Society, for instance, adamantly refused to co-operate with the Zionists for fear of losing their identity in the new organization. To make matters worse, the wealthiest elements in the city, whose support was essential if the community building were to materialize, could not be persuaded to acquiesce in the venture. At Holy Blossom, there was opposition from a sizable faction, despite Rabbi Jacobs' support for united action.

This factionalism, therefore, coupled with the financial difficulties which descended in 1913, put an end to the effort. A group of young peoples' clubs, which had awaited the new building with anticipation, now divorced themselves from the project and formed a loose organization called the Hebrew Association of Young Men's and Young Women's Clubs. They attempted to co-ordinate their activities, but for the time being gave up hope of meeting in a single location. They would wait almost a decade before this would be possible, but in the interim, theirs would be the nucleus of the modern YMHA.

VII

The war years, therefore, found Toronto with a fragmented and struggling Jewish educational system. All admitted its inadequacy, but there seemed to be no means to enlarge it. Toronto, however, reflected a universal problem in North American Jewry, and its educational facilities compared favourably to those of many localities in the United States. Few centres the size of Toronto had a *talmud torah* like Simcoe Street which, despite its limitations, was among the most progressive on the continent. Even in the congregational school movement, Toronto did not lag far behind. Indeed, it might be said that educational efforts here were in advance of some American cities.[29] Moreover, the very existence of the Talmud Torah helped to elevate private educational efforts. Although charlatans continued to operate *chedorim*, the sincere proprietors were able to raise their own standards by inviting an examiner in the person of Ben-Zion Nathanson from Simcoe Street, and the availability of such professional educators doubtless improved the quality of the congregational schools as well.

NOTES

1 Joseph H. Lookstein, "Traditional Judaism in America", *Jewish Quarterly Review*, New Series, XLV (April 1955), p. 323; Moshe Weinberger, *Ha Yehudim Veha-Yahudut Be-New York*, quoted in Aaron Rothkoff, *Bernard Revel* (Philadelphia: Jewish Publication Soc. of America, 1972), p. 11.

2 Quoted *ibid.*, p. 4.

3 Berkowitz had previously served in Ithaca, N.Y., and had answered a call to Goel Tzedec through an advertisement in the orthodox New York Yiddish daily, the *Yiddishes Tageblatt*. His predecessors could not be persuaded to stay in Toronto. A Reverend S. Cohen had served for only two years in the 1880s. A Mr. Eidelman appears to have lasted only a short while early in the 1890s. Reverend Alexander Newman became reader in 1887 and remained for almost a decade, but he left for Pittsburgh, where he became superintendent of a Jewish old folks' home. This information is based on Toronto city directories, on personal interviews with Mrs. Ida Siegel, Mrs. M. Goodman and on Alex J. Goldman, *Giants of Faith* (New York: Citadel Press, 1964), pp. 235-56.

4 Rabbi Gordon was instrumental in the establishment of the Free Burial Society and the Associated Hebrew Charities. For Rabbi Gordon's own account of his arrival, see "Reminiscences of a Toronto Rabbi" (Yiddish) in *Jewish Daily Eagle* (Montreal) 25th Anniversary issue (1932), clipping in Rabbi J. Gordon Papers, Canadian Jewish Congress Archives, Montreal.

5 J.B. Salsberg, personal interview, Jan. 15, 1973; Shemen, "Orthodoxy . . .," p. ii.

6 Ida Siegel, personal interview, July 29, 1971. In this period there were perhaps three or four qualified *melamdim* in Toronto.

7 Interviews: A.S. Socol, March 29, 1973 (Jewish Oral History Project); Ida Siegel, Aug. 12, 1971.

8 *Jewish Times*, Sept. 29, 1899, p. 343.

9 Ida Siegel, personal interviews, Oct. 7, 1971, July 29, 1971; *Jewish Times* Dec. 28, 1906, p. 37.

10 Mrs. Siegel continued to operate a sewing school for girls under Zionist auspices. In 1912, between 200 and 250 children were being taught (*Jewish Times*, Dec. 6, 1912), p. 30.

11 Edmund Scheuer, *Text Book of the Zionists' Jewish Free School*, (Toronto, 1915). The *Star Weekly* noted that Scheuer's curriculum emphasized "tolerance and respect for the creeds of others," inculcated loyalty to the monarchy and in general promoted good citizenship. It described his efforts as "a fine and patriotic work . . ." (Toronto *Star Weekly*, Feb. 12, 1916).

12 Samuel Kurtz, personal interview, Nov. 27, 1972.

13 Ida Siegel, personal interviews, Oct. 7, 28, 1971.

14 *Evening Telegram*, June 10, 1907.

15 The Tarbut schools of Eastern Europe, unlike the *talmud torah*, taught secular as well as religious subjects. The Toronto school made no attempt to do this, but the method of using Hebrew as the language of instruction was patterned directly upon the Tarbut system.

16 Hart, *op.cit.*, p. 183; Ida Siegel, personal interview, Oct. 28, 1971.

17 Samuel Kurtz, personal interview, Nov. 27, 1972.

18 This account of the early years of Talmud Torah Eitz Chaim is based upon Harry Korolnek, personal interview, Dec. 26, 1972; Leibush Nobel, "Vegen Ohnhoib fun Talmud Torah Eitz Chaim" ("Concerning the Beginning of Talmud Torah Eitz Chaim") in N. Shemen and L.J. Zuker, eds., *Jubilee Book, Talmud Torah "Eitz Chaim,"* pp. 77-78; and N. Shemen and

J.I. Wohlgelernter, "Ontshteyung un Ontviklung fun Talmud Torah Eitz Chaim" ("Establishment and Development of Talmud Torah Eitz Chaim") *ibid.*, pp. 127-86. The latter consists of excerpts from the minute books of the school, which have since disappeared.

Far more than did the Simcoe Street Talmud Torah, Eitz Chaim retained its character as a school for the poor. Not only was tuition offered free, but a ladies' society was organized in connection with the school when it moved to D'Arcy Street. The purpose of the Halboshas Arumim ("Clothing the Naked") Society was to raise money for the *talmud torah*, but also to provide clothing for poor students.

19 Wilferd Gordon, personal interview, Jan. 8, 1973.

20 After its eviction from the Zionist Institute several months after the opening, the Radical School moved farther north on Simcoe Street. In 1912 premises were rented at 260 Richmond Street W., and finally, in 1914, a house on Beverley Street north of Baldwin was purchased.

21 In Toronto, the Folks Shulë had opened in 1914, but it was apparently not officially under the auspices of the Labour Zionists. Until 1917, they supported both the Radical School and the Folks Shulë, but the latter was a private effort operated by a Mr. Shubin.

22 Speech by Edmund Scheuer to Goel Tzedec, 1929 (Edmund Scheuer File, Canadian Jewish Congress Archives, Montreal). The Toronto directories for 1892-94 list a school superintendent at Goel Tzedec. Mrs. Ida Siegel, who arrived in 1893, cannot recall a school at the synagogue after her arrival (Ida Siegel, personal interview, Aug. 12, 1971). The school probably met Sunday mornings after the pattern of Holy Blossom.

23 Clipping from Toronto *World* dated 1904, in Edmund Scheuer Scrapbook, Holy Blossom Archives.

24 *Jewish Times*, Apr. 11, 1913, p. 28; Feb. 21, 1913; pp. 28-29; Sept. 6, 1912, p. 20.

25 Rabbi Gordon quoted in *Jewish Times*, June 13, 1913; Scheuer quoted in *Jewish Times*, June 20, 1913. Rabbi Gordon's comment was undoubtedly directed at Goel Tzedec, which had just engaged the already renowed Cantor Bernard Wladowsky. The McCaul Street Synagogue was so anxious to

attract a celebrity that they were offering high wages and advertising themselves as "di greste shul in Kanada" ("the largest synagogue in Canada"). *Yiddishes Tageblatt*, Mar. 23, 1913; May 8, 1914; May 12-14, 1914.

26 Rabbi Price was apparently not impressed with what he found. He insisted that there was no school whatever when he arrived and that he himself generated the project (letter from Rabbi Julius Price to the author, Sept., 1971). The *Hebrew Journal*, however, appreciated Mrs. Siegel's role in the effort (*Hebrew Journal*, Sept. 7, 8, 1914).

27 The United Synagogue of America, founded in 1913, is the organization of synagogues affiliated with the Jewish Theological Seminary of America and is the lay organization of the Conservative movement. See Solomon Goldman, "Towards a National Synagogue," in Mordecai Waxman, ed., *Tradition and Change: The Development of Conservative Judaism* (New York: Burning Bush Press, 1958), pp. 205-06, and Davis, *The Emergence of Conservative Judaism*, pp. 323-25.

28 Louis Gurofsky in *Jewish Times*, Oct. 11, 1912, p. 23. The Zionists, who had occupied a house on Simcoe Street since 1908, had found it inadequate by this time, had sold it at a handsome profit and were now in the process of looking for new premises. Many influential Toronto Jews at this period, including Rabbi Jacobs, believed that a new community centre would satisfy all concerned (*Jewish Times*, Oct. 25, 1912, p. 23).

29 See "A Survey of Jewish Education in New York City (1909)" in Lloyd P. Gartner, ed., *Jewish Education in the United States* (New York: Teachers College Press, Columbia University, 1969), pp. 118-126; Adler and Connolly, *op.cit.*, p. 240; Rockaway, *op.cit.*, p. 172.

Judah Joseph, the first permanent Jewish settler in Toronto. (Arthur D. Hart, (ed.) *The Jew in Canada*)

Rabbi Solomon Jacobs. (Toronto Jewish Congress / Canadian Jewish Congress Central Region Archives)

Rabbi Jacob Gordon. (Author's collection)

Slova Greenberg, founder of the Ezras Noshim Society. (Author's collection)

Shirt factory operated by Galician Jews, Church Street, 1905. (Toronto Jewish Congress / Canadian Jewish Congress Central Region Archives – courtesy Fish Moskoff)

Ida Siegel (second from left in back row) with Herzl girls, *ca.* 1905-1906. (Courtesy Ida L. Siegel)

Holy Blossom Synagogue, Bond Street, 1925 (Public Archives of Canada, PA 87061)

Elizabeth Street and Foster Place, *ca.* 1913-1915. (James Collection – City of Toronto Archives)

Goel Tzedec Synagogue,
University Avenue, 1926.
(Yankel Jessel Collection)

Dorothy Dworkin (centre) with members of the Mount Sinai Hospital Ladies'
Auxiliary, 1920s. (Dorothy Dworkin Collection)

Wolfish family at their drygoods shop, Elizabeth Street, 1913. (Toronto Jewish Congress / Canadian Jewish Congress Central Region Archives)

Children of the old community: (L-R) Roy, Egmont, and Carl Frankel, *ca.* 1905. (Toronto Jewish Congress / Canadian Jewish Congress Central Region Archives – courtesy of the family of Carl M. Frankel)

Looking northwest to Agnes and Teraulay streets (Dundas and Bay) from the Eaton factories, *ca.* 1913. Note Lyric Theatre and Teraulay Street Synagogue (right foreground). (James Collection – City of Toronto Archives)

Jewish Old Folks Home, Cecil Street, *ca.* 1920 (Signs are superimposed on photograph). (Toronto Jewish Congress/Canadian Jewish Congress Central Region Archives)

✡ JEWISH OLD FOLKS HOME ✡

29-31 CECIL STREET

אל תשליכנו לעת זקנה

סאראנטער מושב זקנים

דיא זקנים וזקנות שיקען אייך אַ פורים פרעזענט

Brunswick Avenue Talmud Torah (centre). (Author's collection, courtesy of Samuel A. Kurtz)

Buying poultry on Kensington Ave., 1922. (Public Archives of Canada, PA 84811)

Spadina Avenue, 1925. A University of Toronto graduate engineer, Mr. Hyman became a Hebrew teacher and bookseller. (Courtesy Benzion Hyman)

א גרופפע פון די וואלאנטערן־קאלעקטארס פון דעם מלחמה הילפס קאנפערענץ אין טאראנטא קענעדע

Maurice Goldstick (2), Henry Dworkin (1) with volunteer collectors of the Conference for Jewish War Sufferers, 1919. (Toronto Jewish Congress/Canadian Jewish Congress Central Region Archives)

City Committee, Labor League, 1935. (Toronto Jewish Congress/Canadian Jewish Congress Central Region Archives)

CHAPTER 12

DIVISIVE
AND UNIFYING FORCES,
1880 – 1918

Social stratification in Canada, as in other former colonies, is seldom based upon race alone. It is, rather, intimately connected to date of arrival. The earliest settlers tended to consider themselves superior and either ignored newcomers or attempted to mould them into an acceptable form. It was to be expected, therefore, that social division between the old Jewish community and the new should appear in Toronto; indeed, it was characteristic of Jewish communities throughout North America. The old community, extremely sensitive to criticism by the Gentiles, attempted to divest themselves of their peculiarly Jewish features and, since their dominant tone was initially English, they had little difficulty doing so. Most East Europeans, however, reacted to their new environment by clinging tenaciously to traditional practices, a feature which came increasingly to embarrass the earlier arrivals who feared a resulting upsurge of anti-semitism.

Even the empathetic Alfred Benjamin fell into this pattern. Referring to the East European Jews at the opening of the Bond Street Synagogue, he remarked that "Every effort is being made to Anglicize them and to render them proud of the glorious privilege of being citizens of this beloved Canada of ours." The attempt to dominate the East European community in religious matters and the efforts at speeding acculturation through old-community organizations such as the Jewish Girls' Club further reflected this attitude, as did the encouragement of boys from the Ward to attend functions at Holy Blossom and to sing in their choir.

With the exception of a few individuals, Holy Blossom and the East Europeans rarely mixed socially in the early years of the twentieth century; even in most communal ventures the older congregation remained aloof after Benjamin's death, except when they could be the dominant force.[1] Residentially, the two groups were segregated, and even commercially, they seldom had contact. With the possible exception of the Frankels, who bought stock from the rag-pickers, most members of the old community had little reason to deal with the newcomers; the East Europeans concentrated in the clothing and salvage trades, while the former dealt in optical supplies, jewellery, tobacco, hardware, insurance and retail merchandising.

Many East Europeans were not displeased with this separation. Certainly the wealthy and the social aspirants among them would have welcomed entry into the circle of the "East End" elite; it would signify that they had arrived. Most, however, considered the members of Holy Blossom little different from non-Jews. They were too liberal in their religious practices outside the synagogue and even their services were strange. They seldom spoke Yiddish even among themselves and their English was flawless. Moreover, they were a threat to tradition. "Those who are not orthodox Hebrews are nothing," one traditionalist told the *Star*, "for they live up to the principles of no faith."[2] It is not surprising, therefore, that many East Europeans would have shunned Holy Blossom even if the old community had attempted to treat them as equals, an attitude bolstered by the preachings of Rabbi Gordon against the religious aberrations at Bond St.* Despite the relative traditionalism of Holy Blossom compared to reform synagogues in the United States, the East Europeans in Toronto were aware of the trend away from orthodoxy among the old communities in American centres and had seen how far Holy Blossom had already strayed from its orthodox beginnings.

Holy Blossom, nevertheless, professed to speak for the entire Jewish population. The congregation considered themselves the proper voice of local Jewry, able to present the best public image to the rest of the city. In addition, they were projected into the role of spokesman by the local press and the municipal authorities, who sought the opinion of members of the old community rather than of recent arrivals on issues which affected the Jews. These opinions were not always shared by the East Europeans, who bristled in indignation. One incident from this period illustrates the point. In 1915 a group of fifty-two Jewish organizations in Toronto – all East European – asked the city for

* Prior to the arrival of Rabbi Gordon, the ministers of the new community were on good terms with Rabbi Jacobs. This was especially true of Reverend Halpern of Shomrai Shabboth. Even Rabbi Weinreb was well disposed toward him. Rabbi Gordon, however, was very defensive for orthodoxy and discouraged East European families from sending their children to school at Holy Blossom.

permission to hold a tag day in aid of Jewish war victims in Russia. The chief of police refused on the grounds that there was no precedent for such permission and also because the request, he asserted, was not representative of Jewish opinion in the city. To determine the latter, he had asked Rabbi Jacobs as well as Magistrate Jacob Cohen, a member of Holy Blossom who, according to the chief, "thoroughly understands the Jewish feeling of the city, and he recommended that the permission not be granted in view of the fact that it was purely sectarian in its appeal and was of interest merely to the Jews." Although it is true that the extreme orthodox among the East Europeans probably disapproved of the request because it would have made the Jews too conspicuous, and perhaps also because the leaders of the movement were secularist socialists such as Maurice Goldstick, Henry Dworkin and Shimshon Koldofsky, a supporter of non-religious Jewish education, there was certainly enough interest to warrant the tag day. A mass meeting to protest the refusal attracted large numbers. But most significant was the resentment generated against Cohen and against Holy Blossom for daring to speak for all elements. Cohen, Goldstick complained, "has at no time received the endorsation of Jewish people to represent them . . . ."[3]

II

Within the East European community itself there was neither homogeneity nor harmony. The same forces which produced a supercilious attitude on the part of Holy Blossom manifested themselves among the East Europeans. Lithuanians and Galicians who came in the nineteenth century, for instance, tended to consider the latecoming Poles inferior, even after the latter constituted a majority of the Jewish population. This situation was aggravated by economic divisions. The earlier arrivals often became employers of the newcomers and it became common to equate ethnic background with economic position.

Coupled with developments in Toronto were parochial attitudes transported from Europe. The average Russian Jew, for example, had had little contact with Jews in Galicia or in Poland. Indeed, it was not unusual for a Jew from another province barely a hundred miles away to be considered with curiosity and even with suspicion, especially if he employed a different Yiddish dialect. Each group developed stereotypes of the other: Lithuanians were *tzeylem-kep*, skeptics, with a cold, unemotional approach to religion; Galicians were *greitzer*, stingy and hot-tempered; Russians were *kozak'n*, noisy and unkempt;

191

the Polish *dripkes* were slovenly and not to be trusted. Consequently, the immigrant generation established synagogues composed of their own *landsleit*, went into business partnership only with Jews from their localities in Europe and even discouraged marriage outside the ethnic group, frequently concocting religious prohibitions to justify the restriction. Admittedly, the Polish and the Galicians got on better with each other than either did with the Russians, but sharp divisions remained between these as well.

The dispute among the orthodox over educational practice was as much an extension of ethnic prejudice as a disagreement over pedagogic methods. In the rift between the orthodox and the secularists over education and over the attitude to religious life generally, ideology played an important role. The secularists, who were often class-conscious international socialists, did not divide on ethnic lines at all, and the doctrinaire among them formed an enclave within the East European community, refusing until the mid 1930s to participate in any communal activities. They were, however, neither numerous enough nor sufficiently militant to unite the orthodox in opposition to them. The relationship between the religious and the secularists was more mutual disdain than actual friction.

It was in the economic sphere that tension was greatest within the East European community. At first, however, it appeared that this would be the principal unifying issue. By 1911, a substantial segment of the Jewish population of the city was employed in the ready-made clothing factories. Indeed, 80 per cent of Eaton's twelve hundred factory workers were Jewish.[4] Local Jewish socialists such as Koldofsky and Abraham Kirzner had by this time been expounding the theory of unionism with little effect for almost a decade. Most immigrants were too happy to have employment, and thus hasten the process of transporting relatives, to be concerned about bargaining with their employers.

As early as 1907, however, a group of fourteen recently arrived Polish- and Russo-Jewish cloakmakers, "labour intellectuals" fresh from the revolution of 1905, organized themselves into an independent cloakmakers' union with the intention of tackling the employers. With the development of unionism in the garment trades in the United States, local advocates could draw upon organizers from New York, most of whom were Jewish and able to use the Yiddish language to attract supporters. Abraham Rosenberg, who arrived in Toronto in 1908 to organize a branch of the International Ladies' Garment Workers' Union, was

192

perhaps the most important of these, and he probably came unsolicited. By the fall of 1909 the local Cloakmakers' Union was an operating concern, although it still remained independent of American organizations despite overtures from union agents and suggestions that affiliation with the International or the Amalgamated would be in their best interests.*

First of the employers to be confronted was the Robert Simpson Company, which had adopted a policy of discharging union members. The union called a brief strike and succeeded in forcing Simpson's to recognize the organization. While other employers thus threatened did not transform their premises into union shops, they did at least compromise somewhat on working conditions. These successes, coupled with a feeling of solidarity with other workers generated during the New York garment workers' strike of 1910, caused large numbers to flock to the local union and imbued the organization with confidence. The enthusiasm of the strike now drew the local union into the International Ladies' Garment Workers' Union, the formal affiliation being completed in 1911, just in time for action against the largest single employer of Jews in Toronto, the T. Eaton Company.

Discontent in the Eaton shops had been brewing for several months and revolved around the company's demand that linings formerly sewn by hand were now to be prepared by machine. Eaton promised that no jobs would be lost, but the workers felt that they were entitled to more than a verbal guarantee. Then, in the spring of 1912, Eaton's began to insist that its tailors work overtime to prepare advance orders for the rush season, and when they refused, the company locked them out. The cloakmakers, already aroused over the linings issue and now affiliated with the ILGWU, walked out in sympathy, and the public was supplied with a long list of grievances, ranging from low wages and the acceptance of graft by management personnel to homework, unsanitary washrooms and child labour. Union advocates, both local and imported, succeeded in persuading the strikers that conditions could be ameliorated only through the introduction of a union at Eaton's, and this became the major issue of the strike.[5]

Eaton's adamantly refused to negotiate, despite the attempts of Rabbi Jacobs, Magistrate Cohen and even Mayor Geary to arrange a conference. The Jewish community was infuriated and the East Europeans, especially, immediately united in support of

---

* The Amalgamated Clothing Workers and the International Ladies' Garment Workers' Union were the major organizations in the clothing industry. Both were based in New York and, in this period, were dominated by Jews.

the workers. The newly formed Associated Hebrew Charities undertook to supply food to the families of Jewish strikers and, until the practice was forbidden by the city, Jewish women's organizations attempted street collections for them. Financial support came from local Jewish benefit societies and the parent union in New York.

Nevertheless, despite this show of strength, augmented by the decision of the ILGWU to hold its convention in Toronto to demonstrate sympathy for the strikers, the battle was lost after weeks of hardship and bitterness. The union was not admitted at Eaton's and workers were to be rehired only on the company's terms. The failure of the strike hampered the growth of unionism until renewed labour unrest emerged following the First World War. The strike also produced some damaging rifts in the Jewish community; there was hostility between those who refused to work and those who did not, and afterwards against workers who refused to join the union. Violence, even among Jews, erupted more frequently as the union became increasingly defensive.

It is essential to realize that although probably a majority of the strikers at Eaton's were Jewish, the strike did not acquire a specifically Jewish tone. The Toronto Trades and Labor Council, with whom, incidentally, the local Jewish socialists had long maintained contact, took up the issue as their own. This was a period of labour unrest generally, and not alone among the Jews. The Council sponsored a parade in solidarity with the strikers and a mass meeting at Massey Hall. Moreover, collections from the general public to provide funds for the strikers were most successful, an unlikely occurrence if the cause and image of the strikers had been a particularly foreign and Jewish one. James Simpson, a leader in the council and later mayor of Toronto, urged all races "to fight together with the Jew in the common cause."

In any case, the strike virtually destroyed the Eaton monopoly in the manufacturing of women's clothing. Groups of strikers set up their own rival shops and before long tension was growing between Jewish manufacturers and their employees over the same issue of unionization. This antipathy spread into the benefit societies and the synagogues, remaining latent in normal times but, during the next quarter-century, emerging full-blown whenever a strike hit the garment district. It was a division that at first was based upon ethnic group, but once Polish Jews themselves became entrepreneurs, the phenomenon evolved increasingly into one of division by class.

The Eaton strike also did not improve the East European opinion of Holy Blossom. Although Rabbi Jacobs did attempt to negotiate with the company, his sympathy lay with the workers as individuals and not with unions, and this reflected the sentiment of his congregation generally. Moreover, one of the principal managers at the Eaton factory was Sigmund Lubelsky, a member of Holy Blossom. While a number of Jewish foremen joined the workers on strike, he did not. Consequently, it was not difficult to brand the old community as hostile to the working class and unsympathetic to the lot of their fellow Jews.

If the patriotism of the war years kept unrest in the factories to a minimum, the domestic economic problems produced by the conflict gave rise to other tensions among the East European Jews of Toronto. The major one, perhaps, erupted in May 1917 and revolved around the Jewish bakers' decision to raise the price of a loaf of bread to 12 cents. When customers objected and refused to buy, they were merely told that they had better make their purchases immediately since the price would soon increase again.

A group of Jewish housewives then organized a committee to investigate the justification for the increase and discovered to their consternation that thirteen out of the fifteen Jewish bakeries in Toronto had pre-shortage agreements with mills to purchase flour below the current market price. Consequently, the women organized a boycott of the bakeries, visiting private households, groceries and restaurants, and demanding that no further business be done with the Jewish bakers until the prices came down. Women were encouraged to bake their own bread and the committee set up picket lines in front of bakeries, a practice which resulted in the temporary closing of all fifteen of them. There were breakings of windows, public meetings and altercations between picketers, the bakers and their prospective customers, both in the Ward and in the Spadina Avenue district.

As the women grew more impatient with the recalcitrance of the bakers, a group broke the front window and forced their way into Sherman's Bakery on Elizabeth Street with the intention of burning the flour, but were persuaded to retreat after one of them fainted in the excitement. In one establishment on Agnes Street, coal oil was actually poured over the bread on the counter, but perhaps the most important accomplishment of the protesters was to stop the delivery of bread. "The bakers say that the safety of their drivers was in danger," the *Telegram* reported, "and some were attacked by infuriated women, who pulled their hair and upset their bread baskets on the street." "Our drivers are afraid to go out," one baker complained. "One of them had the shirt torn off his back."

The bakers attempted to defend their position by maintaining that the boycott was not being carried on by the "better class of people" and insisted that since the poor would not be able to afford the cost of coal and flour to bake their own bread, the bakers were actually performing a service for them even at the 12-cent price. Consequently, they assured the public that the boycott would fail.

In truth, the respectability of the protesters was beyond doubt, as is evidenced by the fact that they met either in the Zionist Institute or at the McCaul Street Synagogue. Moreover, they considered violent action only out of desperation and constantly sought a legal solution by petitioning the federal government, through their public meetings, to appoint a food commissioner to regulate prices.

In the meantime, Jewish commercial establishments dependent upon bread were suffering. Some Jewish grocers started to bake their own and Goldenberg's restaurant purchased a supply of matzoth. The customers were apparently displeased with the unpalatable substitute and the proprietor was forced to buy bread surreptitiously. The protesters discovered the action, however, and one Saturday night, a hundred women stormed the premises and confiscated 120 loaves which were subsequently distributed to the poor. Goldenberg apparently continued to purchase bread and the following week several hundred protesters blocked the entrance to his restaurant, while fights broke out between opposing factions at Agnes and Elizabeth streets.

The bakers remained adamant, maintaining that they could not survive if the price were lowered. The protesters, on the other hand, attempted to persuade the non-Jewish public to strike against the Gentile bakers, but the latter's association sent funds to the Jewish bakers to encourage them to hold out. A meeting in the Elm Street Synagogue failed to achieve a settlement and the violence continued. When the Gentile bakers finally dropped their price to 9 cents a loaf, the frustrated Jewish boycotters insisted on an 8-cent price from their Jewish counterparts.

By the end of May the boycott had spread to the West Toronto Junction, where the women, again belying the claim that they were neither respectable nor representative, organized around the synagogue and volunteered to teach housewives to bake their own bread.

As economic conditions eased, however, prices were gradually lowered and the dispute subsided. In the field of baked goods, a price war produced a favourable situation for the consumer. But the bread strike of 1917 must have left considerable hostility and indicated that the potential for disunity within the Jewish community was very great indeed.[6]

III

The troubled opening decades of the twentieth century, however, were not devoid of forces working to bind the Jewish community into an organic whole; especially significant among these was the attitude of the children of the immigrants. Within the East European community parents attempted to imbue the younger generation with ethnic prejudice, but their offspring would have none of it. The native-born occasionally had prejudices of their own against the heavily-accented children who had come from Europe, but even this passed. Although synagogues and *landsmanshaften* divided ethnically, youth organizations did not and frequently the youth brought adult organizations closer together. For instance, the young people of Goel Tzedec and Chevra Tehillim got on well together even at the height of cool relations between the two congregations, and the pattern was strengthened after the children of the latter began to attend Sunday School and the youth club (later the Young People's League) at Goel Tzedec. By the First World War marriage between individuals of different ethnic groups was commonplace despite the objections of the older generation, and a principal meeting place came to be the charity ball of the Hebrew Ladies' Aid Society. There were even increased numbers of marriages involving East Europeans and members of Holy Blossom.[7]

By 1914 ethnic divisions were breaking down even among the parent generation. This was simply because each came to know the other through proximity and long acquaintance. Contact, however, was in some respects forced upon them by outside factors. The necessity of reacting to the pogroms in Kishinev and elsewhere, and to missionary activity in Toronto itself, drew East Europeans together and even brought them closer to Holy Blossom. Philanthropic efforts, too, culminating in the establishment of the Associated Hebrew Charities, served a similar unifying function.[8]

The closing of the gap among the various East European groups and between the new community and Holy Blossom was also accelerated by the quest for status. As economic conditions improved for some East Europeans with length of residence, these sought to solidify their new middle-class role within the Jewish community in some tangible way. For most in this position, the desire was expressed through synagogue buildings and membership.

First among the East Europeans to develop this syndrome in large numbers were the Russians and Lithuanians of the two senior congregations, Goel Tzedec and Chevra Tehillim. In 1905 Chevra Tehillim succeeded in purchasing the impressive New Richmond Methodist Church on McCaul Street and, having fitted it up, renamed themselves the Beth Hamidrash Hagodol, "The Great House of Study," and began to advertise for a professional cantor. Normally, this building would have been far beyond the financial reach of the congregation. However, the Methodists had miscalculated in their move to McCaul Street in the 1890s and now found themselves with few worshippers. Consequently, they were glad to release the structure for a fraction of its worth in order to move to a more favourable location. (Incidentally, Queen Victoria had held a mortgage on the church building and this was transferred to the synagogue, a fact which heightened the status of the congregation.)

Not to be outdone, Goel Tzedec decided to build a synagogue of its own, one which would serve as its own status symbol. In fact, plans were in the offing as early as 1896, the action being prompted not by the proposed move by Chevra Tehillim but rather by the drifting of some of Goel Tzedec's wealthier members into Holy Blossom, whose structure on Bond Street was considered the only synagogue of consequence in the city.

Holy Blossom held a number of attractions. Its services were Anglicized and ceremonious, in contrast to the relative disorder of the East European congregations. But most important, membership was indicative of social achievement and, as East European professionals and manufacturers became more affluent, they were drawn to Bond Street. Indeed, many who were appalled by the formality and the organ, and who hardly understood the English prayers, were persuaded by socially ambitious wives to join. This movement would eventually bring Holy Blossom closer to the East European community; by 1915 East Europeans or native-born Jews whose antecedents lay in the Ward constituted the majority at Bond Street.[9]

Goel Tzedec, however, saw nothing good in the movement. Consequently, they embarked upon an ambitious building project before they were financially prepared for it. The new synagogue, projected for University Avenue south of Agnes, was to be the showplace of the East European community. It was hoped that by thus attaching prestige to membership in Goel Tzedec, the

198

desertion to Holy Blossom could be halted. The commission for the new edifice went to W.L. Symons, who had been a designer in the firm of W.R. Strickland, architect of the Richmond Street Synagogue, and who now himself had a fashionable practice in the city. The congregation was so anxious for a landmark that they allowed him three years to study Jewish ritual and symbolism before submitting the final design, and the result was a spectacular structure seating twelve hundred people, far more than could be accommodated at Holy Blossom. The Norman design, which bore remarkable similarities to the Roman Catholic Cathedral of Westminster, reflected the symmetrical twin-tower design popular in the United States from about 1860 and which had already appeared in the Bond Street synagogue.[10]

The University Avenue Synagogue was dedicated in February 1907 with great aplomb and, while the new building appears to have attracted little notice in the city, Goel Tzedec considered its goal accomplished. The *Jewish Times* congratulated the Toronto community "on the proof of the prosperity shown by the erection of the synagogue that will befittingly impress members of other creeds with the dignity of our faith . . . ."

The interior is a picture of magnificence. Supported by great arches is a magnificent dome, and both are illuminated by electric lights . . .which add greatly to the effect of the stained glass panels of the dome. The ark and altar are illuminated by six huge brass heavers . . .each holding six electric lamps. The ark and altar cost nearly $2,500 . . . . The Goel Tzedec may be said to represent the most modern element of Toronto's Jewish population.[11]

The residents of the Ward gloated over the structure as a symbol of their own self-respect and proof that Holy Blossom was not the only synagogue worthy of public attention.

The new Goel Tzedec succeeded to a degree in slowing the flow to Bond Street, although that movement would never cease altogether. It also changed the character of the congregation from a Lithuanian to an ethnically mixed one. Now a synagogue was available which one could join to enhance one's social status without having to experience the "deitsch" (assimilated) atmosphere at Holy Blossom. As a result, the affluent and the second generation from all groups, especially the Galician and later the Polish, flocked to Goel Tzedec, often maintaining simultaneous membership in their old congregations. Consequently, by 1914 ethnic divisions were rapidly disappearing among the second generation of Toronto Jews and, among the adults, were being displaced increasingly by those based upon economics and ideology.[12]

IV

Zionism, however, was one ideology which fostered relative unity as early as the turn of the century, drawing together not only the generations and the various groups of East Europeans, but to a degree the recent arrivals and the old community as well. Indeed, it was Zionism which provided the first organizational link between Jewish communities across Canada. The birth of political Zionism at Basle in 1897 and the leadership of Theodor Herzl soon had their effect in this country, for within two years, Zionist groups would be active not only in Toronto but also in Montreal, Kingston, Ottawa, Hamilton and Winnipeg. And as pogroms increased in Russia early in the twentieth century, these were prompted to construct a formal national association, the Federation of Zionist Societies of Canada.

Zionism in Toronto blossomed early, within months of the historic Basle conference, emerging, as it did elsewhere in North America, among the East European immigrants. But although the process was well under way in the United States, it appears that Zionist ideas reached Toronto primarily through Montreal.

There was no formal transmission of ideology nor organizational direction from the latter. Influences were far more subtle and indeed frequently unwitting. Some Toronto families, the Samuel Lewises, for instance, became involved through relatives who had been inspired in Europe. Their mentor was a cousin who worked for a clothing manufacturer in Montreal and had stopped to visit his family in Toronto while on business for the firm in 1897. More often, it was Montreal Jewish manufacturers and textile importers, imbued with dreams of a Jewish state in Palestine, who transmitted their enthusiasm to Jewish friends in Toronto when they came to offer stock to local establishments. Their business acquaintances were as a rule not Jews, but while in the city they would attend the local synagogues, stay with families in the Ward and otherwise make contact with their co-religionists. Admittedly, those local families which had had the opportunity to read the New York *Tageblatt* were well acquainted with Zionism in the abstract since that paper was highly sympathetic to the movement, but the principal persuasive thrust came through personal contact via Montreal.[13]

While Zionism in the United States tended to be a second-generation phenomenon, in Toronto many of the immigrants themselves were drawn into the movement. Agudath Zion, the first Zionist society in the city, which Samuel Lewis and his son, Abe, organized in 1898, was composed overwhelmingly of Jews born in Eastern Europe. Toronto Zionism, moreover, was unusual in that all shades of religious opinion were represented. In most North American centres it was common for the long-established families, reformers of the German school and the adamantly orthodox to voice opposition to Zionism. In Toronto, on the other hand, Alfred Benjamin became president of the society and Mr. Levetus, an extreme reformer, was elected vice-president. Even Edmund Scheuer was a member in the early years. As for the orthodox, most of the East European members of Agudath Zion were traditionally observant. Granted, the bulk of the membership at Holy Blossom remained indifferent to Zionism and even those who were sympathetic were interested in its philanthropic rather than its political aspects. The congregation regularly collected funds for the support of Jewish colonists in Palestine.[14] It is true, also, that there were some among the extreme orthodox who preferred to postpone the return to the Holy Land until the arrival of the Messiah, to Zionism, which advocated immediate effort. However in total, Zionism drew to itself a variety of elements in Toronto and although beginnings were small and progress slow, the movement would be infused with new vitality with the increased immigration from Eastern Europe in the first decade of the twentieth century.

Agudath Zion met only sporadically because enthusiasm among the membership waned after the glow of the Zionist Congress had begun to dissipate. Consequently, more recent arrivals organized a second society, Bnai Zion, in 1903. Unlike Agudath Zion, the new group was a mutual benefit society, attracting large numbers of working-class Jews who probably knew little of Zionism prior to their affiliation. Another attraction was the fact that the group concentrated as much on social as on specifically religious or Zionistic activities.

Frequent geographic moves by an organization within a city may indicate another rapid growth or serious difficulties. In the case of Bnai Zion in its early years, the latter explanation certainly applies. The group apparently either did not wish to be associated with a synagogue or the religious organizations would not offer them accommodation. They met first, therefore, at Richmond Hall, then at the Labour Temple on Church Street, then for a brief time in the basement of Goel Tzedec at University and Elm and finally, in 1905, in a rented store on Elizabeth Street. Here it will be recalled, the Sewing School was offered space.

No. 16 Elizabeth Street was ambitiously foreseen by Bnai Zion as the Jewish community centre in the Ward. There were plans to set up a library, to produce plays, to hold English classes for immigrants and even to establish a *talmud torah*. Indeed, in 1905 a school with forty-five boys was actually set up. Lack of funds, however, forced its dissolution within six months. Financial difficulties were the major problem, but lack of enthusiasm in the city was another, a fact that Rabbi Gordon noted when he arrived in that year. Bnai Zion consequently had to relinquish the store and accept the invitation of Mr. Rogul, a member of the group, to meet in the living room of his house on Adelaide Street.[15]

A number of factors were to revive Zionism in Toronto and ensure its success as an agency of unification. The first was the enthusiasm of the young, a circumstance for which the ubiquitous Ida Siegel was in no small measure responsible. Her plan was to set up a social group for girls and indirectly to involve them in Jewish activities, among these the Zionism in which her father and brother were already engaged. The nucleus of the group was ten neighbourhood girls who formed what was to become the first women's Zionist organization in Canada, the Toronto Daughters of Zion (1899). Although initially most of the girls would have preferred a purely social group, she soon had them selling shares of the Jewish Colonial Trust door-to-door and collecting money for Jewish colonists in Palestine through the Jewish National Fund. An annual ball provided funds to rent a clubroom on Queen Street; both of these features drew larger numbers into the organization and the girls were eventually infused with Zionism.

For younger girls, many of whom already attended her sewing school, Ida Siegel formed a group called "Shomrai Shabbos," which met in her home on Saturday afternoons. After Theodor Herzl died in 1904, she persuaded the club to call themselves the Herzl Girls (1906) and to collect money for the Jewish National Fund. In 1905 her brother, Abe, together with Barnet Stone, organized a group of boys, the Zion Cadets, with the same anti-delinquency and anti-missionary purpose. Here, the attraction was not the dances but rather weekly drills and athletic activities at the University Avenue Armouries.[16]

The influx from Europe in 1905 after the events in Russia, altered the situation considerably and perhaps the European persecutions themselves prompted Jews already here to think more seriously of a Jewish homeland. From 1906 onward, prospects for Zionist activity in Toronto improved visibly, enhanced also by the decision to hold a convention of Canadian Zionists in the city. The event, which took place at the Labour Temple, was a great success. Local dignitaries such as Lieutenant-Governor Clark, Edmund Bristol, Member of Parliament for Centre Toronto and J.J. Foy, Attorney General of Ontario sent telegrams of support. Finally, Toronto was recognized within the movement by the election of Ida Siegel as vice-president of the federation.[17]

The convention spurred local Jews to action. The Zionist youth groups under Ida Siegel became especially active, while donations to the Shekel Fund (Jewish National Fund) and purchases of Colonial Trust shares soared. Funds were collected even at weddings and at other family celebrations. A women's Zionist society, B'noth Zion Kadimah, was formed, while a group of teenaged boys who had set up the Toronto Jewish Social and Literary Club were inspired by the convention to become the Zion Literary Club.

Increasingly, prominent Zionists from Montreal and from the United States accepted invitations to speak in Toronto, thereby reinforcing local efforts. An indication of the new enthusiasm which had been generated was the mass meeting which local Zionists called at the new Goel Tzedec synagogue in the spring of 1907. "So great was the crowd," the *Jewish Times* reported, "that hundreds had to be turned from the doors, and standing room was at a premium." Bnai Zion increased to such an extent that it would eventually absorb the old Agudath Zion, while such a host of Zionist societies, catering to various age groups, sprung up in the city that a Local Central Council (later called the Toronto Zionist Council) had to be formed to promote united action.[18]

Local rabbis encouraged the movement as well. Rabbi Weinreb had, immediately upon his arrival, advised the Agudath Zion on the conducting of their activities, despite the fact that some of the most vehement opposition to Zionism came from the ultra-conservatives in the Galician community. By 1907 he and Rabbi Gordon had joined with a number of laymen, including Ben-Zion Nathanson, principal-elect of the Talmud Torah, and Paul Levi, a prominent member of Goel Tzedec, to form a chapter of Mizrachi, an organization advocating orthodoxy and Zionism. Even Rabbi Jacobs, who had in a sermon once equated Zionism with socialism and anarchism, appeared at a Zionist meeting in 1908 and declared himself in sympathy with the movement. By that time Zionism in Toronto was prospering financially and had a growing membership which cut across ethnic and religious lines. Now at last, the Zionists were able to acquire their own building on

Simcoe Street. Named the Zionist Institute, the building, originally a residence, was fitted up with meeting rooms, a library of Hebrew and Zionist literature and a small gymnasium. Plans to erect a new assembly hall behind the house and a bowling alley in the basement never materialized. "The painting, fitting-up and decorating of the building was done entirely by Jewish workmen, in conformity with the Zionist principle of encouraging the training of skilled artisans among the Jewish people."[19]

It should not be assumed, however, that all elements in the city rallied to the Zionist cause after the convention. While orthodox opposition waned as a result of the support of rabbis Gordon and Weinreb and the growing enthusiasm of the younger generation, Holy Blossom for the most part remained indifferent and its offshoot, the Council of Jewish Women, was unequivocally hostile. Indeed, among those who considered themselves the elite of Jewish society in Toronto, to be a Zionist was to be considered slightly disloyal to Canada, an insinuation seldom heard from the non-Jewish community. The majority at Holy Blossom, however, ignored the political aspects of Zionism and, while remaining officially aloof, saw the movement as important on the local scene as a counterforce to the missions. This was probably Rabbi Jacobs' motive in supporting Zionism. Consequently, Holy Blossom never officially condemned the movement.

Vocal condemnation in the first decade of the twentieth century came from the doctrinaire workers' organizations, Bundists and communists, who considered Zionism chauvinistic. But here, too, opposition was muted as the missions arose and, with the founding of a secular pro-Zionist organization, the Jewish National Workers' Alliance (Farband, later Poalei Zion) about 1914, increased numbers deserted the internationalists.

The Balfour Declaration of 1917 assured the legitimacy of the Zionist movement, but for large numbers of Toronto Jews no such assurance was necessary. Between 1910 and 1913, Zionist youth groups proliferated; indeed, by the latter year the Simcoe Street building could no longer accommodate them all. Unable to come to an agreement with the YMHA over the erection of a community centre and hampered by the economic difficulties of the period, the Zionists purchased a house at Beverley and Cecil streets, which itself became immediately overcrowded. During the First World War, the trend continued: a local branch of the Jewish Legion grew out of the Herzl Zion Club formed in 1911; a Toronto chapter of Hadassah, founded in 1916, soon absorbed B'noth Zion Kadimah; other societies emerged to attract English-speaking Jews, high school and university students, among them the

Nordau Zion Club, Herzl Zion Club, Beaconsfield Club, the Queen Esther Cadets and later Young Judaea. The position of the British government in 1917 was indeed good news in the long term, but for the Jews of Toronto, it was especially significant because it assured the continuation of an immediate consolidating trend within their own community, a reinforcement of common ground upon which all could stand. Zionists did not agree on all issues. Secularist and religious Zionists formed the two major disparate groups. Revisionists formed a third. However, their relationship, even in disagreement, was not hostile; they could co-operate when the necessity arose.

NOTES

1 Personal interviews: Ida Siegel, Feb. 3, 1972; John J. Glass, Dec. 3, 1972. For example, Holy Blossom refused to participate in an East European movement to purchase a hearse for Jewish burials (*HBM*, Feb. 16, 1902).

2 *Star*, Jan. 1, 1916.

3 *Star*, July 21, 1915.

4 Sam Kraisman, "Half Century of Progress, Growth and Achievement" in Toronto Joint Board Cloakmakers' Union ILGWU, *Souvenir Journal: Golden Jubilee* (Toronto, 1961), p. 7.

5 Leaflet in Eaton Company History Scrapbook of Newspaper Clippings, 1900-1912, p. 234 (T. Eaton Co. Archives); *World*, March 21, 1912. Other complaints included the elimination of the Saturday half-holiday in the busy season, and the absence of lockers, so that wraps had to be thrown together with a resulting spread of disease. The strikers also claimed that when workers applied for jobs, they were required to reveal how much rent they paid, how much their clothing cost and their cost of living generally. This, it was charged, was to enable Eaton's to keep wages as low as possible (*World*, March 25, 1912).

6 *Star*, May 25, 28, 29, 30, 31, 1917; *Telegram*, May 25, 1917. See also *Star*, Feb. 1919, *passim* and especially Feb. 15, 1919, "West Toronto" section.

7 Personal interviews: Ida Siegel, Aug. 12, Oct. 28, Dec. 23, 1971; J.J. Glass, Dec. 13, 1972; Mrs. H. Salb, Dec. 28, 1972.

8 See Clippings from Toronto *World*, undated, in Anglo-Jewish Association file, Canadian Jewish Congress Archives, Montreal.

9 At least one member of Goel Tzedec, whose wife wanted to attend Holy Blossom, bribed her with an expensive gift so that he could remain a member of his old synagogue. (Confidential interview.)

10 The Bond Street synagogue, designed by John W. Siddall, was the first in the city to introduce twin towers capped by domes, and although many of the Moorish details appear to have been inspired specifically by Temple Beth El in New York City, the twin tower motif reflected universally popular preference. The use of twin towers and domes by both Holy Blossom and Goel Tzedec would influence a series of synagogue structures which were to be erected in the 1920s and 1930s by less prestigious congregations.

11 *Jewish Times*, May 18, 1906, p. 209; Feb. 8, 1907, p. 82.

12 So many members of other congregations descended upon Goel Tzedec that the synagogue had to suspend its by-law which provided that any member who belonged to another congregation could not hold office. Here, as was the case with the movement to Holy Blossom, socially ambitious women exerted pressure on their husbands to join Goel Tzedec. This was perhaps indicative of North American influence on the community; in Europe, wives could seldom have directed their husbands in religious matters. This contention is supported by W. Lloyd Warner, who maintains that in North America women tend to be more class-conscious than men (W.L. Warner, *Social Class in America* [Chicago: Science Research Associates, 1949], p. 88). Marriage also drew Polish and Galician Jews into Goel Tzedec.

13 Ida Siegel, personal interviews: July 29, Oct. 7, 1971; *Yiddishes Tageblatt* (*The Jewish Daily News*), Dec. 28, 30, 1897.

14 The congregation was not actually hostile to Agudath Zion although most members did not join; they granted the society free use of a schoolroom in the Bond Street synagogue for meetings, provided "that there...be no smoking and no damages to furniture" (*HBM*, May 7, 1899). The attitude at

Holy Blossom was perhaps best expressed by Leo Frankel, then president of the congregation, in an address to the 11th [Canadian] Zionist Convention held in Toronto in 1910. Although he believed "that there was already a Zion in England and in the United States, and certainly that there was a Zion in Canada," he nevertheless considered "any movement for the benefit of mankind" to be worthy of support (*Jewish Times*, Dec. 30, 1910, p. 6).

15 Louis Rasminsky, ed., *Hadassah Jubilee* (Toronto, 1927), pp. 105 ff.; Rabbi Jacob Gordon, "Reminiscences of a Toronto Rabbi," *Kanader Adler*, 25th Anniversary Issue.

16 Ida Siegel, personal interviews. Typescript resume of Zionist beginnings in Toronto (5 pp., n.d., copy in the author's possession); Rasminsky, *op.cit.*, p. 98; *Jewish Times*, July 26, 1907, p. 287. About 1903 a mixed group of young adults called Ahavath Zion, "Love of Zion," was formed, but this dissolved within six months because, as Samuel Lewis put it, there was too much "love" and not enough "Zion."

17 *Jewish Times*, July 13, 1906, p. 279. A large number of prominent non-Jews attended the convention. Even Wilfrid Laurier expressed sympathy for the movement (Laurier to C.I. de Sola, Dec. 11, 1905, Laurier Papers, Public Archives of Canada).

18 Among the constituent organizations were Bnai Zion, Toronto Daughters of Zion, B'noth Zion Kadimah, the Young Men's Zion Club and the Zion Literary Society. Joint action was principally in the field of campaigns for membership and the dissemination of Zionist literature. The individual societies remained autonomous (*Jewish Times*, Jan. 10, 1913, p. 37). Actually, a Zionist Council had been formed as early as 1904, but it appears to have existed only nominally (*Jewish Times*, Aug. 12, 1904, p. 303).

19 *Jewish Times*, March 7, 1908, pp. 114-117.

PART III

THE COMMUNITY MATURES

CHAPTER 13

INSTITUTIONAL CHANGE AND THE EROSION OF TRADITIONAL PRACTICE, 1900 – 1937

Religious liberalism tends to appear among Jews whenever a Jewish middle class can expect to be accepted by the middle class of the community at large merely by conforming to the mores of the general population. This was true in Germany, where reform Judaism first came into prominence, and in England, where middle-class orthodoxy was modified considerably. This situation was not possible in Eastern Europe where there was either no Jewish middle class or the general middle class was so anti-semitic that there was no hope of acceptance. Moreover, official anti-semitism tended to transform East European Jews into a proletariat. Consequently, religious modifications there took the form of socialism, anarchism and Zionism. In North America, the Jews who arrived in the nineteenth century, even many of those from Eastern Europe, were quick to achieve middle-class status. Their desire for acceptance by the Gentile community, and by their own children who considered North American behaviour the norm, had religious repercussions here as well. Although there were exceptions, as a rule the wealthier one became the greater was the tendency to digress from tradition in one's daily life and to press for the adoption of more "acceptable" practices in the synagogue.

Another factor that appears to have operated in this process was the individual's symbolic placement, as opposed to his economic status, in the community. The long-established families were accorded high status automatically, but the *nouveaux riches* had to aspire to that degree of respectability not only through length of residence but also through participation in status-enhancing communal and philanthropic activities. In the case of

Jews, this also entailed belonging to the status-enhancing synagogue, which had achieved that position through its ability to "impress members of other creeds with the dignity of our faith . . . ."[1]

All congregations in Toronto, except the most reactionary, must have been affected by this syndrome to a degree. The majority altered their behaviour very little, perhaps because those who might have demanded change left for the more liberal synagogues. Most susceptible to the phenomenon of seeking status through acculturation were the oldest and wealthiest synagogues, Holy Blossom and Goel Tzedec. As was the case with similar congregations throughout the continent, it was here that departure from tradition in the synagogue service was most evident.

By the time Rabbi Jacobs arrived at Holy Blossom in 1901, alteration in the service on the English model was well under way: the regular English sermon had been introduced, voluntary offerings had been severely restricted and, in general, steps had been taken to ensure decorum.[2] But aside from the installation of an organ, few changes after the pattern of German and American reform had appeared. By that year, however, many of the traditionalists in the congregation were passing from the scene, either through death or movement into the more traditional East European synagogues, and Scheuer's faction was pushing inexorably into the forefront.

The influx of status-seeking East Europeans complicated this trend. The second generation, who gravitated to Holy Blossom in revolt against the traditionalism of the Ward, augmented Scheuer's forces; on the other hand, the refugees from Goel Tzedec, Chevra Tehillim and Shomrai Shabboth could not divorce themselves easily from the service to which they had been accustomed. These rallied to the traditionalist wing at Bond Street.

It was a beleaguered Rabbi Jacobs who had to keep the balance between the two factions, for the reformers lost no time in demanding changes to suit the new century and to draw back to the synagogue a religiously indifferent old community. Jacobs, himself a traditionalist, attempted to achieve this purpose without a radical assault on tradition by offering compromise measures during the first years of his tenure. At the Yom Kippur services in 1902, he read a portion of the prayers in English and, during the previous Hanukkah, he had allowed men and women to sit together in the synagogue for this occasion only. He also permitted the choir to sing occasionally in English and agreed to close services with a formal benediction from the pulpit. The ritual committee of the congregation, however, now dominated by the reformers, was by no means satisfied; they confronted the rabbi with a barrage of proposals for what they considered improvements, most of them in line with developments in the United States.

The most radical of these was the demand for the seating of the sexes together during the services and the abolition of the requirement that men cover their heads at prayer. In Europe such practices were rare even among the most liberal congregations; only among reform synagogues in the United States, where the attempt at conformity to Protestant usage was especially strong, had these changes become commonplace. For the time being, the traditionalists were able to vote down the motion, but only by a slim majority and after the entire membership had been called to discuss the matter; the margin became narrower each time the issue was raised. Despite the fact that the revised bylaws of the synagogue repeated in 1904 the condition, in force for over thirty years, that services would be conducted in accordance with the orthodox *minhag*, the reformers continued to press for changes, while the traditionalists had to be satisfied with compromise. For instance, in 1903 the ritual committee managed to pass proposals that the traditional Sabbath Eve service at sunset Fridays be replaced by a late service which would not follow the order of the Prayer Book. They urged further that references to angels and sacrifices be omitted, that three instead of eight people be called to the reading of the Torah on Sabbath mornings, and that the organ be used even on Yom Kippur.*

The traditionalists seem to have remained indifferent until the following year, when Scheuer urged that mixed seating be introduced at the late Friday services. They were willing to compromise on the issue since the orthodox would not attend these services in any case, but they demanded their price. In return for "family pews" at the late services, the orthodox sunset service was reinstated, the organ was not to be played on Yom Kippur and the traditional number of worshippers were once again to be honoured during the Sabbath morning Torah reading.

---

* The moderates seem to have lacked leadership after Benjamin's death. Since Rabbi Jacobs was a traditionalist, they should have been able to rally around him. The rabbi, however, was unpopular with a large number of members, so much so that when his contract expired he was re-engaged only on a monthly basis. It is probable that the difficulty lay in matters apart from the issue of reform. Otherwise, one side or the other would have made use of him in the dispute.

Between 1904 and 1906, increased numbers of traditionalist members resigned and appeared in Goel Tzedec, probably alienated by the friction at Holy Blossom and certainly attracted by the rising new University Avenue synagogue. By 1906 so few of the practising orthodox remained that the traditional Friday evening services, a barometer of those who closed their businesses on the Sabbath and those who boycotted the reform late services, had to be discontinued. Granted, those left were still vocal enough to prevent the playing of the organ on Yom Kippur and there remained even some critics of the mixed choir which, by 1909, had become a common feature at Bond Street. However, Scheuer's supporters were gaining ground. By 1912 reforms were being approved by large majorities and only the old four-fifths clause, which had been written into the letters of incorporation of the synagogue, was inhibiting the host of radical changes being advocated by the trustees. Scheuer now prepared to persuade the provincial legislature to invalidate the provision.

The minutes of the congregation for the first decade of the twentieth century provide little specific detail of the role played by Rabbi Jacobs in blocking such changes, and the synagogue records between 1912 and 1920 have been lost. It is evident, however, that as long as Jacobs remained at Holy Blossom, wholesale rejection of orthodoxy was impossible. Although he was obviously willing to tolerate concessions to the liberals, by 1911 he was considered the leader of the traditional element, at least by the reformers. So unpopular had he become that they attempted several times to oust him, ostensibly on grounds that he was a poor speaker, unable to attract large Sabbath attendance, but actually in the hope of replacing him with someone more amenable to reform. Each time, however, enough moderates, and others with non-religious motives, were able to assure his continued tenure.[3]

By 1912, the dispute over religious liberalism was being debated openly in the Jewish press. The *Times*, speaking as usual for the acculturated but traditional English element and always eager to give advice to Toronto, stated categorically that "Holy Blossom synagogue is not a Reform Temple but an Orthodox house of worship . . . ." and urged that the laymen of the congregation accept the guidance of Rabbi Jacobs and not "flirt with reform customs." The editor deplored the fact that Jacobs had to dance to the tune whistled by the trustees.[4]

Rabbi Jacobs, always the diplomat, refused to give his own views on the proposed innovations, but there can be little doubt as to his position. Scheuer's petition to the province for the elimination of the four-fifths clause was probably unsuccessful

214

because Jacobs refused to support it; the authorities would not likely have interfered with the operation of a religious institution against the wishes of its minister.

But the best foundation for the contention that Jacobs almost single-handedly blocked reform is the rapidity with which Holy Blossom attached itself to the reform movement in the United States following the rabbi's death in 1920. No longer did the congregation look to England for guidance, nor make a pretence at seeking an acculturated orthodox minister as had been the case ten years earlier. The reformers, now clearly in the ascendancy, secured the appointment of a graduate of Hebrew Union College, Isaac Mayer Wise's seminary of Cincinnati.

Rabbi Barnett R. Brickner was a reformer, but not a doctrinaire one. His own background was traditional and he was sensitive to the value of established custom. He was prepared, therefore, to continue the practical policy of modified orthodoxy if the congregation wished it.[5]

Before long, however, the rabbi realized that the majority of his flock were amenable to more fundamental changes in ritual and orientation. This was not to be achieved without opposition, but the traditionalists were now far outnumbered and after some tactful politicking, Brickner secured the four-fifths majority necessary to introduce the American reform *Union Prayer Book* at Sabbath services in the spring of 1921 and for Holy Blossom to affiliate with the association of reform synagogues in the United States, the Union of American Hebrew Congregations. Under his direction, the congregation gradually exchanged its English connections for American ones, and the erosion of orthodoxy now began in earnest. In line with American reform, the wearing of the tallith was made optional and mixed seating was approved. By 1924 the assault on tradition was virtually completed with the introduction of the reform prayer book on the High Holy Days. The *Star* could now describe the "Brickner Jews" as being "rather like the Maitland Street Quakers, in that they have discarded some of the rigidities of former times."[6]

By the time Brickner left Holy Blossom in 1925, the congregation had adopted the practice of American reform except for a single custom, the requirement that men cover their heads. The least suggestion that this be eliminated brought heated opposition even from some ardent reformers, and Rabbi Brickner, who had no desire to introduce reforms merely to spite the traditionalists, did not press the issue.

For a brief time after Brickner's resignation, the congregation again considered seeking an English rabbi, an indication that

American reform was not yet entrenched. The reformers, however, were in the majority and the pattern was established of securing rabbinical leadership from Hebrew Union College. Rabbi Ferdinand Isserman, who served between 1925 and 1929, was prepared to hold the line where his predecessor had left off. While he endeavoured to cement the relationship between Holy Blossom and Hebrew Union College, he was nevertheless hesitant about introducing further reforms himself. The radical element at Bond Street, however, was not to be deterred and continued to agitate for the removal of hats and abolition of the four-fifths provision regarding ritual changes.[7]

For the most part, they were unsuccessful. But the reformers did initiate one more departure from tradition, the holding of a major service on Sunday mornings. During Brickner's tenure, the late Friday evening services had been well attended, but a good 40 per cent of the regular congregants were not members of the congregation while a significant number of non-Jews were also attracted, drawn by the rabbi's eloquence. By the time Rabbi Isserman arrived, most of those members of Holy Blossom who attended any services at all were women.

A similar phenomenon had long been evident in liberal congregations in the United States where, in an attempt to attract the male membership who worked on Saturday, the Sabbath morning service was suspended and replaced by a major assembly on Sunday. Holy Blossom was still too traditional to abolish Saturday prayer, but in 1927, a formal Sunday morning service with choir and sermon was instituted to replace that of Friday evening.

The reformers were undoubtedly pleased since at this service the wearing of hats was made optional, a ruling which drew little criticism from the traditionalists who continued to attend on Saturdays and did not consider the Sunday assembly a genuine service. The Sunday service attracted large numbers, but it did not fulfil its function, since frequently the majority in attendance were not Jewish. Eventually it was discontinued.

By the end of the decade orthodoxy was effectively dead at Holy Blossom; only its symbol, the yarmulke (skull-cap), remained. While both Brickner and Isserman were able to tolerate it, and perhaps even favoured its continued use, their successor, Rabbi Maurice N. Eisendrath, could not.[8] Arriving in 1929, Eisendrath, at twenty-seven, was imbued with the spirit of change. Typical of the reform rabbinic graduates of the period, he stressed the rationalistic, ethical and universal aspect of Judaism. His only dogma was that traditional ritual was a bane to the modern Jew and must be discarded.

Eisendrath found his new synagogue an anomaly. His experience with reform congregations in Chicago and Cincinnati had not prepared him for a city in which reform Jews were in a minority, in which the most liberal congregation, his own, still prayed with covered heads, and in which a few of the members still observed the dietary laws and were uncomfortable with the mixed choir and abridged service. In the trend of North American reform, he felt, Holy Blossom was nothing less than reactionary.

By 1929, marriages between members of Holy Blossom and the rest of the Jewish community were commonplace; it will be recalled that East Europeans now constituted the majority at Bond Street. At such ceremonies, both a traditional rabbi and the rabbi of Holy Blossom would officiate, and Eisendrath was appalled by the insistence of the orthodox family that he and his congregants cover their heads. He resolved, therefore, to eliminate the practice at his own synagogue, this to be done not by four-fifths majority, but rather by *fait accompli*.

Just prior to the High Holy Days in 1929, Eisendrath called a congregational meeting to discuss the issue of making the head-covering optional. Those who appeared were primarily the old families who were most sympathetic to reform, and, despite an attempt by one traditionalist present to filibuster until he could rally more of his supporters, the question was decided by the rabbi's argument that each member must be allowed to follow his own conscience. It was a close victory, but a victory nonetheless.

On the eve of Rosh Hashana, a minority of worshippers left their hats at home. Even these, however, were astonished when Eisendrath, himself, appeared bareheaded; few had conceived that the option should apply to the rabbi as well. "A thousand gasps, gathering into bursts of whispers spread through the congregation," Eisendrath recalled, "and exploded across the pews like a clap of long-delayed thunder." After the service, some of the members almost came to blows in the lobby over the issue, but the majority was apparently content with the situation, after the initial shock had passed. The next morning, half the congregation did not don their skull-caps and over the next few months the number of those who covered their heads dwindled to a handful.[9]

II

Changes at Goel Tzedec were less radical, but they were prompted by at least one factor similar to that operating at Holy Blossom

– the presence of young, increasingly affluent and socially mobile individuals who desired to make the synagogue a symbol of status. It is significant, however, that in contrast to the situation at Bond Street, the advocates of change at Goel Tzedec were influenced as much by developments in Montreal as by those in the United States, and that they had strong loyalties to their ethnic group as well as to the traditional ritual. Consequently, while Holy Blossom drifted into the camp of the radicals at Cincinnati, Goel Tzedec followed the lead of many of the older orthodox congregations on the continent by attaching itself to the Jewish Theological Seminary of America and to what would develop into the Conservative Movement.

It is essential to understand the development and position of the Jewish Theological Seminary if the subtle changes at Goel Tzedec are to be placed in proper prospective. The Seminary had been founded in the 1880s in opposition to the radicalism of the American reformers, and as an institution for the training of Americanized orthodox rabbis. Its leadership represented the older Jewish settlers, heavily influenced by the Sephardim who looked to England and Holland, and by Germans who, although they remained traditional, had often been trained in secular universities and consequently "tended to translate their concepts of Judaism into the idioms of modern culture."[10] Like Jews' College, London, and the modern rabbinical seminaries at Berlin and Breslau, the Seminary, which combined the teaching of secular and religious knowledge, became the rallying point for the native-born and acculturated traditionalists in its early years, but unfortunately it was chronically short of funds. By 1902 many of the older leaders had died and the institution's financial difficulties had necessitated a reorganization, accompanied by the injection of large sums of money by old German-Jewish reform families in New York and Philadelphia, who wanted a rabbinical school which could produce English-speaking orthodox rabbis to act as agents of acculturation for the masses beginning to arrive from Eastern Europe.

The Jewish Theological Seminary might have achieved this had the institution remained unequivocally orthodox. However, the reorganization included an invitation to Dr. Solomon Schechter of Cambridge to assume the leadership of the school. As a result, the Seminary became a paradox; that is, a school emphasizing loyalty to traditional religious practice but at the same time advocating critical examination of the sacred texts to determine the historical development of law and ritual, an implied denial of the orthodox position that the complete corpus of Jewish law had been transmitted through Moses on Mount Sinai.

Schechter's stand on textual criticism was the major factor encouraging East European immigrants to set up their own rabbinical school, the Rabbi Isaac Elchanan Theological Seminary (RIETS), to draw some of the native orthodox away from the Jewish Theological Seminary and to brand the older institution as an instrument of reform. The Jewish Theological Seminary, on the other hand, continued to maintain that it had remained essentially orthodox and that only this scientific orthodoxy, coupled with its practice of producing acculturated rabbis, would ensure the survival of traditional Judaism in North America.

Once the new University Avenue Synagogue had been completed, its proponents began to struggle with the problem which had beset synagogues of similar age, size and stage of acculturation across the continent. If the congregation were to have status enough to inhibit the flow of the wealthy into Holy Blossom and to attract the younger generation back to the synagogue, more than an impressive building was necessary. The latter would appear merely an expression of conspicuous bourgeois consumption if it were not accompanied by changes in the atmosphere of worship appropriate to the dignity of the new sanctuary and worthy of an acculturated middle class. To the layman, the Jewish Theological Seminary and Conservative Judaism connoted not scholarly traditionalism and cautious radicalism, but rather respectably Americanized and decorous orthodoxy, precisely the element considered essential for the successful development of Goel Tzedec.

The Seminary had a number of attractive features which, in addition to the projected image of refinement, operated to draw Goel Tzedec closer to its circle. For one thing, it was still not considered anathema even by the immigrant orthodox. Indeed, as late as 1926 there was an attempt to merge the pristinely orthodox Rabbi Isaac Elchanan Yeshiva with it, and indications are that the failure of the effort was not due to the greater or lesser orthodoxy of the Seminary. Even the most committed traditionalists in Toronto raised no objection when their sons chose to study for the rabbinate at that institution.

The second popular element was Schechter's program for an American Judaism: regular English sermons, decorum at services and the use of modern pedagogic methods in Jewish education, with the Seminary as a resource centre to assist individual congregations. Unlike either organized American reform or immigrant orthodoxy, where the laity was dominant and communication with constituent synagogues was weak, the Seminary under Schechter strove to be a directing force, an important attribute for congregations seeking assistance in curriculum planning and the acquisition of textbooks, in publicity to attract new members, in the organization of youth work, men's clubs and women's auxiliaries – all to stem the tide of reform and religious indifference. Some members of Goel Tzedec, while in the United States on business or to visit relatives, had already been impressed by Schechter's reputation and had seen his influence at work in congregations there. Those involved in educational efforts and youth activity at University Avenue, including Abe Lewis and Ida Siegel, wrote often to him for advice.

A third attraction was the character of the Seminary graduates. The supporters of the Jewish Theological Seminary believed in "the inevitability of the occidentalization of the Jew, seeing in the culture of the enlightenment and in modern citizenship affirmative values for Jews and Judaism."[11] In the early twentieth century, the Seminary produced young rabbis equipped to adhere to tradition and, at the same time (since without exception they were American college graduates) ready to assist the integration of their congregants into North American life.

Toronto Jewry had the opportunity of observing just such an individual in the person of Rabbi Herman Abramowitz, minister of Shaar Hashomayim Congregation in Montreal. Like Goel Tzedec in Toronto, Shaar Hashomayim was the senior orthodox congregation in the city; it was older and its membership considerably more affluent than its Toronto counterpart, and by the turn of the century it had reached the stage of insisting upon middle-class dignity at its services. Perhaps the principal manifestation of this development was the choice of Abramowitz, a graduate of the Jewish Theological Seminary, as its rabbi about 1902.

Relations between the two synagogues were close and cordial. For one thing, the Montreal congregation contributed financially toward the erection of the University Avenue Synagogue; but more important was the role played by Rabbi Abramowitz. Prior to the arrival of Rabbi Gordon, and even afterwards, he was a frequent visitor to Goel Tzedec, speaking about Zionism and education, and perhaps performing the occasional wedding as well. Indeed, on many ceremonial occasions which required an English orator, it was Abramowitz who was invited, and he probably had several opportunities to expound the advantages of

Conservative Judaism. For instance, while in Toronto for the laying of the cornerstone for the new synagogue, he addressed a joint Sabbath service of Goel Tzedec and Chevra Tehillim at McCaul Street. "He pointed out that the strength of Conservative Judaism lay in the fact that it meets the religious wants of old and young alike and is capable of harmonising and uniting all the elements in Jewry. He quoted copiously from rabbinnic [sic] authorities to prove that true orthodoxy meant order, refinement and decorum," and he urged parents to provide their children with "a beautiful service and an enlightened Judaism."[12]

The precise influence of each of these factors on Goel Tzedec is difficult to ascertain. Certainly, the opening of the University Avenue Synagogue brought no sweeping changes in the ritual. Once it became obvious that the new building alone had not succeeded in attracting large numbers of congregants, the status-seeking element and the small group of progressives genuinely concerned with moderate change as a vehicle for making orthodoxy workable in North America, began increasingly to press for improvement. For the most part this group, composed primarily of members under forty years of age, advocated no radical departure from the traditional ritual or ideology. They demanded only increased decorum and the appointment of an English-speaking rabbi who would preach regularly, attract the native-born generation and be an acceptable representative of the congregation in the community at large. Rabbi Gordon did not preach each Sabbath and, despite the fact that he spoke English well, refused to use it in the pulpit.

Rabbi Gordon's attitude was not mere recalcitrance; it was a response to the altered role of the rabbi in North America. This was considerably different from the traditional one and it presented a difficulty for European rabbis who came to serve acculturated orthodox congregations in Canada and the United States. In Europe, the rabbi had been appointed by the community as a whole, as their interpreter of Torah and arbiter of religious questions. Consequently, he possessed a kind of transcendent authority. In North America, on the contrary, since few cities had centralized Jewish communal organizations, the importance of the individual synagogue was enhanced considerably. The rabbi was hired by a particular congregation and was expected to conform to their wishes. Moreover, the rabbi now had to assume the roles of preacher and pastor, functions for which European-trained rabbis were usually unprepared and tended to avoid. Graduates of the American rabbinical schools, on the other hand, were trained to be comfortable in the pastoral role.* Throughout the first decade of the twentieth century, the progressives at Goel Tzedec agitated in vain for an English-speaking rabbi, but the congregation seemed more concerned with engaging a virtuoso cantor. However, the demand appeared more rational, even to a minority of the older members, as the alienation of the native-born generation became more evident. By 1911 the progressives had the support of two officers of the congregation, Isaac Brodey and Elias Pullan, and through their intervention the trustees were persuaded to invite Eugene Kohn, a rabbinical student in his final year at the Jewish Theological Seminary, to preach during the High Holy Days. Apparently the trustees agreed reluctantly and only on condition that the group who wanted Kohn, not the congregation, pay his fee.

The ultra-traditionalists, who still constituted a majority, saw Kohn as the first wedge of reform and received him as an enemy. Many refused to house him and one member threatened to obtain an injunction to prevent his speaking in English. Then, when he did rise to preach on the first day of the holiday, he was drowned out by the thunderous pounding heels of the ultras.

After the initial shock had subsided, the Holy Days passed without further incident and the congregation grew accustomed to having an English preacher each year. The acculturated group now began to demand the engagement of an English-speaking rabbi on a permanent basis and at the expense of the congregation. Years of delay brought no results, for even after the idea was approved, action was constantly postponed. Finally, late in 1913, perhaps in response to the need to combat the missionaries, the congregation appointed Dr. Julius Price, a graduate of the Seminary.[13]

Price was not enthusiastic about coming to Toronto. The reception given Kohn was common knowledge in New York and Price was more interested in scholarly research than in a pulpit. His teachers at the Seminary, however, felt that he could do for Goel Tzedec what Abramowitz had done in Montreal and this argument, together with a promise of financial support from some of the wealthier members of the congregation, persuaded him to accept the call.

---

* In Europe, orthodox rabbis would preach formally in the synagogue only twice a year, on the Sabbath before Passover and on that prior to Yom Kippur. The extreme conservatives in the orthodox rabbinate observe the practice to this day. The weekly Sabbath sermon in the vernacular was introduced by nineteenth-century German reformers in an effort to make the services meaningful to congregants who did not understand the Hebrew prayers. It is now common in most North American synagogues.

The ultras at Goel Tzedec greeted him with little more amiability than that with which they had received Kohn. Whenever he began to speak, they would march conspicuously out of the synagogue and return at the conclusion of the sermon. They soon discovered that Price was preaching no heresy and so the exodus gradually came to an end, but they continued to resent his presence as a possible threat to orthodoxy and an infringement on the position of Rabbi Gordon.[14]

Rabbi Gordon himself did nothing to indicate that he objected to Price's appointment, and the pattern was set for a friendly division of responsibility that would continue between the traditional rabbi and his English-speaking counterpart at Goel Tzedec until Gordon's death in 1934. Rabbi Gordon continued to perform the traditional rabbinical duties: he remained the final authority in questions of Jewish law; he arbitrated disputes between members and studied Talmud with them; he supervised *kashruth*. And on the two Sabbaths a year when it was customary for him to speak formally in the synagogue, Rabbi Price deferred to him.*

Price, on the other hand, preached every Sabbath and was the congregation's public relations agent to the Jewish community and to the non-Jews. He helped form the first Jewish Masonic lodge in the city, itself a sign of acculturation. He spoke throughout Ontario to encourage enlistment in the armed forces during the First World War and he attended Zionist conventions in Montreal. At home, he was active in the Anti-Missionary League, and superintended and expanded the congregational school begun at Goel Tzedec by Mrs. Siegel, while Rabbi Gordon concentrated his communal efforts in the Simcoe Street Talmud Torah.

The new rabbi attempted no doctrinal alteration of the prayers; he merely included an English petition before the ark prior to the scriptural reading and an English blessing of the congregation at the conclusion of services. The former disturbed very few since the practice was already commonplace in many orthodox congregations in the United States and probably also at Shaar Hashomayim in Montreal, which no one could brand as reform. The concluding blessing, however, infuriated the ultras, no doubt because it was a Christian practice and was reminiscent of the pattern of innovation at Holy Blossom. In addition, a large segment of the congregation was alienated by Price's stinging criticism of their lack of decorum during services, a tactless move

---

* Goel Tzedec could afford two rabbis because Rabbi Gordon was paid very little and served other congregations as well.

on his part considering the difficulty that many at Goel Tzedec had in accepting a modern rabbi in the first place. Before long, he was extremely unpopular and came to feel increasingly uncomfortable. Although he left of his own volition in 1916, many were relieved to see him go.[15]

Services at Goel Tzedec now fell back into the old pattern. No mention of a possible successor to Price appears in the congregational minutes, but it is difficult to determine whether the drain on manpower during the war made rabbinical graduates too scarce or whether the majority at Goel Tzedec merely had had enough of Americanized rabbis for the time being.

The trend of increased attachment to the organizations surrounding the Jewish Theological Seminary, however, did not abate. In 1913 Schechter had founded a congregational association affiliated with the institution and called the United Synagogue of America. Modelled on the United Synagogue in London,[16] this was to be essentially a union of traditionally-oriented congregations of English-speaking Jews and was to be the agency through which the communication of an Americanized orthodoxy was to be maintained between the Seminary and the interested laity. Mrs. Schechter strove to do the same for Jewish women's societies by creating the National Women's League and, although no effort was made to connect Goel Tzedec officially with the United Synagogue, the women's auxiliary did maintain informal contact with the League from the inception of the latter in 1918.

The same year, Ida Siegel established a federation of women's synagogue organizations in Toronto, called the Women's Orthodox Auxiliary, comprising the ladies' auxiliaries of Goel Tzedec, McCaul Street, Adath Israel and Hebrew Men of England, to finance the expansion of Jewish education for children in the individual synagogues, something to which the male members were largely indifferent. Since the National Women's League was still considered orthodox and since it offered a variety of advantages, including a speakers' roster and advice on publicity and activities, it was an easy task to transform the local group into a branch of the League. The congregations involved did not officially recognize the affiliation as applying to themselves, but the beginnings of formal contact with the embryonic Conservative Movement had begun. Local women travelled to conventions where they were infused with the goals of the League and brought back to Goel Tzedec a variety of printed materials produced by the New York organization.

The changes which took place at the University Avenue

Synagogue between Price's departure and the engagement of the congregation's second English-speaking rabbi in 1921 were due largely to female influence. Efforts were made to enlarge the congregational school and to provide cultural and social activities for young people along the lines suggested in New York and demanded by the native-born. It is significant that expansion of the school facilities in the basement of the University Avenue Synagogue was achieved in this period at the expense of the ritual bath (mikva). Most of the women at Goel Tzedec, especially the younger ones, had dispensed with it by this time and had no compunctions about advocating the elimination of the bath to provide more classroom space. There was a mikva nearby in Mendel Reimon's Turkish bath on Centre Avenue, they maintained, and those who still wished to use one would not be deprived.

It would be interesting to know the degree to which the women's movement to eliminate the mikva was motivated by the belief that its use was inappropriate because the practice did not conform to middle-class values. Whatever the case, the ultras among the men raised violent objection and attempted to stifle the plan by insisting that funds were unavailable to refurbish the mikva as a classroom. The more liberal male element, however, supported the women's efforts to secure the money through fund-raising projects and, by the end of the decade, additional classrooms had been created by the installation of movable partitions in the basement assembly hall, similar to those used at Holy Blossom, and the mikva had become a kitchen.

None of these changes affected the order of services at Goel Tzedec. But by 1921 demands had been renewed for an English-speaking rabbi and for the elimination of pledged offerings during the scriptural reading – a custom regarded as undignified commercialism which had disappeared at Holy Blossom decades before. So important was it considered to be rid of the uncouth practice that it was done while Goel Tzedec was seriously short of funds.

Goel Tzedec, however, was not yet completely committed to the Jewish Theological Seminary; Rabbi Julius Siegel, Price's successor elected in 1921, was a graduate of the more orthodox Rabbi Isaac Elchanan Theological Seminary. Whether his appointment represented a reaction against the Jewish Theological Seminary by the extreme traditionalists is unclear. Certainly, they had not objected to Price on ideological grounds, but merely opposed his use of the English language. Consequently, it is possible that either a Jewish Theological Seminary graduate was not available or, more probably, that Rabbi Siegel seemed the most likely to please all factions in the congregation.

Whatever the case, Siegel was immensely popular, even with the ultras. Modern, yet traditional, he introduced a variety of young people's and adult social and educational clubs, as well as late Friday evening lectures. These talks were well attended, even by non-members, but unlike the late Friday activities at Holy Blossom, there was no service. The traditional prayers continued to be held at sunset. Moreover, Rabbi Siegel refused to take sides in the developing dispute between the orthodox rabbinate in the United States and the Jewish Theological Seminary, with its attendant animosity in the individual congregations. He kept Goel Tzedec neutral by attending conventions both of the ultra-orthodox rabbinical association, the Agudath Harabonim, and the Conservative United Synagogue.

By the early 1920s Goel Tzedec was well on its way to exhibiting the characteristics of the middle-class traditional synagogue of the period; decorum was demanded at services, offerings had been largely eliminated and the status of women had been enhanced through the formation of a ladies' auxiliary. In many congregations in the United States and at Holy Blossom in Toronto, the liberal elements further assured female status by demanding mixed seating at services. Goel Tzedec, too, would be confronted with this problem, but not for another decade. At this juncture, it was still too conservative for any such departure from tradition; women continued to occupy the gallery.

Another feature of the middle-class synagogue evident at Goel Tzedec was the increased importance attached to the English-speaking rabbi at the expense both of the cantor and the European-trained rabbi. When Rabbi Siegel arrived, his annual salary was only $500, while Rabbi Gordon received $1,000 and the cantor almost twice that amount. By 1923, however, Rabbi Gordon's salary had been reduced to $650 and, although the cantor's had been increased slightly, Rabbi Siegel was now the highest paid official of the congregation.[17]

Siegel left Goel Tzedec in 1924 to continue his studies at Yale and with his departure a decision had to be made whether to choose a successor from RIETS or from the Jewish Theological Seminary. Once again, the congregation was not prepared to make a choice on ideological grounds; it determined to elect the most qualified candidate regardless of his background and affiliation. But the congregation was now beginning to see a difference between the two organizations. In 1925, Goel Tzedec was invited to join both the Union of Orthodox Hebrew Congregations and the United Synagogue of America, but is was decided to defer a decision until a new rabbi had been appointed. Apparently there was fear that a Seminary graduate might be uncomfortable in the orthodox union and that a graduate of RIETS, conversely, might object to affiliation with the increasingly suspect United Synagogue.

However, there were other factors which came into play. The graduates of RIETS, although the majority had been born in the United States and had superior talmudic training to those of the Jewish Theological Seminary, lacked the polish necessary to commend them to congregants who were acculturated or seeking to become so. The RIETS rabbi tended to come from recently arrived immigrant families and reflected somewhat the narrow cultural environment of the *shtetl*, whereas his Seminary counterpart came as a rule from families already Americanized. Moreover, his training did not equip him with secular subjects; unlike the Seminary, RIETS did not demand a university degree from its graduates. As a result, graduates of the Jewish Theological Seminary tended to be accepted over RIETS graduates even by very traditional congregations. At Goel Tzedec, the choice fell to Rabbi Jesse Schwartz.[18]

Even after Schwartz arrived, however, the congregation remained ambivalent toward organized orthodoxy and organized Conservatism. When the synagogue was invited to send delegates to the convention of the Union of Orthodox Hebrew Congregations, it neglected to do so only because the notice had arrived too late. Rabbi Schwartz, however, was determined to convince his congregation to affiliate formally with the United Synagogue and his efforts succeeded not because Goel Tzedec had any particular liking for the philosophy of Conservatism but rather because, as a result of affiliation, each member would receive the periodical of the organization. In 1926, therefore, Goel Tzedec sent its first delegates to the United Synagogue convention in Washington, D.C. and formal commitment to the organizations of the Conservative Movement was complete.

Rabbi Schwartz noted in his installation address that he and Rabbi Gordon appealed to "different elements in the synagogue," but he hoped for "friendliest cooperation." Although the congregation invited Rabbi Gordon to remain, with Rabbi Schwartz the liberalization of Goel Tzedec began seriously. The English-speaking rabbi appears to have had control of the ritual, while the laity made increased demands for conformity to middle-class standards. Decorum was considered a major priority and late Friday services were introduced to offset falling synagogue attendance. Schwartz was even prepared to permit the installation of microphones, as had just been done at Holy Blossom, and the issue was dropped not because of religious scruples, but rather because the cost was prohibitive. He did, however, retain the traditional prayer book and Hebrew as the language of worship.[19]

By the time Rabbi Schwartz left Toronto in 1926, there was no longer any question that his successor would be a graduate of the Jewish Theological Seminary; no representation whatever was made to RIETS to supply a rabbi. Even when none of the new Seminary graduates was found suitable, Goel Tzedec sought advice from the Rabbinical Assembly of America, the association of rabbis affiliated with the Jewish Theological Seminary. Through their efforts, Rabbi Samuel Sachs, a Seminary graduate, was elected.*

The congregation, nevertheless, were not prepared to divorce themselves from organized orthodoxy, nor did they see their association with the Jewish Theological Seminary as a departure from it. When RIETS decided to establish a secular college under its auspices, Goel Tzedec forwarded a list of its officers to be placed in the cornerstone of the new building and attempted to raise funds for the institution during the High Holy Days services in 1927. The following year, Goel Tzedec appointed a committee to participate in the establishment of an association of orthodox synagogues in Canada. Rabbi Sachs, certainly having more insight into the subtle ideological distinctions between orthodoxy and the Seminary than did the laity, did not consider himself orthodox. He was, however, intensely traditional and opposed any radical alteration of the ritual. But even minor changes brought heated opposition from the leaders of the congregation. In 1928, for example, when Rabbi Sachs introduced a slight abridgement of the service, the Board of Trustees approved it only after vehement debate. The only assault upon tradition that Sachs attempted was the dispensing with the *duchenen*.† When he first suggested it in 1930, there was great objection on grounds that the change would be contrary to orthodox practice. Although the

* Rabbi Sachs was ideal for Goel Tzedec because he had been born in Lithuania (1894) and had studied at a European *yeshiva* as well as at RIETS. He had been ordained by the Jewish Theological Seminary of America in 1916 and held a degree from Columbia College. Consequently, he was familiar with both the European and American types of orthodoxy, as well as with the Conservative philosophy. He would remain at Goel Tzedec until his retirement in 1946.

† This is a ceremony included in the synagogue service on holy days re-enacting the blessing of the congregation by the priests in the Temple at Jerusalem.

custom would eventually be dropped as a result of Rabbi Sach's efforts, its elimination would not be achieved during the period of this study.

The 1920s and 1930s was a period of experimentation at University Avenue. While Holy Blossom moved confidently into the sphere of reform, Goel Tzedec was caught up in the myriad forces working to modify orthodox practice without destroying orthodoxy itself. It was a period of uncertainty and fluidity in which the congregation sought modernization and acculturation without assimilation. The adjustment was difficult and was achieved slowly, but at least by the end of the 1920s certain changes had come to be accepted. For one thing, the English-speaking rabbi and the weekly Sabbath sermon were now beyond debate and in 1928, the *bimah** was ordered lowered so that the congregation could better see the pulpit. During the same period, activities exclusively for young people were inaugurated; separate Friday evening services were introduced and a group affiliated with the United Synagogue Young People's League was in operation at University Avenue. In addition, Rabbi Sachs attempted to draw young people into the synagogue and improve the quality of instruction in the congregational religious school by instituting a teachers' training course for teenagers in 1928.[20]

These changes were innocuous compared to those at Holy Blossom and in some synagogues similar to Goel Tzedec in the United States, and, it must be emphasized, they had little effect on the actual form of worship, nor did they pose a threat to orthodoxy. However, by the early 1930s increased demands directed at the service itself began to be heard. Predictably, they began with insistence upon the adoption of practices to make worship even more orderly and more palatable to the middle class. The English-speaking rabbi was given full control of the service, including the right to introduce English prayers "wherever permissible and suitable," increased congregational singing and uniform prayer books. The Prophetic Portion *(Haftarah)* was to be recited only by the professional reader and, in response to the enhanced status of women, it was proposed that they be permitted to sit on the ground floor.

With this last proposal, a real potential threat to orthodoxy had at last come to the fore at Goel Tzedec. By the early 1930s some liberals in the congregation were apparently in favour not only of dispensing with the women's gallery but also of seating the sexes

---

* A platform from which the Torah is read and the cantor conducts services. In the traditional Ashkenazic synagogue it is placed approximately in the centre of the hall of worship.

229

together. This demand was probably an attempt to improve the status of women in the synagogue, in line with middle-class values, and a device to attract greater attendance at services rather than an actual reform tendency, but it had the effect of arousing bitter opposition from the traditional majority. "A very considerable and heated discussion" characterized the general meeting at which the issue was debated in 1933, and it was decided that the congregation must have an authoritative rabbinic opinion on its permissibility. It is significant that advice was sought both from the unequivocally orthodox and from the Jewish Theological Seminary. Rabbi Moses S. Margolies, president of the Agudath Harabonim, who represented the former, offered the expected reply: any tampering with the women's gallery would be absolutely in contradiction of Jewish law. Professor Louis Ginzberg, a distinguished talmudist, answered for the Seminary. In his opinion, it would be permissible for men and women to sit on the same floor, provided they were separated. The congregation, attempting to find the mean between orthodoxy and change, therefore rejected outright the proposal for family pews and adopted Professor Ginzberg's solution. Women were seated on the extreme sides of the ground floor and separated from the men's section by velvet cords.

For the remainder of the period of this study, and for a considerable time afterwards, Goel Tzedec conformed to this condition. In 1937, the cords were removed to widen the aisles, but mixed seating would not be approved until the congregation moved to suburban Forest Hill in 1955. Granted, late Friday evening services were introduced with great success, but in all probability the traditional sunset services continued as well. The trend toward liberalism had been set, however, and after Rabbi Sachs' departure in 1946,[21] a less traditional rabbi would have little difficulty in abridging and doctrinally modifying the service.

Some comment, in conclusion, is in order concerning developments at Beth Hamidrash Hagodol Chevra Tehillim (McCaul Street Synagogue), which stood second in the hierarchy of the East European congregations and consequently might have been expected to follow Goel Tzedec in its modification of orthodoxy. This however, did not occur during the period considered here. Until his death in 1934, Rabbi Gordon remained in control at McCaul Street and he appears not to have experienced the pressure for change that was felt at Goel Tzedec. Chevra Tehillim remained less status-conscious and consequently more traditional than its sister synagogue; demands for alteration of the service and for mixed seating were seldom, if ever, heard. The sole significant change in this period was the engagement of an English-speaking orthodox rabbi to preach on the High Holy Days beginning in the mid-1920s. Only in 1937, when a successor to Rabbi Gordon was sought, was a shift in the position of the congregation evident. The new minister, Rabbi Reuben Slonim, was a Seminary graduate and he took the lead in introducing whatever modifications did occur. These would follow a pattern similar to that at University Avenue: increased decorum and an English sermon before any alteration in the actual service.

NOTES

1 The theory of symbolic placement is based upon W. Lloyd Warner's concepts of "Evaluated Participation" and his "Index to Status Characteristics," both presented in his *Social Class in America*. Although Warner admits that religious institutions are not infallibly reliable for the exact placement of individuals in social classes because they cut through many social levels (p. 96), when the limitations of the theory are considered, it can still be useful and certainly applies in the case of the Jewish community of Toronto. See, for instance, Milton M. Gordon, *Social Class in American Sociology* (Durham, N.C., Duke University Press, 1958), chap. 4.

2 As far back as 1889, no layman was permitted to officiate at services on the Sabbath and on holy days. Then in 1902 it was decided that "no one except the officiating minister...be permitted to pray aloud," and finally in 1904 laymen were forbidden to conduct services even on weekdays, "unless in cases of necessity." (*By-laws of the Toronto Hebrew Congregation Holy Blossom 1889; HBM*, Sept. 14, 1902; *By-laws of "The Holy Blossom" Toronto Hebrew Congregation, 1904*). Much of the material in this chapter is based on information contained in the Minute Books of Holy Blossom and Goel Tzedec synagogues. Detailed references are to be found in the author's dissertation, footnotes to Chapter 13.

3 *HBM* Oct. 22, 1911; personal interviews: Arthur Cohen, Dec. 15, 1971; Ben Geldsaler, Sept. 28, 1972. At one point prior to 1910, support for the rabbi was organized by two young agnostics in the congregation who wanted to see Jacobs remain because they were courting his daughters.

4 *Jewish Times*, Sept. 6, 1912, pp. 12, 14.

5 Brickner's scholastic credentials were above reproach. In addition to his ordination, he held two Masters' degrees from

Columbia University, one in education, and a Ph.D. from the University of Cincinnati. He also studied at the traditional Teachers' Institute of the Jewish Theological Seminary in New York. Prior to his advent to Toronto, he had been one of the organizers of the Young Judaea movement in the United States, he had served as Director of Extension of Jewish Education for the Bureau of Jewish Education in New York City and, during the First World War he had been director of the training school and personnel division of the Jewish Welfare Board of the United States army and navy.

6 There is some debate about the exact date of the introduction of mixed seating. The *Canadian Jewish Review* (Dec. 29, 1922, p. 4) insists that it had been the practice as early as 1916, but while it was admittedly permitted at the late Friday services and on isolated occasions otherwise, it is improbable that Rabbi Jacobs would have tolerated it as a universal practice. The *Review* probably refers instead to the practice of allowing women to sit on the ground floor of the synagogue, but still separately from the men. Although no specific mention of the seating of the sexes together is made in the surviving minutes until 1927, after Brickner's departure, the consensus of opinion among those who can recall the period is that Rabbi Brickner introduced the practice.

7 It should not be assumed, despite his caution in introducing new reforms, that Isserman was as sympathetic to tradition as Brickner. In an address shortly after his arrival, Isserman remarked that "The two main groups in the Jewish race, the reform and the orthodox, are opposed to one another just as are modernist and fundamentalist in the Christian religions." The final determinant of religious life, he believed, was "in the individual himself, and not in traditional authority ..." (quoted in *Star*, Aug. 18, 1925).

8 Both Brickner and Isserman left Holy Blossom after receiving invitations from larger congregations in the United States. Brickner went to Cleveland and Isserman to St. Louis.

During their terms in Toronto, both were active outside the Jewish community as well as within it. Brickner was president of the Toronto Federation of Jewish Philanthropies and the Ontario Jewish Immigrant Aid Society. He was a founder of the Jewish Boys' Club and participated actively in the establishment of a Jewish farming school at Georgetown. He served, in addition, as president of the Ontario Social Hygiene

Society, and belonged to the General Ministerial Association of Toronto. His relations with Christians were cordial and he addressed Protestant congregations and other non-Jewish groups on a number of occasions. He was also active in the disarmament movement and was appointed to a municipal committee to examine methods of caring for the mentally ill. His communal activity and his position in social causes made him extremely popular.

Rabbi Isserman was especially active in the general community. He led a campaign to abolish corporal punishment in the public schools; he initiated the first Canadian exchange of pulpits between a rabbi and a Christian minister, this being with Reverend E. Crossley Hunter of Carlton Street United Church in 1928. This attracted thousands to the church ("It was like going to a football game," Mrs. Isserman recalls), and so alarmed the orthodox that some engaged a court stenographer to record his address in the hope of securing enough evidence to effect his expulsion from the rabbinate.

9 This account is based upon Rabbi Eisendrath's own recollections, which are substantiated in large part by those of the older members of the congregation. Maurice N. Eisendrath, *Can Faith Survive: The Thoughts and Afterthoughts of an American Rabbi* (New York: McGraw-Hill, 1964), pp. 226–228.

10 Ben Zion Bokser, "Conservative Judaism," *Jewish Quarterly Review*, New Series, XLV (Apr. 1955), p. 338.

11 Davis, *The Emergence of Conservative Judaism*, p. 321.

12 *Jewish Times*, May 18, 1906, p. 203. Abramowitz also spoke at the dedication ceremonies the following year.

13 It was not possible to obtain a minister from the unequivocally orthodox Rabbi Isaac Elchanan Theological Seminary, since that institution would not be opened until 1915 and would not ordain rabbis until 1919. Besides, Goel Tzedec had already had considerable contact with the Jewish Theological Seminary and so a request went out to Dr. Schechter for a recommendation. Price, a native of Worcester, Mass., held a Ph.D. in Semitics, Sanskrit and Greek from Columbia University.

14 Letters from Rabbi Price to the author, Aug. 17, Sept. 1971.

15 *Canadian Jewish Review*, Jan. 13, 1923, p. 6; Rabbi Samuel

Sachs, interview in Santa Monica, Calif., by Mr. Jack Provost of the Federation Council of Greater Los Angeles, Aug. 13, 1973, at the author's request; Rabbi Price to the author, Sept. 1971.

16 This was an association of Ashkenazic synagogues, formalized in 1870. By the turn of the century, it was an efficient centralized organization for cooperative action, fostering traditional orthodoxy and supporting the authority of the Chief Rabbi.

17 Goel Tzedec, "Balance Sheet for year ending Oct. 31, 1921"; Goel Tzedec, "Financial Statement 1922-23." Holy Blossom had reached this position about the time that the Bond Street synagogue had opened. The last cantor of stature resigned in 1905 and no effort was made to replace him.

18 Rothkoff, op.cit., pp. 166-67; Canadian Jewish Review, Aug. 1, 1924, p. 1.

19 A sign of the decline in religious observance is the fact that increased numbers of new members at Goel Tzedec in this period did not live within walking distance of the synagogue. Observant Jews would have joined synagogues in their immediate vicinity. The new members were probably attracted to University Avenue because of the prestige attached to it.

20 The Young People's League was run according to a program outline received from New York. Despite its affiliation with the United Synagogue, one advertisement for the organization stated that all "inclined towards orthodoxy are welcome" Canadian Jewish Review Dec. 23, 1921, p. 11).

21 Rabbi Sachs, in line with the practice of his predecessors and with what Goel Tzedec had come to expect of its rabbis, was active in communal work outside the synagogue. He became president of the Ontario region of the Canadian Zionist Federation, head of the local B'nai Brith Anti-defamation League and a member of the Board of Education for the Toronto Hebrew Free School. He was active in the Jewish Big Brother movement and the Family Welfare Bureau of the Federation of Jewish Philanthropies. He was also chairman of the Public Relations Committee of the revived Canadian Jewish Congress (see below) and chaired the Advisory Board of the Ontario Cloak and Suit Industry. The latter was a government position responsible to the Ontario Department of Labour.

CHAPTER 14

CULTURAL DEVELOPMENT IN THE NEW COMMUNITY

The immigrant Jews of Canada were hungry for culture – for their own and for that of their new surroundings. Consequently, they insisted upon education for their children beyond the compulsory age, patronized libraries and established literary, dramatic and political clubs. This was J.S. Woodsworth's assessment in 1909 and, to a significant degree, it was correct.[1]

Perhaps because of Toronto's proximity to the Jewish cultural heartland of New York, few Yiddish writers emerged here, in contrast to Montreal or Winnipeg. "It is to be regretted," the *Jewish Times* complained in 1913, "that aside from Zionist propaganda, purely literary work is somewhat lacking in evidence." This was true also because the Toronto Jewish community remained primarily working class, attracting few resident intellectuals. On the other hand, the local Jewish population was far from being indifferent to intellectual pursuits. By the First World War there were at least two shops where one could purchase Jewish books – Dworkin's for the secular and socialist, and Simon's for the religious – and door-to-door book peddlers from Europe and New York were commonplace in the Jewish neighbourhoods. Significant, too, was the fact that in 1911 the Nordau Zion Club felt it necessary to persuade the Public Library Board to authorize a Yiddish and Hebrew collection.[2]

The same period saw a variety of purely cultural organizations emerge in the Ward. In 1909 a Hebrew Literary Society developed around the staff of the Simcoe Street Talmud Torah, while the Folks Farein would grow out of a Yiddish literary club. These would set the pattern for a host of others which would appear during the next two decades and would include a Yiddish group at the University of Toronto (1916); a "self-education club" (1917) through which young immigrants studied English, Yiddish poets and the political issues of the time; a Yiddish Verein Kultur (1921); a Hebrew Culture Club (Tarbut, *ca.* 1922), and probably many more of which no trace exists and which might have gathered without formal organization at the Zionist Institute or at Walerstein's ice cream parlour on Spadina Avenue. Primarily, however, Toronto Jews drew their cultural breath from the United States, especially from New York. In the field of Zionism, if the initial contact came through Montreal, American centres continued to provide most of the visiting orators, and the same was true in the cultural sphere. Those attracting large crowds – the renowned author Sholem Asch, for example, and "Yehoash," the popular Yiddish poet – came invariably from New York.

Domination from the United States was apparent also in the two major fields of expression for Jewish culture outside the synagogue, the Yiddish theatre and the Yiddish press. Prior to 1910 indigenous efforts in both of these areas had been dismal failures. In 1906 an attempt was made to publish an English and Yiddish journal of news and literary items called the *Toronto Jewish Weekly*, while the following year, another publication called the *Toronto Yiddishe Presse* appeared, following a format similar to the *Weekly*. Neither lasted more than a few months and most local Jews continued to import the New York Yiddish press. The religious and the middle class read the *Tageblatt*, while secularists preferred the *Forward*. The *Kanader Adler* of Montreal was also read by the Yiddish-speaking, but the New York papers were the most popular. Only Jews whose native language was English looked to Montreal and the *Jewish Times*. Indeed, a branch office of the *Times* was set up in Toronto in 1910, but apparently lasted only a short while.

The attempt to open a Yiddish theatre staffed by local performers met with similar disappointment. For instance, in 1906 a certain Michaelson, who operated an ice cream parlour at Agnes and Elizabeth streets, together with a Mr. Abramov, a self-styled local actor and director who probably made his living by some more practical means, opened a hall for Yiddish performances on Elizabeth Street. Michaelson and his wife had aspirations as actors and the three became the company. The effort was unsuccessful.[3]

It soon became apparent that Yiddish theatre would be practical only if local impresarios imported companies from the United States. Even here, the first effort had been a failure because there were too few Yiddish-speaking Jews in the city who would support the venture. In 1897 a company of Jewish actors from the United States had attempted to open a theatre in a vacant church on Richmond Street. The English-speaking old community and the second-generation East European immigrants who knew little Yiddish did not understand the linguistic nuances or the allusions dependent upon European experience. Those to whom these would have appealed, the parent generation of Yiddish-speaking immigrants, saw the theatre as irreligious and therefore took little interest in it.

A decade later, however, things had begun to change. Increasingly there were Jews who had seen Yiddish theatre in the United States or in the larger cities of Eastern Europe. Increasingly, also, there were secularists and those who, while remaining religious, were more tolerant. For the Yiddish theatre served an important psychological function for the Jewish immigrant; it was a place where he could laugh uproariously after a day in the factory, where he could rise out of the indignity of his existence as a rag-picker to heights unattainable outside the fantasy of the stage, where the catharsis of weeping simultaneously over one's own lot and over the tragedy of the fictional character was to be had for ten cents.

Charles (Chanina) Pasternak, an able entrepreneur who had achieved success through the judicious purchase of properties in and adjacent to the Ward, was the first to see new possibilities for success with Yiddish theatre. When Goel Tzedec moved into its grand new structure in 1906, he purchased the old synagogue at University and Elm and a powerful cultural vehicle in Toronto was born. The People's Theatre, as he named it, drew a few local artists but primarily attracted American touring companies which, for lack of accommodation, had had to perform previously in the Orange Hall on Queen Street, east of Yonge. This was inconvenient to the Ward and consequently performances had been poorly attended. Actually, the People's Theatre did not do well either at first. Perhaps it acquired an unfavourable reputation because its balcony nearly collapsed at one performance and the men in the audience had to hold it up while its occupants made their escape. The unpopularity of the People's Theatre was certainly not due to a lack of desire for Yiddish performances. When the local Zionists, in an effort to raise money to refurbish their building, brought Jacob Adler's company from New York in 1909, two thousand local Jews filled Massey Hall.[4]

Pasternak was quick to capitalize on the situation by joining forces with another enterprising businessman, Simon Rabinowitch, and moving to the former Agnes Street Methodist Church at Agnes and Teraulay in 1909. Renamed the National, after the popular New York Yiddish playhouse of the time, the

237

remodelled church held nine hundred people and, for several weeks following the opening, it was "packed to the very doors" as family groups flocked to see a Yiddish version of *Hamlet*.

The new impresarios, however, realized shortly that the only feasible means of continuing was to lease the theatre to American managers. Soon renamed the Lyric, the theatre became the site of a variety of productions during the next decade, including the New York Yiddish Opera and what the *Jewish Times* called "the better class of Yiddish dramas...." The three weekly performances in the season between September and May attracted almost capacity audiences, but the frequency with which the lease changed hands suggests that Yiddish theatre was not a profitable concern in Toronto. There was still competition. The really famous New York troupes of Jacob Adler, Boris Tomashefsky, David Kessler and others, who would perform plays by Ibsen and Shakespeare, came usually to Massey Hall and not to the Lyric, often sponsored by the Zionists in efforts to raise money for their proposed new headquarters or for colonists in Palestine. The result was that although Toronto Jews were served well in the theatre, local talent never had the opportunity to develop. Although a few aspiring local actors did succeed in joining the Lyric company, most of the group continued to be professionals from New York.

Performances at the Lyric took place Friday and Saturday evenings and Saturday afternoons, much to the consternation of the orthodox, many of whom objected to the theatre as an irreverent pastime. Some of the religious element would attend Saturday evenings after the Sabbath, but the extreme orthodox would not enter the building. Indeed, the strictest congregations expelled members for attending the theatre or at least deprived them of the privilege of leading services. On the other hand, the more acculturated orthodox congregations, Goel Tzedec for instance, were not above holding benefit performances at the Lyric.

By the early 1920s, the Ward was no longer sufficiently Jewish to warrant continued operation of the Lyric, the management having been reduced to renting the theatre for boxing matches on Thursday evenings. But even before it closed, plans were afoot to open a new Yiddish theatre on Spadina Avenue. The sponsoring group included some of those involved in the Lyric – Pasternak, and Isidore Axler, a bright young entrepreneur. The projected new Standard Theatre was to be the first in Canada actually built as a Yiddish playhouse and it would accommodate twelve hundred people. Public interest was to be aroused by selling shares, the possession of which would entitle the holder to seats at a discount.

From the time of its opening in August 1922, the Standard was a success, due in large measure to the perspicacity of Abraham Littman, who assumed the position of manager. Abe Littman was no stranger to Toronto; for a brief time in 1912 he had taken over the Lyric and his tenure was one of its few profitable periods. He had since returned to Brooklyn, but just prior to the opening of the Standard had been recalled to the Lyric and was in the process of turning the tide again. It is not surprising, therefore, that he should have been asked to direct operations at the Standard.

Littman managed the theatre for two years, during which he assembled one of the finest Yiddish theatrical companies on the continent. Indeed, the Toronto company played Cleveland, St. Louis, Chicago and Detroit, and even performed regularly in New York. After he was persuaded to leave for Detroit, however, a steady decline set in. The Standard company struggled on for a few years, but increasingly came to be superseded by visiting troupes from New York.[5] By the mid-1930s, attendance had fallen off considerably because of the increasing acculturation of the second generation and the advent of sound motion pictures and radio. The presentation of live Yiddish performances, never a financially sound proposition in Toronto, now became an unqualified liability; by 1935, the Strand, as it was now called, had become a movie house.

The demise of the Standard did not eliminate Yiddish performances in Toronto. Touring companies still played at public facilities such as Massey Hall, or at Alhambra Hall on Spadina Avenue. These, however, were invariably sponsored by local organizations in fund-raising efforts. By the 1930s, few impresarios would seriously consider Toronto without such an invitation.[6]

II

If Toronto Jewry ever tried to escape American cultural domination (and there is no evidence to indicate that it did), this would have been more successful in the journalistic sphere than in the theatrical. Following the disappearance of the *Weekly* and the *Presse*, a number of futile attempts were made to establish a Jewish periodical in the city, and at last, in 1911, some progress was achieved.

The precise origin of the *Hebrew Journal (Der Yiddisher Zhurnal)* is obscure. Abraham Rhinewine, who later became editor of the paper, insists that it was founded by the co-operative effort of several individuals.[7] However, if any others were involved, only the name of Harry Winberg survives.

Winberg, a man of varied ambitions, had arrived in Toronto from the United States early in the twentieth century and immediately plunged into a multiplicity of pursuits, of which the establishment of a Yiddish newspaper was only one.[8] Undoubtedly, the success of the paper was due to Winberg's employment of a professional editor, who decided not to compete with the New York dailies. Under the auspices of H. Hirsch, the *Journal*, which began as a weekly, concentrated at first on local news and serials, leaving the international field and ideological matters to the *Tageblatt* and the *Forward*. By the end of 1914, Hirsch had been lured to Montreal to edit the well-established *Kanader Adler*, but he left the *Journal* a prospering concern. The increasing local Jewish population had found the paper to their liking and this, together with a thirst for European news as the war approached, enabled the *Journal* to publish daily.[9]

The paper attracted gifted writers to its staff, some of whom eventually acquired a partial interest in the periodical. These included Rhinewine and H.M. Kirshenbaum. Almost without exception, they were secularist and socialist immigrants from Russian Poland, and some had emigrated in order to escape arrest for revolutionary activity.

Considering this situation, the *Journal* remained remarkably impartial. Since the traditional community constituted a majority in Toronto, the paper had to serve them as well as the secularists, and the former never felt it necessary to found their own publication. Politically, the *Journal* leaned toward socialism and generally supported socialist or pro-labour candidates, non-Jewish as well as Jewish. A few of them occasionally appeared on the local scene, but in national and provincial politics, where only the two major parties were in contest, the paper invariably chose the Liberals. This was due to the political outlook of the staff and continued into the 1930s, as long as Rhinewine remained at the helm. It was due also to the fact that the Liberal party had been in power federally when most of the staff arrived in Canada, and Jewish immigrants in Toronto, like those elsewhere in North America, tended to support the party which they first came to identify with the freedom of the New World.[10]

After Rhinewine's death in 1932, a former staff writer, Shmuel Meir Shapiro, purchased the paper from Winberg and his remaining partners. Shapiro was a Conservative and, at one point during Rhinewine's editorship, when the paper had supported socialist Henry Dworkin in a municipal race, Shapiro had, with Conservative financial support, set up a rival Yiddish daily called *Di Yiddishe Velt (The Jewish World)*. This, however, dissolved immediately after the election and, once Shapiro gained control of the *Journal*, he tended to support whichever political party was in power, probably in order to maintain government advertising. He, too, managed successfully to steer the middle course between the religious and the secularist communities.

The *Hebrew Journal* did not long remain alone in the field of Yiddish journalism in Toronto. In 1915, the *Kanader Adler* attempted to publish a Toronto issue entitled *The Daily Advertiser*; the same year, the Cloakmakers' Union issued *The Cloakmakers' Bulletin*, while two years later a working-class paper called the *Arbeiter-Tzeitung* appeared, supported by the Jewish locals of the trade unions and by working-class benevolent societies, and probably meant to be a successor to *Di Neie Tzeit*, a local workers' paper of the immediate prewar period. None of these lasted for more than a few issues, and the *Advertiser* never reached the news-stands.[11]

Jewish periodicals of a purely literary nature fared little better. Twice during the 1920s, Shapiro attempted to publish humorous and satirical works, first *Der Mazik (The Jester)* and then *Der Besem (The Broom)*. In the same period, a paper appeared called *Kanader Yugend (Canadian Youth)*, devoted to literary criticism. These were all short-lived, as were numerous others which remain nameless. By 1926, the *Journal* and the *Kanader Adler* were the only daily Yiddish publications in Canada, and few others were appearing with any regularity.

The English-language Jewish press, on the other hand, had a more auspicious career. Since the late nineteenth century, Toronto had been served by Montreal publications, the *Jewish Times* and its successor, the *Jewish Chronicle*. By the early 1920s, however, English-speaking Toronto Jews had grown numerous enough to support their own weekly, the *Canadian Jewish Review*. This was the brainchild of George W. Cohen, a journalist from Buffalo who made the periodical a success by means of three techniques. First, since Cohen had joined Holy Blossom, he persuaded Rabbi Brickner to become contributing editor; Brickner's successors, rabbis Isserman and Eisendrath, followed suit. A second successful policy was the paper's support for open immigration, which undoubtedly won over even the Yiddish-speaking sector of the population. Finally, and perhaps most important, the *Review* appealed to the socially arrived and the socially aspiring. The members of Holy Blossom, the *nouveaux riches* in the East European community, especially at Goel Tzedec and at the McCaul Street Synagogue, and the rising second generation revelled in the accounts in the paper of their social events and peregrinations. So popular did it become in the 1920s, that the *Review* could be sharply critical of the local Jewish community and survive.

The community, however, would not tolerate an attack on the concept of a Jewish homeland in Palestine. Under the editorship of Rabbi Brickner, the *Review* had been unreservedly Zionist. Isserman, similarly enthusiastic, appears to have continued this policy.[12] Eisendrath, on the other hand, was another matter. He had little use for traditional Judaism and still less for Zionism. Assuming the editorship of the *Review* in 1929, as had now become customary for rabbis at Holy Blossom, he immediately alienated a large segment of the community. A band of Arabs had just massacred a large part of the Jewish population of Hebron and Eisendrath took the editorial position that the Arabs were merely nationalists fighting for their own land. A furor broke out in the city and even a number of Eisendrath's own congregants demanded that he resign as editor and leave the pulpit. He refused to do either and consequently a sizable secession from Bond Street took place.

More important was the action taken by a group of local Zionists headed by Rose Dunkelman, the wife of a local clothing manufacturer and member of Holy Blossom, herself a tireless worker for the Zionist cause. Assisted by others of substance, including Samuel Kronick and Moses Gelber, Mrs. Dunkelman sought to counter Eisendrath's influence by establishing a rival weekly with a pro-Zionist stance.

A second Jewish weekly had already begun in Toronto, but within months was on the verge of bankruptcy. The Zionist group purchased the paper, renamed it *The Jewish Standard* and imported the eloquent Zionist editor, Meyer Weisgal, from New York to head the venture.[13] Weisgal conducted a weekly debate with Eisendrath during the two years he remained in Toronto and by the time he left, the *Review* was rapidly losing circulation. By 1931, however, despite their ideological success, the Zionist group found themselves unable to carry the *Standard* in the midst of the depression. Consequently, once they sold the paper, its ideological flavour dissipated and it became primarily a magazine dealing with literature and personalities. From this period, the *Hebrew Journal* remained the major disseminator of local news and the spokesman for the Jewish community.[14]

NOTES

1 James S. Woodsworth, *Strangers Within Our Gates* (Toronto: Missionary Society of the Methodist Church, Canada, 1909), p. 157.

2 A number of attempts, especially on the part of the Zionists, had already been made to establish a Jewish public library in the city using a room in the Zionist Institute as a nucleus. None, unfortunately, had been successful and the resort to the public institution was the result. Even after the Jewish collection was established, however, independent Jewish efforts did not abate. A small non-circulating library was set up in 1921 at the Zionist building on Beverley Street, but its contents were devoted primarily to political topics and Rabbi Siegel continued to agitate for a library of wider scope. Later in the decade, Henry Dworkin would insist that the service being provided by the public library was inadequate and would urge the Jewish trade union locals to sponsor a Jewish library at the newly remodelled Labour Lyceum on Spadina Avenue. None of these efforts bore fruit and Toronto would have no Jewish public library until the early 1940s.

3 Bossin, *Stars of David*, p. 45.

4 *Ibid.* Numerous interviews substantiate the incident of the balcony.

5 *Hebrew Journal*, June 3, 1926; B. Hyman, personal interview, Oct. 8, 1972; *Star*, May 19, 1924; June 15, 1925.

6 It has been remarked earlier that Jews tended to gravitate to professions with a degree of stigma attached because here there was little competition. Outside the salvage trades, the motion picture industry is a good example of this phenomenon in Toronto. By 1915, a majority of the independent movie theatres in the city were owned by Jews, a situation which obtained until the mid-1920s when most were bought out by a syndicate, Famous Players Canadian (Ben Geldsaler, personal interview, Sept. 28, 1972).

7 Rhinewine, *Der Yid in Kanada*, I, p. 217.

8 For instance, Winberg, having become involved in real estate, erected a multi-storey apartment block at the corner of Agnes and Elizabeth streets in 1905. This might have started a trend toward "high-rise" development in the area, but popular

opposition forced the city to prohibit further such construction. Winberg also ran periodically for mayor, with no real hope of winning.

9 *Jewish Times*, Jan. 10, 1913, p. 5. A.B. Bennett, personal interview, Oct. 3, 1972.

10 Kirshenbaum joined the paper in 1913 and became a partner in 1919. Rhinewine (1857-1932), a Socialist-Territorialist who favoured the establishment of Jewish colonies in the Canadian West, became city editor in 1912 and editor-in-chief in 1915. He was one of the founders of the I.L. Peretz School and taught at the National Radical School. Winberg was a Conservative, but he did not commit the paper to support the party (J.J. Glass, personal interview, Dec. 13, 1972).

11 Rhinewine, *Der Yid in Kanada*, I, pp. 216-18.

12 For Isserman's sympathetic attitude to Zionism, see Rabbi F.M. Isserman to H.H. Smith, Nov. 14, 1928 (Collection of Mrs. Evelyn Goodman, Toronto) and his editorials in the *Canadian Jewish Review*, Jan. 15, 1926, p. 1; April 9, 1926 pp. 1, 5; Feb. 1926.

13 Actually, the first editor of the *Jewish Standard* was Hyman Edelstein, a Jewish poet originally from Ireland. Edelstein soon found that the purpose of the new journal would be political rather than literary, and consequently he resigned. Weisgal had been editor of *The New Palestine* in New York and had accepted the Toronto post in order to escape disputes within the Zionist movement in the United States. Meyer Weisgal, *Meyer Weisgal...So Far* (London: Weidenfeld and Nicolson, 1971), pp. 92-93.

14 A number of other Jewish periodicals emerged in Toronto in the 1920s and 1930s. Among them was a Yiddish communist paper which appeared in the twenties; the *Canadian Jewish Tribune*, published by Rhinewine and Kirshenbaum when they were *persona non grata* at the *Journal* in the early thirties; and a Yiddish weekly called *Canadian News*, which was founded in 1935 and for twenty years catered to the labour element. None, however, had either the longevity, the circulation or the influence of the *Journal*.

CHAPTER 15

POLITICS

If Woodsworth had written twenty years earlier, he would surely not have included political activity as an evident characteristic of Toronto Jewry. The old community voted, as befitted good citizens, but they apparently had little desire to become involved in politics themselves. Only one local Jew sought public office in the nineteenth century. Newman Leopold Steiner, born in Bohemia, had lived in New York and Buffalo before arriving in Toronto in 1852. A sculptor and marble dealer, Steiner did a thriving business in tombstones and memorial tablets, became prominent in upper middle-class social circles in the city, a master of the local Masonic chapter and president of the German Benevolent Society. In 1870 he was appointed a justice of the peace and, an ardent Reformer (Liberal) in politics, he ran successfully for alderman in St. James's Ward in 1880. Throughout the decade, he was returned with overwhelming majorities in his constituency, which, it should be noted, had few Jewish voters. Steiner, however, cannot be considered a member of the Jewish community. Although he was still Jewish when he arrived and had married within the faith in 1876, he apparently did not associate with Holy Blossom and by the 1890s had become a Lutheran.[1]

The old community in Toronto, therefore, unlike its counterpart in the United States, eschewed political activism. The political interest of the Jews in the United States during the nineteenth century has been ascribed to the fact that, for the most part, they were Germans and consequently were anxious to demonstrate their loyalty to the Republic. They appeared, therefore, in elected positions and in appointive offices dependent upon party patronage. Perhaps this was not the case in Toronto because entrenched interests prevented non-Protestants from holding office. Discrimination, especially by the Orange Order, was an influential factor, but more important was the fact that most Toronto Jews prior to the arrival of the East Europeans were either English by birth or had acquired British attitudes. They felt little pressure, therefore, to prove themselves as citizens and preferred (like Lewis Samuel and Edmund Scheuer,) to concentrate their public activities in commercial organizations such as the Board of Trade and in fraternities such as the Canadian and the National clubs. But even these excursions were rare. Most Jews were not attracted to organizations and many did not commit themselves even to the synagogue. True to the Victorian ethos, they treasured their privacy. Only Scheuer and Frank Benjamin ventured into public service; both were appointed justices of the peace in 1902.

The first East European immigrants were likewise initially indifferent to politics. This was not due, as might be supposed, to fear of the state; on the contrary, they saw in Canada and the British Empire all that was just and predictable in government. Two factors kept them out of politics in the nineteenth century. For one thing, many had no conception of loyalty to a state; they hardly understood the concept. Even Zionism was for them a messianic rather than a political idea. Secondly, representative government was outside the experience of most; those who did grasp it believed it to be the preserve of the Gentiles, and they had been conditioned by their European past to avoid non-Jews.

After a few years, however, apprehension was superseded by confidence. "As soon as you come here, you're affected by the air around you," one immigrant recalled. Political participation was taken seriously in Toronto.[2] Furthermore, the Yiddish-speaking community were avid readers of the American Jewish press, which exhorted Jews to take advantage of the opportunities of liberty and enfranchisement in North America, a position which would later be taken up by the *Hebrew Journal*.

But although the majority soon were anxious to exercise their franchise as an obligation of citizenship, large numbers were attracted by the personalities of the candidates whom, especially on the municipal level, they had the opportunity of hearing personally, and through the influence of the ward heeler. Once again operating principally in the municipal arena, these agents, in Toronto as in other centres, saw immigrants as an easily manipulated bloc of votes to bolster the political establishment. Political issues were usually irrelevant to the immigrant Jew in the early twentieth century, but the personality and reputation of his prospective representative were not. Nor were the ward heelers and occasionally the candidates themselves above offering a dollar for a vote correctly cast. Few accepted the bribe, but the majority, now eager to vote and flattered at being personally approached by what seemed to them a member of the elite, were susceptible to verbal persuasion.

Besides the appeal of the candidate, the ward heeler had other devices to secure immigrant votes. Especially important in the case of Toronto Jews was the promise of a peddler's licence, the distribution of which was regulated by quota, or the suggestion that the authorities might be persuaded to ignore the illegal stabling of a horse in a particular locality. It is not unreasonable to assume that some East European Jews who had witnessed, or themselves experienced, unjust arrests in the old country, might have seen in the opportunity to curry favour with the ward heeler a chance to fend off the possibility in Toronto by having a friend at City Hall. More practical and universal considerations also came into play. For instance, in the period prior to the First World War, a deposit of ten dollars was required for gas services in the city, a severe hardship for most immigrant Jews. The deposit, however, was waived if a responsible person guaranteed payment of the rates. The ward heeler could act as guarantor himself, or assure the voter that his candidate would so do. This device was used to great advantage on the municipal level by the Conservative party.[3]

By the end of the first decade of the twentieth century, the political consciousness of the new community had come alive. A number of Jews with East European antecedents had already run, albeit unsuccessfully, for city office and, in the municipal election of 1910, 60 per cent of the eligible Jews voted, despite the fact that the balloting took place on Saturday. Two Canadian centres, Winnipeg and Ottawa, already had a Jewish alderman, and at the opening of the Teraulay Street Synagogue (Machzikei HaDas) in 1907, both Edmund Bristol and Claude Macdonell, the local members of Parliament, had predicted similar development in Toronto.[4]

The more astute and acculturated East Europeans recognized the growing political awareness of the local Jews and sought both to purge it of corruption and channel it in directions beneficial to the immigrants. In the autumn of 1909, a Hebrew Ratepayers' Association was formed, apparently at the behest of A.P. Lewis. Prompted by increased taxes in the Ward and an appeal to the city for funds by missionary societies, Lewis indignantly declared at the organizational meeting at Goel Tzedec that the Jews were not to be labelled as foreigners, that they were "citizens of a free, broad Dominion, bearing our share of the load, and expecting our portion of the freedom and privileges of British subjects . . . ." The

Association was to be non-partisan, formed "solely to educate its members as to what are and what are not their rights and privileges; and also to influence the district to a higher standard of citizenship, and a healthier view of life." The Hebrew Ratepayers' Association, therefore, would act as a lobby to protect the interests of the Jews of the Ward and an agency to help Jews participate in civic life by educating them in political practice and encouraging them to become naturalized citizens.

Toronto Jewry did not fall into the stereotype pattern of voting en bloc for one party, or unanimously for Jewish candidates. Admittedly, in the early twentieth century most East European Jewish immigrants were loyal to the Conservative party, representative of the administration in power in Ontario and in Toronto at the time of their arrival. Only the wealthy and acclimatized English and German Jews felt secure enough to oppose the majority trend in Toronto by supporting the Liberals.[5] By the early years of the twentieth century, the doctrinaire socialists were also voting Liberal, as were a number of the older middle-class East European families. But primarily, the Ward continued to vote Conservative.

By 1911, however, the atmosphere was beginning to change and more East European Jewish voters were dividing between the parties, especially in the federal arena, and large numbers were being caught up in the enthusiasm of the electoral spectacle. "At the recent Federal Election," Rohold observed in a description of local Jewry the following year, "in no other part of the whole of Canada, was the contest more real and fierce, than amongst the Jews in St. John's Ward. For weeks before the election, night after night all the available meeting places were taxed to the utmost capacity . . . . All kinds of promises were made to the supposed electors, who had votes and who had not. In fact, every man, woman and child in the ward was a politician . . . ."[6] How much of this was due to the efforts of the Hebrew Ratepayers, or of individuals such as Magistrate Jacob Cohen, to dissuade the Jewish voters from attaching themselves blindly to one party is unclear. The phenomenon was probably the result of length of residence and the arrival of the acculturated younger generation to political awareness.

Jewish candidates fared poorly, even in their quest for the Jewish vote, during much of the period preceding the First World War. An apologist for the Jewish community might attribute this situation to an altruistic attitude on the part of Jewish electors. After all, Abe Lewis made it the avowed purpose of the Hebrew Ratepayers to support the best candidate and not exclusively

Jewish ones. In actuality, however, a less disinterested motivation was in force. Most immigrant voters were concerned with the practicalities of politics. On the municipal level, where most activity took place and unnaturalized immigrants could vote as soon as they had acquired property, the best government, it was felt, was one which could get things done. There were problems of sanitation, of taxes, of dealing with landlords, of licensing, of obtaining immigration permits, possibly of securing grants for Jewish charities, and numerous others which required decisive action, and for that, power was imperative. The immigrant feared that a Jewish elected official might, by virtue of his background, be isolated at City Council and thus be deprived of an effective voice. Besides, the political establishment, Gentile, Protestant and Orange as it was, had been only too glad to court the Jewish voter and had effectively demonstrated its ability for action.[7]

Most Jews, therefore, rallied behind the nominees of the establishment and, in Tory Toronto, that meant the Conservatives. It was within the Conservative party that Jewish ward heelers first began to appear and that a Jewish political association first emerged. The Jewish ward heelers were not employees of the political machine, and probably did not envisage themselves as active political manipulators. They were, rather, thrust into the position by virtue of their prominence in the Jewish community and often because of their occupations. Steamship agents, widely known because of their help in bringing relatives from Europe, and court interpreters, for instance, exerted influence in this regard. They were especially active among the Polish Jews, the poorest element and so most in need of favours from the establishment, but they were not unknown among the Galicians and Russians as well. By 1910 a Hebrew Conservative Association was active in the Jewish neighbourhoods and was being taken seriously by the local members of Parliament, Macdonell and Bristol. Its membership in the period numbered four hundred and it was considered "representative of an influence which controlled thousands of voters throughout the city."

The case of Jacob Cohen is illustrative of how one local Jew rose to political prominence. Cohen had been born in Poland and had emigrated to the United States, working as a clerk and peddler in New York, Tennessee, Louisiana and Texas. Having amassed some capital, he moved to Toronto where an elder brother had already settled. From 1873 to 1878 he peddled jewellery in the Ontario hinterland, finally opening a shoe store on Queen Street close to City Hall and to the police courts. Because the Conservatives had been in power when he arrived, Cohen gravitated to the party and began to attend meetings of the local association, where he struck up an acquaintance with Colonel George Taylor Denison, then a police magistrate. By the 1890s the Yiddish-speaking population of the city had increased and a number of Jews were appearing in court on minor infractions, usually for violation of peddling regulations. Whenever Denison needed an interpreter, he would call across the street for "Jake" Cohen, who spoke Polish as well as Yiddish. As such incidents increased in frequency, the process of interpretation became too time-consuming and Denison arranged for Cohen to be appointed a Justice of the Peace and a bail magistrate, so that he was able to sit on the Bench himself (1910). Upon Denison's retirement in 1918, the magistrate designated Cohen as his successor.

Even prior to his appointment as a J.P., Cohen had been ex-pected to deliver the Jewish vote whenever there was an election. The Conservative party supplied him with funds for a campaign, but considering his integrity on the Bench, it is unlikely that he used any for bribery. The Jewish community, on the other hand, looked to him for intercession at City Hall.

The development of Jewish political associations did not meet with unanimous approval in the Jewish community. Opposition to peculiarly Jewish political associations was especially vocal in Holy Blossom, where a majority favoured as few distinctions as possible from the general population. If members such as Cohen supported the Hebrew Ratepayers and the Hebrew Conservative Association, others condemned their formation. In response to the establishment of a Hebrew Citizens' League, probably a forerunner of the Hebrew Ratepayers, Edmund Scheuer had urged the Jewish community to abandon such efforts and to participate in politics with a minimum of publicity. "A solid Jewish vote would indeed be a calamity for Canadian Jewry," he maintained. Canadian Jews had no need to organize as Jews or to be informed politically in the Yiddish language.[8]

By the end of the 1920s, exclusively Jewish political associations would have disappeared and the Jews integrated themselves into the general ward associations of both parties. In fact, those associations which encompassed wards with a large Jewish population would often be dominated by Jews, but they would no longer be exclusively Jewish. Prior to 1920, however, the educative process was still in progress and the defensive attitude predominated. Despite Scheuer's complaints, another Jewish political association was formed in 1915. Like the Hebrew Ratepayers, this was established "by the best of the younger element of the Jewish citizens for the purpose of educating their co-religionists" in politics at all levels, so that they might take an "intellectual interest" in political affairs. The group professed to be non-partisan, but its composition suggests that it was Liberal.

II

The pre-World War One years were ones of change in many aspects of Jewish life in Toronto. The sudden increase in population, the establishment of the Associated Hebrew Charities, the development of unions and the growth of political associations were all indicative of a maturing community. This period was marked also by the first successful entry of Jews into the official life of the city. In the federal election of 1911 Jewish enumerators had appeared and by 1913 Dr. John Shayne, president of Bnai Zion, had been appointed immigration inspector. A brace of Jewish candidates contested the municipal elections for 1913. Harry Winberg ran for alderman with the support of C.A.B. Brown, a prominent non-Jewish politician; Abraham Nisnovitz, a real estate agent, ran for the Board of Education with the backing of the socialists.

More significant, however, was the success of Louis M. Singer in the aldermanic contest in Ward 4 the following year. Singer, a recent law graduate and member of a wealthy East European family which had joined Holy Blossom, had long been active in Conservative political circles, as well as in the Hebrew Ratepayers' Association. Singer's victory marks a watershed in the political life of Toronto Jews, but it also illustrates the level of the community's maturity. His opponent, also a Jew, had based his campaign on ethnic appeal, styling himself "candidate for the Jews." Singer, on the other hand, had concentrated on issues and hardly mentioned his antecedents at all. Yet, despite the tactics of his opposition, the *Hebrew Journal* remained neutral and tried to persuade its readers merely to vote. On the day of the election, the Jews supported Singer overwhelmingly.

The attitude of the public was also interesting. Most local papers were sympathetic to Singer and none made an issue of his religion. The *Star*, especially, supported him as a "man of action" and even published his photograph prior to his election, an unusual practice at that period. In the final vote, a large number of non-Jewish electors favoured Singer as well.[9]

For almost forty years following Louis Singer's election, Jewish municipal candidates sought only those positions which it was possible to achieve through a substantial Jewish vote; that is, the post of alderman and Board of Education trustee in wards 3 and 4, where the majority of the Jews resided. Even so, because of the boundaries of the wards, none of these could expect to be elected on the basis of Jewish support alone. The office of mayor, which required much broader support, was generally avoided as being beyond reach. Only Harry Winberg had the confidence to contest the mayoralty, an action which required even greater audacity since he was not a member of any political party. Several times between 1915 and 1925 he offered himself as a candidate and each time he was taken seriously neither by his opponents nor by a majority of the voters.

The events surrounding Winberg's first candidacy in 1915, though hardly significant in the political life of the Jewish community and even at times bordering on farce, were important for the attitudes they exposed in the Jews and in the general population. Winberg made no secret of his Jewishness and stated categorically that he was proud of it. Yet, he had been nominated by Gentiles and got considerable support in areas where Jewish population was sparse. Moreover, the *Star*, captivated by his immigrant success story, gave him far more space than it provided for his Orange opponent, Mayor Church. The paper urged his defeat not because he was a Jew, but rather because of his opposition to a by-law concerning radial railways. Most Jews, on the other hand, withheld their support from Winberg despite his prominence in the Jewish community. As one Jew remarked after the election, "the probability of better treatment from a Hebrew mayor did not enter into their considerations."[10]

Throughout the remaining period of this study, Jewish candidates were reasonably successful on the municipal scene. Joseph Singer, elected alderman in 1919, was serving on the Board of Control by 1923. Nathan Phillips won an aldermanic post the following year and would continue on City Council until he was elected mayor in 1955, the first Jew to hold that office. Usually, however, a seat on the Board of Education was considered the logical stepping stone to a political career. Samuel Factor, elected in 1923, later went to City Hall and eventually became the first Jew from Toronto to enter Parliament (1930); John J. Glass, who became a member of the provincial legislature (1934-43), also began his career on the Board of Education (1928) and then progressed to the post of alderman. Joseph Gordon, elected to the Board in 1925, advanced to City Hall in 1928. There were only two notable exceptions to the rule at this period. E.F. Singer, the first Jewish member of the Ontario legislature, had held no previous political office, but his rapid ascent was no doubt due to

252

the long residence, wealth and influence of his family. Ida Siegel, in contrast, successfully elected to the Board of Education in 1931, was defeated when she sought an aldermanic post in 1933. She appears to have been deserted by Jewish voters because the Jewish ward heelers campaigned against her. They felt that since she was not a lawyer and a woman at that, she could not be an effective spokesman for Jewish interests. Consequently, they supported the Orange candidate, from whom favours could be assured.[11]

On the federal scene, the difficulties were greater. As early as 1917, Jews had been nominated for federal seats in the ridings of West Toronto and Centre Toronto, but none had been elected. By the mid-1920s, politically concerned Jews were anxious to have an explicitly Jewish candidate who would speak for Jewish interests without ulterior motive and whose prestige would reflect upon his constituents. This was the case in Montreal, where the Jewish community had been represented in the House of Commons by Samuel W. Jacobs since 1917.

But if Rabbi Brickner had looked forward to the election of a Jewish member, his successor at Holy Blossom did not. Commenting on the provincial election of 1926, Rabbi Isserman objected to the demands by Jewish politicians that a Jew be nominated. The injection of religion into politics, he maintained, leads only to malice and bigotry. The prospect of a Jewish candidate, he insisted, was repugnant to Jews "who consider themselves Canadians and who do not consider the Jews a political party." Isserman had also opposed a Jewish candidate in the federal election of 1926, an action for which he had been severely criticized in the Jewish community. "I am of the opinion," he asserted, "that Jews as Jews need no representatives . . . ."[12]

By 1925 the possibility of success for a Jewish candidate was very real, especially in the newly created federal riding of Toronto Centre West, which encompassed the bulk of the Jewish community. Toronto had consistently returned Conservative members to Ottawa and the local Liberal machine saw the opportunity of winning a seat on the ethnic issue. Jews were therefore welcomed into the ranks of the Liberal party in Toronto at the Ontario Club, and a successful campaign was undertaken within the local Liberal riding association to win the nomination for Alderman Joseph Singer. True to their habitual practice, however, the Jews refused to be cajoled into voting for a Jewish candidate *per se*. In fact, one Liberal spokesman reported that thousands of Jews were against Singer. Consequently, he was defeated.[13]

A variety of explanations could be advanced to explain Singer's rejection by the Jewish community. Some contemporaries believed that the Jews, affected by the Tory atmosphere of Toronto, simply refused to vote for a Liberal. Another factor was that the Jewish factory workers failed to turn out and that Jewish manufacturers refused to support a Liberal.[14] It would be interesting to know if there was any relationship between the two phenomena. In any case, it is probably true that many factory workers refused to vote for Singer because of his upper-class connections.

Singer's very Jewishness also worked against him. The Orange Order and the non-Jewish Masonic lodges apparently spent considerable amounts to see that a Jew was not elected. Some Jews, also, preferred a Gentile for the same reasons that they had hesitated to elect Jews to municipal office early in the century. Finally, even Singer's Jewish supporters avoided appealing to Jews solely on the basis of his being Jewish. Granted, they brought Sam Jacobs from Montreal to speak for him, but on the whole, Jewish Liberals, being from the more acculturated elements and consequently tending to minimize parochialism, urged Jews to vote for Singer because of his policies and not his religion.[15]

Singer nevertheless drew a respectable number of votes considering his party and his background, and some in the Jewish community felt that the Jewish Conservatives should now lobby for the nomination of a Jewish candidate in their party. Hardly waiting for the advice, the Hebrew Conservative Association nominated Louis Singer in the provincial riding of St. Andrews in 1926. The Orange-dominated riding association, however, refused to approve either a Jew or a Catholic and the Jewish Conservatives were vocal in their disapproval, maintaining that the party had ignored "the Jewish community's rights to representation." Singer ran, in any case, as an Independent against the official nominee, but the machine was too entrenched and, as the *Star* remarked, he was "crushed."[16]

It now became apparent, even to Jewish Conservatives, that if any breakthrough for the Jews were to be made beyond the municipal sphere, this would most likely come by way of the Liberal party. The Conservative party had consistently refused on grounds of religion to nominate a Jew. However, as the Jewish population came increasingly to dominate particular ridings, it was not inconceivable that the party would have swallowed its prejudice if a suitable Jewish nominee were put forward. The difficulty was that the Conservative Jewish leadership consisted of men of the East European immigrant generation who did not possess enough facility in the English language to be successful, and the few who did lacked the self-confidence to run. The Liberals, on the other hand, had been attracting the native-born and the college-educated professionals. Here, there was a plethora of Jewish potential candidates. Moreover, for politically active Jews and for the rest as well, party divisions faded considerably for a few years following 1926. Because of past frustrations in attempting to get Jews elected, it now became vital to the self-respect of the community to send a Jew to Parliament. Although even at this juncture the Jews did not vote *en bloc*, large numbers did shift to the Liberal party as the possibility of a Jewish nominee increased.[17]

By 1930 the Liberals in the federal riding of Spadina had nominated Samuel Factor in the approaching election. His Conservative opponent, Tommy Church, a former mayor who had always been able to count on Jewish support, probably expected little difficulty. The Jews, however, were now no longer concerned with issues or personalities; they were concerned only with the election of a Jewish member and, with Jewish voters constituting a majority in the riding, that was a real possibility if for once they voted together. The *Hebrew Journal*, which had refused to support Joseph Singer five years earlier, now threw itself behind Factor with full force.

For once the ethnic tactic worked, assisted no doubt by Factor's Yiddish-speaking immigrant and working-class background. Factor was successful and was soon joined at the provincial level by John Glass, another Liberal. However, the Conservatives had seen the writing on the wall and had already nominated E.F. Singer for the forthcoming provincial election.

For a brief time after the initial election of Jews to federal and provincial office, the experience appears to have served a cathartic purpose and the Jewish community fell back into the pattern of dividing between the parties. The Depression, however, fostered a concentration on issues over party or ethnic loyalty and Jews, like everyone else in search of economic panaceas, divided their support not only between the traditional middle-class parties, but among a variety of socialists and communists as well. On the other hand, persecution of Jews abroad and discrimination at home produced an increasingly defensive attitude, and pressure mounted to elect Jewish representatives who could be trusted to defend Jewish interests by advocating open immigration policies and by condemning domestic anti-semitism. While the East Europeans were undoubtedly affected most by these sentiments, the scions of the old community were not indifferent, especially as Nazi barbarities became more evident.

The 1930s, therefore, set a pattern for Jewish political behaviour in Toronto which prevailed certainly until after the Second World War and, to a significant degree, continues to this day. The old immigrant practice of voting out of deference or in the hope of favours had largely disappeared, replaced by two sometimes conflicting determining forces: on the one hand, the desire to vote purely on issues which affected the public good, and on the other, the feeling that security was to be had only in the election of Jews to public office, regardless of issues and party.

NOTES

1 *History of Toronto and County of York* (Toronto: C. Blackett Robinson, 1885), II, p. 154; City of Toronto, *Minutes and Proceedings of the Council of the Corporation of the City of Toronto 1883* (Toronto: E.F. Clarke, 1884), Appendix 2, p. 11.

2 Julius Seltzer, personal interview, Feb. 15, 1972.

3 Personal interviews: Arthur Cohen, Dec. 20, 1971; Julius Seltzer, Feb. 15, 1972; Ida Berk, Feb. 4, 1972; Ben Zion Hyman, Oct. 8, 1972. These practices by ward heelers were not confined to the relationship with Jews. Other immigrant groups were approached in a similar manner. The Jews were merely the most obvious and the most convenient to brand as potentially corruptible. As late as 1919, the *Telegram* would condemn "the so-called Christian politicians who seek to corrupt and befool the Europeans of Toronto."

> Every Canadian of Hebrew origin, including many Canadian Hebrews of European birth, is sick at heart of the methods employed in dealing with the so-called Hebrew vote in this city. The Canadian-born heirs to British freedom take the so-called glorious names of Liberalism and Conservatism into their pursuit of the Jew vote. There never was a general election or a bye-election in the semi-European constituencies of Toronto where the successful candidate could not be unseated, and Liberal and Tory workers could not be put in jail for their share in organized attempts to educate the foreign voters with whiskey, beer and money (*Telegram*, editorial, Oct. 9, 1919).

4 Since it is forbidden to write on the Sabbath, most Jews asked the returning officer to mark their ballots for them. This was

the situation whenever voting was scheduled for Saturday. Even the rabbis voted in this manner. In 1916, for instance, over 75 per cent of eligible Jewish voters turned out, despite the Saturday voting (*Star*, Jan. 1, 1916).

In 1906, J.S. Granatstein ran for alderman in the Jewish neighbourhood; Paul Levi ran in the same period. Abe Lewis ran for Board of Education early in the century and in 1909 he, Levi and Louis Gurofsky ran for the aldermanic post (*Jewish Times*, Dec. 14, 1906, p. 22; Jan. 8, 1909, p. 75).

5 This was true elsewhere in North America as well. See Lawrence H. Fuchs, *The Political Behavior of American Jews* (Glencoe, Ill.: Free Press, 1956).

6 Rohold, *The Jews in Canada*, pp. 13-14.

7 For instance in 1911 one municipal candidate, Charles Alfred Maguire, appealed to the Pride of Israel, and probably to other Jewish organizations as well, to help him to secure the Jewish vote (Pride of Israel *Souvenir* 1930, pages not numbered). There is no mention of whether the society acquiesced.

8 Scheuer in *Toronto News*, undated clipping, *ca.* 1900-1910, Edmund Scheuer Scrapbook, Holy Blossom Archives.

9 *Star*, Dec. 27, 30, 1913; Jan. 2, 1914; Nov. 6, 1915.

10 *Star*, Jan. 1, 1916. In the same period, Henry Dworkin, a Jew, was nominated as aldermanic candidate for the Socialists in one of the ridings, but he declined in favour of James Simpson, a Gentile labour leader who later became mayor (*Star*, Dec. 24, 1915). Dworkin later did run, but was defeated, probably because he was a socialist and not because he was Jewish.

11 Two trustees sat for each ward. By the late 1920s, it was possible to elect a Jewish trustee in Ward 4 because a tacit arrangement could be made with influential Gentiles in the northern part of the ward who might, by unfavourable comment, have assured the defeat of a Jew. They would accept the Jewish nominee provided that the Jewish politicians would approve whomever they put forward (confidential interview).

Some Jewish candidates ran initially for specifically Jewish reasons. John Glass, for instance, sought to eliminate the tacit refusal to hire Jewish teachers. He was helped in his campaign by the Sons of Jacob Benevolent Society and other candidates probably received similar assistance from their own organizations (J.J. Glass, personal interview, Dec. 13, 1972).

12 *Canadian Jewish Review*, Aug. 8, 1924, p. 1; Nov. 5, 1926, p. 16; Nov. 19, 1926, pp. 1, 17.

13 G.N. Gordon to S.W. Jacobs, May 1, 1925 (telegram, Jacobs Papers, Public Archives of Canada); Louis Gurofsky to S.W. Jacobs, Oct. 6, 1925 (telegram, *ibid.*).

14 S.W. Jacobs to Joseph Singer, Nov. 5, 1925; Dr. Abraham Brodey to Jacobs, Oct. 31, 1925; Joseph Singer to Jacobs, Oct. 30, 1925 (Jacobs Papers).

15 *Ibid.*: L. Gurofsky to Jacobs, Oct. 30, 1925 (Jacobs Papers). One additional factor might be mentioned in connection with Singer's defeat, the belief that a Liberal government might restrict immigration from Eastern Europe. Sam Jacobs believed that to be an issue, but it appears not to have been discussed openly in Toronto. See Jacobs to Singer, May 20, 1925, Jacobs Papers.

16 *Ibid.*, Brodey to Jacobs, Oct. 31, 1925. *Star*, Oct. 21, Nov. 12, Dec. 1, 2, 1926.

17 Personal interviews: David E. Newman, Aug. 24, 1974; Rabbi S. Sachs, Aug. 13, 1973. See also Samuel Factor's address to the Ontario Zionists, quoted in *Star*, Apr. 24, 1933.

CHAPTER 16

TWO ATTEMPTS AT UNITY: THE FEDERATION OF JEWISH PHILANTHROPIES AND THE CANADIAN JEWISH CONGRESS, 1916 – 1929

The First World War wrought many changes in the Jewish community of Toronto. The troubled years which preceded it had resulted in an unprecedented influx of Jews into the city. The war itself, creating a scarcity of commodities and housing, meant substantial profits for merchants fortunate enough to have stored up stock prior to the outbreak or those who had made wise purchases of real estate. Both Jews and non-Jews fell into these categories. Indeed, the war years produced within the Jewish community a number of prosperous individuals who now had the leisure for communal work and the experience to handle its financial aspects. Finally, as peace approached, the prospect of Jewish national dreams being realized in Palestine grew more likely following the Balfour Declaration. Throughout the world, organizations were being formed to speak for the Jews at Versailles. In Canada, too, a national organization was to emerge.

During the first years of war it was necessary to absorb thousands of new immigrants to Toronto. The Jewish community reacted by establishing numerous philanthropic agencies, co-operating through the Associated Hebrew Charities. The Associated Charities, however, was merely an information depot, with minimal control over the distribution of relief and none whatever over the collection of funds. In addition, it united only a handful of charitable organizations. The result was an improvement over the situation prior to 1912 but, in the field of fund-raising, chaos nonetheless. Charitable funds were collected through a variety of devices: benefit concerts, raffles, bazaars, indiscriminate and frequently unauthorized door-to-door collections. Money was not plentiful to begin with, but the constant solicitation was making the public increasingly cynical and tight-fisted. Moreover, philanthropic agencies found it impossible to carry out their functions because a great deal of their time was occupied in raising money. This became especially serious when the flood of immigrants made expansion of services essential.[1] The solution to both problems would be a fusing of the information centre with an independently structured fund-raising organization: in short, a federation. Under this system, constituent organizations would maintain their separate identities but would unite for fund-raising and planning.

The principles of such an organization were not strange to the Jews. In many European centres, organized Jewish communities – *Kultus gemeinden* or *kehilloth* – had for centuries imposed taxes for the support of charitable projects and institutions. The ethnic diversity of North American Jewry made the transplanting of such communities impossible. Nevertheless, co-ordination of services was imperative, producing the Associated Hebrew Charities in 1912.

By this time, many Jewish communities in the United States had recognized the need for common fund-raising efforts and the majority chose federation over consolidation. Chicago, Philadelphia, Cleveland, Milwaukee, Detroit, Syracuse and Buffalo had all established federations by 1904 and Pittsburgh followed suit in 1912. Canadian Jews joined the movement as well; Montreal and Hamilton were in the process of organizing federated systems.[2] These federations, founded in times of prosperity, were conspicuously successful, encouraging Toronto Jewry to embark upon such an effort in 1916, at the outset of a period of economic decline.

For Jewish charities in Toronto, 1916 was a year of crisis. Money was not forthcoming even for basic relief, let alone for the maintenance of physical facilities. The ladies' societies, approaching bankruptcy because of the financial crisis, were unable to supply coal to their dependent families, and preparations were under way to sell the Associated Charities building on Simcoe Street to pay the taxes. Communal welfare would now have to take precedence over organizational chauvinism.

The federation concept had been filtering into the Jewish community for years. The American press, Jewish and non-Jewish, abounded in articles on the subject and communal workers were becoming increasingly aware of its advantages. Three individuals deserve mention in this connection, for the collective memory of the Jewish community variously accords to them the distinction of having initiated the Federation of the Jewish Philanthropies of Toronto. These were Edmund Scheuer, Abraham Cohen and Ida Siegel.

Scheuer maintained an academic interest by collecting articles on federation from American papers. Cohen, on the other hand, a young lawyer active in Goel Tzedec, undertook to study federations in other cities and had become convinced that one would work in Toronto. Ida Siegel shared this opinion as a result of her frequent visits to American centres such as Pittsburgh, Rochester and Buffalo, all of which had federated Jewish charities.[3]

It was Mrs. Siegel who attempted to test public opinion on the subject by calling a meeting at the Zionist Institute on Beverley Street in the fall of 1916, to which workers in synagogues, societies and charitable organizations were invited. The meeting was less than successful; only Leo Frankel, president of Holy Blossom, Alderman Louis Singer and Abraham Cohen appeared. Frankel, seeing the poor response, promptly left. Singer, too, was pessimistic, believing that a fragmented and parochial community such as Toronto could never organize a federation. He suggested that a prominent individual whose mere presence could generate confidence should be sought to head any co-operative effort and he refused to participate further until there was such a commitment. Mrs. Siegel and Cohen, determined that a federation must be established, agreed. The logical candidate to lend his name was Edmund Scheuer, by this time the elder statesman of Toronto Jewry. Scheuer had known Ida Siegel as his student at Holy Blossom Sabbath School; he liked her and so she was in a position to approach him. Scheuer accepted the presidency, but insisted that he not be asked to participate actively. The problem remained, therefore, of drawing other prominent individuals into the organization and persuading them to take an active part.

A catalyst emerged in J.J. Allen, prominent on the local theatrical scene and an individual with a circle of acquaintances encompassing the whole spectrum of the Jewish community. In addition, he maintained membership both at Holy Blossom and at Goel Tzedec. Allen had become wealthy through the ownership of newly popular motion picture theatres and was sympathetic to many aspects of charitable work. Moreover, Mrs. Siegel had long been friendly with his wife, Ray, who persuaded her husband support the federation concept.

The list of individuals who attended the organizational meeting of the Federation of the Jewish Philanthropies at Scheuer's grand Rosedale residence in October 1916, illustrates Allen's success in attracting prominent supporters from a variety of elements in the community. The group resolved that a federation be formed immediately, and circulated in the Jewish community the call for an election of officers. As might have been expected, the initiative came from Holy Blossom and Goel Tzedec, the two principal congregations, and from the philanthropic groups associated with them. However, a provisional board of trustees, elected later that month, included not only additional synagogue-affiliated individuals, but secularists and socialists as well.*

The principal object of Federation was efficient fund-raising through a single annual campaign. The board members contributed the cost of publicity, which consisted initially of notices in English and in Yiddish. These were prepared by Archie Bennett, who had wide journalistic experience, and were distributed by mail throughout the city. The *Hebrew Journal* attempted through its editorials to prepare the Jewish community for the first campaign, planned for February 1917 with a goal of $30,000. In the meantime, volunteers were organized to canvass potential subscribers.

Despite these efforts, Federation had great difficulty achieving its initial structure. As Scheuer later recalled, "We had to meet opposition from within our ranks and without."[4]   As soon as the amount to be raised had been announced, a number of supporters, and even some members of the board, defected, refusing to serve as canvassers on the grounds that it would be impossible to raise such a monstrous sum. Others believed that there were too many disparate factions in the city to contemplate a united campaign. So serious did this collapse of morale become that four days before the campaign was to start, thirty-three new people had to be invited by special delivery letter to infuse new vigour into the operation by serving on the board.[5]

Additional problems also plagued the fledgling Federation. The Ladies' Montefiore, although they participated, were not enthusiastic about a new system. The East European women's

* In addition to Allen, Mrs. Siegel and Cohen, these included Leo Frankel, president of Holy Blossom; Mrs. Loeser of the Ladies' Montefiore; Mrs. Lewis of Hebrew Ladies' Aid; Barnet Stone, a prominent Zionist; Sam Factor, Archie Bennett, a journalist; and several prominent members of the East European community, Moses Gelber, Louis Levinsky and J.S. Granatstein. The provisional board would also include socialists such as Henry Dworkin and Abraham Rhinewine.

societies were also reluctant to submerge themselves in a colossus which would be inimical to their independent identities and would demand an annual report of activities, income and expenditure. Their independent philanthropic organizations had been a source of self-respect which they could not easily surrender. Then, to add insult to injury, the board approved a constitution which excluded women, despite their having been the backbone of Jewish philanthropy in Toronto since the 1860s. After a protest by Ida Siegel, who was also active in the women's suffrage movement, they agreed to admit one female. Ironically they chose not Mrs. Siegel, but rather a member of the Montefiore, who had initially opposed Federation, a circumstance not likely to please the East European women.

The Federation of the Jewish Philanthropies survived the initial turmoil and a variety of organizations, far exceeding that encompassed by the Associated Hebrew Charities, was persuaded to affiliate.[6] Constitutionally, Federation followed similar organizations in Baltimore and Pittsburgh. Individuals sponsored Federation by becoming members at six dollars per year and all funds collected in this manner were apportioned among the affiliated groups. Beneficiary organizations were closely controlled, having to submit detailed annual reports and to obtain permission to increase their obligations and facilities. Although Federation publicity emphasized the continued autonomy of affiliated organizations, in fact restriction was the dominant, and perhaps the necessary, consequence of affiliation. All powers of the Federation were vested in a Board of Trustees consisting of forty-five people.[7]

At first, the opening campaign appeared to be a great success. Three days prior to the official starting date, fifty people had pledged over $7,000, a feat accomplished by the Allens, who contributed a substantial sum and challenged others to match it. This met some of the immediate needs of the community, such as the provision of coal to the poor and the redeeming of the Associated Charities. In total, however, the first campaign was a dismal failure; the $20,000 raised was insufficient to provide the necessary services, and some of the wealthy board members had to supplement the treasury by increasing their own contributions. Moreover, although it did eliminate Jewish street beggars, Federation failed to stop independent fund-raising efforts, despite the request that members refuse contributions to any charity not approved by the organization. Charitable societies continued to multiply, much to the distress of the Federation officers

Nevertheless, it weathered its first critical years, despite an influenza epidemic which taxed its resources to their limit. Food, fuel, rent and transportation for medical help outside Toronto were provided for the poor. In 1918-19, the Ladies' Co-operative Board alone cared for seventy-two families, and the Federation as a whole opened an enlarged Free Dispensary on McCaul Street and operated a kosher soup kitchen which supplied 193 families during the epidemic.[8]

By the end of 1918, the new organization had gained the confidence of Toronto Jewry. "The question of the advisability of organizing a Federation of Jewish Philanthropic activities in Toronto, has without any doubt been answered affirmatively," the Board of Trustees announced. "The ultimate object of the amalgamation is now clear to the community . . . ." Over two thousand had now acquired membership and the total subscription had exceeded $50,000. Moreover, Federation had been incorporated under the province and was now receiving an annual municipal grant of $1,000. It appeared, therefore, that considerable unity had at last been achieved and that the financial problems of the Jewish charitable institutions had been largely reduced.

The financial success was qualified but real, but the supposed unity was only superficial. Scheuer maintained correctly in 1918 that the Federation board was "composed of representatives of all classes of Jews of Toronto";[9] it was indeed broadly based and had drawn together practically all elements of the Jewish community. Relatively unified action was now the rule, but not under conditions favoured by many of the constituent organizations. The ladies' societies, especially, found their relationship with Federation distasteful.

Scheuer thought he understood the reasons for dissatisfaction within Federation and the refusal of some groups to join. In calling for communal harmony in an early speech, he was sharply critical of individuals who, he maintained, "continually organize new societies for the purpose of holding office."[10] Political ambition and parochialism, however, were not the principal sources of dissension. The very factor that gave the appearance of unity proved the alienating element: that is, the domination of Federation by members of the old community, its adoption of their philosophy of scientific philanthropy and the tendency for East Europeans on the board and in many of the constituent agencies to defer to them.

With the nominal presence of a single woman on the board, the Federation of the Jewish Philanthropies was a male-operated enterprise. In the East European community, organized charity, except for immigrant transportation, free burial and a few lesser activities, had been left to women. Even the Associated Hebrew Charities gave few East European men the experience of running a philanthropic organization, and most probably preferred to let their wives continue their active role. In Federation, however, men assumed leadership and since members of the old community constituted the most prosperous segment of the population, with time to devote to administration, they naturally rose to prominence in the organization. This was not an attempt by Holy Blossom to govern the city's Jewish philanthropies as the Ladies' Montefiore had tried to do earlier in the century. Members of the old community were merely propelled into the position of leadership, reinforced by prosperous East Europeans who had either affiliated with Holy Blossom or deferred to its members in matters of policy.

That policy was one of strict economy and efficiency – "scientific philanthropy." A thorough and objective system of investigation was introduced to root out the undeserving and the Board insisted that the womens' organizations distribute relief with restraint. Originally, Federation had had no investigators of its own; it used the volunteers of the ladies' societies, which were constantly criticized for their open-handedness and badgered for written reports. In fact, when these were not submitted, Federation refused to disburse funds to the society concerned.

Frustrated by the rigidity of Federation, one by one the East European ladies' societies began to withdraw, including the Montefiore, despite the old-community complexion and scientific approach of the Board. Each probably hoped to continue its personal approach independently, but the bulk of the contributors to Federation considered the new system a success. Most local Jews had lost their taste for individual philanthropy; they preferred to leave everything to Federation. The ladies' societies, therefore, denied Federation resources, either dissolved or continued informally on a much reduced scale. Of the societies which withdrew, only Maternity Aid continued to prosper because it had never had to receive funds from Federation and because it performed services that Federation could not provide.

As the ladies' societies disappeared, Federation began to assume their functions. This necessitated the appointment of professional administrators. Almost immediately after its establishment, it had engaged someone to take charge of the central office, receiving requests for relief and calling the appropriate society to investigate. After the dissolution of the ladies' societies, Federation had to employ its own paid visitors.[11]

With Federation taking on more responsibility and with another increase in immigration at the conclusion of the war, it was felt that an expert executive director should also be appointed. Since Canadian professional social work was still in its infancy, Samuel B. Kaufman was brought from Indianapolis as director in 1921.

Kaufman's major duties were to be the keeping of accounts and the administration of the office, but he also offered suggestions for expansion and rationalization of Federation services. He recommended methods for improvement of the information clearing house in order to reduce duplication and called for the establishment of a Health and Sanitation Committee to co-operate with non-Jewish agencies such as the City Welfare Department, the Board of Health, the Mothers' Allowance Commission and the Neighbourhood Workers' Association. He was largely responsible for the replacement of volunteer workers by professionals, and among the first of these to be employed were two natives of Toronto. Miss Malca Halpern, a graduate in nursing from Mt. Sinai Hospital in New York, took charge of Federation's medical functions, while Miss Judith Bronstein, a graduate of the newly established Social Service Department at the University of Toronto, was assigned responsibility for children's work.

In addition, an immigrant aid society was established to deal with postwar refugee problems and set the groundwork for a revitalized free loan society to reduce the dependence of the needy on communal handouts. In this project, Kaufman was assisted by a revived B'nai B'rith lodge which had come into existence in 1919. In 1922, the Toronto Lodge, contemplating a social service project, approached Rabbi Brickner for a suggestion. He recommended a new free loan society financed by B'nai B'rith and administered by Federation. Samuel Kronick, a millinery manufacturer and a member of the lodge who had for years been quietly offering interest-free loans out of his own resources, was placed in charge of the enterprise together with Nathan Phillips, the president of the lodge.[12]

During Kaufman's tenure, from 1922 to 1924, Federation expanded its activities to include appropriations for a boys' camp established by the B'nai B'rith on Lake Couchiching in 1921 and a Girls' Fresh Air Cottage at Whitby run by the Council of Jewish Women. It also brought two consultants from the Bureau of Jewish Social Research in New York to organize a campaign for a new orphanage, an effort which resulted in the purchase of a building on Annette Street in the West Toronto Junction in 1922. Having had its original headquarters in the Zionist Institute on

Beverley Street, Federation had now taken over the lower floor of the Associated Hebrew Charities building on Simcoe Street, where the orphanage was also located. When the institution vacated the premises, its portion of the building was fitted up as the Jewish Boys' Club, which was financed through Federation. Federation itself soon found that its increased activities required additional space, and in 1928 the community purchased Edmund Bristol's residence at Beverley and Baldwin streets, renaming it Scheuer House. This would serve as headquarters for Federation and for many of its affiliated organizations for the next quarter century.[13]

When Sam Kaufman resigned in the summer of 1924, there was opposition to the importation of another high-priced expert from the United States. Some believed that a home-grown product commanding a smaller salary would be preferable. Fortunately, the majority of the board favoured the extra expense of an experienced director, calculating a saving in eventual efficiency. They chose Joseph A. Woolf of Cleveland, a social worker trained at the University of Chicago, with wide experience there and in Pittsburgh. Thereafter, Federation always insisted on a professional director.

Despite its administrative efficiency, Federation was a financial failure. A few successful campaigns in the early 1920s now gave way to increased shortages of funds. Response to appeals was disappointing compared to that in cities with Jewish populations of similar size. Pledges went unfulfilled and the organization was forced to borrow from private individuals to meet its commitments. Even so, Jewish institutions were short of funds.

There were several reasons for this financial difficulty. First, the Jewish population of Toronto was primarily working-class; consequently, large sums of money were simply not available. Secondly, although the annual municipal grant to Federation had been increased to $2,500 in 1922, it was nominal compared to the needs of the organization which, by accepting the subsidy, obligated itself to care for all the Jewish poor. This situation, moreover, coincided precisely with the growth of Jewish educational and welfare institutions, the necessity of employing salaried professionals and the arrival of hundreds of potentially dependent European immigrants. Consequently Federation's efforts to deal with welfare problems in the Jewish community were less than successful and would collapse under the onslaught of the Great Depression.

Federation, however, must be credited with one outstanding, if unwitting, accomplishment; its work constituted a step toward unification of the Jewish community of Toronto. No other events prior to the emergence of Naziism in the 1930s generated as much co-operative action as the Federation campaigns. No other idea, including Zionism at this period, drew as many disparate elements of the community together as did the prospect of a successful and nearly comprehensive philanthropic system. Nothing worked as well to lower the barriers between old community and new.

It should not be supposed that distinctions disappeared altogether. This could be accomplished only by developments of overriding historical significance, such as the destruction of European Jewry during the Second World War and the establishment of the State of Israel. Indeed, whatever unity was achieved through Federation in the 1920s was done on Holy Blossom terms, operating principally with old community leadership and East European deference, and under old community principles. Resentment continued to smoulder in the new community, especially among the most recent arrivals who felt that Federation, dominated by the affluent and the acculturated, was oblivious to their problems. These preferred to be served by organizations such as the Folks Farein which chose to remain independent.

II

A second force in this period promised to bind local Jewry together. During the war, a movement for Jewish national conferences had emerged in various Central European countries and in the United States to protest against anti-semitic violence in Poland, Hungary, the Ukraine and elsewhere. These conferences sought to create organizations to assist Jewish war victims and to establish organized local Jewish communities. Some also looked forward to the end of hostilities, when the issue of Jewish national self-determination might be promoted at a peace conference. Canadian Jewry, too, was not immune to these sentiments.

The movement which was to give birth to the Canadian Jewish Congress had its origins in Montreal. In February 1915 the local branch of the Jewish National Workers' Alliance convened a meeting of all Jewish organizations in the city to help Jewish war victims in Europe. It was projected that a national Canadian organization of Jews, the Canadian Jewish Alliance, would be formed to petition the federal government to facilitate immigration, make land available for colonization and promote Jewish representation at the peace conference. Reuben Brainin, celebrated Hebrew and Yiddish author and editor of the *Kanader Adler*, was elected its president and immediately set about eliciting nationwide support.

In Toronto a Conference for Jewish War Sufferers had been active almost from the outbreak of hostilities, collecting money to be sent overseas through the American Joint Distribution Committee. The Toronto Conference tended to attract the labour-oriented and the secularists, a similar element to that in Montreal urging formation of the Canadian Jewish Alliance. It is not surprising, therefore, that the Toronto group responded to Brainin's call almost immediately and discussions were begun with him and with East European Jews in Winnipeg with the aim of calling a national congress.

Much of the struggle within Canadian Jewry which preceded the establishment of the Canadian Jewish Congress took place in Montreal, but it bears consideration at this point because the nature of the division in Montreal elucidates the situation in Toronto and the motivation behind support for the Congress movement here.

While the Alliance was in the process of formation, opposition had broken out in Montreal, spearheaded by the Zionists, the reform and the Jewish press. In November, 1915, this group convened a Conference of Canadian Jews at Montreal, with Zionist delegates from across Canada, attempting to fortify their position by arranging for the attendance of prominent individuals such as Arthur Meighen, Louis D. Brandeis and Dr. Shmarya Levin. The organizational meeting of the Canadian Jewish Alliance, on the other hand, took place in Toronto in February, 1916, no doubt an indication of the enthusiasm for the movement in the city. Here there had been no outcry, either from Holy Blossom or from the Zionists.

The Canadian Jewish Alliance and the Conference of Canadian Jews avowed similar objectives: a national Jewish assembly, the fostering of Jewish rights at the peace conference, the support of the Canadian government for this purpose, and the relief of Jewish war victims. The real issue underlying the division, therefore, concerned who should comprise the new organization and by what means the representatives should be chosen. The movement which had begun as an attempt to support Jewish interests abroad had become a dispute over who should dominate at home, a struggle between the old community and the new.

Since its inception, the Federation of Canadian Zionists had had old-community leadership from Montreal in the person of

Clarence I. de Sola, son of the late minister of the Spanish and Portuguese Synagogue. In addition, the old community elite had dominated philanthropic federations and, perhaps most galling for the recent immigrant majority, had gained control of overseas relief as well. They now evidently sought also to assume the leadership of the Congress movement, producing a conservative organization consisting of representatives elected through deference. For a maturing new community, this was intolerable and the Alliance pushed for an organization dominated by recent immigrants, supported by labour unions and the widest possible number of "popular" organizations, and consisting of democratically elected representatives.

As peace approached, it seemed that the movement for a national assembly of Canadian Jewry would disappear. The size of the two opposing factions prevented either from calling together a broadly representative body and, to make matters worse, Brainin accepted an editorial post in New York. Events in the United States, however, infused new life into the Canadian movement. The month following the armistice saw the election of representatives to an American Jewish Congress at Philadelphia. The actual meeting encouraged East European labour groups in Winnipeg and the *Hebrew Journal* in Toronto to build on the foundations laid by the Canadian Jewish Alliance. In Toronto, the Conference for Jewish War Sufferers under the leadership of Maurice Goldstick became the nucleus for the Congress movement. This had now become virtually synonymous with the local Alliance relief committee. In Montreal, the formerly unsympathetic papers, especially the *Chronicle*, now began to favour the Congress idea and significant numbers of Zionists, especially of East European background, were drifting into the movement. Despite opposition from the old community, a national "Congress Committee" was established, its support based primarily in Toronto and in Winnipeg, an indication of the growing maturity of those Jewish communities outside Montreal.

The headquarters of the organization, however, continued to be in Montreal. It was decided that the first meeting of the Canadian Jewish Congress would take place in Montreal in March 1919 and local communities were instructed to elect delegates.

The nature of the organization was determined at a meeting in Toronto in February, attended by representatives of organizations from across the country. Congress was to be a broadly based democratic assembly with one delegate for each 750 Jews, except in small towns, where each group of one hundred was to be allowed a representative. Moreover, every Jewish national

organization was entitled to a delegate, assuring the representation of every variety of opinion. Representatives were to be
chosen directly and by secret ballot, with any Jew, male or
female, over eighteen being entitled to vote and to stand for office
after payment of a registration fee of ten cents. To ensure that the
less affluent would not be deterred from running, every delegate's
fare to the Congress was to be paid from a central fund.

In Toronto the election was greeted with great enthusiasm by
all groups except Holy Blossom. The latter did nothing to oppose
the movement as the old communities had in Montreal and in the
United States; it merely remained aloof. The new community,
however, seeing in Congress a chance for the East Europeans, the
working class and the recent immigrants to have a voice at last in
the organizational structure of Canadian Jewry, flocked to the
polls. Of Toronto's fifteen thousand Jews, over seven thousand
registered their votes, the younger generation being especially
anxious to support the concept.[14]

In Toronto, therefore, the plight of European Jews and the
opportunity for the new community to assume the leadership of
Canadian Jewry had the effect of uniting virtually all elements
within the East European community behind the Congress
movement. Recent immigrants, especially, saw Canadian Jewish
Congress as their representative and temporarily forgot their
ideological differences in their backing of it. Deference, too, was
minimized. The ballot for Toronto delegates emphasized the
importance of the secret vote. "You must have no fear of drawing
someone's anger if you do not vote for him," electors were told.
The list of candidates cut across the whole spectrum of Toronto
Jewry, rich and poor, religious and secularist, manufacturer and
union leader. Even Holy Blossom, which officially avoided
association with the movement, was vicariously represented by
several of its members. Despite the reduction of ideological
differences, the electors were asked not to vote indiscriminately.[15]

The results of the election in Toronto reflected those across the
country. The overwhelming number of successful candidates were
East Europeans, Yiddish-speaking and non-affluent. Recent
immigrants predominated; few of the delegates had arrived prior
to 1900. The election, therefore, was rightly seen as a victory for
the "common people." Those elected, for the most part, were the
active members of the community, irrespective of their wealth or
social standing.[16]

Canadian Jewish Congress offices were set up in Montreal,
Toronto and Winnipeg. In Toronto the local section of the
Congress Committee called a meeting in May to "lay before the

public questions of the day in Jewish life, particularly the question of the situation in Poland and that of immigration into this country," two of the major issues discussed in Montreal. Although Sam Jacobs of Montreal was unable to speak as requested, he sent another member of Parliament and the meeting was a profound success.

After the initial Congress, however, popular enthusiasm waned considerably. Toronto delegates, returning with a mandate to set up an organized Jewish community (*kehillah*) and an immigrant aid society, got little support in their attempt at implementation. An important reason for this, perhaps, was the failure of the Canadian Jewish Congress, in the midst of its idealism in 1919, to set up any mechanism beyond the three regional offices to generate enthusiasm and to keep the organization alive between the proposed annual conferences. Consequently, few delegates appeared at the congresses called during 1920 and 1921, and by the following year, it had been decided to dispense with national meetings altogether.

In Toronto a rudimentary organization was maintained in a storefront office on Spadina Avenue, but it was a far cry from the grand plan envisioned by the first Congress. It did perform one function of an organized Jewish community by settling occasional disputes affecting Jews in various localities throughout Ontario and it did arrange lectures on Jewish problems. Its principal activity, however, was to lobby in Parliament for the admission of immigrants and to assist with the paperwork for those attempting to bring relatives from Europe. In fact, the only lasting effect of the Canadian Jewish Congress in Toronto was the local branch of the Jewish Immigrant Aid Society, founded in 1920 and administered at the Congress office. By the middle of the decade, the office had been closed as a result of local apathy, the JIAS had been taken over by Federation and, as the aftermath of war faded, the unity which had prevailed in 1919 dissipated as well.

NOTES

1 By-laws of the Federation of the Jewish Philanthropies of Toronto in the *2nd Annual Report* 1918-19, p. 3.

2 See Harry L. Lurie, *A Heritage Affirmed: The Jewish Federation Movement in the United States* (Philadelphia: Jewish Publication Society of America, 1961), pp. 30-46, 416,

and resolution passed by the organizational committee of the Federation, Oct. 1916, reprinted in Hart, *The Jew in Canada*, p. 218.

3 See Edmund Scheuer Scrapbook, esp. article from *Albany Herald*; Ida Siegel, personal interview, Aug. 26, 1971.

4 Speech, March 1918, quoted by Ben Sadowski, "History of Jewish Social Welfare Development in Toronto" (address delivered Sept. 1951; typescript in archives of the United Jewish Welfare Fund of Toronto), p. 4.

5 "The Development of the Social Services in the Toronto Jewish Community" (mimeograph, 14 pp., *ca.* 1965, Canadian Jewish Congress Central Region Archives, Toronto), p. 11.

6 These included the Ladies' Co-operative Board of Jewish Charities, the Jewish Orphans' Home and Day Nursery, the Hebrew Burial Society and the Hebrew Free Loan Society (i.e., all the basic operations of the Associated Hebrew Charities), the Jewish Girls' Club, the Hebrew Ladies' Maternity Aid Society, the Jewish branches of the Big Brother and Big Sister movements formed recently as an anti-delinquency measure, the Jewish Free Dispensary and a Sewing School operated by the Council of Jewish Women.

7 The Federation of the Jewish Philanthropies of Toronto, *2nd Annual Report 1918-19*, pp. 12-14.

8 *Ibid.*, pp. 20-21.

9 "Report of the President," *ibid.*, p. 24.

10 Speech, March 1918, in Sadowski, "History of Jewish Social Welfare Development . . .," p. 4.

11 Since the records of Federation no longer exist, this account has been based upon inferences in the *2nd Annual Report*, on Hart, *The Jew in Canada*, on Sadowski's article and on personal interviews with Mrs. Ida Siegel, Dec. 26, 30, 1971. Schipper's view of the founding of Federation (in Rose, ed., *A People and its Faith*, p. 38), which emphasizes the role of Scheuer and Cohen, is unsubstantiated. As the eventual spokesmen for the organization, they were probably credited by the public with its founding.

12 A free loan society had been established in 1911 and had operated under the Associated Hebrew Charities. It worked

on an informal basis with promissory notes being guaranteed by prominent individuals. By 1917, however, it was deeply in debt and had only two dollars in the treasury. (Sadowski, *op.cit.*, p. 3.) Information on Samuel Kronick's personal philanthropy was obtained in a personal interview with Mr. Archie Bennett, March 7, 1973.

13 The orphanage building on Simcoe Street had become intolerably overcrowded as early as 1918 and children were being refused for lack of space ("Report of the Jewish Orphans' Home" in Federation, *2nd Annual Report*, pp. 27-28). The institution, also called the Jewish Childrens' Home, had a special relationship with Federation. Of all the affiliated organizations, this one alone retained practically complete autonomy. Operated by an efficient society jealous of outside influence, the orphanage accepted monetary and planning assistance from Federation, but would brook no interference. Eventually, however, its functions would be taken over by the latter; by 1932, adoption and the placing of children in foster homes had come to be recognized as being preferable to institutional care. The orphanage was therefore used only as a temporary or emergency facility, and the responsibility for child care was assumed by the Jewish Children's Bureau, an agency of Federation which had been set up in 1921 and had shared the function of placing dependent children with the Maternity Aid Society. Maternity Aid was itself absorbed by the Children's Bureau in 1933. The orphanage closed in 1936.

The Jewish Boys' Club was the closest that Toronto Jewry ever came to setting up a Jewish settlement house. When it was first established, it was fused with the Jewish Big Brother movement. As the necessity for specialization became evident, however, the latter separated and by 1933, the two organizations were operating independently. The boys' club did maintain a close association with the B'nai B'rith camp until its absorption by the YMHA in 1937 and during this period clearly contributed to the decline of delinquency among Jewish boys.

14 Morris [Maurice] Goldstick, interview by Julius Hayman, *ca.* 1957 (typescript, Canadian Jewish Congress Archives, Montreal); Archie B. Bennett, personal interview, Oct. 3, 1972.

15 "Canadian Jewish Congress Ballot for Toronto," 1919 (Canadian Jewish Congress Central Region Archives, Toronto).

16 For example: Ben-Zion Nathanson, orthodox principal of the Simcoe St. Talmud Torah and popular orator on the subjects of education and Zionism; Henry Dworkin, newsagent, socialist, active in immigrant aid; Shimshon Koldofsky, labour organizer; Maurice Goldstick of the Toronto Conference; Abraham Rhinewine, editor of the *Hebrew Journal*; Isaac Matenko of the Jewish National Radical School; Dr. M. Schwartz, active Zionist; Moses Gelber, wholesaler, active in Goel Tzedec, orthodox education and Zionism; A. Bromberg and Ben-Zion Hyman, Hebrew teachers; Samuel Weber, founder of the Free Burial Society; Samuel Factor, lawyer; Charles Pasternak, active in theatre and philanthropy; Rabbi Jacob Gordon; A.B. Bennett, journalist. Of Holy Blossom members, only Louis Singer and Joseph Singer were elected; they were acceptable because of their East European antecedents and because they were known through their activity in politics and philanthropy.

CHAPTER 17

THE KEHILLAH MOVEMENT AND THE DECLINE OF RABBINIC AUTHORITY, 1912 – 1937

Although the Toronto branch of the Canadian Jewish Congress failed to evolve into a central administrative agency for the Jewish community, other efforts were developing a structure which would attempt to unite at least the religiously observant in the city. The Kehillah of Toronto, as it came to be called, emerging in 1923, was a far less ambitious venture than those centralized local Jewish community bodies projected by the Canadian Jewish Congress or organizations of the same name in Europe. *Kehilloth* in Europe were, in certain matters, the supreme source of communal authority, superintending Jewish education and philanthropy, guilds and markets, regulating competition, supervising the preparation of kosher food for public consumption, approving or disqualifying rabbis, *shochtim*, teachers, judges and other religious functionaries, arranging for the arbitration of disputes within the community; they were even empowered in some countries to tax local Jews for communal purposes. In Toronto no attempt would be made at an all-inclusive jurisdiction, at least at the outset. The local *kehillah* would confine itself solely to the regulation of *kashruth* in the city and it would profess authority only over the orthodox Jews. Unlike the Canadian Jewish Congress, its origins lay not in an international crisis but rather in a local one, the decline in religious observance and rabbinic authority in Toronto.

If the Rabbi of Slutsk had overstated his case somewhat by branding the stones of America impure, he had at least perceived that North American life held innumerable dangers for traditional religious practice. While there was never a universal rejection of traditional observances in North America, the drift from orthodoxy was everywhere evident. The observance of the Sabbath and the dietary laws was the most vulnerable element of the tradition and here, especially, the greatest weakness appeared.

The English and German Jews who arrived in Toronto at mid-century were relatively strict about *kashruth*; they employed a *shochet* for the purpose. When it came to Sabbath observance, however, they were notably lax. As the elder generation of the old community passed away or became imbued with liberal religious ideas, indifference to traditional observance and to the synagogue itself became commonplace at Holy Blossom. At the same time as membership increased, attendance at services declined, along with the number of members' children enrolled in the Sabbath School. By 1913 the younger generation had been largely alienated and Mrs. Frankel, principal of the congregational school, was complaining how difficult it was to attract them to Sabbath services when their mothers were down town shopping. "How can we expect our children to attend synagogue," she asked, "when the parents attend only once or twice a year."[1]

Unlike those East Europeans who had emigrated in the 1860s and 1870s and were generally indifferent to Judaism, those who fled the pogroms of the decades following 1881 at first clung adamantly to traditional ways and attempted to provide themselves quickly with synagogues and religious leaders in their new surroundings. Rabbi Gordon recalled that when he arrived in Toronto in 1905, the Sabbath was strictly observed in the Ward. Jewish factories and stores closed on Saturday, despite financial loss. Some opened Sunday out of economic necessity and despite the possibility of prosecution. Jews employed by non-Jewish firms attempted to avoid working on the Sabbath, the younger generation at the insistence of their parents, and made up the time in the evenings. In this period, the prospect of a Jewish secularist riding his bicycle on Saturday would produce consternation, while on the afternoon of the first day of Rosh Hashana, the residents of the Ward would gather on the bridge at the foot of York Street to symbolically cast their sins upon the waters in the traditional *tashlich* ceremony.[2]

By the first decade of the twentieth century, however, the tide had begun to turn. As early as 1904 one pious Jew moved his family east of Yonge Street, away from the Jewish neighbourhood, in order that his children might not be corrupted by seeing Jewish youngsters violating the Sabbath. When the Lyric Theatre opened in 1909, the *Jewish Times* complained that some

Jewish women visited the synagogue on Saturday morning and attended the matinee at the theatre in the afternoon. "Too much effort cannot be devoted to doing away with the practice," the paper exclaimed, "and it is hoped that the time will come when Jewish Toronto...will frown upon theatre going on the Sabbath." Social pressure against the practice was apparently breaking down. Indeed, by 1915 a few Jewish shops along Agnes Street were opening on Saturday.[3]

By the outbreak of the war there were other signs of weakening tradition as well. As late as 1913 Magistrate Cohen was still able successfully to refer civil disputes between Jews to Rabbi Gordon for settlement, but within two years many would prefer to see the action carried out in the secular courts. Moreover, when Rabbi Gordon issued a ban against the National Radical School for holding a picnic on the Sabbath in 1912, it had no effect; and there were incidents of Jews at this period preferring civil marriage. Perhaps the most dangerous indication of all was the increased audacity and public acceptance of the violators. About 1915 one storekeeper advertised in the *Hebrew Journal* that he had been elected cantor for the High Holy Days in a local synagogue. He also stated his business hours which included the Sabbath and holy days.[4]

Following the war the decline accelerated, even among the members of scrupulously traditional synagogues. The 1920s saw a reduction in the number of local Jews affiliated with synagogues, and Goel Tzedec was having difficulty obtaining a quorum for weekday morning services.[5] Jewish stores were increasingly conducting business on Saturday, not only those in the major commercial thoroughfares such as Yonge Street, but also in the solidly Jewish Kensington Market. Even some bakeries and groceries, formerly the strictest in Sabbath observance, were beginning to remain open.

Two simultaneous attempts were made in 1922 to put an end to this practice, one from Rabbi Gordon's circle and another from the Polish community. Paul Levi, a member of Goel Tzedec and the individual who had moved out of the Jewish neighbourhood to preserve the piety of his children, organized the Sabbath Observance Investigation Committee to locate jobs for young people which would enable them to observe the Sabbath. At the same time, Rabbi Y.L. Graubart, who had succeeded Rabbi Judah Rosenberg as the spiritual guide of the local Polish Jews, launched a campaign against Sabbath violation, urging synagogues not to elect Sabbath violators to office, holding open-air sermons in the

Kensington Market, and insisting on a boycott of offending stores. He encouraged the picketing of these establishments and so incensed the storekeepers that some attempted to assault him. Rabbi Graubart also published notices urging Jewish workers and manufacturers not to work on Saturday, and including lists of Sabbath-observing and forbidden shops. He even approached the unions in an attempt to persuade Jewish manufacturers to let their employees off for holy days and exhorted the community to ask government permission for Sabbath-observing workers to make up time either on Sunday or in a longer working day.[6] All these efforts had little effect, however, in closing the Jewish stores. The public grew accustomed to the convenience of Saturday shopping and the practice spread.

The decline in orthodox practice in Toronto is easily explained. For most, the reason was simply economic. In the retail trades, Saturday was the principal business day; as for the factories, it was necessary to work Saturday mornings in most non-Jewish firms and as competition for jobs increased, so did the anxiety of being discharged for Sabbath absence.

Another factor was the appearance of increased numbers of Jewish secularists. Granted, these had been present in Europe, but social pressure had forced them either to keep their religious violations secret or branded them as outcasts. Moreover, in any particular *shtetl*, they had been relatively few. The persecution of social radicals in the late nineteenth and early twentieth century, however, forced thousands of them to emigrate and in North America, while still a minority, they organized far more openly. More important, centralized religious authority was no longer present to make them pariahs. Consequently, they were able by example to exert considerable influence.

A third factor was the attitude of the second generation, for whom real integration into Canadian life was a possibility. Imbued in the public schools with non-traditional ideas, influenced by Gentile and non-observant Jewish acquaintances, and often seeing traditional Judaism as an archaic hindrance to citizenship, they ignored parental strictures in religious matters.

In the field of *kashruth*, there was a similar deterioration in the standards of observance from those prevailing in Europe, but this was not the result, as with the Sabbath, simply of popular laxity. In fact, most Jews in Toronto, even the secularists, preferred to purchase kosher meat. The decline was due rather to unscrupulous butchers and meat wholesalers who attempted to defraud the public by advertising forbidden meat as kosher and to the influx, in the mass immigration early in the century, of unqualified self-styled *shochtim* who, in the absence of an authoritative body to pass on their competence, were accepted by an unwitting public.

The rabbis of Holy Blossom in the nineteenth century made no effort to supervise the supply of kosher food beyond their own congregation. The East Europeans probably would not have accepted their supervision had it been offered. The earliest East European rabbis who arrived attempted immediately to establish their traditional authority over the preparation of kosher meat. Rabbi Weinreb supervised the work of several *shochtim* and members of the Galician congregation would patronize only those butchers selling meat from animals slaughtered by them. Even so, a great deal of non-kosher meat was still being sold in the city. After Rabbi Gordon's arrival in 1905, the two joined forces to widen rabbinic administration by forming a Va'ad HaKashruth (*kashruth* regulation board). Under this system, all congregations accepting the authority of the rabbis agreed to employ only the eight local *shochtim* approved by them. The synagogues collected a fee from each butcher for the services of the *shochet* and this in turn provided remuneration for the *shochtim* and for the supervising rabbis. It appears that Rabbi Levy, and later even Rabbi Jacobs, were eventually also brought into the Va'ad.[7]

The rabbis strove to prevent slaughtering for Jewish consumption without their supervision and to drive incompetents out of the field. In July 1908 they announced in the *Kanader Adler* that a "Congregational combine" existed in Toronto, operating "with the consent of the whole city" and insisted that slaughtering outside of the eight kosher slaughterers appointed by the congregation (that is, approved by the Va'ad) was non-kosher and unfit for consumption. "Ask your butcher who his shochet is," they demanded. "Do not have your fowl killed by Shochetim who have been declared unclean and incompetent." They also proclaimed that anyone disobeying the decree of the Va'ad by slaughtering without authority would be worthy of excommunication.[8]

This position seems to have been acceptable to the laity, but the unauthorized *shochtim* were furious. Early in the Va'ad's existence, one of these, Marcus Dickman, distributed circulars in the local synagogues urging the public to ignore the rabbinic ban. Then in 1912, when the Va'ad publicly named Dickman as incompetent, the *shochet* replied with a letter to Toronto Jewry in the *Hebrew Journal*, insisting that in fact the meat prepared under the rabbis was non-kosher. Dickman further attempted to foment public opposition to rabbinic authority by issuing a pamphlet supposedly discrediting the rabbis. He charged Rabbi Weinreb with using money belonging to the Va'ad HaKashruth for his own purposes and Rabbi Gordon with doing the same with funds from the Simcoe Street Talmud Torah and the Associated Hebrew Charities.[9]

Despite this vituperation, the rabbis refused to withdraw their statements and Dickman sued each for libel, seeking damages for deprivation of livelihood, an indication that the public supported the rabbis. The rabbis were forced to defend themselves in court and the case dragged on until February 1914, when both parties, frustrated at the lack of progress, dismissed the action without costs.

Although it is evident from the Dickman incident that the Jewish public was willing at this point to submit to some rabbinic authority, the rabbis themselves were unable to unite for any length of time. Rabbis Weinreb and Gordon, who usually got on well together, occasionally disagreed over matters of supervision and the authorization of *shochtim*. This hampered the authority of the Va'ad HaKashruth, but it was not a serious threat to its existence. The position taken by Rabbi Yehuda Rosenberg after his arrival in 1913 was another matter. It has already been remarked that the engagement of Rabbi Rosenberg signified an increase in and a consolidation of the local Polish Jews. With it came ethnic pride and a tendency to revive the old prejudices against Lithuanians and Galicians represented by the Va'ad. Rosenberg, after a brief affiliation in 1915, dissociated himself from it and attempted to establish an independent system of *kashruth* supervision for the Polish community. He even went so far as to permit the consumption of meat slaughtered by *shochtim* who had refused to affiliate with the Va'ad HaKashruth and who consequently had been prohibited by Rabbis Weinreb and Gordon. Rosenberg, moreover, attacked the legitimacy of the Va'ad's claim to authority, necessitating a reply by Rabbi Gordon in the press.

The war years, therefore, were ones of chaos in the field of *kashruth*. Each faction forbade its followers to purchase meat supervised by the other, rabbis Gordon and Weinreb because they considered their Va'ad HaKushruth the only authority empowered in these matters, and Rabbi Rosenberg, because he insisted that since the Va'ad did not constitute an organized Jewish community (*kehillah*) in the legal sense, it could not prohibit independent rabbis from certifying *shochtim*. In the meantime, confusion reigned and butchers flagrantly sold unfit meat as kosher.*

The Va'ad HaKashruth apparently did not attempt to supervise the production of kosher products beyond meat. In the case of shortenings and cooking oils, where animal fats might possibly be used, Rabbi Gordon arranged for supervision independently. These independent contracts, and the fact that the Va'ad was constantly collapsing and having to be reorganized, indicate the failure of the organization to establish exhaustive and universally recognized *kashruth* supervision. This was due to the inability of the rabbis to agree among themselves.

The problems of the Va'ad HaKashruth were not confined to rabbinical discordance; the very existence of the organization rankled with the *shochtim*, who disliked the close surveillance and resented having to share their congregational salaries with the supervising rabbis. In 1918, therefore, these organized an association called the Agudath Hashochtim, for collective action against attempts by the Va'ad to monopolize control of kosher products. By 1920, the *shochtim* had succeeded in ameliorating their situation; they were now to be employed either by the meat wholesalers or by the abattoirs, rather than by the congregations affiliated with the Va'ad. They were to be paid a uniform rate according to the weight of the bullock slaughtered, whereas under the old system, each *shochet* had negotiated his terms of employment with the individual congregations. The rabbis, however, continued to be paid by the congregations out of the fee charged to the producers for supervision.

This situation improved the economic circumstances of the *shochtim*, but was hardly encouraging for the prospects of the Va'ad. The organization, already weak, continued technically to

---

* At this juncture, it is necessary to understand a technical point of Jewish law. It is generally agreed in rabbinic legal literature that a communal governing body comprising a majority of the rabbis and recognized by a majority of the Jewish inhabitants of a city constitute a proper *kehillah* and, as such, it reserves the exclusive right to make decisions in religious matters concerning the entire city. Even meat prepared by qualified *shochtim* and supervised by qualified rabbis outside the *kehillah* could be considered non-kosher.

The matter, however, was complicated by the fact that in North America the Jewish communities were heterogeneous. In such circumstances, an independent rabbi governing a particular ethnic element often insisted that since his followers had never recognized any *kehillah* when it was founded (as Rosenberg claimed), they were not bound by its dicta. Jewish law does not resolve this problem and consequently this has been a point of contention in Toronto and in many other North American communities.

exist, but effectively, it had been destroyed. The slaughterhouses could now deal directly with the *shochtim* without having to treat either with rabbis or with congregations. The union of *shochtim*, therefore, put an end to the fiction of a unified Va'ad HaKashruth and the consequent disorder did nothing to enhance rabbinical prestige.

II

At an early meeting of the Associated Hebrew Charities, it was proposed that a variety of communal problems might be solved if a *kehillah* on the European model were formed in Toronto to deal with religious, educational and philanthropic matters. By the early 1920s, the need was greater than ever, especially in view of the disorder in the religious life of the city. Federation had solved many of the philanthropic difficulties, but confusion prevailed in the field of rabbinical jurisdiction.

The potential did exist for a workable *kehillah* in Toronto. Despite the erosion of traditional practice, a large proportion of the local Jewish population still leaned toward orthodoxy, in contrast to the situation in many other North American cities. In 1919 Rabbi Gordon, commenting on this feature, could still refer to Toronto as "The Jerusalem of Canada."[10] The difficulty, however, lay in forging all orthodox elements into a single community recognizing the authority of a united local rabbinate.

That difficulty was compounded by the very effort of the Polish community to create unity. Their number in Toronto was growing, and by the 1920s it must have been apparent that they would shortly constitute a majority. Without a spiritual guide since Rabbi Rosenberg's departure in 1918, local Polish Jews diligently sought a successor in Europe; it was unthinkable that they should once again submit to the authority of the Galician or the Lithuanian rabbi. Their plan was simple. They would bring over a rabbi of indisputable scholarship, widely known throughout the Jewish communities of Europe and America, and appoint him "Rav HaKolel" (chief rabbi) in Toronto. Everyone would then recognize his authority, disputes would cease and rabbinic prestige would be restored

In 1920 chaos reigned in Russian Poland. Added to the economic upheaval and physical destruction of the war was the contest between the Whites and the Bolsheviks; typically, the Jews found themselves trapped between the two adversaries. For- tunately for the Polish Jews of Toronto, these were precisely the conditions which would make North America inviting to a European rabbi.

Rabbi Yehuda Leib Graubart, to whom the invitation was extended, satisfied all the criteria for a Rav HaKolel, according to Toronto's Polish Jews. He was the descendant of a prominent rabbinical family and had had a long and successful career in the rabbinate himself. Since 1905 he had been serving in Stashov, in the district from which most of Toronto's Polish Jews had emigrated. There he had become a leader of Polish Jewry, renowned for his religious knowledge and published works, as well as for his efforts in creating rabbinical associations throughout Poland and Russia. Finally, he was an enthusiastic Zionist, a position likely to sit well with Toronto Jewry.

Toward the end of his life, Rabbi Graubart, who had immense difficulty in adjusting to North American life, would withdraw from communal work and concentrate almost exclusively on his writings, but when he first arrived in Toronto in 1920, he plunged into public activity with alacrity and enthusiasm. He took charge of the Eitz Chaim Talmud Torah and endeavoured to improve Sabbath observance in the city. The deplorable situation in the distribution of kosher meat, however, forced him to focus his major efforts in that direction, and here he came into conflict with the rabbinic establishment personified by rabbis Gordon and Weinreb.

Shortly after Rabbi Graubart's arrival, the lay leaders of the Polish community, who had long resented the activities of the Va'ad HaKashruth, united nine Polish congregations into an independent kashruth supervision organization. The United Polish Jewish Communities Khal Adath Israel, headed by Itshe Meyer Korolnek, resolved to recognize only Rabbi Graubart's authority in matters of kosher food. The Agudath Hashochtim, who preferred the chaotic situation which existed under the Va'ad HaKashruth, feared that Rabbi Graubart's zeal might endow him with real power. Consequently, they attempted to mobilize public opposition to the new organization. Nevertheless, the Khal Adath succeeded in entrenching itself among the Polish Jews. Meanwhile, yet another remodelling had taken place in the old Va'ad HaKashruth; it now began to call itself a kehillah, thereby implying that all authoritative religious pronouncements would have to come from that body. Alarmed by the founding of the Khal Adath, this kehillah worked out a modus vivendi with the shochtim to minimize the effectiveness of the Polish organization. The shochtim probably agreed to supervision by the kehillah because they thought it would be more flexible than that imposed by Rabbi Graubart.

Throughout 1921 the kehillah and the Khal Adath fought a

"quiet war," the latter implying that rabbis Gordon and Weinreb were not strict enough and the established rabbis insisting that Rabbi Graubart had no authority to undertake independent supervision. The established rabbis urged the *mashgichim* (supervisors appointed by the *kehillah* to oversee the work of the *shochtim*) to report only to them and not to Rabbi Graubart. Rabbi Graubart, on the other hand, exhorted the *shochtim* to slaughter only under his supervision. By January 1922, both sides had realized that their bickering served only to enhance the profits of unscrupulous butchers, wholesalers and *shochtim*. The two factions, admitting that they were "exhausted," met at Goel Tzedec to initiate a move for unity. "One more day," the *Hebrew Journal* observed, "and we shall have . . .peace, kosher meat and . . .a united *kehillah*. Hopefully for many years."[11]

The constitution of the United Synagogues, as the new *kehillah* was called, and the exact relationship of Rabbi Graubart to the other rabbis within it, are obscure. In any case, regardless of whatever terms had been agreed upon in January, by April the accord had broken down and each side was again prohibiting meat supervised by the other. The crux of the difficulty was Rabbi Graubart's insistence that he be recognized as the chief rabbi of the city. After all, he had been invited to be Rav HaKolel, albeit only by the Polish element, and he was unaccustomed to having to compete with other rabbis for authority. Rabbis Gordon and Weinreb certainly did not question his scholarship, and were prepared to accept him into the *kehillah* on terms of equality with themselves. They could not, however, countenance the prospect of submitting to his authority. Rabbi Weinreb had been in the city for over twenty years and Rabbi Gordon almost as long. And although he had never formally claimed the title, Rabbi Gordon had long been recognized unofficially as the dean of the Toronto rabbinate. Each, therefore, considered the other's position an affront.[12]

By the summer of 1922 the dispute had become more complex. As the moderates in both camps strove frantically to arrange peace conferences which might keep the new *kehillah* together, other groups held their own meetings in opposition to *any* rabbinical control. Since under the *kehillah* the *shochtim* were once again to be paid by the community, and since the *kehillah* was to be a monopoly, neither the *shochtim* nor the labour unions were pleased. Moreover, since increased supervision involved a rise in the price of meat in order to pay the supervisors, there was opposition from some butchers and even from orthodox members of the public. The unions, which professed to speak for the Jewish worker, were interested in this aspect as well and called for opposition to the *kehillah*. At one point, meat authorized by the *kehillah* was actually doused with gasoline.

The constant feuding over kosher meat evoked sharp criticism within the Jewish community. Holy Blossom, after Rabbi Jacobs' death in 1920 safely divorced from the orthodox rabbinate, was perhaps the most vocal. "A pretty mess some of our Orthodox co-religionists have made of Bosher-Kosher [*sic*: kosher meat]," Rabbi Brickner remarked. "We are even frank in admitting that we regarded the whole 'business' with some little amusement . . .," he wrote, seeing the dispute as indicative of lack of immigrant acculturation. He feared that if discord reached the courts, Jews would be considered ridiculous by the general community. Discounting the legal-religious aspects of the division between the *kehillah* and Rabbi Graubart's forces, he maintained that the problem was financial and that all would be solved if the orthodox congregations paid their rabbis a suitable wage.[13] Even the Yiddish-speaking element was disgusted. "Do we not have any more important questions to deal with," the *Hebrew Journal* complained, "that we dispute day and night over kosher meat?" By the end of the year, all pretence of unity between the *kehillah* and the Polish Jews had collapsed, and the *Journal* commented wearily that perhaps it was as well "that the *kehillah* is at an end, if only to be rid of the disputes."[14]

For several months afterward, rabbinical authority was virtually non-existent. Each faction distributed leaflets in the synagogues defending its position and condemning the opposition with bitter invective. In yet another attempt at unity, therefore, the old Va'ad HaKashruth was reorganized still another time, in this instance on the model of the *kehillah* established in New York City in 1908.

The New York institution went far toward reproducing the European *kehillah*. It sought to control education, charity and the certification of religious officials, to arbitrate disputes within the community, to be a liaison with government, to be the arbiter of Jewish social behaviour and even to bring Jewish criminals to justice. Although by the early 1920s it was on the verge of collapse, it provided a model for Toronto's new communal organization. The Kehillah of Toronto, incorporated in October 1923, by no means shared the ambitious scope of its counterpart in New York. Its purpose was merely to provide uniform and scrupulous supervision of the slaughtering of cattle for kosher meat. Unlike the situation with its predecessors, however, surplus funds, acquired through supervision fees paid by butchers and a surtax on meat paid by the consumer, were to be distributed among local Jewish charitable and educational institutions, an indication that once the question of kosher meat was settled, the Kehillah would perhaps expand its activities into the educational and philanthropic fields. It must have been apparent to its organizers that in the Kehillah lay potentially bountiful financial resources for communal use and especially for the support of Jewish schools. The feature immediately modelled on New York was the method of representation. All orthodox synagogues and interested organizations were invited to elect delegates who would then constitute a lay board of directors which would elect officers from among themselves to administer financial aspects of the organization. The rabbis were to form an autonomous committee within the Kehillah, responsible for the certification and supervision of *shochtim*. Under this system, the rabbis were to agree upon standards and offer a single declaration. In matters of *kashruth*, no individual rabbi was to engage in independent action. The public was informed of the existence of the new organization by notices sent to all synagogues and by announcements published in the daily press and posted in butcher shops.

The initiative in the founding of the Kehillah of Toronto came from the laity in the Galician, Lithuanian and Russian communities, the adherents of rabbis Weinreb, Gordon and Levy, and most of the synagogues of these ethnic groups affiliated, as did a number of *landsmanshaften* and even some Jewish unions and butchers' associations. The Polish community was invited to participate as well.

In the interest of unity, Rabbi Graubart apparently agreed to some sort of informal contact with the Kehillah, although he signed no contract agreeing to abide by its decisions. He would affiliate formally only on condition that the other rabbis recognize him as Rav HaKolel, and when after several months it became evident that none of them was prepared to do so, he severed all connection with the Kehillah of Toronto and proclaimed his Khal Adath a legal *kehillah*, authorized to invalidate the pronouncements of the other organization. Once again, each rival *kehillah* was declaring unfit the meat approved by the other. As butchers and wholesalers took sides between the two groups, a confused public found itself confronted not only with *trefa* meat being sold as *kosher* but also technically *kosher* meat being prohibited by one rabbi and permitted by the other, simply because of the dispute over jurisdiction. An infuriated Rabbi Brickner insisted that any chief rabbi would have to be elected by the entire community and so Rabbi Graubart could not claim the title. The dispute between the rabbis, he maintained, was making a farce of religion, and he urged a quick settlement before the younger generation was alienated from Judaism as a result.[15]

In Toronto at this period, all slaughtering had to be carried out in the municipally owned abattoir where individual meat producers leased stalls. Under an agreement with the city, the Kehillah had the exclusive authority to prepare *kosher* meat in the abattoir. Only their approved *shochtim* were permitted there; those of the Khal Adath were excluded, as were independents operating under the aegis of the Agudath Hashochtim without rabbinical supervision. An attempt to arbitrate the dispute within the Jewish community in 1924 had failed and the disagreement did nothing to improve relations between Rabbi Graubart and the other rabbis.

Supporters of the Kehillah intensified their efforts by attempting to induce the kosher butchers to purchase only from wholesalers approved by the Kehillah. Feelings ran so high that at one meeting violence broke out between butchers of the opposing factions. By the spring of 1925, the butchers of the Khal Adath, together with the *shochtim* excluded from the abattoir, protested to the Board of Control and later to Mayor Foster, but the city officials refused to take action, believing the matter could best be settled among the Jews themselves. A third protest to the city early in 1926 still brought unsatisfactory results for the excluded parties. The Board of Control left the decision to the manager of the abattoir, who followed the path of least resistance and favoured the Kehillah. The Polish community repeatedly threatened court action and Rabbi Brickner repeatedly warned that "no doubt we shall all be treated to some startling headlines in our daily newspapers as the case progresses."[16]

The action which eventually brought the question into the courts was not one in which the Kehillah and the Khal Adath were the initial antagonists but, in the course of events, the case developed along those lines. In the summer of 1925, while hostility between the two associations was at fever pitch, a local butcher named Cohen, whose shop was under Kehillah supervision, discovered that he could obtain meat more cheaply by purchasing from wholesalers supervised by the Khal Adath. Several other butchers had done the same, but Cohen was singled out for public condemnation because he had been seen violating the Sabbath by riding a streetcar. The rabbis of the Kehillah then published a notice in the Yiddish press, including Cohen in the list of forbidden butchers.[17] At first Cohen sought an injunction against the Kehillah in a lower court, but the judge hesitated to grant it, especially in light of the position taken by the Yiddish press in support of the Kehillah. Even some secularists, unconcerned about dietary laws, supported the Kehillah as the beginning of a more comprehensive communal organization.

An injunction was finally granted, however, restraining the rabbis from publishing their notices, but the rabbis circumvented it by announcing merely that they were not responsible for the fitness of Cohen's meat and that their supervisors did not visit him. This was done because Cohen had had the effrontery to place a notice in his window maintaining that he was under the supervision of all the orthodox rabbis of the city; but, threatened with a charge of contempt of court, the rabbinic authorities had to withdraw the notice and apologize to the Bench.

In the interim, Cohen had brought suit against the four Kehillah rabbis who had appended their names to the notice of prohibition, rabbis Jacob Gordon, Joseph Weinreb, Samuel Silverstein and Meyer Berger, claiming injury to his business and reputation.* The rabbis defended themselves by asserting that their statements were without malice and that these had been published as a religious duty to the Jewish community.

The case, heard in the Supreme Court of Ontario before Mr. Justice W.H. Wright, attracted considerable attention, even in the non-Jewish community, because it was a peculiar religious dispute and because of the notable attorneys secured by both sides. Cohen engaged Gershon Mason, lawyer for the Eaton family and a prominent layman in the movement which would produce the United Church, while the Kehillah chose Isidore Helmuth, son of the former Anglican Bishop of Huron.

Cohen's argument against the Kehillah rabbis was that since the preparation of his meat had been under the supervision of Rabbi Graubart, whose credentials could not be questioned, it was indeed kosher and consequently the Kehillah announcement was libellous. The Kehillah authorities replied that Rabbi Graubart's qualifications were indeed above reproach, but since the Kehillah of Toronto constituted an organized Jewish community, a kehillah as defined by Jewish law, Rabbi Graubart had no right to make independent pronouncements, the Khal Adath Israel was not a legitimate kehillah and so Cohen's meat was technically non-kosher. Before the issue between Cohen and the rabbis could be decided, therefore, the definition of a legitimate kehillah had to be established.

* Rabbis Silverstein and Berger had recently arrived in Toronto and, recognizing the legitimacy of the Kehillah, had affiliated with it.

Three rabbis were called in to testify concerning the definition and function of a *kehillah*, one from Albany and two others from Montreal. Stacks of Hebrew legal works were brought into the courtroom as intricate issues of Jewish religious practice were discussed. To make matters worse for Justice Wright, many of the witnesses could be examined only in Yiddish, thus necessitating the use of interpreters and additional attorneys. One newspaper observed that all of this "gave the court-room procedure the air rather of a theological lecture than a civil action." Testimony was long, contradictory and heated. The *Telegram* remarked that when the president of the Kehillah was examined, he "broke loose in a long oratorical outburst which might have been like Tennyson's stream if his Lordship had not intervened." The Kehillah forces insisted that since the Polish congregations, as well as the others, had supported the original Va'ad HaKashruth, the Kehillah was legitimate, whereas Rabbi Herschon of Montreal, brought in by the Khal Adath, maintained that *kehilloth* were designed to meet conditions in countries where Jews and Gentiles lived apart; they did not apply in a "free country" such as Canada. Moreover, Rabbi Graubart insisted that since some of the Kehillah rabbis engaged in business (Rabbi Gordon had dabbled in real estate and sold some religious articles), they were unfit to render religious opinions. The proceedings eventually assumed a comic opera air, with the two Gentile lawyers arguing over the interpretation of the *kehillah* concept in the *Shulchan Aruch*.* It was decided that the real problem was whether two *kehilloth* could exist in the same city simultaneously.

After several days of deliberation, Justice Wright, confused by a bombardment of conflicting interpretations of Jewish law, suggested that the case be decided by a tribunal of rabbis, one chosen by the plaintiff, one by the Kehillah and one by the Union of Orthodox Rabbis (Agudath Harabonim) in New York. The rabbinical court (*beth din*) would sit in Toronto with the powers of a royal commission and Justice Wright would make their decision a decree of the Supreme Court. The three scholars, Rabbi Israel Rosenberg of Brooklyn, president of the Agudath Harabonim, Rabbi Joseph Konvitz of Newark, New Jersey, and Rabbi A.S. Pfeffer of New York, arrived in the city in July 1926 and immediately created a favourable impression.

---

* A code of Jewish law compiled by Rabbi Joseph Karo in the sixteenth century, and considered authoritative by most orthodox Jews.

They are venerable figures [the *Star* observed in a front-page article] in black skull caps and black robes . . . . Rabbi Pfeffer, the oldest of them, has a beard of Biblical grandeur . . . . Their keen alert intellectual features attest the fact that Jewish fundamentalism is the most exacting kind of scholarship.

No judges could be more scrupulously impartial than these three rabbis. Since coming to Toronto they have been immured in their hotel chambers [at the Prince George] only leaving them at night for an automobile airing. They have not even given audience to local Hebrews anxious to pay their respects. They have been the acme of impersonality.

Yet they are not impersonal . . . . Though they wear black caps they are not hanging judges . . . . The Star met them this morning and found them the most charming and amiable of men.

They are jolly men. Their eyes twinkle. They have not long faces, but round faces, continually rippling with smiles. Evidently what is genuinely Rabbinical is not lugubriously puritanical. They come as peacemakers, and they radiate good will. Meeting them was like receiving a patriarchal benediction.[18]

The judgement of the *beth din* vindicated Rabbi Gordon and his fellow defendants. The visiting rabbis found that the Kehillah of Toronto did indeed constitute an organized community and declared that only one such organization could exist in a city at a given time. If one rabbi in the community disagreed with the others, the decision of the majority was to be binding. Furthermore, the tribunal ordered all butchers and *shochtim* claiming to be kosher to submit to the regulations of the Kehillah and announced that the rabbis were in duty bound to publish the names of offenders as they had done with Cohen. They ordered that the Kehillah was to be reorganized within thirty days, during which time each rabbi could decide for his own congregation what was kosher, but communal matters would be decided by Rabbi Weinreb, the senior orthodox rabbi in the city. After the reorganization, however, only the Kehillah definition of *kashruth* was to be legal. The Khal Adath Israel was to be absorbed into the Kehillah and the majority was to rule in all decisions. All other organizations for religious matters were to be prohibited.[19]

In an effort to satisfy Rabbi Graubart, who still considered the scholarship of his colleagues inferior to his own, the *beth din* allowed for a modification of the Kehillah structure. All the orthodox rabbis were to unite in a new Vaad Harabonim (Rabbinical Board) within the Kehillah. This would decide communal religious matters by majority decision, but personal matters were permitted to be dealt with by the individual rabbis without contradiction by any of the others. The presidency of the Vaad Harabonim was to alternate every four months among Rabbi Gordon, Rabbi Weinreb and Rabbi Graubart. Each of the rabbis was to be accorded an honorarium for his work in *kashruth* supervision and, in order to placate Rabbi Graubart, the latter was granted a larger one than the others and was made the first president of the Vaad. The *shochtim* and supervisors under Rabbi Graubart were to be admitted to the Kehillah and so also to the city abattoir, and the Kehillah was to add an officer of the Khal Adath to its executive. In the interest of peace, the Kehillah was to pay court costs, even though the tribunal had found in its favour. All further disputes were to be submitted to the same *beth din*.[20]

The Khal Adath Israel merged with the Kehillah of Toronto in accordance with this decision, but the union was an uneasy one. "The erstwhile enemies have, metaphorically speaking, kissed and made up," Rabbi Brickner remarked, "to live happily ever after – until the next ruction."[21] The nine synagogues supporting Rabbi Graubart officially entered the Kehillah, but since their total membership was not large, they feared that they might be out-voted in some areas (the Kehillah had one delegate for every fifty members of an affiliated organization). Consequently, in preparation for eventual secession, the Khal Adath retained its identity within the larger body. A rift was to be expected also because of the strained relations between Rabbi Graubart and the rest of the Vaad Harabonim. The former continued to maintain that none but himself was fit to supervise *kashruth* and while Rabbi Weinreb, who was a man of gentle nature and who liked Rabbi Graubart personally, tended to give him latitude, Rabbi Gordon did not. As a result, Rabbi Graubart refused to attend meetings of the Vaad Harabonim whenever Rabbi Gordon presided.[22]

The Kehillah did, however, succeed in surviving these temperamental differences and indeed enjoyed several years of successful operation. During the last years of the decade substantial surpluses were achieved which, in line with the charter of the organization, were distributed to charity and especially to the Talmud Torah Eitz Chaim and the Brunswick Avenue Talmud Torah. Even the secularist Peretz Shulë received a grant.

Despite the apparent triumph of the Kehillah in the late 1920s, its control was not as effective as it should have been and substantial public resentment was growing against it. One serious blow to its effectiveness was its failure to secure a definition of *kashruth* in Ontario law. In February 1926, a delegation of Kehillah supporters had approached Premier Ferguson for legislation to prevent butchers and restauranteurs from advertising their establishments as kosher without rabbinical (presumably Kehillah) authorization. The Premier, however, asserted that federal or municipal governments should deal with the matter, but governments at all levels took the view that they ought not to become involved in religious matters and the Cohen case, which interrupted these negotiations, probably confirmed this opinion. Consequently, when the Kehillah attempted to prevent some delicatessens from importing meat from Winnipeg and the rabbis called the owners to appear before them, the summons was ignored.[23]

A second difficulty encountered by the Kehillah had its roots in European economic conditions and in a weak point of the *beth din's* decision. The mid-1920s was a period of great financial hardship for the Jews of Eastern Europe, especially those in Poland. Large numbers emigrated, accompanied by rabbis who found that their communities could no longer provide them with an adequate standard of living. Suddenly, North American cities found themselves inundated with rabbis and those professing to be such, and Toronto also experienced the influx. Most recognized and affiliated with the Kehillah, as the membership of the Vaad Harabonim indicates. Some, however, refused to do so and could take advantage of a technicality in the decision of 1926 to retain some independence.

Although the *beth din* had declared that the Kehillah was the only legitimate supervisory agency for communal *kashruth*, it also recognized the impossibility of establishing the authority of a European *kehillah* in America. Consequently, while it attempted to unite the rabbinate by facilitating Rabbi Graubart's entry into the Kehillah, it did not demand that all rabbis join. The tribunal further allowed that an unaffiliated rabbi might declare permissible, *for his own followers and not for the community*, meat prohibited by the Kehillah, provided that the basis for the prohibition was not improper slaughtering, but rather the absence of communal supervision.

This presented no problem in 1926 because all the local rabbis had affiliated with the Vaad Harabonim, but later in the decade some recently arrived rabbis preferred to remain aloof, either because they did not recognize the legitimacy of the organization and resented its control,[24] or because they needed to augment their incomes through independent *kashruth* supervision. They could not oppose the Kehillah in the supply of beef since all cattle had to be slaughtered in the municipal abattoir, where the Kehillah had a monopoly. They could, however, cause difficulty in the slaughtering of fowl, which could be killed in the *shochet's* own premises and over which the Kehillah had, as yet, no jurisdiction. Individual rabbis, even members of the Vaad Harabonim, made their own arrangements for supervision in this area. Obviously, this was a potential blow to the Kehillah and by 1929, Rabbi Gordon was urging exclusive Kehillah control over fowl slaughtering.

This effort brought to a head resentment against the Kehillah which had been brewing among some elements ever since its inception. Some complained that its leadership was an oligarchy and that the organization should be run in a more democratic fashion. Others were displeased with the financial disbursements of the association; even the Kehillah itself admitted that money was handled in a haphazard manner and that accounts were kept in insufficient detail. *Shochtim* charged that they were being exploited and that the rabbis received the major share of the income for slaughtering, while butchers and members of the public complained that the attempt to use the Kehillah income to support the Jewish schools, and the necessity of supporting newly arrived *shochtim* who had to be admitted to the Kehillah, unduly increased the price of meat.

Besides these specific local problems, the Kehillah of Toronto generated hostility from recent immigrants who had experienced *kehilloth* in their homelands and recalled them with distaste. Since European *kehilloth*, the machinery of Jewish autonomy within a given state, were consequently responsible for the misdeeds of a community, they had to have real power over the individual, an attribute infuriating to the independent minded in the community. At their peak, especially in seventeenth-century Poland, however, the *kehilloth* were presided over by rabbis of great scholarship and by dedicated lay elders, usually the wealthy and the educated. They worked well and consequently were tolerated even by the non-religious and free-spirited. With the collapse of the Polish state, the calibre of the elders declined. Subject to crushing taxation and no longer feeling morally obliged to do otherwise, they often shifted the burden to the already impoverished community. Some used the *kehillah* to achieve personal power. Consequently, educational standards and rabbinic leadership declined, as did the prestige of the organization, while divisions within the community were aggravated by class antagonism.[25] By the middle of the nineteenth century, some *kehilloth*, especially those in the Russian Empire, were required to enforce conscription and to collect taxes for other than Jewish communal purposes. Especially painful was the tax on food (*taxe*) used to maintain Russian municipal governments.

It is not surprising, therefore, that East European Jews had a tradition of loathing for *kehillah* officers and indeed for any communal authority, a feeling augmented by the rise of socialism and secularism which opposed all religious restriction. The intellectuals, the Zionists and the poor were alienated from the traditional *kehillah* and tended to form their own associations apart from it. In the ethnically heterogeneous Jewish communities of the New World, class-consciousness (increased by experience with the factory and with unionism), the flourishing of Jewish socialism, the gradual decline of religious observance, the tendency toward individual initiative and the desire for integration into the community at large all militated against the transplantation of the European communal organization. The Kehillah of Toronto, which by no means aspired to the authority of its European predecessors and certainly was far less corrupt, albeit unsophisticated, in financial matters, consequently came to be identified with recollections of self-seeking communal elders, and its supervision fees were interpreted as an effort to reimpose the *taxe*. The Kehillah, which might in other circumstances have been the agency for communal unity, a security-enhancing body for the immigrant, was seen rather as an instrument of separation and coercion.

It was at the height of this ill feeling that the Kehillah attempted to extend its control over fowl slaughtering. The action brought protests from *shochtim* who wanted to avoid surveillance, from members of the public who suspected an increase in the price of chicken, and from poultry dealers who feared a decline in their profits. When the *shochtim* who refused to submit to the Kehillah were advertised as unfit, some dissenters sought the support of the cloakmakers' union, which in turn arranged a public protest meeting at the Labour Lyceum on Spadina Avenue. The outcome of the gathering was the establishment of a rival supervisory body named United Jewry. The new organization, also called the Vaad Hoir, at first attempted only to compete with the Kehillah in the area of poultry slaughtering, but its intention was eventually to

295

break the monopoly at the civic abattoir as well. Chief among its supporters was the Central Butchers' Association, which had been formed by Jewish retailers a decade before to engage in co-operative buying and price-fixing. Displeased with the strict surveillance of the Kehillah, they sought to destroy it by throwing their weight behind the Vaad Hoir.[26] There was also considerable support from Jewish labour organizations and from societies such as the Pride of Israel, who were unhappy with their lack of voice in Kehillah operations.

Throughout 1929 and 1930, the authority of the Kehillah was seriously endangered by its inability to bring the poultry *shochtim* under its control. Moreover, the advocates of the Vaad Hoir began to distribute leaflets labelling Rabbi Gordon an ignoramus, Rabbi Graubart an enemy of the masses and the lay leaders of the Kehillah profiteering hypocrites. To make matters worse, the Vaad Hoir engaged two recently arrived rabbis, who had legitimate credentials but did not recognize the Kehillah, to supervise for them. These individuals, Rabbi Israel Hurwitz and Rabbi Zvi Yehuda Kelman, were now placed in a position similar to that of Rabbi Graubart in 1926. As a result, despite the threat of public exposure by the Kehillah rabbis, some butchers and even some congregations began to deal with the Vaad Hoir.

An attempt to settle the dispute without recourse to ad-judicators outside the Jewish community failed. When a *beth din* from New York, headed by Rabbi A.S. Pfeffer, was approached by the Kehillah once again, the dissidents refused to recognize it and the Vaad Hoir intensified its anti-Kehillah campaign. In order to attract butchers away from the Kehillah, the Vaad Hoir offered to have its *shochtim* slaughter for them free of charge. It even went so far as to arrange a mortgage for one retailer, on condition that he would affiliate with the Vaad Hoir. At the same time, the Vaad Hoir approached the city for redress because the management of the civic abattoir had refused to allow its *shochtim* to slaughter there and had even called in the police to have them forcibly removed. The Vaad Hoir accused the Kehillah of all manner of offences: they were dictators unduly raising the price of meat by using supervision fees to support schools; they mismanaged funds; they were a combine impinging on public liberty, since they would not slaughter for butchers who refused to submit to Kehillah regulations. In 1932 the Board of Control at last agreed to appoint an arbitrator, Judge Tytler of the County Court.[27]

Tytler urged that the Kehillah and the Vaad Hoir jointly call a conference of local Jewish organizations for the purpose of

296

reorganizing the Kehillah on what he considered a more democratic basis. It had been decided that only delegates from religious organizations could vote within the Kehillah on religious matters; consequently most societies and unions had withdrawn. At this point, only those societies which conducted services on the High Holy Days were admitted. The Kehillah had previously agreed to absorb the synagogues represented by the Vaad Hoir, but understandably refused to participate in any such convocation. For one thing, to agree to joint sponsorship with the Vaad Hoir would be to imply the legitimacy of that organization and thus impugn the prestige of the Kehillah. Secondly, "democratic" representation, according to the dissidents, would involve the inclusion of delegates from secular organizations such as the Workmen's Circle, the Masons and the Jewish locals of the labour unions. With a delegate appointed for each 50 members, the Amalgamated Clothing Workers alone, with a membership of 1,800, would be entitled to 36 members, whereas the largest synagogue, Goel Tzedec, could elect only 12. It was obvious that in such circumstances the religious elements would soon be swamped and since the purpose of the Kehillah was primarily religious, such a situation would be incongruous. At this juncture, therefore, Judge Tytler had no choice but to launch a formal inquiry into the entire kosher meat supervisory structure in the city, much to the chagrin of many of the local Jewish leaders who hoped to keep the dispute out of the English-language press.[28]

Although the hearing was complicated by numerous tangential issues and class hostility between unionists and the middle-class lay leaders of the Kehillah, the basic question remained the same as that which had supposedly been settled by the rabbinical tribunal six years before; that is, whether the Kehillah did in fact constitute an organized Jewish community with all its implied authority. The Vaad Hoir maintained that since the sole purpose of the Kehillah was to tax meat and since no organization had ever existed in Europe with only that function, the Toronto group did not in fact fulfil the criteria for an authoritative body.

After weeks of testimony, in which many of the arguments raised in the debate between Rabbi Graubart and the Kehillah were resurrected, Judge Tytler decided for the Kehillah, coming to the conclusion, despite denials by the Vaad Hoir, that the latter organization had been formed not to democratize the Kehillah but rather to destroy it. He was convinced that the Kehillah had not misused its funds and stated that no rabbi outside the organization had the right to oppose it in any matter. With this decision, the difficulty should have been settled, but unfortunately, Judge

Tytler refused to order the city to enforce it. " . . . This is for all the Jewish people to decide," he asserted, "and not for any one outside of their religious law."[29]

The judge's report pleased no one; one controller observed that it was "not worth 15 cents,"[30] while Tytler's failure to take action effectively destroyed the Kehillah's power. The Vaad Hoir continued to operate, while the Kehillah was forced to admit increased numbers of secular organizations in order to maintain popular support, thus weakening its religious legitimacy from within. Furthermore, the Kehillah, with its monopoly over the abattoir, was always in a position to offend someone, especially *shochtim* and supervisors seeking employment, and complaints were both vocal and frequent.[31] Finally, the constant bickering and especially the court proceedings had disillusioned many with religious practice in general and with orthodox communal organization in particular.

In 1933 a group of local women active in philanthropy, education and Zionism, led by Rose Dunkelman and Mattie Rotenberg, attempted to mobilize popular support for the Kehillah, which they saw as potentially providing the basis for wider Jewish communal government and a source of revenue to support Jewish institutions during the Depression. Although the movement persuaded large numbers of women to purchase only meat approved by the Kehillah, it did not solve the problem of the organization's unpopularity and impotence. Many still bought meat from unaffiliated stores and Rabbi Graubart had now again begun to criticize the standards of his colleagues. And once again, butchers began to sell non-kosher meat as kosher.[32]

By the time of Rabbi Gordon's death in 1934, the Kehillah was merely a shell, devoid of power and prestige, even though the Vaad Hoir was falling into obscurity under the weight of the depression and because of public apathy. Increasingly, the Polish Jews, now a majority in the city, began to assume control of the Kehillah. There was an effort to raise its prestige by offers to provide free supervision. This was unsuccessful, as was the attempt in 1937 to appoint "an outstanding Orthodox Rabbi" to head up the community. By this time, the local rabbinate was powerless and supervision chaotic. When some of the so-called *kosher* butchers began to remain open on the Sabbath, only the unions could force them to close.

The Kehillah of Toronto finally collapsed in 1939 for lack of public support and under a barrage of complaints about its management. No doubt the domination of the Polish Jews, lacking refinement and the qualities of leadership in the opinion of the Russians, alienated the latter and caused many to withdraw. Typical of the public attitude is the following item on Toronto in the *Canadian Jewish Year Book*, 1939/40: "The various synagogues are not organized or united in any way, except indirectly in the Kehillah, which functions very sporadically and unsatisfactorily, devoting itself almost exclusively to the supervision of Kashruth and to the interminable squabbles with the butchers."[33]

IV

The specific events in the turbulent career of the Kehillah of Toronto are only superficial explanations for its demise. The deeper cause was not unique to Toronto; it plagued Jewish communities throughout North America and was perhaps best explained by Rabbi Judah L. Magnes in a Presidential address to the New York Kehillah in 1918.

> The European notion of a uniform . . . all-controlling . . . kehillah cannot strike root in American soil . . . because it is not in consonance with the free and voluntary character of American religious, social, educational, and philanthropic enterprises. . . . The only power that the kehillah can exercise is moral and spiritual in its nature, the power of an enlightened public opinion, the power of a developed community sense.[34]

The voluntarism of North American life militated against that community sense, and in the Jewish community it was aggravated by ethnic diversity and the irrelevance of the issue of unity to a working class concerned with earning a livelihood. In addition, synagogues, *landsmanshaften*, fraternal organizations and labour unions fulfilled the functions of the traditional *kehillah* and bolstered the voluntarist idea. Unity and submission to communal authority would be generated only by the crises of the 1930s, the Depression and the eruption of anti-semitism abroad and in Toronto.

NOTES

1 Quoted in *Jewish Times*, June 13, 1913, p. 26.

2 Rabbi Jacob Gordon, "Reminiscences of a Toronto Rabbi," *Kanader Adler*, 25th anniversary edition, 1932 (Yiddish,

clipping in Rabbi Jacob Gordon Papers, Canadian Jewish Congress Archives, Montreal).

3 Mattie Rotenberg, personal interview, Jan. 25, 1972; *Jewish Times*, June 18, 1909, p. 619; J.B. Salsberg, personal interview, Jan. 15, 1973.

4 Paul Frumhartz, interview by Julius Hayman, March 17, 1957 (typescript, 6 pp., Canadian Jewish Congress Archives, Montreal); Shemen, "Orthodoxy . . .," p. 15.

5 By the end of the decade, the congregation was having to employ men to form the *minyan*. An indication of the religious decline at Goel Tzedec is the fact that members no longer lived within walking distance of the synagogue and consequently drove to services, if they came at all. (See addresses given in New Years' greetings in *Canadian Jewish Review*, Sept. 26, 1924, Ida Siegel, personal interview, Oct. 7, 1971, Goel Tzedec *Minutes*, Nov. 28, 1926; Feb. 5, 1928; Feb. 17, 1929).

6 *Canadian Jewish Review*, Apr. 7, 1922, p. 8; Shemen, "Orthodoxy . . .," p. 13; leaflet published by Chevrai Shomrai Shabbos, (Rabbi Jacob Gordon Papers).

7 Evidence taken "in the matter of certain grievances of Max Goldman, of the City of Toronto, in the County of York, Butcher, and Others, against the management of the Civic Abattoir, in the City of Toronto, and the Kehillah Incorporated, of the same place" [hereafter referred to as the *Kehillah Enquiry*], pp. 817 ff (Folio #36, City of Toronto Archives); *Star*, June 22, 1926, p. 17; "Agreement between Shochtim and Rabbis of Toronto," Oct. 30, 1915 (Canadian Jewish Congress Archives, Montreal).

8 Quoted in translation in the Statement of Claim, Dickman *vs.* Winreb (*sic*), p. 4 (Supreme Court of Ontario, File for Action #908/1912).

9 Statement of Defense and Counterclaim, Dickman *vs.* Winreb, p. 4 (Supreme Court of Ontario, File for Action #908/1912); Marcus Dickman, *The Way of Peace, a Panacea for all Ills* (pamphlet, Yiddish, 1912, quoted in translation in Counterclaim, Dickman *vs.* Gordon, pp. 4-7 [Supreme Court of Ontario, File for Action 22/1912]). There is little doubt that the allegations were absurd.

10 Rabbi Jacob Gordon in *Hebrew Journal*, Feb. 21, 1919.

11 *Hebrew Journal*, Jan. 22, 1922.

12 See *Daily Jewish News* (Chicago), May 14, 1915 and *Kanader Adler*, Sept. 10, 1916. In his early public pronouncements, Rabbi Graubart had styled himself "Rabbi of Toronto." (See e.g., *Canadian Jewish Review*, Dec. 23, 1921, p. 13.)

13 Quoted in *Canadian Jewish Review*, July 28, 1922, p. 4.

14 *Hebrew Journal*, Sept. 13, 1922, editorial; Dec. 22, 1922, author's translation.

15 Supreme Court of Ontario, Action #1813/25 "Cohen *vs.* Silverstein *et al.*," testimony of Rabbi S.Z. Silverstein; Samuel A. Kurtz, personal interview, Nov. 27, 1972; Brickner, quoted in *Canadian Jewish Review*, Nov. 2, 1923, p. 6.

16 Brickner, in *Canadian Jewish Review*, March 14, 1924, p. 7.

17 Supreme Court of Ontario, Action #1813/25, "Cohen *vs.* Silverstein," p. 43. Examination of Rabbi Meyer Berger; Henry S. Rosenberg, personal interview, May 4, 1973. *Hebrew Journal*, July 31-Aug. 7, 1925, notice entitled "What Jews in Toronto must not forget" (translation). The announcement stated flatly that Cohen sold non-kosher meat and urged all other butchers to be exacting concerning their supervision. On Aug. 14 and 16, Cohen was named singly.

Toronto Jews take care of your houses. Do not contaminate your souls. Beware of Cohen's butcher shop, 170 Dundas West. He sells you meat unfit according to law. Buy kosher meat only, that is stamped with the Kehillah stamp.

(*Hebrew Journal*, Aug. 14, 16, 1925, author's translation).

18 *Star*, July 19, 1926.

19 "Award of the Hebrew Religious Tribunal 1926," translated in *Kehillah Enquiry* transcript, pp. 826-28.

20 "Peace Settlement," quoted in *Telegram*, July 21, 1926.

21 *Canadian Jewish Review*, editorial, July 30, 1926.

22 Shemen, "Orthodoxy...," p. 24; N. Shemen, personal interview, March 5, 1973; Rabbi Samuel Sachs, interview, Aug. 13, 1973.

23 Supreme Court of Ontario, Action #1813/25, "Examination of S.Z. Silverstein"; Rabbi Gordon in *Hebrew Journal*, May 18, 1925.

24 One of these, Rabbi Zvi Kelman, believed that the laws

pertaining to the *kehillah* do not apply in the diaspora (*Kehillah Enquiry*, pp. 1, 133).

25 Arthur A. Goren, *New York Jews and the Quest for Community: The Kehillah Experiment, 1908-1922* (New York: Columbia University Press, 1970), p. 9. For a detailed account of the European *kehilloth* in their prime, see Salo W. Baron, *The Jewish Community*, 3 vols. (Philadelphia: Jewish Publication Soc., 1948), esp. I, pp. 267-82.

26 It is probably no coincidence that the president of the Central Butchers' Association was the same Jacob Cohen who had been involved in the dispute with the Kehillah in 1926.

27 *Kehillah Enquiry*, pp. 27-32, 982-1016.

28 *Ibid.*, pp. 779, 1222, 1014, 1293-96. Edmund Scheuer to Shmuel Meyer Shapiro, May 9, 1932 (MSS. copy, Holy Blossom Archives).

29 Judge John Tytler to Mayor Wm. J. Stewart, July 8, 1932 (City of Toronto Archives). "Report by His Honour Judge Tytler re: Kehillah Enquiry," 1933 (City of Toronto Archives).

30 Quoted in *Evening Telegram*, July 11, 1932.

31 See Kehillah of Toronto, *Ballot 1932* (Canadian Jewish Congress Archives, Montreal); G. Tellson to E. Pullan, Oct. 30, 1933 (courtesy Mr. Samuel A. Kurtz). At one point, the Kehillah was compared to Czar Nicholas ("Committee of Unterdrichte poor rabbis and chicken shochtim and butchers of Toronto," leaflet, 1933, Rabbi Jacob Gordon Papers).

32 Rabbi Gordon in *Hebrew Journal*, March 30, 1934; Announcement of Rabbi Rizenman to Toronto Jewry (Yiddish, leaflet in Rabbi Jacob Gordon Papers); *Hebrew Journal*, Aug. 8, 1934. For an indication of the lack of public co-operation with the Kehillah in this period, see advertisement in Toronto Hebrew Free School, *Theatre Night Programme*, March 9, 1936 and Henry S. Rosenberg to Rabbi B. Treiger, March, 1935 (Associated Hebrew Schools Archives, Toronto).

33 M. Frank, "The Jews of Toronto," *Canadian Jewish Year Book*, 1939/40 (Montreal: privately printed, 1939), p. 333. After the dissolution, each rabbi again embarked upon independent supervision. Only the Polish community, which had preserved the Khal Adath, continued some semblance of united action, first under Rabbi Kaminetsky and then after the

Second World War under Rabbi David Ochs. The organization still exists today as the Agudath Shomrai Hadas. No attempt at universal supervision would be attempted again until the Orthodox Division of the Canadian Jewish Congress set up a Rabbinical Vaad Ha'Kashruth in the 1950s. It is still operating and is successful, but it is by no means universally accepted and has little power beyond moral suasion.

34 Quoted in Goren, *op cit.*, p. 252.

CHAPTER 18

THE NEED FOR
UNITY, 1920 – 1937

The 1920s was a decade of intense activity in Jewish Toronto, a period in which the community, still in its formative stage, was beginning to experience a growing self-assurance. Despite the disruptive effects of the Kehillah dispute, the weakening of traditional values and practices, and the necessity of absorbing numerous postwar immigrants, this was a time of progress, for the experiments of the previous twenty years were at last beginning to bear fruit.

The new confidence was best typified by the new synagogue buildings opened in this period, as the community shifted westward toward Spadina Avenue. The Polish Jews, formerly the fewest in number, the poorest and least visible, took the lead with their monumental Beth Jacob synagogue on Henry Street, dedicated in 1922. Aptly named "The Great Synagogue," the new structure in the Romanesque "round style" continued the twin-tower fashion popularized in the city at Holy Blossom and Goel Tzedec, but it also had an impressive vaulted ceiling capped by a massive central dome and four smaller ones. There were carved oak interior furnishings, elegant stained-glass windows, a weekday chapel, a ritual bath, a meeting room with a movable roof for use on the festival of Succoth, an apartment for the sexton and an assembly hall in the basement. Most important, however, was the fact that the congregation had enough confidence in Jewish professional and scientific ability to employ a Jewish architect to design the building, the first time this had been done in Toronto.[1]

Other congregations followed suit, some, such as Hebrew Men of England and Anshei Ostrovtze, purchasing churches and remodelling them (1921, 1925), but many erecting synagogues of their own. For instance, Anshei Kiev produced another twin-tower edifice which was opened in 1926; Agudath Israel Anshei Sfard opened a "round style" building on Palmerston Avenue in

1925 and Anshei Minsk completed its eclectic Russian-Romanesque affair on St. Andrews Street in 1930. Others built farther west, on Shaw Street and Ossington Avenue.

The educational and philanthropic organizations, whose maturity in this period was exemplified by the acquisition of new buildings, had their roots in the previous decade. Principal among the welfare institutions to expand in this way were the Jewish Old Folks' Home, the Jewish Childrens' Home, and the Mount Sinai Hospital.

The Jewish Old Folks' Home (Moshav Zekenim) originated in a women's society called the Ezras Noshim, which had been founded by Mrs. Slova Greenberg about 1913. The society had begun as a mutual benefit organization for immigrant women; sick members were visited and assisted with housekeeping duties during their illnesses.

The increase in the Jewish population just prior to the First World War created a need for a communal organization for the elderly who could not be cared for by their families. As early as 1913 the Hachnosas Orchim building on Grange Avenue had been converted into a home for the aged by the Associated Hebrew Charities, but it apparently never functioned well. Various private individuals provided some assistance to the destitute aged, but these efforts were too haphazard to be effective. In 1916, therefore, the Ezras Noshim decided to embark upon a formal program and in the following year were able to purchase a house on Cecil Street. The adjoining building was later acquired and by the early 1920s the institution, then called the Jewish Institute for Aged Men, was accommodating about thirty residents.*

Next to expand was the Jewish Childrens' Home. It will be recalled that since 1910 the orphanage had been occupying the upper floors of the Associated Charities building on Simcoe Street. Always inadequate and severely criticized by the municipal authorities, the institution was already seeking better facilities in 1919 when the subject of a new orphanage was proposed by the Maternity Aid Society. For some reason, an attempt to secure property in the centre of the city was unsuccessful and in 1922 the institution purchased a twenty-room mansion on Annette Street, in the West End.

* The incident which prompted the Ezras Noshim to establish a Jewish old folks' home was the case of a pious woman in her nineties, who had been committed to a home for incurables, was being given non-kosher food and was unable to make her protests understood to the English-speaking staff. The Jewish Old Folks' Home opened in January 1920 and by 1934 would house seventy-five residents.

The improvement was phenomenal. The number of children who could be accommodated far exceeded the number who needed care. A graduate nurse was appointed superintendent and dispensary facilities were provided. By 1924 the institution was housing sixty-one children and, in recognition of its effectiveness, was receiving both municipal and provincial grants, in addition to its support from the Federation of Jewish Philanthropies. A variety of educational and recreational activities was offered. Children were registered at local public schools and most attended the Sunday School at Holy Blossom as well. Some boys were provided with a more intensive Jewish education in the daily orthodox *talmud torahs*. In addition, volunteers from the Jewish community offered music, sewing and dancing lessons, while the B'nai B'rith and Oddfellows lodges organized outings.

The orphanage operated until the early 1930s when, in line with developments across the continent, it was replaced by a system of foster homes. But while in the United States there was a tendency to give this work over to non-denominational public agencies, in Toronto it was kept in Jewish hands.

The institution which best indicated the maturing of the Jewish community, however, was the Mount Sinai Hospital. The Jewish Dispensary had been considerably successful in its early years in providing medical attention to Jews who had no need of hospital care or were afraid to enter hospitals. As the Jewish population grew, however, its limited services became increasingly inadequate and the need for a Jewish hospital more urgent. For one thing, the public hospitals refused to admit Jewish physicians to staff positions; their patients entering hospitals had to be treated by unfamiliar doctors. This was especially unnerving for recent immigrants, who saw hospitals only as places in which to die.

A second problem revolved around the language barrier and the provision of kosher food. The Folks Farein and the Maternity Aid Society each visited Jewish patients and did some interpretation, but the system was too sporadic. The same could be said of the Folks Farein's attempt to supply kosher meals.

Efforts to generate support for a Jewish hospital prior to 1914 had ended in failure, as did an effort by Reverend Kaplan to convince the Toronto General Hospital to provide a wing with a kosher kitchen and a Yiddish-speaking staff. As one of the principal *mohelim* in Toronto, Kaplan spent a great deal of time in the hospitals and was acutely aware of the problems. His plan was to have the Ezras Noshim partially finance the outfitting of the wing, but hospital officials were unsympathetic.

A majority in the Jewish community agreed that Toronto Jewry was financially incapable of supporting an independent hospital. Nevertheless, while Kaplan had been negotiating with the Toronto General, Maternity Aid had taken over two rooms in the Hachnosas Orchim building which had, by this time, been vacated by the Old Folks' Home, for care of maternity cases. This they hoped would expand into a full-blown maternity hospital.[2]

By 1921 it had become evident that Kaplan's rebuff by the Toronto General was irrevocable. Mrs. Greenberg, still heading the Ezras Noshim, then mobilized its members for the establishment of a Jewish hospital. Many of the women involved had participated in the founding of the Old Folks' Home and were adept at fund-raising by door-to-door collection. During the next difficult year public support was generated, principally by the efforts of Dorothy Goldstick Dworkin, a force, it will be remembered, behind the Jewish Dispensary. Support came especially from Jewish doctors, who offered both money and services in order to assure themselves of a hospital where they could treat their patients. By 1922 sufficient funds had been raised to purchase a building occupied by the Lyndhurst Hospital, a small private institution on Yorkville Avenue.

The twenty-bed Toronto Jewish Convalescent and Maternity Hospital, as its name suggests, made no claims to comprehensive services, and these did not expand after it was renamed Mount Sinai the following year, after the noted New York Jewish hospital. Conditions bordered on the primitive. The institution had no sterilizer; instruments and bandages had to be disinfected at nearby Women's College Hospital. There was no elevator; patients had to be carried to upper stories by hand. The permanent staff in 1923 included Miss Pickles, the nursing superintendent, four graduate and two undergraduate nurses, a cook, a laundress, a housemaid and a janitor, while the thirty-three Jewish doctors in the city all donated some time.

Besides its deficiency in physical facilities, the hospital faced the problem of public acceptance. Despite its being the only kosher hospital in Canada, it was nevertheless a hospital and consequently, according to immigrants, to be feared. So reluctant were patients to be admitted during its first year that the Mount Sinai had to lure them with the promise of a free baby carriage for the first child born.[3]

These fears were dispelled as the public accepted invitations to tour the premises and discovered that maternity patients at Mount Sinai actually survived to raise their children. But acceptance brought only increased financial burdens and greater strain on the physical facilities. Unable to meet the standards for a provincial grant, the institution relied on the fund-raising power of the Ezras Noshim and, while the women certainly expended a commendable effort, being for the most part East European immigrants they lacked the prestige to tap the real sources of wealth in the community. In addition, the Ezras Noshim had insufficient experience to administer a large institution.

These difficulties stemmed principally from the fact that, unlike similar institutions in many North American cities, the Mount Sinai Hospital was not the creation of the financially secure old community or even of the established East Europeans, but rather of the most recently arrived East European element, who were least capable of maintaining it. This was a natural development in Toronto, since the acculturated old community was practically unaware of the difficulties encountered by hospitalized immigrants and by Jewish doctors. The Holy Blossom circle were unencumbered by a language barrier, a fear of hospitals or concern about kosher food. They patronized non-Jewish doctors as a rule and consequently could be served without difficulty when they entered a hospital. Perhaps most important, they tended to oppose any institution which would separate Jews from the community at large. Therefore, not only did they fail to take the initiative in the founding of a Jewish hospital, they also declined to support Mount Sinai once it had been established.[4]

As the hospital deficit mounted and the necessity of renovating the old building increased in urgency, it became imperative that a link with the old community and with the affluent sector of the new be established. The catalyst once again was J.J. Allen, who used the same device now as he had in the case of the Federation of Jewish Philanthropies: he donated a large sum to the hospital and persuaded others to match it. Through his membership in Holy Blossom and Goel Tzedec, he succeeded in drawing in a number of capable entrepreneurs and professionals, including E.F. Singer, soon to be a member of the provincial legislature.

These men, however, agreed to lend their support only on condition that the Ezras Noshim relinquish control in favour of a board of directors. The former reluctantly acquiesced and the transfer of power was accomplished late in 1923. The board consisted almost exclusively of men, primarily members of Holy Blossom or Goel Tzedec. Singer, who assumed the presidency, was a diplomat *par excellence*, able to fuse the disparate elements supporting the hospital. He was especially effective in placating members of the old community, who were unaccustomed to dealing with East Europeans, and in suppressing the rampant jealousy prevalent among the staff doctors.

After the takeover the Ezras Noshim effectively withdrew from the hospital organization, but in the spring of 1924 Mrs. Dworkin was able to attract some remaining women into a Ladies' Auxiliary, whose principal purpose at first would be the raising of money through social functions. The hospital was financed by these, by membership dues in the same manner as the Talmud Torah, by Federation allotments and, after 1925, by provincial grants. Both paying and charity patients were accepted and the institution was non-sectarian. The professional staff was upgraded with nine fully trained nurses, and students ceased to be employed, but the Ladies' Auxiliary often had to act as volunteer nursing aides. In fact, in 1926, when cooks and other support staff could not be engaged, the Ladies' Auxiliary provided meals and mended linen.[5]

Even under the new administration, however, things did not run smoothly. The hospital constantly fell into debt as services expanded. A particular drain on its resources was the acceptance of interns and the opening of an out-patient department to replace the Dispensary late in the 1920s. This necessitated campaigns for extra funds, an extremely unpopular move with the leadership of the Federation. "It is unfortunate," the executive director reported in 1925, "that in the founding of this Hospital the Federation was not consulted . . . . It is a violation of Federation principles for one of its organizations to be under the necessity of appealing separately to the community for the additional necessary assistance." This attitude no doubt reflected the continued animosity of some of the old community, who had not yet come to terms with the concept of a Jewish hospital. Nevertheless, the hospital continued to supplement its treasury with bazaars, baby contests and moderately successful door-to-door collections. By the end of the decade, the institution was so popular that it had become overcrowded and plans for expansion were under way.[6]

The Depression seriously inhibited this development. In the early thirties Mount Sinai was in such difficulty that some board members had to make personal loans to keep it open. When a campaign to raise money for an addition to the building was proposed, no member of the local Jewish establishment would head the venture, so low had the prestige of the institution fallen. Fortunately, O.B. Roger, an English Jew recently arrived to take up a post with an oil company in Toronto, was anxious to prove his good citizenship and agreed to superintend the campaign.

Under his aegis and despite the financial crisis, a modernization, including expansion to eighty-six beds and the addition of surgical facilities, was completed in 1934. These would serve the Jewish community for another two decades.

II

Educational development took place both in secular and in religious schools. In the former, the Farband Shulë, under the auspices of the Poalei Zion, saw the greatest growth, following its founding in 1922. The principal advance in the field of Jewish education, however, resulted from the expansion of the Simcoe Street Talmud Torah.

By the conclusion of the First World War the need for change was urgent since enrolment stood at about 250, far too many for the limited space available and too few to meet the needs of a growing Jewish community.[7] Moreover, the residential concentration of the community had now shifted westward, enrolment was declining and if the Talmud Torah were to continue to attract students, a relocation was necessary.

Rabbi Gordon had begun to advocate a move as early as 1917, when a sharp decline in enrolment had raised the spectre of collapse for the Simcoe Street school. Together with Louis Levinsky, president of the institution, he embarked upon a personal fund-raising campaign. Within a year, sufficient money had been pledged to plan a new building and enough was in hand to purchase a lot on Brunswick Avenue, north of College Street.

Construction, however, did not begin until 1922. Besides the difficulty in persuading contributors to honour their pledges in a period of tight money, there was the problem of deciding how ambitious the project was to be, how large the new structure and whether it should include an auditorium and athletic facilities. Curriculum, too, was a problem. There was little uncertainty about the continued use of the *ivrit be'ivrit* system, but the role of Yiddish and of secular studies had to be reassessed if the school were to attract all elements. All agreed that the new school would be non-denominational, Hebraist, religious and Zionist, concepts implied by the name Toronto Hebrew Free School. However, in accord with Rabbi Gordon's patriotic position, and indeed with the stand of the established members of the community from Goel Tzedec, Chevra Tehillim and even Holy Blossom, who were the principal supporters of the institution, the school would endeavour to develop a positive attitude toward Canadian citizenship.[8]

310

It was decided that no effort would be spared in the new facilities. Committees were dispatched to Philadelphia and New York to examine the highly developed communal *talmud torahs* in those cities, both as to buildings and curricula. Benjamin Brown, whose Henry Street synagogue had impressed the community, was engaged to prepare a design, which would include accommodation for 800 students in 15 classrooms, a 1,300-seat auditorium-banquet hall, a library and a chapel, a novel suction system to provide ventilation, fireproof concrete flooring and, at the urging of YMHA, athletic facilities consisting of a gymnasium, a swimming pool, showers and lockers. By the time construction began, the new Talmud Torah was apparently being seen as more than merely a religious school; it was being planned as a Jewish community centre on the model of those springing up throughout the United States, providing social and educational facilities for adults as well as children. The *Canadian Jewish Review* was quick to add that it would be a building "for a large Jewish community that is rapidly becoming thoroughly Canadianized."[9]

Although the basic educational requirements of the non-Polish orthodox element had provided the initial motivation for the new building, the image of the Talmud Torah-Jewish Centre as an agency for dealing with the problems of Canadian life within the Jewish family was a major asset in attracting support. Able to draw both orthodox and liberal Jews, the Brunswick Avenue building could act as a "medium for real Canadianization," permitting young people to engage in activities popular in this country, but in a Jewish milieu. This would encourage acculturation, but at the same time lessen the cultural gap between the generations.

In December 1925 the Brunswick Avenue Talmud Torah finally opened. With no plans to interfere with public school education, the Toronto Hebrew Free School continued the Simcoe Street policy of afternoon instruction. However, the organizers of the new school hoped that it would supersede all other institutions of Jewish learning in the city, with the probable exception of Eitz Chaim.

At first this seemed realistic. The nature of the enrolment indicated that the Free School held wide appeal. Congregations with their own Sunday schools supported it, as did Rabbi Brickner, who urged members of Holy Blossom to avail themselves of its facilities. So staunch a supporter was Brickner, in fact, that the officers of the Talmud Torah invited him to speak at the opening ceremonies along with rabbis Gordon and Weinreb.[10]

By 1926 the Talmud Torah had expanded to include a high

311

school department and adult classes, and plans were under way to force private *chedorim* to affiliate with it. When the institution had first opened, large numbers of parents, who had previously patronized private *melamdim* and *chedorim* had begun to send their children to Brunswick Avenue. Since the institution was in need of additional teachers, a number of capable local professionals accepted an invitation to give up independent instruction and join the faculty, but most did not, and the staff came increasingly to consist of knowledgeable recent arrivals from Europe. Some of these worked in factories during the day, but there were also professionals from the United States who had either answered advertisements in the American Jewish press or had been approached through the New York Jewish teachers' association.

In 1926 the new principal, Moses Emmanuel, (who had been imported from Rochester after Nathanson had been unceremoniously retired in a quest for younger personnel), attempted to deal a final blow to the private institutions by demanding that members of the executive board of the Talmud Torah, who comprised forty to fifty of the wealthiest members of the community, set an example by sending their own children exclusively to Brunswick Avenue. At first the board responded *en masse* at the expense of the private *melamdim*, but the movement was short-lived. Some students objected to the structured nature of the instruction, while some parents, who supported the institution out of a feeling of communal responsibility and perhaps also because of its role as a community centre, objected to the religious emphasis. Consequently, many students were soon withdrawn, with the result that the Toronto Hebrew Free School would never be able to eliminate all private instruction, let alone the established congregational schools and the secularist institutions. While Montreal had been able to establish a system of co-operation among its various Jewish schools as early as 1917, and other centres on the continent would do likewise, Toronto Jewry was unable to unite in this regard. The first effective co-operation did not come until the early 1950s when the Bureau of Jewish Education was established.

In the meantime, the 1920s saw other educational expansion. Eitz Chaim again had expert direction after Rabbi Graubart's arrival. Although the language of instruction continued to be Yiddish, more Hebrew was introduced in line with the rabbi's Zionist leanings, and an upper school, Yeshiva Shaarei Torah, was established in 1923. Now, too, Eitz Chaim was placed on a firm financial footing and, after a fire in 1928, the D'Arcy Street facilities were greatly enlarged. In the same period, *talmud torahs* were established at the extremities of the city, in the West Toronto Junction and on Berkeley Street, in connection with the Congregation Eastern Children of Israel.

The twenties witnessed expansion also in young people's organizations. By 1922 the Jewish Boys' Club was operating out of the Federation building on Simcoe Street, while the Council of Jewish Women had acquired 44 St. George Street for use as a headquarters and girls' club. However, the need remained for a central meeting place for the various young people's clubs in operation around the city – in short, a YMHA.

With the collapse of the community centre movement prior to the First World War, a federation of young people's clubs had been established and by the end of the decade, after meeting sporadically at the University Avenue Synagogue and in the Zionist Institute, the group was using a cottage on Brunswick Avenue, on property owned by the Talmud Torah. The organization operated with relative success, but its activities were restricted merely to the affiliated clubs for adolescents. Expansion was inhibited by lack of funds and accommodation. Moreover, the group was run with only marginal leadership from the adult community. Edmund Scheuer was named honorary president, but appears to have taken little interest, and an informal advisory board (composed of Ida Siegel, E.F. Singer, Joe Harris and Mr. and Mrs. Henry Rosenthal) offered only occasional advice. The solution lay in a reorganization which would draw in young businessmen and professionals who themselves would take an active part.

As long as the YMCA continued to satisfy that element's desire for athletic activity, this was impossible. In 1918, however, a sudden rash of anti-semitism broke out in the YMCA; the organization adopted a policy of setting up separate athletic groups for its Jewish members. This infuriated many, especially veterans of the war, who promptly resigned and attempted to mobilize community support for a rival Jewish institution. In the difficult postwar years, however, they had to be content with rented premises, first in the Racquet Club on Russell Street and then on the upper floors of a commercial building at the corner of Brunswick and College. When this opened in 1921, the federation of young people's clubs, which had been meeting in the cottage next door, was brought in.

The combined organization had now been formally constituted as the Toronto YM and YWHA, with an executive board consisting of experienced young professionals and merchants. All adult

313

social and recreational groups were invited to affiliate; in fact, over seventy did so.

In 1922, when plans for the new Talmud Torah building were being finalized, the YMHA proposed that the organization and Talmud Torah pool their resources and erect a community centre which would provide educational and recreation facilities for the Jewish community. The intention was to produce an institution unique in North America, in which "Y" members could be influenced religiously and the Talmud Torah students would have the use of athletic facilities.

Despite the immense practicality of the suggestion, the officials of the Talmud Torah felt that the introduction of a wider organization would dilute the institution's principal purpose, that of education. The "Y" proposal, however, did add thrust to the movement for the inclusion of athletic facilities in the new building for use by the students. For one thing, Rabbi Gordon favoured physical as well as intellectual exercise; moreover, two "Y" activists, Harry Pullan and Hyman Smith, whose fathers exercised considerable influence on the board of the Talmud Torah, were able to do some persuasive convincing on the matter among the laity. The result was that the "Y" took over maintenance of the athletic facilities and had use of them after school hours, while the students could utilize them while classes were in progress. A liaison system was thus established between the two institutions, allowing the Talmud Torah to develop into a genuine Jewish community centre in the next decade.

III

The 1920s saw some old problems disappear, to be succeeded by new ones. For instance, the proliferation of Jewish educational, welfare and recreational facilities was successful in frustrating the efforts of the missionaries. As early as 1919 the Anglicans had noted that the presence of Jewish religious schools was making it virtually impossible to attract boys to the missions. Only athletic facilities were popular with Jewish children and attendance fell off here too when the Brunswick Avenue building opened. By 1926 the Anglican Church had virtually given up attempts at outright conversion and missionaries were complaining of the aloofness and devoutness of the Jew.[11]

Singer and Rohold were also experiencing difficulties. Singer's mission did not survive the move out of the Ward and in 1919, he left for Detroit where he thought his efforts would be more successful. At this time also, the Presbyterian mission was in

314

trouble. Attendance was poor except at the dispensary and Rohold was complaining of the refusal of Jews to attend the mission.[12] By 1923 he had left for Palestine and his successors found their efforts fruitless. The fact that the mission had now become a liability is indicated by the refusal of the United Church to assume responsibility for it when church union was effected in 1925. The Elizabeth Street building, therefore, remained under the auspices of the Presbyterian Church, which appointed Reverend Morris Zeidman, a converted Jew, to head missionary efforts. Zeidman soon realized the futility of the work and began to concentrate his efforts on the unemployed. As for the United Church, by 1929 it had given up separate missions to the Jews. Although the various denominations which comprised it had participated in proselytizing activity, the newly formed United Church had shown little interest in continuing these efforts.[13]

Another problem which had been plaguing the Jewish community began to dissipate in the 1920s as well. This was the social gap between the old and new communities. The trend toward co-operation, under way for nearly a decade, gained momentum as at least the affluent joined forces in political ventures, in social organizations such as the Primrose Club[14] and the Oakdale Golf Club, and in support of Federation, the Mount Sinai Hospital, the YMHA, the boys' and girls' clubs and the Hebrew Free School.

It was during Rabbi Brickner's term at Holy Blossom that the feeling of solidarity and the spirit of co-operation between the old community and the new became apparent. Indeed, he was in large measure responsible for it, striving to break down the snobbishness in his own congregation and showing the East Europeans that Bond Street was not a centre for apostasy. "None of our forefathers came over on the 'Mayflower'," Brickner wrote in 1922. "None of us therefore arrogate to ourselves any distinctions that arise from the claim that priority is equivalent to superiority." If any at Holy Blossom did not concur, they kept their objections to themselves. Brickner's advocacy of the Talmud Torah was extremely important in rallying old community support for that institution and his work on behalf of Jewish refugees in the Ukraine gave him entry into many an East European institution. His support for open immigration also drew him closer to the new community, as did his sympathy with Zionism.[15]

But Brickner was too optimistic when he observed in 1925 that the Jewish community of Toronto was "signally without fences between the elements – orthodox, Reform, Zionist and non-Zionist – which are all too prevalent in older communities";[16]

315

there were still serious rifts between the religious and the secularist, as well as within each camp itself. The rift in the secularist movement was due to the growing militancy of its communist wing.

It will be recalled that, as a working-class Jewish community, Toronto had been extremely favourably disposed toward socialism. The Workmen's Circle and the Poalei Zion were forces to be contended with in the city, although both would decline in the 1930s as more people began to rise in the economic scale. In the twenties socialism was rampant among the Jewish factory operatives and strikes were commonplace. Despite the injection of support from union agents from the United States, who arrived periodically in Toronto, these were usually futile. Added to the workers' frustration was the fact that few of them had been factory operatives in Europe; they had often been petty tradesmen and in Toronto they found their status reduced. They were prepared, therefore, to listen to intellectuals of the socialist type. Many believed that the unions lacked militancy and these began to drift to the radical left. If the union organizers from the United States had done little else, they had at least generated class-consciousness. Finally, Jews, especially recent arrivals, were attracted to the communist movement by its condemnation of anti-semitism.

By the early twenties considerable tension had developed between social democrats and communists within the Workmen's Circle. The former were leaders of the trade unions and opponents of the Bolshevik Revolution. (Rhinewine and the *Hebrew Journal* fell into this category.) These were accused by the class-conscious left wing of having betrayed the principles of the organization, with the result that the Workmen's Circle had begun to expel a number of the extremists. The growing animosity came to a head in 1922, when the Workmen's Circle held its National Conference in Toronto. The left wing became furious when the membership refused the platform to Dr. M. Olgin, the editor of *Freiheit*, a radical American Yiddish periodical. Moreover, the convention voted overwhelmingly to condemn Russian-style communism generally.[17] The communists within the Workmen's Circle, who had been attempting since 1918 to assume control of the organization branch by branch through the winning of offices, now set up a "shadow" executive to direct extreme left-wing activities. In addition, they adopted the tactic of attempting to attract Jewish factory workers and their families by organizing cultural activities emphasizing the survival of the Jews as a people. Universalism appears to have found little place among the Jewish communists.

About 1923, the communist Freiheit Club was opened in Alhambra Hall on Spadina Avenue. A choir called the Freiheit Gezangs Farein was formed. An orchestra and athletic teams were organized and a women's group (the Jewish Association of Progressive Women) was set up, which began to operate a children's summer camp at Long Branch and by 1925 was sponsoring Saturday morning classes in ideology for Jewish children at the Freiheit Club.[18]

These activities disturbed the social-democratic Workmen's Circle, which finally expelled its communists in 1926. The latter promptly formed a mutual benefit organization called the Labor League (now the United Jewish People's Order), which united all communist cultural activities in the Jewish community, began to publish a Yiddish-language paper, *Der Kampf* (now the *Vochenblatt*) and later began to run political candidates.

The percentage of the total Jewish population which affiliated with the communist movement was not large, but the Labor League proved an embarrassment to the community. To the orthodox, they were merely the lunatic fringe whose spiteful antics on Yom Kippur could be ignored, especially since most Labor League sympathizers were opposed to them as well. To the socialists, however, the communists were a real encumbrance. Despite the fact that the Labor League was not a branch of the Communist Party, nor were all its members communist, communism was its principal ideological aspect and the Workmen's Circle saw it as a threat to socialism. There were even incidents of violence between the two groups, especially when Morris Spector, leader of the Jewish communists, attempted to speak at socialist gatherings. As the tendency increased for newspapers to identify Jews with communism, socialist Jews strove to divorce themselves as completely as possible from the stigma.

Nevertheless, much of this division was minor compared to the internal discord in other centres, and there was indeed the beginning of real friendship and co-operation in Toronto.[19] For the most part, however, in the 1920s this co-operation appeared on an individual rather than on a communal scale. Toronto Jewry seemed incapable of united action. This was most evident in the Federation of Jewish Philanthropies. If the organization did unite its active workers, from old community and new, it could not generate support among the Jewish public and was soon in financial difficulty. The occasional successful campaign during the decade failed to offset the contrast between the state of organized Jewish charity in other cities and that in Toronto. Whereas the existence of organized Jewish charity elsewhere was taken for granted and agencies there were generally well-endowed, Federation in Toronto was in constant difficulty. To a perceptive guest editor of the *Canadian Jewish Review*, the explanation was obvious. "This insecurity of our charity institutions," Archie Bennett wrote in 1926, "reflects the indefiniteness of our communal character." In the United States, he observed, reform was dominant and in Montreal, orthodoxy was most powerful. In each instance, communities were able to unite in support of communal ventures. In Toronto, reform was weak and orthodoxy experimenting in search of means of adapting to North American life. Consequently, Bennett believed, the Toronto community was still fluid, diverse and immature, unable to think in terms of communal action.[20]

As the decade progressed, however, new problems arose which required wider co-operation, notably the increasing evidence of domestic anti-semitism and the threat of a restrictive governmental immigration policy.

It has been observed earlier that prior to 1920, hostility to Jews in Toronto manifested itself principally in actions against individuals and that wholesale condemnation of Jews as an ethnic group tended to be rare or at least to remain latent. After the initial postwar exhilaration had passed, however, a wave of insecurity swept North America. The factors fostering fear of social, religious and economic change in the United States were operating no less in Canada and were expressed in a desire to preserve social values and the quality of life against European contamination. Immigrant paupers, radicals and, in general, those who resisted assimilation were seen as the greatest threat to the status quo.

Toronto Jews by the 1920s had grown used to social and occupational discrimination. They had come to expect restrictions when they attempted to move north of Bloor Street; they had accepted the fact that it would remain difficult for Jews to find employment in the public school system or for Jewish doctors and nurses to train at the major hospitals.[21] Some local papers continued to point out the Jewishness of persons involved in unpleasant incidents, whereas they ignored the religions of others in similar situations. Summer resorts and professional associations tacitly refused admission to Jews, and even members of Holy Blossom had resigned themselves to exclusion from Gentile golf courses and other social clubs.[22] But added to these slights in the 1920s, and increasingly alarming to the Jewish community, was a growing anti-semitism directed in blanket condemnation of the Jews as a group.

One might cite numerous incidents of continued good relations between Jew and Gentile, on the public level if not on the private. The period abounds in scenes of apparent cordiality such as a "Canada Night" held by the Toronto Lodge of B'nai B'rith at the King Edward Hotel, at which "Jews and Gentiles, Catholic priests and Protestant ministers..., orangemen and knights of Columbus, stood together...with bowed heads before the seven-branched menorah."[23] There were addresses by the rabbi of Holy Blossom to various non-Jewish organizations and ministers invited to speak at Bond Street, culminating in an exchange of pulpits between Rabbi Isserman and Reverend E. Crossley Hunter of Carlton Street United Church in 1928. There were glowing reports in the press about the positive attitude of Jewish schoolchildren toward education at all levels, of their good deportment and the willingness of their parents to co-operate with school authorities. Descriptions of Jewish holy days were published often, as were accounts of Jewish social events and the arrival of rabbis. The *Star*, especially, expressed sympathy to Jewish causes, deploring the plight of Jews in Poland, providing detailed coverage of Zionist conventions in Toronto and expressing support for Zionist fund-raising campaigns. The paper even supported Jewish aldermanic candidates in this period. Even the usually anti-semitic *Telegram* occasionally struck a sympathetic note. In 1925 the paper actually offered a contribution to the Federation of Jewish Philanthropies, as did a number of private non-Jewish individuals.

Nevertheless, there were disturbing signs, especially in newspaper comment stereotyping the Jew as a radical and otherwise as being a danger to Canadian society. Postwar economic difficulties, coupled with the "Red Scare," produced widespread paranoia and xenophobia in Toronto. Moreover, because Jews had been active in movements for social change in Europe and because Yiddish was so closely related to German, the language identified in the local press with Bolshevism, some Torontonians began to see all Jews as revolutionaries.

One of the first victims of this attitude was Ida Siegel's Mothers' Club at Hester How (Elizabeth Street) School. Complaints in 1919 about the use of Yiddish at meetings brought an order from the Board of Education that only English be employed. "The Jews came to Canada and should become English in every way as soon as they could," the chief inspector declared.[24] When Mrs. Siegel argued that she was solidly patriotic and that her object was not

319

to foster Yiddish but rather to use it to translate Red Cross circulars and instructions in health and education, the board remained adamant, its position hardened by a recent meeting in the Labor Temple at which Bolshevism was cheered and several socialists were arrested.

Throughout the next two years the press abounded with descriptions of Jews as radicals and undesirables. The *Telegram* singled them out as ringleaders in local labour disputes. *Saturday Night* suggested that all Jews were Bolsheviks and cited the leftist leanings of the editor of the *Hebrew Journal* as proof.[25]

The twenties were also rife with other unfavourable comment about Jews, branding them as dangerous aliens infiltrating cities and positions of influence in the country and refusing to assimilate. As early as 1921, the *Globe* had complained of a Jewish invasion of the public schools and in 1923 published an editorial enumerating the number of Jews prominent in American big business, attributing the fact to an inherent instinct for commerce.[26] Another editorial the same year attributed German anti-semitism to the fact that Jews refused to assimilate and that they were "admittedly the brains of the Communist movement in Germany as in Russia and elsewhere."[27] The *Telegram*, too, branded the Jew as disloyal. Prompted by Rabbi Brickner's attendance at an anti-war rally, the paper charged that "Toronto Hebrews have allowed the local leadership of their people to be largely monopolized by a gang of Europe first and Canada last and British anti-conscription politicians.... Their only idea of leadership is to Europeanize the Hebrew people of Toronto, to lure British subjects and their children away from Britain and towards Europe."[28]

Hostility became explicit also over the issue of religion in the public schools. When Sam Factor, as a Board of Education trustee, objected to the suggestion in 1924 that Christian instruction be introduced and complained that Jewish children were already being compelled to participate in the singing of Christian hymns, he received a stinging reply from a non-Jewish member. "Are we a Christian nation or a Jewish nation? As long as we remain a Christian nation we are not to be dominated by the Jewish people."[29] An objection by Rabbi Isserman two years later, over the assignment of New Testament passages as memory work and the fact that Jewish children who did not wish to participate in religious instruction were required to leave the room, elicited a less than satisfactory response. Isserman had complained that the situation "draws a line of distinction between Jewish children and the Christians, ...[whereas] they should all be regarded as

320

Canadian boys and girls." Trustee Wanless replied that since Canada "is a Christian country" the Jews "must recognize that they cannot dominate our educational system." The Jews, he said, "are not and cannot be citizens of any country except their own – and that is Palestine."[30]

In 1926 the official Anglican Good Friday message warned of the menace of the Jew as an unbeliever, taking over sections of cities, attending university and exerting influence in "the press, high finance, drama and politics" and demanding a voice in educational policy. The statement, shocking as it was at the time, merely reflected the fear during the previous two years of a supposedly insidious influx of Jews into Toronto. The *Globe* had long been commenting upon the growth of slums in the centre of the city and, although the Jew was not singled out for criticism, there was certainly condemnation by implication. The *Telegram*, typically, was less subtle. "ANOTHER NEW SYNAGOGUE," the paper announced in 1922 after the opening of Beth Jacob. In 1900, it noted, there had been only two large synagogues; now there were twelve. "The rate of increase compared with that of the Hebrews, does not put the Gentiles in a winning place. The Jews are not creeping in. They are coming by leaps and bounds, establishing churches and schools, etc. all over the city." Despite Jewish objections, the viciousness of the *Telegram's* articles increased, perhaps reaching their nadir in September 1924.

An influx of Jews puts a worm next the kernel of every fair city where they get a hold. These people have no national tradition . . . . They engage in the wars of no country, but flit from one to another under passports changed with chameleon swiftness, following up the wind the smell of lucre. They are not the material out of which to shape a people holding a national spirit. They remain cosmopolitan, while war drains the blood of the solid citizens of a nation. Not on the frontiers among the pioneers of plough and axe are they found, but in the cities where their low standards of life cheapen all about them.

. . .Jews of all countries should be discriminated against as a race by a poll tax so high that friends in Montreal and Toronto and Winnipeg would have their resources strained to the utmost to lend their tribesmen through foreign post more than enough to bring a baker's dozen per annum. . . .[31]

These statements did elicit opposition, not only from the Jews but from the community at large as well. The *Star* called them a

"Gross Libel" and commented that "An attack like that should be repudiated by all decent people . . .. It does not represent Toronto opinion." Nonetheless, there were indications that all did not disagree with the *Telegram*. In 1923, for instance, there were applications to the municipal Building Assessment Committee requesting reductions of valuation on the grounds that an influx of Jews into certain neighbourhoods had depreciated property values. Of significance, perhaps, was the acceptance by the *Star*, a week after its objection to the *Telegram* article, of the following advertisement:

> Public notice! An erroneous impression as to the racial origin of this house has been scattered throughout the city, and the name of Glass Bros. is being associated with Jewish or Hebrew nationality. Without prejudice or intended offense, we beg to state that this house is strictly gentile, owned and managed by Canadians in Canadian interests.[32]

The disclaimer suggests that the stereotype of the Jew as alien was prevalent and that at this period there must have been considerable discrimination against Jewish businesses in Toronto.

The Jews responded to this type of anti-semitism with displeasure and, at one point in 1926, a group within the community sued one newspaper because of a scurrilous piece. However, instead of uniting as a community to oppose the practice, the usual reaction of Toronto Jews in the twenties was to be as inconspicuous as possible and to attempt to ingratiate themselves with their Gentile neighbours. Echoing the *Jewish Times* of decades before, the *Canadian Jewish Review* urged Jews to be on their best behaviour at summer resorts; at the Jewish Girls' Club, no dancing was permitted on Sunday in deference to the Christian Sabbath, while at Holy Blossom social functions, members were instructed that "there should be no hilarity on Sundays." Jews appearing before Magistrate Cohen for any misdemeanor were given severe penalties, since Cohen felt that an unfavourable image projected by one Jew reflected upon all. Indeed, on occasion, convictions of Jews for violations of the Lord's Day Act were overturned by non-Jewish judges in higher courts. The entire reaction to discrimination in the twenties reflects a lack of confidence and maturity on the part of the Jewish community, often in contrast to other immigrant groups. For instance, when the famous tenor Giusseppi Martinelli sang in Toronto in 1924, the local Italians claimed him as their own, flocking to his concerts and cheering unabashedly. When a Jewish virtuoso such as Jascha Heifetz arrived, on the contrary, he was billed as a Russian. Comparing Jews and Italians, the *Canadian Jewish Review* observed that "Jews though much stronger in numbers are afraid to be that natural. . . ." If the Jew was proud of his artist, he remained silent about it.

There were times in the twenties when local Jews did express confidence in the light of anti-semitism, but it was confidence in the basic integrity of the general community rather than in themselves. In 1925, for example, an organization styled the Ku Klux Klan was organized in Toronto to combat the "propaganda of the Roman Catholics and of the Jews." When one of its members declared that "The Jews are gradually taking possession of all the industries of the continent," and its publication repeatedly described Jews as a criminal element, the Jewish community did not act.[33] Rabbi Brickner was sure that the organization would be stopped by the non-Jewish community. "I have faith enough in the good sense of our Protestant neighbours in Toronto," he remarked, "to feel sure that the movement will meet with failure." Scheuer expressed similar pious sentiments. "There is no place for the K.K.K. in any country where the British flag waves," he observed.[34] He was correct, but the Jews played no role in defending themselves against the attack. The self-assurance evident in institutional development was largely absent when it came to dealing with the community at large.

NOTES

1 The architect was Benjamin Brown, the first Jew to practise architecture in Toronto. The Henry Street Synagogue, which accommodated eight hundred people, cost $156,000 and was opened by the celebrated Cantor Josef Rosenblatt from New York. Hundreds, unable to secure entry into the synagogue, crowded Henry and Cecil streets during the service. Even the *Telegram*, usually unsympathetic to the Jews, admitted that "seldom has such splendid chorus singing been heard in a Toronto church" (*Telegram*, Aug. 21, 1922).

2 Ida Siegel, personal interview, Nov. 4, 1971. For an account of early negotiation with the Toronto General Hospital, see Louis Gurofsky, letter to the editor of the *Jewish Times*, Feb. 25, 1910, p. 3.

3 Dorothy Dworkin, "Mount Sinai Hospital," in The New Mount Sinai Hospital, *Highlights*, XVI, no. 2 (March 1970), p. 12.

4 *Ibid.*, no. 1 (Oct. 1969), p. 13. Confidential interview.

5 Mount Sinai Hospital, Toronto, Ladies' Auxiliary, *Calendar & Dues Book 1933-34*; D. Dworkin, "Mount Sinai Hospital," in *Highlights*, Oct., 1970, p. 14.

6 Report of the Executive Director of Federation, reprinted in *Canadian Jewish Review*, Apr. 10, 1925, p. 20; D. Dworkin, in *Highlights*, Oct., 1970, p. 14; March, 1970, p. 12.

7 Hart, *op.cit.*, p. 182; Dr. Alexander Brown, interview, March 30, 1973 (Jewish Oral History Project).

8 Dr. L. Jacober, interview, March 30, 1973 (Jewish Oral History Project); Alexander Brown, "Half a Century of Jewish Educational Achievements" (typescript, 6 pp. 1957, Associated Hebrew Schools Archives, Toronto.) For Rabbi Gordon's views on the necessity for and the role of the new Talmud Torah, see his articles in the *Hebrew Journal*, Dec. 30, 1919; June 18, 1923.

9 *Canadian Jewish Review*, Dec. 26, 1924, p. 40.

10 Goel Tzedec *Minutes*, Aug. 25, 1925. The Simcoe Street Talmud Torah remained open until 1928 when the building was sold and classes merged with Brunswick Avenue.

11 Church of England in Canada, *Journal of the Incorporated Synod of The Church of England in Canada in the Diocese of Toronto 1919* (Toronto: Parker, 1919), p. 213. [Hereafter referred to as *Anglican Synod Journal*, Toronto.] *Anglican Synod Journal*, Toronto, 1920, p. 224; 1922, p. 221; 1925, p. 201; 1926, p. 209. The opening of the new Jewish Girls' Club on St. George Street, as well as Jewish summer camps, also had the effect of minimizing missionary influence. From 1926 to 1936 there was a steady decline in Anglican missionary activity. In 1931, the Anglican report on proselytism observed that missions were a failure because of "family, national and business ties" among the Jews (*Anglican Synod Journal*, Toronto, 1931, p. 160). But most significant is a report of 1936:

> We report with regret a decrease in some of our children's activities. . . . We believe this is due to the increasing

number of clubs supplied by the Jewish authorities, very often at the same time, of the same character, and in the same neighbourhood as our own. Whether it is by intent or merely a coincidence, we do not know, but we have every reason to believe that efforts are made to supply almost identical groups for the Jews under Jewish leadership as we offer in our programme (*Anglican Synod Journal, Toronto, 1936*, p. 148).

For the intention of the Jewish community to do precisely that, see *Canadian Jewish Review*, Sept. 22, 1922, p. 10. By 1937, Anglican missionary efforts were admitted to have failed (*Anglican Synod Journal*, Toronto, 1937, p. 133).

12 Christian Synagogue, Toronto, "Statistical Report for 1919" (typescript, United Church Archives). Rev. S.B. Rohold, "Brief Statement for the Committee," Oct. 2, 1919 (typescript, *loc. cit.*).

Social pressure was important in keeping Jews out of the mission. "It is very hard when they come to the mission and go back to their own Jewish friends and have everything knocked out of their heads . . ." (*ibid.*). Converted Jews were dismissed by Jewish firms and expelled from Jewish boarding houses and Jewish philanthropic organizations refused relief to those who frequented the mission. See also Rev. S.B. Rohold to Rev. J. McP. Scott, Nov. 13, 1919, and Grace Bredehoft to Rev. J.M. Scott, 1919 (United Church Archives) for accounts of Jewish activities drawing prospective converts away from the missions.

13 Mrs. Annie Zeidman, interview, April 25, 1973 (Jewish Oral History Project); F.C. Stephenson and Sarah Vance, *That They May Be One* (Toronto: Board of Home Missions, United Church of Canada, 1929); Edmund H. Oliver, *His Dominion of Canada* (Toronto: Board of Home Missions and The Women's Missionary Society of the United Church of Canada, 1932). The author is grateful to Rev. Glenn Lucas, Archivist of the United Church, for clarifying a number of perplexing issues related to the missions.

14 The Primrose Club had originated in 1907 as an elite Jewish men's society called the Cosmopolitan Club, its membership consisting almost exclusively of the old community. However, as more East Europeans acquired wealth and status, they were accepted to membership. Indeed, the affluent in the new community sought status in the Cosmopolitan as they sought

it at Holy Blossom, this being true especially of young professionals. Activities at the Cosmopolitan were exclusively social and offered an opportunity for real fraternity to develop between the two elements.

In 1921, the organization vacated its Beverley Street meeting house and occupied a luxurious building on Willcocks Street, complete with ballroom and oak-panelled billiard room. The building is now the Faculty Club at the University of Toronto.

15 During the High Holy Days of 1924, Brickner spoke both at Goel Tzedec and at the McCaul Street Synagogue (*Canadian Jewish Review*, Oct. 10, 1924, p. 10).

16 Editorial, *Canadian Jewish Review*, June 5, 1925, p. 1.

17 Julius Seltzer, personal interview, Feb. 15, 1972; *Globe*, Apr. 18, 28, May 2, 4, 1922.

18 It appears that the instructors here were non-Jews; despite the "Red Scare," communism had by this time become fashionable among a number of non-Jewish intellectuals, especially Rev. A.E. Smith, a Methodist minister and president of the Ontario Labour Party. Indeed, the communist movement in Toronto was predominantly Gentile. Morris Spector, the leader of the Jewish communists of the period, was seldom identified with the Jews and even the usually anti-semitic *Telegram* seldom equated Jews with communism (see e.g. *Telegram*, Apr. 29, 1922).

19 For instance, in 1925 Rabbi Isserman joined Rabbi Gordon in installing Rabbi Schwartz at Goel Tzedec, and in the same year he officiated with rabbis Gordon and Berger at the opening of the Palmerston Avenue Synagogue (*Canadian Jewish Review*, Nov. 27, 1925, p. 21; Dec. 18, 1925, p. 16). For good relations between Goel Tzedec and Holy Blossom, see Goel Tzedec *Minutes*, Nov. 29, 1927.

20 *Canadian Jewish Review*, Oct. 22, 1926, pp. 1, 19.

21 Dr. Anna Gelber, personal interview, July 29, 1973. Some non-Jewish employers refused outright to hire Jews (*Canadian Jewish Review*, Aug. 3, 1923, p. 6; see also Willinsky, *A Doctor's Memoirs*, p. 23).

The issue of restrictive covenants came to a head in the Supreme Court of Ontario in 1945. A report of the proceedings indicates their commonplace existence. See Edwin C. Guillet, *Racial Discrimination* (Famous Canadian Trials, Vol. 33, 1945, typescript, Metropolitan Toronto Central Library); see also *Canadian Jewish Review*, Aug. 24, 1923, p. 7.

22 Gilbert E. Jackson, "Anti-Semitism," speech to the Empire Club of Canada, Toronto, Dec. 9, 1939, in The Empire Club of Canada, *Addresses Delivered to Members during the Year 1939-40* (Toronto: Hunter-Rose, 1940), pp. 190-91; B.G. Kayfetz, "Only Yesterday: From Discrimination to Acceptance," *The Chronicle Review*, Sept. 1972, pp. 25-34; Nathan Strauss, interview, March 8, 1973 (Jewish Oral History Project). Strauss notes that Jews were excluded from a lawyers' club founded about 1923-24.

The founding of the Oakdale Golf Club in 1925 was indicative of this trend. It was established principally by members of Holy Blossom, with some from Goel Tzedec as well, in direct response to the rejection of Jews by Gentile clubs. Tongue in cheek, the editor of the *Review* remarked that Jewish golf clubs actually strengthened Judaism by reminding members of their unacceptability in Gentile society (*Canadian Jewish Review*, Oct. 16, 1925, p. 10).

23 *Star*, Nov. 18, 1924.

24 *Star*, Jan. 15, 1919.

25 E.g., "Koldofsky and Company orders who are to work in the City," *Telegram*, May 30, 1919.

26 See *Canadian Jewish Review*, Oct. 12, 1923, p. 7; Aug. 31, 1923, p. 6. In a survey taken by the *Globe* of Jewish students in Toronto schools, it was reported that some principals were reluctant to release exact figures because "non-Jewish parents would resent the presence of a large number of Jewish pupils in the schools" (*Globe*, March 21, 1922).

27 *Globe*, Nov. 8, 1923. For Rabbi Brickner's rebuttal, see *Canadian Jewish Review*, Nov. 16, 1923, p. 6. He pointed out the paradox of Jews being accused simultaneously of particularism and internationalism.

28 *Telegram*, July 24, 1923. Brickner replied in the *Canadian Jewish Review* (Aug. 10, 1923, p. 6) that every "peanut politician" was not a Jewish leader, that Jews were pro-British,

and he noted that local synagogues had contributed hand-somely toward relief of victims of a fire at Haileybury in Northern Ontario.

29 Quoted in *Star*, Nov. 13, 1924.

30 Isserman, quoted in *Star*, Feb. 25, 1926. Wanless, quoted in *Star*, Feb. 26, 1926.

31 *Telegram*, Sept. 22, 1924.

32 *Star*, Oct. 3, 1924.

33 Klan member, quoted in *Star*, Feb. 19, 1925.

34 Brickner and Scheuer, quoted in *Star*, Feb. 20, 1925.

CHAPTER 19

UNITY AT LAST?

Several problems, among the many that confronted Toronto Jewry in the twenties and thirties, combined with particular force to impose increased solidarity upon the local Jewish population. The prospect of immigrant restriction, the emergence of Naziism in Germany and incidents of violence against Jews at home, and finally the Depression generated a degree of maturity in the Toronto Jewish community which, if left to its natural development, might have taken additional decades to accomplish.

The movement for immigration restriction had emerged in the immediate postwar period as a reaction to economic difficulties and the fear of European radicalism. Its advocates were most vocal in the United States, but restrictionist sentiment had begun to filter northward, heightened by the prospect of the United States closing its doors and of Canada being inundated with European refugees. By 1919 even the *Toronto Daily Star*, usually sympathetic to the immigrant, was urging the government to adopt a more cautious immigration policy.[1]

During the early 1920s Jews constituted a major proportion of those seeking asylum in North America.[2] In Toronto, as elsewhere, they suddenly appeared conspicuously everywhere, aggravating local fears of unemployment, overcrowding, social unrest and Jewish influence. In 1922, for instance, the *Globe* issued a strong protest against Jewish immigration. "It is said that there are not enough ships to carry all the Jews of Roumania, Poland, Lithuania, Russia, and elsewhere, who would come if they could be sure of admittance," the paper declared, noting that these would surely flock to the cities where they would aggravate urban problems. Moreover, the *Globe* maintained, "no matter how poor the Jewish immigrant, he seems to have a friend at court with influence and money." Mrs. A.E. Gooderham of Toronto, president of the Protestant Federation of Patriotic Women of Canada, deplored the projected immigration of six thousand Jews in 1924 and advised the encouragement of immigrants from Britain and from Northern Europe. Similar sentiments were expressed against other immigrant groups from Southern and Eastern Europe as well, but the Jews were most frequently singled out for criticism, especially because of their association in the public mind with radicalism. In 1926, for example, when the Ontario section of the Canadian Labour Party held its annual convention at London, Ontario, *Saturday Night* was quick to point out that a Yiddish version of the "Red Flag" had been extremely popular with a majority of the delegates, most of whom, it was observed, had come from Toronto. "When this country puts up its bars against further immigration from certain parts of Europe . . ., we will know where to start."[3]

Local Jews were in a quandary. As wage earners they sympathized with the demands of non-Jewish labour organizations for restriction to minimize the threat of unemployment. On the other hand, most of those seeking entry were their co-religionists and *landsleit*, even their own relatives. Consequently Toronto Jewry, old community and new, was unanimous in opposition to restriction and constantly petitioned the federal government to that effect, at times charging the Department of Immigration with anti-semitic policies.[4]

There had been informal efforts to assist immigrants in Toronto since the late nineteenth century. Only following the First World War, however, were immigrant assistance efforts formalized, beginning in 1920 with the Toronto Branch of the Jewish Immigrant Aid Society, the only actively functioning offspring of the first Canadian Jewish Congress. But the group was poorly organized, and collapsed for lack of funds. It was reorganized in 1922 by Rabbi Siegel as a co-operative effort of Federation, B'nai B'rith and the Council of Jewish Women. The following year the local JIAS was completely absorbed by Federation.

The new organization engaged in the practical work of finding accommodation and employment, loans and help in transporting relatives for new immigrants. But it also had a beneficial effect upon Toronto Jewry in providing another forum in which Jewish leaders could develop a sense of communal solidarity. Although much of the actual immigration procedure was handled in Montreal, local branches of JIAS were important in mobilizing anti-restriction opinion, initiating *habeas corpus* proceedings to prevent deportations and attempting to influence local politicians to speak favourably for Jews.[5] More importantly, it kept alive, through national conferences and petitions, the idea of co-operation of Jews across Canada, a concept which had been temporarily fruitful in the Canadian Jewish Congress of 1919 and which required organized communities on the local level.

Hitler's rise to power added urgency to the efforts to assure entry to European Jews and prompted North American Jewry to organize in protest against the growing number of anti-Jewish acts by the Nazis. In Toronto, these events served to fuse together the disparate elements in the community, orthodox, reform, secularist, Zionist, workers and employers, as a Toronto Jewish Conference was organized to promote co-operative effort. The Conference elected a committee in the spring of 1933 to propose methods of dealing with the situation and, by the end of April, a protest organization called the League for the Defense of Jewish Rights had been formed under the leadership of Rabbi Samuel Sachs of Goel Tzedec and Shmuel Meir Shapiro, editor of the *Hebrew Journal*. The League immediately joined similar organizations in Montreal and Winnipeg in advocating a revival of the Canadian Jewish Congress.[6]

In June, the League for the Defense of Jewish Rights (Toronto), the Western Jewish Congress Committee (Winnipeg) and the Pro-Congress Committee of Montreal sponsored a conference in Toronto to protest Nazi atrocities. By the end of the meeting, a plan had been formulated to re-establish the Canadian Jewish Congress. According to its platform, Congress was to protect the social and economic rights of Jews in the light of European events, relieve Jews forced to leave Germany and petition Canadian governments to refuse incorporation to Nazi groups. It also proposed to combat anti-Jewish prejudice by educating the Canadian public, "as well as by recourse to legal methods."[7]

Although, like its predecessor, the revived Congress met initially in Montreal and would have its headquarters there, there was considerable activity in Toronto as well, as the city became the rallying point for the Central Division. Maurice Goldstick, socialist, Labour Zionist and admitted agnostic, assumed the chairmanship of the committee to reorganize the Central Division, while Rabbi Eisendrath led Holy Blossom into the movement and orthodox congregations of all varieties elected delegates. Only the Jewish communists were excluded, not because they declined to join, but rather because the organizers of Congress believed that their internationalism made them untrustworthy and it was felt that their presence would tarnish the image of the organization, whose success was largely dependent upon public approval.[8]

The Central Division office was opened in Toronto in 1934 under the directorship of Archie Bennett, former editor of the *Jewish Times*, publicist for the Federation of Jewish Philanthropies, long-time advocate of communal organization and a

331

driving force behind the revival movement. It is evident, however, that the initial unity which gave birth to Congress would probably have dissipated quickly in Toronto, as it had a decade earlier, but for the disturbing local events of the preceding year. A spate of overtly anti-semitic incidents erupted in Toronto during 1933. In January, for instance, a local insurance company cancelled most of the policies of Jewish holders and was persuaded to reinstate them only after E.F. Singer had forced action by the Ontario legislature. Discrimination in employment continued. Jews were denied leases to apartments in the better residential areas and were excluded from numerous hotels and resorts in the district surrounding the city. A "Gentiles Only" sign appeared on the dance hall at Lambton Park. "The fire [of anti-semitism] is dormant in Canada," Singer observed in April, "it has not blazed up, but the spark is there."[9]

In August, however, the pyrotechnics began. The scene of the first disturbances was Balmy Beach, at the eastern end of the city. Convenient both to the Ward and to Spadina Avenue via the Queen Street streetcar line, the eastern public beaches had become, in the postwar period, a popular location for one-day outings and picnics for families from the central part of the city. Jews, especially, favoured the Beaches, much to the distress of the local Anglo-Saxon residents and the exclusive canoe club which occupied part of the waterfront. These deplored the presence of boisterous immigrants, non-Jews as well as Jews. Throughout the 1920s, however, complaints from the Beaches concentrated primarily on Jews, the most easily identified of the unwelcome groups. They were accused of demoralizing the beaches by nursing babies openly and by changing into bathing attire in automobiles.

Balmy Beach was also a favourite haunt for unemployed youths, who loitered on the boardwalk and harassed passers-by. By 1933 there were several "clubs" meeting in the area, some composed of this element, some of more respectable local residents and some consisting of a mixture of the two. The Balmy Beach Swastika Club, formed in 1933 ostensibly to keep the beach free of "obnoxious visitors," fell into this last category. Some members were sincerely attempting to preserve the character of the area, but others were merely seeking the pretext to give vent to their anti-semitism.

In July there had been a few clashes between Jews and non-Jews on the beach, but all had been minor. The Jews were disturbed, however, at the prominent display of the swastika, the harassment of Jewish women on the neighbouring streets and the fact that youths would drive by the homes of Jewish residents and fling garbage on the porches while shouting Nazi slogans. The police apparently refused to take the matter seriously, especially in light of statements by the Swastika Club denying anti-semitic motives, but the Jews were horrified.

Matters came to a head early in August, when the club organized a dance at their meeting house on the beach and erected swastika signs on the building. At this juncture, about fifty Jewish youths took matters into their own hands and marched on the clubhouse, where they were met by club members armed with broom handles and lacrosse sticks. Fortunately, the club had gotten wind of the raid and had hastily removed the signs. The police also suspected trouble and arrived in full force. Consequently no violence ensued, but the club members cancelled their dance and marched off down the boardwalk, taunting the Jews to the tune of "Home on the Range":

Oh give me a home where the Gentiles may roam,
Where the Jews are not rampant all day,
Where seldom is heard a loud Yiddish word
And the Gentiles are free all the day.[10]

The initial public response was sympathetic to the Jews. Although Mayor Stewart announced that he would not tolerate any group's taking the law into their own hands, he condemned the Swastika Club's activities as "un-British and un-Canadian." A number of Christian clergymen and politicians also spoke against the use of the swastika. The *Jewish Standard*, echoed by Rabbi Sachs, charged that this was not merely a Jewish matter, but that the attitude exhibited by the Balmy Beach Club was a threat to all Canadians. The mayor did prohibit the wearing of the swastika emblem on the beach after the club had refused to disband at his request, but characteristically, the *Telegram* continued to maintain that the group had a right to demonstrate, so long as they remained within the law, while the *Star* advocated ignoring the club rather than taking action against them.

The League for the Defense of Jewish Rights, now recognized by Jews as the spokesman for the community, refused to issue a call for the cancellation of Jewish picnics, although the Jewish newspapers did caution their readers to avoid incidents on the beaches. Consequently, outings continued and the following weekend Jews were attacked at Kew Beach, adjacent to Balmy Beach, by a group wearing the swastika. A near riot followed, but the police were able to force the attackers to retreat.

Despite the incident, the consensus in Toronto appears to have been expressed by the *Star*, which maintained that the movement was merely one of raucous youths and that the police would deal with it. The paper insisted that there was actually no large-scale anti-semitic movement in Toronto; only time was needed for common sense to reassert itself. The Jews were therefore advised to take no action.[11] Within the Jewish community, too, there was confidence that things would improve with time. While the *Jewish Standard* carried articles throughout August describing Nazi efforts to stir up anti-semitism in Canada, the leaders of the community maintained that Canadian justice and British tradition would be sufficient to put an end to the movement. One Jewish shopkeeper interviewed by the *Star* believed that "people here are too broadminded" to let Naziism spread in Canada.[12] Mayor Stewart called a meeting of conciliation between the Swastika Club and the League for the Defense of Jewish Rights, promising to end abuses on both sides.

A week later, however, the battle was raging again. At Christie Pits a group in the audience watching a baseball game between Jewish and non-Jewish teams suddenly displayed a swastika sign with the exclamation "Hail Hitler" and, after the game, proceeded to paint the symbol on one of the park buildings. They openly admitted their intention to exclude Jews from the park. A similar incident occurred at a game at Christie Pits a few days later amidst a crowd of about ten thousand, but this time, Jewish players and onlookers were actually assaulted. A gang of Gentile youths known as the "Pit Gang" descended on the park with baseball bats and lead pipes. Following the incidents at Balmy Beach, groups of Jewish youths, schoolboys and young factory workers had begun to organize self-defence clubs. When news of the attack at Christie Pits reached the Jewish neighbourhood, scores of Jewish toughs hastily assembled at the YMHA on Brunswick Avenue and were transported to the park in trucks. The fighting, which continued for six hours, spread to the surrounding streets. Jewish shops along Bloor Street were vandalized, while members of the "Pit Gang" roamed the area looking for Jews, whom they accosted and sometimes attacked. One resident stated that his Jewish neighbours were afraid to walk several blocks to shop. Police were stationed at the entrances to the park, warning Jews not to enter.

In typical fashion, the *Telegram* blamed the Jews for the incident and suggested that the League for the Defense of Jewish Rights had had a difficult time stopping Jewish militants from importing gangsters from the United States to defend the community, a fact denied by the police. The *Star* took a more realistic approach, but continued to see the movement as isolated and easily controlled by the authorities. The paper, therefore, urged Jews not to resort to violence.

The Jewish community, for the most part, agreed with the *Star*, but did not share its confidence. The defence groups which had been organized earlier in the summer now united; few agreed with the magistrate when he dismissed charges against those involved in the Christie Pits incident on the grounds that the provocation of the Jews was intended as a joke. Violent incidents tended to peter out, especially after the swastika gangs discredited themselves by harassing non-Jews at Riverdale Park in search of "Reds." However, a national swastika association "to defend Gentile Rights" was formed and soon spawned the Union Party, a group sympathetic to Hitler. The result was a consolidation of the Jewish community behind the League for the Defense of Jewish Rights and its successor, Canadian Jewish Congress, a trend strengthened further by discrimination against Jews in the Toronto Island parks and on the beaches in the western part of the city, by vandalism at the Jewish cemetery on Roselawn Avenue, and by threats to the life of Rabbi Sachs who, as head of the local B'nai B'rith Anti-Defamation League, had been planting agents in the Union Party to monitor their activities.* Each of these incidents served to keep alive enthusiasm for Canadian Jewish Congress until its existence came to be taken for granted.

II

While anti-semitism was uniting the community politically, economic factors were forcing consolidation of philanthropic and fund-raising activities. The Federation of Jewish Philanthropies had never evoked an enthusiastic response from the Jewish public, despite the appearance of great vitality on the part of its leadership. By 1932 Scheuer, still honorary president, was complaining of the laxity in support despite the fact that many local Jews still had money for recreation. Once the Depression came to be felt in full during 1933 and 1934, Federation found itself in even greater difficulty. The campaign that year fell $30,000 short of the amount estimated necessary for operation. So hard had the majority of Toronto Jews been hit by the Depression that in 1933, the average per capita contribution to the organization was only 92 cents. Federation warned that it would have to curtail or discontinue some of its activities. A reduction of services would be a serious difficulty for Jews, who were often worse off than other groups. Immigration restriction, which had

*The relationship between this group and the Unity Party which existed at that time is unclear.

335

now been introduced, divided families, reduced their earning power and made the sending of funds overseas a necessity.

In 1932, Federation had attempted to rationalize the use of funds by merging the Co-operative Board of Jewish Charities with Federation's Social Service Committee to form the Jewish Family Welfare Bureau.[13] This was an improvement, since casework could now be dealt with by a single agency, operating autonomously of the Federation fund-raising machine itself. However, its burden was enormous and was lessened very little by the establishment of the municipal Department of Public Welfare in 1935. Although the latter provided food and fuel, many Jewish immigrants were ineligible for public relief because they failed to satisfy the necessary residence requirements and because, initially, public assistance was offered only to couples. Divided families, therefore, were at a disadvantage. In addition, many who did qualify refused to avail themselves of the opportunity because they considered the acceptance of public charity a disgrace. Only intensive efforts by Rabbi Sachs and others to persuade local Jews that public aid was a right of citizenship, with no stigma attached, eventually relieved some of the pressure on the Jewish agencies.[14] Nevertheless, Federation was far from able to cope with community problems.

In 1935 there was an effort to make the use of Federation funds still more efficient by combining another group of agencies. The Jewish Family Welfare Bureau, the Jewish Children's Bureau which had developed out of the Orphanage, the Jewish Big Brother and Big Sister organizations and the Jewish Employment Bureau, all formerly autonomous, merged to create the Jewish Family Welfare Bureau, now the Jewish Family and Child Service, the result of an amalgamation with the Jewish Child Welfare Bureau in 1940. Once again by treating the family as a unit, this agency succeeded in eliminating much expenditure through overlapping and confusion of function.

Federation began to see some light on the horizon as the efforts of these consolidations came to be felt. Moreover, the fund-raising campaign for 1935 was surprisingly successful. Although it collected much less than the $90,000 projected, the Jewish community did appear to rally to its support. Three hundred women volunteered as canvassers and the result was at least enough to keep the agencies dependent upon Federation in operation.

If the survival of Federation in 1935 was due to Jewish efforts, it was also in large measure the result of widespread support from the general community. The local papers, especially the *Star*, were quick to perceive the plight of the local Jews, a factor rightly attributed to the nature of their community.

> There are, in Toronto, some 48,000 Jews. Among these there is said to be only one man of exceptional wealth; and fewer than might be thought of really substantial means. In most American cities it is otherwise; the Jewish organizations have many rich individuals and corporations on whom they can depend. In Toronto the Jewish population is largely made up of people of the working class, together with light manufacturers and small shop-keepers, most of them hard hit by the depression.[15]

Both the *Star* and the *Mail and Empire* urged Christians to contribute to the Federation campaign and noted substantial pledges from a number of local department stores, banks and manufacturers.

Nevertheless, it was obvious that the funds collected in 1935 served only a stop-gap function. If Federation's beneficiary agencies were enabled to continue, at least temporarily, the campaign did nothing for Jewish educational and welfare institutions which did not fall under the aegis of the organization. Mount Sinai Hospital, for example, despite its new addition or perhaps because of it, was rapidly approaching bankruptcy. As for the Toronto Hebrew Free School, the crisis was already at hand.

The Brunswick Avenue Talmud Torah had never been entirely free of financial difficulty, but its tribulations were magnified by the Depression. With over four hundred pupils by 1932, it was reported to be in a "difficult and unfortunate state." Various congregations had offered contributions, while the Kehillah continued its attempt to use profits from the supervision of kosher meat to support the institution. Despite these efforts, the Talmud Torah's deficit increased; by 1935 it had reached the point of being unable to pay the salaries of its teachers. Although these continued their instruction without pay for twelve weeks, the school finally had to admit bankruptcy and close its doors.

The collapse of the Talmud Torah alarmed even those who had previously been indifferent; during the nine agonizing weeks the school remained closed, the Jewish community bordered upon panic. Numerous suggestions were offered to effect a reopening, but none of the existing communal organizations was able to produce any satisfactory plan. The initiative came from a group of younger men, mostly from orthodox families but a number also from Holy Blossom, who were already raising money for the school. These undertook to reorganize the institution and place it on a solid financial footing. Manufacturers, merchants and salesmen, this group, which included Samuel Kronick, I. Brodey, Samuel Godfrey, Mark G. Cohen and Bernard Vise, had considerable business experience and was prepared to unite with the older generation to save the Talmud Torah.

The association decided upon a division of labour to accomplish their objectives, separating into "Group A" and "Group B." The former was charged with the responsibility of financing the capital debt of the school, whereas "Group B," enlarged by Bernard Vise, was to be responsible for obtaining operating expenses.

The "Group B" plan for generating public enthusiasm and rationalizing the use of funds was an expansion of the Jewish centre idea of the previous decade, using the Brunswick Avenue building as a base. The new Jewish Centre of Educational and Communal Activities would include the Toronto Hebrew Free School and a variety of communal recreation and educational organizations.[16] Each group would operate autonomously, with the Jewish Centre board being composed of representatives from each constituent organization. Since the concept had been encouraged by the success of similar ventures in the United States, especially that of Rabbi Mordecai Kaplan in New York, the latter was invited to address an early planning meeting.

During 1935-36, the Jewish Centre expanded under the capable direction of Bernie Vise. In fact, it included the Jewish Boys' Club and Council House as well, attracting over fifty clubs throughout the city. Education for adults, as well as for children, was emphasized, as was the necessity for unity in the light of growing anti-semitism.

The Centre attempted to raise funds through independent collection and benefit performances, which fended off foreclosure of the mortgage and permitted the school to reopen, but did not promise to provide sufficient funds for long-term operation in light of public indifference to solicitation by a multitude of organizations. The difficulties encountered by Federation, however, had prompted a similar reorganization of that institution by a number of individuals, some of whom were active in "Group B." Following developments in the United States, they took up the idea of a united welfare campaign to provide funds and a planning organization for all Jewish activities in the city. Whereas Federation had done this only for charitable institutions, the new scheme would include the Jewish Centre, Mount Sinai

Hospital and others as well. An expert was invited from New York to plan the initial structure and, by the spring of 1937, the United Jewish Welfare Fund of Toronto had been established, incorporating the Federation of Jewish Philanthropies, the Jewish Centre and Talmud Torah, the United Palestine Fund, the Joint Distribution Committee, the overseas relief organizations (Geverkshaften), the Old Folks' Home, Mizrachi, ORT, the Hebrew Free Loan Society and the local office of Canadian Jewish Congress.

The first campaign was to be an experiment to determine whether the new approach would increase efficiency and elicit larger contributions. By 1938, its success was so evident that plans were already under way to make the organization permanent. It was also decided that a major fault of Federation had been its failure to exercise control over its beneficiary organizations. By insisting on at least limited control, the initiation of which was possible only because many of the constituent organizations were desperate for funds, the United Jewish Welfare Fund was able to prepare workable budgets. The Welfare Fund therefore served as a unifying force for most local institutions, creating the machinery for unity which would enable the Jewish community of Toronto to deal with problems of common concern and to absorb large numbers of European immigrants following 1945.[17]

If the United Jewish Welfare Fund succeeded in creating relative institutional unity in Toronto, Canadian Jewish Congress enabled effective defensive action to be taken both on the national and the local level. For example, it attempted to keep immigration open in 1934 by guaranteeing responsibility for as many German-Jewish refugees as the government would admit. On the local scene, it organized a boycott of German goods. It also attempted to maintain a good public image for the Jew by reviving an arbitration court which kept Jews out of the public eye and by opposing the election of Jewish communists who were seeking office. Congress also attempted to combat discrimination in recreational facilities and in employment.

Canadian Jewish Congress in this period, however, was far more successful in its national aspects than in its local ones. It served to bind Canadian Jewry together and could indeed act as its spokesman, but on the local scene and particularly in Toronto, it fell short. One of its purposes, according to its organizers, had been to create standardized *kehilloth* in local centres, capable of dealing with all communal problems, from *kashruth* and education to philanthropy and anti-semitism. Admittedly, some of the tasks were accomplished in Toronto. By 1937, Congress committees were discussing means of encouraging better attendance at Hebrew schools, curriculum controls and the establishment of a Jewish public library. But Congress did not even attempt to exercise control in the area of religious practice. The community was too diverse and such efforts in the previous decade had been an obvious failure. Moreover, neither Congress nor the Welfare Fund had succeeded in creating sustained psychological unity in the Jewish community to accompany its institutional consolidation. Both organizations had grown out of crises and it was still possible for public enthusiasm to wane as soon as these had passed. Despite their limitations, the two organizations had nevertheless unified Toronto Jewry as never before, establishing the institutional structure through which psychological unity could mature and find expression during the next four decades.

NOTES

1 *Star*, editorial, May 3, 1919.

2 See Louis Rosenberg, *Canada's Jews* (Montreal: Bureau of Social & Economic Research, Canadian Jewish Congress, 1939), esp. Table 92, p. 136.

3 *Globe*, Jan. 14, 1922; W.J. Egan to Mrs. A.E. Gooderham, March 6, 1924 (Department of Immigration Papers, Public Archives of Canada); *Saturday Night*, editorial, Apr. 10, 1926.

4 Perusal of confidential correspondence between senior officials of the Department of Immigration in the Public Archives indicates that the charge was not without foundation.

5 E.g., E.J. O'Connell to W.R. Little, Oct. 13, 1920 (Department of Immigration Papers).

6 One example of the co-operation which the crisis fostered between various Jewish groups was the anti-fascist conference organized by the Left Poalei Zion at this period. Jewish employers closed their shops so that workers could attend the demonstration at Queen's Park. It was estimated that 20,000 workers did so (Max Federman, interview, March 13, 1973, Jewish Oral History Project).

7 Congress platform, quoted in *Star*, June 12, 1933.

8 See e.g., Goel Tzedec *Minutes*, Feb. 1, 1934; Congregation Tifereth Israel Bikur Cholim Anshei Ostrovtze *Minutes*, Oct. 17, 1933; J.J. Glass, personal interview, Dec. 13, 1972.

9 Singer's address to Ontario Zionists, quoted in *Star*, Apr. 24, 1933.

10 Quoted in *Star*, Aug. 2, 1933.

11 *Star*, Aug. 10, 1933.

12 Quoted in *Star*, Aug. 9, 1933. See also Scheuer's statement expressing confidence in Canadian justice and opposing violent action by Jews, *Telegram*, Aug. 12, 1933.

13 The Social Service Committee had been formed in 1918 to deal with cases, such as wife desertion, transportation for medical treatment in the United States and loans to establish immigrants in business, which did not fall within the domain of any of Federation's constituent organizations (Federation, *2nd Annual Report*, p. 43).

14 Those directly involved believe that there was considerable discrimination against Jews in the distribution of public relief in the 1930s. Moreover, public officials did not understand that additional funds for food were required because of the higher cost of kosher provisions. Federation exerted efforts to combat the prejudice and educate the public officials. See Ben Sadowski, "History of Jewish Social Welfare Development in Toronto," *loc. cit.*

15 *Star*, Oct. 29, 1935; *Mail and Empire*, Oct. 29, 1935.

16 These would include the Institute of Jewish Studies, an adult education service; a library; a Jewish Little Theatre; an orchestra; Young Israel, a young people's congregation associated with the Talmud Torah; Young Judaea, a federation of Zionist youth clubs; and the YM and YWHA.

17 See Welfare Fund Files, Canadian Jewish Congress Archives, Montreal and "Welfare Fund Scrapbook," Canadian Jewish Congress Central Region Archives, Toronto, esp. its *Second Annual Report*, 1938; "The Development of the Social Services in the Toronto Jewish Community," p. 14; Sadowski, p. 6.

EPILOGUE:

A GLANCE FORWARD

The forty years following the establishment of the United Jewish Welfare Fund have moulded a Toronto Jewry far different from that of 1937. The community is now largely middle class, no longer concentrated in small shops and in the garment industry. Its communal institutions are now firmly established, mature not only in age, but also in their own perception of themselves.

Toronto Jews have come to grips with many of the problems which confronted them in 1937. Class and ethnic divisions are becoming blurred; communally controlled charity and discipline in planning and expenditure are coming to be taken for granted; common educational standards have begun to be implemented with the help of a Board of Jewish Education; the supervision of *kashruth* under communal auspices has become a model for other North American cities. But most significant are the strides that have been made toward that elusive psychological unity.

Most of these developments had their roots in the formative period described in this volume, but external events have provided a new dimension. The destruction of European Jewry during the Second World War and the establishment of the State of Israel in 1948 compelled Toronto Jews to minimize their internal differences in order to save survivors of the holocaust and provide support for the new state which alone could promise protection against a recurrence. With these events came the realization that integration into North American society did not, of itself, ensure physical and spiritual survival. The future of Toronto Jewry depended upon its ability to deal with its problems efficiently and as a total community.

In January 1976, the United Jewish Welfare Fund and the Toronto component of Canadian Jewish Congress amalgamated to form the Toronto Jewish Congress. The immediate reason for this merger was to enhance the community's administrative and financial efficiency. It is significant, however, that its proponents have continued to describe Toronto Jewish Congress as the successful culmination of a struggle for communal unity, a real

342

kehillah on the model of those originally envisaged by Canadian Jewish Congress.

There is no doubt that Toronto Jewish Congress is the product of the trend toward institutional consolidation evident even forty years ago. In all probability, it is the instrument through which unity of outlook will be generated as well.

REFERENCES

BOOKS AND PAMPHLETS

GENERAL EUROPEAN BACKGROUND

Baron, Salo W. *The Jewish Community: Its History and Structure to the American Revolution*. 3 vols. Philadelphia: The Jewish Publication Society of America, 1948.

Bermant, Chaim. *Troubled Eden: An Anatomy of British Jewry*. New York: Basic Books, 1970.

Elbogen, Ismar. *A Century of Jewish Life*. Translated by M. Hadas. Philadelphia: The Jewish Publication Society of America, 1966. (First published 1944.)

Graetz, Heinrich. *History of the Jews*. Edited by B. Löwy, 6 vols. Philadelphia: The Jewish Publication Society of America, 1956. (First published in English, 1891.)

Greenberg, Louis. *The Jews in Russia*. 2 vols. New Haven: Yale University Press, 1944.

Handlin, Oscar. *The Uprooted*. New York: Grosset & Dunlap, n.d. (First published in 1951 by Little, Brown & Co.)

Johnpoll, Bernard K. *The Politics of Futility: The General Jewish Workers Bund of Poland, 1917-1943*. Ithaca: Cornell University Press, 1967.

Niebuhr, H. Richard. *The Social Sources of Denominationalism*. Cleveland: Meridian Books, 1967. (First published in 1929: New York: Henry Holt & Co.)

Plaut, W. Gunther. *The Growth of Reform Judaism*. New York: World Union for Progressive Judaism, 1965.

Roth, Cecil. *The Jewish Contribution to Civilisation*. London: Macmillan, 1938.

Tobias, Henry J. *The Jewish Bund in Russia from its Origins to 1905*. Stanford: Stanford University Press, 1972.

Woodroofe, Kathleen. *From Charity to Social Work*. Toronto: University of Toronto Press, 1962.

Zborowski, Mark and Elizabeth Herzog. *Life is with People*. New York: Schocken, 1962. (First published 1952: New York, International Universities Press.)

GENERAL: UNITED STATES

Adler, Selig, and Thomas E. Connolly. *From Ararat to Suburbia: The History of the Jewish Community of Buffalo*. Philadelphia: The Jewish Publication Society of America, 1960.

Cahan, Abraham. *The Rise of David Levinsky*. New York: Harper & Row, 1960. (First published in 1917: New York, Harper & Brothers.)

Davis, Moshe. *The Emergence of Conservative Judaism*. Philadelphia: The Jewish Publication Society of America, 1965.

——and Isidore S. Meyer, eds. *The Writing of American Jewish History*. New York: American Jewish Historical Society, 1957.

Drachman, Bernard. *The Unfailing Light*. New York: Rabbinical Council of America, 1948.

Eisendrath, Maurice N. *Can Faith Survive: The Thoughts and Afterthoughts of an American Rabbi*. New York: McGraw-Hill, 1964.

Fuchs, Laurence H. *The Political Behavior of American Jews*. Glencoe, Ill.: Free Press, 1956.

Gartner, Lloyd P., ed. *Jewish Education in the United States*. New York: Teachers College Press, Columbia University, 1969.

Glaab, Charles N. and A. Theodore Brown. *A History of Urban America*. Toronto: Macmillan, 1967.

Glazer, Nathan. *American Judaism*. Chicago: University of Chicago Press, 1957.

Goldman, Alex J. *Giants of Faith*. New York: Citadel Press, 1964.

Gordon, Milton M. *Social Class in American Sociology*. Durham, N.C.: Duke University Press, 1958.

Goren, Arthur A. *New York Jews and the Quest for Community: The Kehillah Experiment 1908-1922*. New York: Columbia University Press, 1970.

Grinstein, Hyman B. *The Rise of the Jewish Community of New York 1654-1860*. Philadelphia: The Jewish Publication Society of America, 1947.

Hapgood, Hutchins. *The Spirit of the Ghetto*. New York: Funk & Wagnalls, 1902.

Hartmann, Edward George. *The Movement to Americanize the Immigrant*. New York: Columbia University Press, 1948.

Herberg, Will. *Protestant-Catholic-Jew*. Revised ed. Garden City, N.Y.: Anchor Books, 1960. (First published in 1955: Doubleday & Co.)

Jones, Maldwyn A. *American Immigration* (Chicago History of American Civilization). Chicago: University of Chicago Press, 1960.

Klaperman, Gilbert. *The Story of Yeshiva University*. New York: Macmillan, 1969.

Lurie, Harry L. *A Heritage Affirmed: The Jewish Federation Movement in America*. Philadelphia: The Jewish Publication Society of America, 1961.

Miller, James A. *The Detroit Yiddish Theatre, 1920 to 1937*. Detroit: Wayne State University Press, 1967.

National Council of Jewish Women. *Proceedings of the First Convention of the National Council of Jewish Women*. Philadelphia: The Jewish Publication Society of America, 1897.

Rischin, Moses. *The Promised City: New York's Jews, 1870-1914*. New York: Corinth Books, 1964. (First published 1962.)

Rothkoff, Aaron. *Bernard Revel*. Philadelphia: The Jewish Publication Society of America, 1972.

Sklare, Marshall. *Conservative Judaism: An American Religious Movement*. Augmented edition. New York: Schocken Books, 1972.

_____ed. *The Jews: Social Patterns of an American Group*. Glencoe, Ill.: Free Press, 1958.

Warner, W. Lloyd. *Social Class in America*. Chicago: Science Research Associates, 1949.

Watson, Frank Dekker. *The Charity Organization Movement in the United States*. New York: Macmillan, 1922.

Wirth, Louis. *The Ghetto*. Chicago: University of Chicago Press, 1964. (First published 1928: Chicago: University of Chicago Press.)

CANADA, GENERAL:

Belkin, Simon I. *Through Narrow Gates: A Review of Jewish Immigration, Colonization and Immigrant Aid Work in Canada, 1840-1940*. Montreal: Canadian Jewish Congress and the Jewish Colonization Association, 1966.

Cohen, Zvi, ed. *Canadian Jewry*. Toronto: Canadian Jewish Historical Publishing Company, 1933.

Figler, Bernard. *From Mandate to State, 1923-1948: The Story of the Zionist Order Habonim*. Montreal: privately printed, 1951.

_____and David Rome. *Hannaniah Meir Caiserman, A Biography, 1884-1950*. Montreal: Northern Printing Co., 1962.

Gordon, M.E. *Political and Legal Aspects of Jewish History in Canada*. Montreal: Canadian Jewish Congress, 1959.

Gottesman, Eli, comp. *Canadian Jewish Reference Book and Directory*. Montreal: Central Rabbinical Seminary of Canada, 1963.

Hart, Arthur D., comp. *The Jew in Canada*. Toronto and Montreal: Jewish Publications Limited, 1926.

Morgan, Henry James. *The Canadian Men and Women of the Times*. Toronto: William Briggs, 1898, 1912.

Rosenberg, Louis. *Canada's Jews: A Social and Economic Study of the Jews in Canada*. Montreal: Bureau of Social and Economic Research, Canadian Jewish Congress, 1939.

347

Sack, B.G. *History of the Jews in Canada*. Trans. R. Novek. Montreal: Harvest House, 1965. (Originally published in Yiddish *ca.* 1945.)

Selick, Abel, ed. *History of Bnai Brith in Eastern Canada*. Toronto: Bnai Brith, 1964.

Splane, R.B. *Social Welfare in Ontario 1791-1893*. Toronto: University of Toronto Press, 1965.

Vineberg, Ethel. *The History of the National Council of Jewish Women of Canada*. Montreal: National Council of Jewish Women, 1967.

Y.L. Peretz School. *Jubilee Souvenir*. Winnipeg: privately published, 1929. (Yiddish.)

TORONTO: PRIMARY

An Account of a Historic Exchange of Pulpits between Rabbi and Minister. Toronto, 1928. (Archives of the Presbyterian Church in Canada, Knox College, Toronto.)

Bureau of Municipal Research. *What is "The Ward" going to Do with Toronto?* Toronto: Bureau of Municipal Research, 1918.

————. *Toronto at a Glance*. Toronto: Bureau of Municipal Research, 1929.

The City of Toronto Poll Book. Toronto: Lesslie Brothers, 1841.

Clark, C.S. *Of Toronto the Good*. Montreal: Toronto Publishing Co., 1898.

Denison, Col. George T. *Recollections of a Police Magistrate*. Toronto: Musson, 1920.

Gunn, William T. *His Dominion*. 2nd ed. Toronto: The Canadian Council of the Missionary Education Movement, 1918.

Hebrew Men of England Congregation. *Souvenir Program of the Twenty-fifth Anniversary*. Toronto: Record Press, 1934.

History of Toronto and County of York. 2 vols. Toronto: C. Blackett Robinson, 1885.

The Jewish Centre of Educational and Communal Activities. Toronto: privately printed, 1938.

Jewish Old Folks' Home, Toronto. *17th Annual Directory 1934-35*. Toronto: privately printed, 1934.

Labor League Mutual Benefit Society, Toronto. *10 Years Labor League*. Toronto: privately printed, 1936. (Yiddish.)

Mulvaney, C. Pelham. *Toronto: Past and Present*. Toronto: W.E. Caiger, 1884.

Oliver, Edmund H. *His Dominion of Canada*. Toronto: Board of Home Missions and The Women's Missionary Society of the United Church of Canada, 1932.

Parkes, J.W. *How the Russian Jews Came to the West*. Toronto: Committee on Jewish-Gentile Relationships, 1938.

Pope, Joseph. *The Tour of Their Royal Highnesses the Duke and Duchess of Cornwall and York through the Dominion of Canada in the Year 1901.* Ottawa: King's Printer, 1903.

Presbyterian Church in Canada, Women's Missionary Society. *The Story of our Missions.* Toronto, 1915.

Pride of Israel Sick Benefit Society. *Silver Anniversary Souvenir.* Toronto: privately printed, 1930. (English and Yiddish.)

Radomer Friendly Society. *10th Jubilee Book.* Toronto: privately printed, 1935. (Yiddish.)

Rasminsky, Louis, ed. *Hadassah Jubilee.* Toronto: Toronto Hadassah Council, [1927].

Rhinewine, Abraham. *Der Yid in Kanada [The Jew in Canada].* 2 vols. Toronto: Farlag "Kanada," 1925, 1927.

Robertson, John Ross. *Landmarks of Toronto.* Fourth Series. Toronto: J.R. Robertson, 1904.

Rohold, Rev. Sabeti B. *The Jews in Canada.* Toronto: Board of Home Missions, Presbyterian Church in Canada, 1912.

_____. *Presbyterian Church in Canada, Missions to the Jews. Historical Sketch.* Toronto: The Christian Synagogue, 1918.

_____. *The War and the Jew: a bird's eye view of the world's situation and the Jews' place in it.* 2nd ed. Toronto: Macmillan, 1915.

Samuel, Sigmund. *In Return.* Toronto: University of Toronto Press, 1963.

Scadding, Henry. *Toronto of Old.* Ed. F.H. Armstrong. Toronto: Oxford University Press, 1966. (First published in 1873 by Willing & Williamson, Toronto.)

Scheuer, Edmund. *Text Book of the Zionists' Jewish Free School.* Toronto: privately printed, 1915.

Shemen, Nachman and Louis J. Zuker, eds. *Yovel-Buch, Talmud Torah "Eitz Chaim" [Jubilee Book, Talmud Torah "Eitz Chaim"].* Toronto: privately printed, 1943.

Stephenson, F.C. and Sarah Vance. *That They May Be One.* Toronto: Board of Home Missions, United Church of Canada, 1929.

Traub, S., ed. *50 Years of History of the Beth Medrosh Hagodol Chevra Tehillim of Toronto.* Toronto: privately printed, 1938.

Toronto Hebrew Free School. *Theatre Night Programme,* March 9, 1936. Toronto, 1936.

_____. *The Liquidation of a Capital Debt.* (25th Anniversary book of the school.) Toronto: privately printed, 1947.

Toronto Independent Benevolent Association. *Silver Anniversary Souvenir.* Toronto: privately printed, 1934. (Yiddish.)

Weisgal, Meyer. *Meyer Weisgal . . . So Far.* London: Weidenfeld and Nicolson, 1971.

Willinsky, Abraham I. *A Doctor's Memoirs.* Toronto: Macmillan, 1960.

Woodsworth, James S. *Strangers within Our Gates.* Toronto: The Missionary Society of the Methodist Church, Canada, 1909.

TORONTO: SECONDARY

Arthur, Eric. *Toronto: No Mean City.* Toronto: University of Toronto Press, 1964.

Bnai Israel – Beth David Congregation. *50th-10th Anniversary Jubilee Volume.* Toronto, 1966.

Bossin, Hye. *A Tattler's Tales of Toronto.* Toronto: Handy Library, *ca.* 1950.

―――. *Stars of David.* Toronto: Canadian Jewish Congress, 1957.

Committee on Jewish-Gentile Relationships. *Facts & Fables about the Jews.* Toronto: n.d. (*ca.* 1938).

Congregation Shearith Israel Anshe Lida. *40th Year Anniversary.* Toronto, 1950.

Eisen, David. *Toronto's Jewish Doctors.* Toronto: Maimonides Medical Society of Ontario and Canadian Jewish Congress, 1960.

Eitz Chaim Schools. *Dedication Journal.* Toronto, 1963.

Goheen, Peter G. *Victorian Toronto 1850 to 1900: Pattern and Process of Growth.* (Research Paper No. 127). Chicago: University of Chicago Dept. of Geography, 1970.

Grace Church on-the-Hill, 1874-1964. Toronto: privately printed, 1964.

Guillet, Edwin C. *Toronto: From Trading Post to Great City.* Toronto: Ontario Publishing Co., 1934.

Hathaway, E.J. *Jesse Ketchum and his Times.* Toronto: McClelland and Stewart, 1929.

Hayman, Julius. *Our First 100 Years.* Toronto: Canadian Jewish Congress, 1957. (mimeograph)

Independent Friendly Workers Circle, Toronto. *20th Jubilee Book.* Toronto: privately printed, 1953. (Yiddish and English.)

Ivansker Mutual Benefit Society. *25th Anniversary Jubilee Book.* Toronto: privately printed, 1957.

Jewish National Fund. *Programme of the Negev Testimonial Dinner 1963.* Toronto: Morris Printing Co., 1963.

―――. *Programme of the Negev Testimonial Dinner 1965.* Toronto: Morris Printing Co., 1965.

Middleton, J.E. *The Municipality of Toronto: A History.* 2 vols. Toronto: Dominion Publishing Co., 1923.

Mozirer Sick Benefit Society. *50th Jubilee Book.* Toronto: privately published, 1955. (Yiddish and English.)

National Council of Jewish Women of Canada, Toronto Section. *Diamond Jubilee.* Toronto: privately printed, 1957.

Pursley, Louis H. *Street Railways of Toronto 1861-1921.* (Interurbans

350

Special #25.) Los Angeles: Electric Railway Publications, 1958.

Rosenberg, Louis. *Population Characteristics of the Jewish Community of Toronto.* (Jewish Community Series #3 – Canadian Jewish Population Studies.) Montreal: Canadian Jewish Congress, 1955. Mimeograph.

Rubinoff, Israel. *The History of the Farband Labour Zionist Order in Toronto.* n.p.: Historical Research Committee, Canadian Jewish Congress, 1957. Mimeograph.

Selicson, Marvin. *The Folks Farein at Fifty.* Toronto: privately printed, 1964.

Sons of Jacob Benevolent Society, Toronto. *Silver Jubilee Book.* Toronto: privately printed, 1943.

Stolnitz, Nathan. *Neginah in Yiddish'n Leben [Music in Jewish Life].* Toronto: Morris Printing Co., 1957.

Toronto Cloakmakers Union. *Silver Jubilee Souvenir Journal.* Toronto: privately printed, 1936.

_____. *40th Anniversary Souvenir Journal.* Toronto: privately printed, 1949.

United Jewish People's Order Mutual Benefit Society. *First National Convention.* Toronto: privately printed, 1945.

Wallace, Elisabeth. *Goldwin Smith: Victorian Liberal.* Toronto: University of Toronto Press, 1957.

Warschauer, Heinz. *The Story of Holy Blossom Temple.* Toronto: Holy Blossom Temple, 1956. (Mimeograph.)

_____. *The Story of Holy Blossom Temple.* 2nd ed. revised. Toronto: Holy Blossom Temple, 1969.

ARTICLES AND PUBLISHED SPEECHES

UNITED STATES

Berman, Jeremiah J. "The Trend in Jewish Religious Observance in Mid-Nineteenth-Century America," *Publication of the American Jewish Historical Society,* XXXVII (1947), pp. 31-53.

Bloom, Bernard H. "Yiddish-Speaking Socialists in America: 1892-1905," *American Jewish Archives,* XII, no. 1 (April 1960), pp. 34-68.

Bokser, Ben Zion. "Conservative Judaism," *Jewish Quarterly Review,* new series, XLV (April 1955), pp. 334-49.

Glazer, Nathan. "The American Jew and the Attainment of the Middle-Class Rank: Some Trends and Explanations," in M. Sklare, ed., *The Jews: Social Patterns of an American Group* (Glencoe, Ill.: Free Press, 1958), pp. 138-46.

Goldman, Solomon. "Towards a National Synagogue," in Mordecai Waxman, ed., *Tradition and Change: The Development of Conservative Judaism* (New York: Burning Bush Press, 1958), pp. 199-206.

Halpern, Ben. "America is Different," in M. Sklare, ed., *The Jews: Social Patterns of an American Group* (Glencoe, Ill.: Free Press, 1958), pp. 23-39.

Honor, Leo L. "The Impact of the American Environment and American Ideas on Jewish Elementary Education in the United States," *Jewish Quarterly Review*, new series, XLV (1955), pp. 451-96.

Liebman, Charles S. "Orthodoxy in American Jewish Life," *American Jewish Year Book*, LXVI (Philadelphia: The Jewish Publication Society of America, 1965), pp. 21-97.

Lookstein, Joseph H. "Traditional Judaism in America," *Jewish Quarterly Review*, new series, XLV (April 1955), pp. 318-33.

Panitz, Esther L. "The Polarity of American Jewish Attitudes towards Immigration (1870-1891)," in Abraham J. Karp, ed., *The Jewish Experience in America*, 5 vols. (Waltham, Mass: American Jewish Historical Society, 1969), IV, pp. 31-62.

Sklare, Marshall. "Aspects of Religious Worship in the Contemporary Conservative Synagogue," in M. Sklare, ed., *The Jews: Social Patterns of an American Group* (Glencoe, Ill.: Free Press, 1958), pp. 357-76.

Stein, Herman D. "Jewish Social Work in the United States 1920-1955," in M. Sklare, ed., *The Jews: Social Patterns of an American Group* (Glencoe, Ill.: Free Press, 1958), pp. 173-204.

Szajkowski, Zosa. "The Attitude of American Jews to East European Immigration (1881-1893)," *Publications of the American Jewish Historical Society*, XL, no. 3 (March 1951), pp. 221-80.

_____. "Emigration to America or Reconstruction in Europe," *Publications of the American Jewish Historical Society*, XLII, no. 2 (Dec. 1952), pp. 157-88.

Ward, David. "The Emergence of Central Immigrant Ghettoes in American Cities: 1840-1920," in Association of American Geographers, *Annals*, LVIII (June 1968), pp. 343-59.

_____. "The Internal Spatial Structure of Immigrant Districts in the Late Nineteenth Century," *Geographical Analysis*, I (Oct. 1969), pp. 337-53.

Weinryb, Bernard D. "Jewish Immigration and Accommodation to America" in M. Sklare, ed., *The Jews: Social Patterns of an American Group* (Glencoe, Ill.: Free Press, 1958), pp. 4-22.

CANADA

Brickner, Rabbi Barnett R. "Immigration and Colonization," in Empire Club of Canada, *Addresses Delivered to the Members During the Year 1922* (Toronto: Macoomb Press, 1923), pp. 83-101.

Bryce, Dr. P.H. "Civic Responsibility and the Increase of Immigration," in *Empire Club Speeches 1906/7* (Toronto: William Briggs, 1907), pp. 186-97.

Caiserman, H.M. "The Canadian Jewish Congress Moves Forward," *The Jewish Standard* (Toronto) Sept. 7, 1934, pp. 16, 17, 65.

Griffin, F.G. "*The Jew in Canada* by A.D. Hart," review, *Toronto Star Weekly*, Jan. 17, 1925, p. 22.

Sack, B.G. "Jews in Transition," *The Jewish Standard* (Toronto), Aug. 15-Sept. 1, 1960, pp. 5, 38-44.

Vineberg, Mrs. Sol. "Council in Canada," *The Canadian Council Woman*, VII, no. 2 (Jan. 1967), p. 11.

TORONTO

Birnbaum, S.J. "The History of the Jews in Toronto," *The Jewish Times*, XV, no. 51 (Nov. 29, 1912), pp. 6-7; XV, No. 52 (Dec. 6, 1912), pp. 7-8; XVI, No. 2 (Dec. 20, 1912), pp. 5-6; XVI, No. 4 (Jan. 3, 1913), pp. 5-6; XVI, No. 5 (Jan. 10, 1913), p. 12; XVI, No. 7 (Jan. 24, 1913), p. 8; XVI, No. 10 (Feb. 14, 1913), pp. 5-6; XVI, No. 14 (March 14, 1913), pp. 5-6.

Boimoil, N. "Rabbi Yehuda Rosenberg" in N. Shemen and L.J. Zuker, ed., *Yovel-Buch, Talmud Torah "Eitz Chaim"* (Toronto: privately printed, 1943), pp. 104-19.

Draimin, Bertha. "Memory Open Your Door," *The Canadian Council Woman*, VII, no. 2 (Jan. 1967), p. 5.

Dworkin, Dorothy. "Mount Sinai Hospital," The New Mount Sinai Hospital (Toronto), *Highlights*, XVI, No. 1 (Oct. 1969), pp. 13-14; XVI, No. 2 (March 1970), pp. 12-13; XVII, No. 1 (Oct. 1970), pp. 14-15.

Eisen, David. "Jewish Settlers of Old Toronto," *The Jewish Standard* (Toronto), Dec. 15, 1965, pp. 4-5, 14-17; Jan. 1, 1966, pp. 4-5, 12; Jan. 15, 1966, pp. 9, 11, 14-15.

Eisen, Sol. "The Toronto Jewish Community," *Toronto Daily Star*, Aug. 11, 1917.

Frank, M[aurice]. "The Jews of Toronto," in *Canadian Jewish Year Book 1939-40*, (Montreal: privately printed, 1939), pp. 333-35.

Frumhartz, P. "Matenko un zeyn Lebensveg," in Workmen's Circle Peretz Schools, *Souvenir Programme, 80th Birthday Celebration of I. Matenko* (Toronto: privately printed, 1955), pp. 6-7. (Yiddish.)

Goodman, H. "Rabbi Jacob Gordon," *Hebrew Journal* (Toronto), Dec. 7, 1937, p. 5. (Yiddish.)

Gordon, Rabbi Jacob. "Reminiscences of a Toronto Rabbi," in *Kanader Adler* (Montreal), 25th Anniversary Edition, 1932 (Yiddish. Clipping in Rabbi Jacob Gordon Papers, Canadian Jewish Congress Archives, Montreal.)

Gordon, Wilferd. "Young Israel" in *Moses Gelber Memorial Book*, mimeo, (Toronto: Toronto Hebrew Free School, 1940), pp. 12-18.

Gorman, Lazarus. "The Beth Tzedec Story," *The Jewish Standard* (Toronto), Aug. 1, 1955, pp. 6-9.

Graubart, Rabbi Philip. "A Fertel Yorhundert Talmud Torah "Eitz Chaim," (A Quarter-century at Talmud Torah 'Eitz Chaim') in N. Shemen and L.J. Zuker, eds., *Yovel-Buch, Talmud Torah "Eitz Chaim"* (Toronto: privately printed, 1943), pp. 51-56.

Greenbaum, A. "The First Fifty Years," in Judean Benevolent and Friendly Society, *Golden Jubilee Book* (Toronto: privately printed, 1955), pp. 5-9.

Haberman, Milton P. "The History of our Congregation," in Adath Israel Congregation, *Golden Jubilee Book* (Toronto: privately printed, 1952), pages not numbered.

Harrison, Eunice. "Camps were and are important in Toronto," *The Canadian Council Woman*, VII, no. 2 (Jan. 1967), p. 8.

Jackson, Gilbert E. "Anti-Semitism," in The Empire Club of Canada, *Addresses Delivered to Members during the Year 1939-40* (Toronto: Hunter-Rose, 1940), pp. 181-92.

Jacobs, Rev. Rabbi [Solomon]. "The Jews and Patriotism," in Empire Club of Canada, *Addresses Delivered to the Members During the Sessions 1915-16, 1916-17* (Toronto: Bryant Press, 1917), pp. 119-27.

Kayfetz, B.G. "The Development of the Toronto Jewish Community," *Tradition*, XIII, no. 1 (Summer 1972), pp. 5-17.

_____. "Only Yesterday: From Discrimination to Acceptance," address to the Toronto Jewish Historical Society published in *The Chronicle Review* (Toronto), Sept. 1972, pp. 25-34.

_____. "Pioneers in Education," *The Jewish Standard* (Toronto), July 1, 1960, pp. 5, 13.

Koldoff [Koldofsky], L. "Azoy iz di Yiddishe Shul Geboyt Gevoren," in Arbeiter Ring Peretz School, *Shul Buch* (Toronto: privately printed n.d.), pp. 22-26.

Kraisman, Sam. "Half Century of Progress, Growth and Achievement," in Toronto Joint Board Cloakmakers' Union ILGWU, *Souvenir Journal: Golden Jubilee* (Toronto: privately printed, 1961), pp. 6-13.

Levy, Mort. "Report on YMHA," in *Moses Gelber Memorial Book*, mimeo. (Toronto: Toronto Hebrew Free School, 1940).

Magerman, A. "Geschichte un Dergreichungen fun der Klokmacher Union in Toronto" [History and Accomplishments of the Cloakmakers' Union in Toronto]. Speech at the 50th jubilee banquet of the Union, Toronto, Nov. 5, 1960.

Mandel, Yaakov. "Ha' Gaon Reb Yehuda Leib" (obituary for Rabbi J.L. Graubart), *Hebrew Journal* (Toronto), Oct. 10, 1937. (Yiddish.)

Nobel, Leibush. "Vegen Unhoib fun Talmud Torah 'Eitz Chaim'" in N. Shemen and L.J. Zuker, *Yovel-Buch, Talmud Torah "Eitz Chaim"* (Toronto: privately printed, 1943), pp. 77-78.

Salsberg, Joseph B. Articles on organization of *shochtim* in *The Canadian Jewish News*, July 14, 1972, p. 5; July 21, 1972, p. 5; July 28, 1972, p. 5.

_____. "Sam Kronick – Product of the Jewish Renaissance," *The Canadian Jewish News*, Nov. 3, 1972, p. 5.

_____. "When Elections brought Coal to the Shtiblach," *The Canadian Jewish News*, Nov. 10, 1972, p. 5.

Schipper, Sidney S. "The Contribution of Holy Blossom to its Community" in Albert Rose (ed.), *A People and its Faith* (Toronto: University of Toronto Press, 1959), pp. 30-42.

"Shamash" (pseud.) [Shmuel Meir Shapiro]. "Finf un Tzventzig Yohr Eitz Chaim Talmud Torah" [Twenty-five years of Talmud Torah Eitz Chaim] in N. Shemen and L.J. Zuker, *Yovel-Buch, Talmud Torah "Eitz Chaim"* (Toronto: privately printed, 1943), pp. 120-122.

Shemen, Nachman. "Rabbenu Yehuda Leib Graubart" in N. Shemen and L.J. Zuker (eds.), *Yovel-Buch, Talmud Torah "Eitz Chaim"* (Toronto: privately printed, 1943), pp. 13-45. (Yiddish.)

Shemen, Nachman and J.I. Wohlgelernter, "Onshteyung un Onviklung fun Talmud Torah Eitz Chaim" [The Establishment and Development of Talmud Torah Eitz Chaim] in N. Shemen and L.J. Zuker (eds.), *Yovel-Buch, Talmud Torah "Eitz Chaim"* (Toronto: Privately printed, 1943), pp. 127-186. Excerpts from minute books.

Shidlowsky, Charles. "From Rags to Riches: Shmatasville Blues on New Old Spadina," *Masada* (Toronto) IV, No. 2 (Oct., 1972), pp. 10-14.

Siegel, Ida L. "Toronto's Talmud Torah: Then and Now," *Canadian Jewish Review* (Toronto), Sept. 16, 1955, p. 16.

Siegerman, Max. "Our Union in the First Years of its Existence" in Toronto Joint Board Cloakmakers' Union ILGWU, *Souvenir Journal: Golden Jubilee* (Toronto: Privately printed, 1961), pp. 29-31.

Sivitz, H.N. "Geschichte fun Tzedoka Klalis in Toronto" [The History of Communal Charity in Toronto], *Kanader Adler* (Montreal), Feb. 23, 1913. (Yiddish.)

Title, Pinia. "An Iberblick fur der Apter Gezelshaftlecher Landsmanshaft in Toronto" [A Survey of the Apter Community in Toronto], *20th Jubilee Banquet Program of the Apter Friendly Society* (Toronto: Privately printed, 1967), pages not numbered. (Yiddish.)

"The Toronto Federation of Jewish Philanthropies," *The Jewish Standard* (Toronto), June 1, 1934.

"Toronto's Oldest Agency," *Canadian Travel Courier*, II, No. 11 (Nov. 17, 1966), pp. 1, 3.

Vise, Bernard. "The Talmud Torah and the Jewish Centre" in Toronto Hebrew Free School, *Theatre Night Book*, March 9, 1936.

NEWSPAPERS AND PERIODICALS
(dates approximate)

The Asmonean [Cincinnati] 1851.
The Canadian Jewish Review [Toronto] 1921-1938.
Daily Mail [Toronto] 1876.
The Globe [Toronto] 1876-1937.
The Hebrew Journal (Yiddisher Zhurnal) [Toronto] 1914-1937.
The Illustrated London News Jan. 3, 1863.
The Jewish Chronicle [Montreal] 1915.
The Jewish Daily News [Chicago] 1915.
The Jewish Messenger [New York] 1862-1865.
The Jewish Standard [Toronto] 1934-1935.
The Jewish Times [Montreal] 1898-1914.
Der Kanader Adler [Montreal] 1913-1919.
Kanader Neies [Toronto] 1935-1937.
Kanader Yugend [Toronto] 1920s.
The Leader [Toronto] 1876.
The Mail and Empire [Toronto] 1897-1937.
Der Mazik [Toronto] *ca.* 1925.
Toronto Mirror 1856-1857.
Montreal Daily Star 1898.
Saturday Night [Toronto] 1898-1920.
Toronto News 1912.
Toronto Patriot 1840.
Star Weekly [Toronto] 1912-1925.
The Evening Telegram [Toronto] 1895-1937.
Toronto Daily Star 1897-1937.
Toronto World 1897-1912.
Yiddishes Tageblatt [New York] 1897-1920.
Y-Time [Toronto] 1938, 1947, 1949.

PUBLIC DOCUMENTS

Canada, Board of Registration & Statistics. *Census of the Canadas, 1860-61*. Quebec: 1863.

Canada, Bureau of Statistics. *Fifth Census of Canada 1911*. Ottawa: 1913.

_____. *Sixth Census of Canada 1921*. Ottawa: 1924.

Canada, Census & Statistics Office. *Fourth Census of Canada, 1901*. Ottawa: 1902.

Canada, Dept. of Agriculture. *Census of Canada 1870-71*. Ottawa: 1873.

_____. *Census of Canada 1880-81*. Ottawa: 1883.

_____. *Census of Canada 1890-91*. Ottawa: 1893.

Evidence taken "in the matter of certain grievances of Max Goldman, of the City of Toronto, in the County of York, Butcher, and Others, against the management of the Civic Abattoir, in the city of Toronto, and the Kehilla Incorporated, of the same place." 1932 (Parts 1-2 in Folio #36, City of Toronto Archives; Part 3, Canadian Jewish Congress Central Region Archives.)

Hansard [Federal]. Session 1906, Vol. I, pp. 226-35.

Hansard [Federal]. Session 1906, pp. 5636 ff., 6279-6317, 6327-6364.

Hastings, Dr. Charles D. "Report of the Medical Health Officer dealing with the recent investigation of Slum Conditions in Toronto 1911." Toronto: Dept. of Health, n.d. (Folio #5, City of Toronto Archives.)

The Ontario Gazette.

Ontario Legislative Assembly. *Sessional Papers*, Vol. XLVI – Part III (1914). Toronto: L.K. Cameron, 1914.

Ontario, Province of. "Letters of Patent Incorporating The Toronto Jewish Old Folks Home (Moshev Zakeinem), March 26, 1918."

_____. "Letters Patent of The Rabbinical Council of Toronto 'Vaad Horabonim' Sept. 28, 1927."

_____. *Report of the Registrar of Friendly Societies of Ontario 1918*. Toronto: King's Printer, 1919.

"Report by His Honour Judge Tytler re: Kehillah Enquiry" 1932 (Typescript copy, City of Toronto Archives.)

Statutory Declaration "In the matter of Certain Complaints made against J.L. Lunney, Dominion Immigration Officer, St. John N.B.," 1921, (Dept. of Immigration Papers RG 76, Vol. 54, File 2240, Public Archives of Canada).

Supreme Court of Ontario. File for Action #22/1912, "Dickman *vs.* Gordon."

_____. File for Action #908/1912, "Dickman *vs.* Winreb."

_____. Action #1813/1925, "Cohen *vs.* Silverstein *et al.*"

Toronto, City of. *Assessment Roll for the City of Toronto 1834.*

_____. *Assessment Roll for the Ward of St. George City of Toronto.* 1856, 1859, 1861, 1874.

_____. *Assessment Roll for the Ward of St. Lawrence City of Toronto,* 1856, 1859, 1861, 1874.

_____. *Assessment Roll for the Ward of St. James City of Toronto,* 1856, 1859, 1861, 1874.

_____. *Assessment Roll for the Ward of St. John City of Toronto,* 1856, 1859, 1861, 1874.

_____. *Assessment Roll for the Ward of St. Andrew City of Toronto,* 1856, 1859, 1861, 1874.

_____. *Assessment Roll for the Ward of St. David City of Toronto,* 1861, 1874.

_____. *Assessment Roll for the Ward of St. Thomas City of Toronto,* 1874.

_____. *Assessment Roll for the Ward of St. Matthew's City of Toronto,* 1885.

_____. *Assessment Roll for City of Toronto made in 1904 for 1905, Ward 3, Division I.*

_____. *Assessment Roll for City of Toronto made in 1910 for 1911, Ward 3, Division II.*

_____. *Assessment Roll for City of Toronto made in 1911 for 1912, Ward 4, Division II.*

_____. *Board of Control Minutes.*

_____. *Minutes and Proceedings of the Council of the Corporation of the City of Toronto 1883.* Toronto: E.F. Clarke, 1884.

_____. *Report of the Charities Commission 1911-12.* Toronto: Carswell, 1912.

_____. Registry Office. Instrument No. 69381 (Deed to the Pape Ave. Burial Ground).

_____. Registry Office. Abstract Index, Plan K-2.

_____. Registry Office. Abstract Index, Plan 8A.

_____. Registry Office. Abstract Index, Plan 514 vo. 486.

_____. Registry Office. Instrument No. 11135A, "Conveyance of land situate on the South of Richmond St. in the City of Toronto Dated 16 July 1875."

_____. Registry Office. Instrument No. 11512A, "Conveyance of land on Richmond St. Toronto in trust for a Jewish Congregation Sept. 11, 1875."

_____. Registry Office. Instrument No. 15101 (York), May 9, 1883, "Martin McKee et eux to Trustees Jewish Burying Ground" [Deed to Jones Ave. cemetery].

LETTERS AND TELEGRAMS
(in chronological order)

D'Arcy Boulton [Attorney General of Upper Canada] to Lieut. Col. Cameron [Colonial Secretary], July 8, 1817 (Colonial Office Records, Public Archives of Canada, Series Q, 322, Part 1, p. 216).

Arthur W. Hart to Robert Baldwin, March 28, 1836 (Robert Baldwin Correspondence A49 #86, Baldwin Room, Metropolitan Toronto Central Library).

Arthur W. Hart to Robert Baldwin, May 3, 1844 (Robert Baldwin Correspondence A49 #87, *loc.cit.*).

C. I. de Sola to Wilfrid Laurier, Nov. 21, 1905 (Laurier Papers, Public Archives of Canada, Vol. 389, pp.103524-5.).

Sir Wilfrid Laurier to C. I. de Sola, Dec. 11, 1905 (Laurier Papers, Public Archives of Canada, Vol. 391, p.104026).

S. B. Rohold to Rev. J. M. A. Scott, Jan. 21, 1908 (United Church Archives, Toronto).

State Medical Board of Ohio to Miss Dorothy Goldstick, May 25, 1909 (Dworkin Papers, Canadian Jewish Congress Central Region Archives, Toronto).

R.P.M. [Prob. Mackay] to Rev. Dr. Taylor, Rochester, N.Y., Jan. 5, 1910 (United Church Archives, Toronto).

Rev. R. P. Mackay [Secretary of the Presbyterian Church in Canada] to Thomas Cline, Boston, Mass., May 28, 1910 (United Church Archives, Toronto).

Rev. J. M. Scott to Rev. J. R. Dobson, Montreal, Dec. 9, 1910 (United Church Archives, Toronto).

Rev. J. M. Scott to Miss Martha Dickson, Peterboro, 1910 (United Church Archives, Toronto).

Rev. J. M. Scott to Mrs. Shortreed [of the Women's Foreign Missionary Soc., Toronto], March 17, 1911 (United Church Archives).

Rev. J. M. Scott to John D. Naismith, March 23, 1911, (United Church Archives).

Rev. J. M. Scott to Rev. S. B. Rohold, March 27, 1911 (United Church Archives).

J. M. Scott to Rev. A. B. Baird, Winnipeg, Apr. 24, 1911 (United Church Archives).

Rev. J. M. Scott to Rev. A. D. Baird, Winnipeg, Dec. 19, 1911 (United Church Archives).

Rev. J. M. Scott to Rev. J. R. Dobson, Montreal, March 14, 1912 (United Church Archives).

Rev. R. P. Mackay to Barnet Stone, June 13, 1913, (United Church Archives).

Edmund Scheuer to the editor of the *Canadian Jewish Chronicle*, March 22, 1915 (Holy Blossom Temple Archives, Toronto).

A. B. Bennett to S. W. Jacobs, Apr. 29, 1919 (S. W. Jacobs Papers, Public Archives of Canada).

A. B. Bennett to S. W. Jacobs, telegram, Apr. 28, 1919 (Jacobs Papers).

A. B. Bennett to S. W. Jacobs, telegram, May 4, 1919 (Jacobs Papers).

S. W. Jacobs to A. B. Bennett, May 5, 1919 (Jacobs Papers).

A. B. Bennett to S. W. Jacobs, May 13, 1919 (Jacobs Papers).

Rev. S. B. Rohold to Rev. J. McP. Scott, Nov. 13, 1919 (United Church Archives).

Grace Bredehoft to Rev. J. M. Scott, 1919 (United Church Archives).

Frank D. Benjamin to Edmund Scheuer, July 8, 1920 (Holy Blossom Temple Archives).

E. J. O'Connell to W. R. Little, Oct. 13, 1920 (Dept. of Immigration Papers, RG 76, File 2240, Public Archives of Canada).

W. R. Little to E. J. O'Connell, Oct. 16, 1920 (Dept. of Immigration Papers, File 2240).

Goel Tzedec Congregation, Toronto, Circular letter, Apr. 19, 1921 (Collection of Mrs. Evelyn Goodman, Toronto).

F. C. Blair to H. M. Mitton, Aug. 4, 1922 (Dept. of Immigration Papers, RG 76, File 541782).

N. L. Nathanson to N. Smith, Jan. 8, 1924 (Collection of Mrs. Evelyn Goodman, Toronto).

W. J. Egan to Mrs. A. E. Gooderham, March 6, 1924 (Dept. of Immigration Papers, RG 76, File 541782).

Mattie Miller to Edmund Scheuer, May 6, 1924 (Holy Blossom Temple Archives).

G. N. Gordon to S. W. Jacobs, telegram, May 1, 1925 (S. W. Jacobs Papers, Public Archives of Canada).

S. W. Jacobs to Joseph Singer, May 20, 1925 (S. W. Jacobs Papers, Public Archives of Canada).

Louis Gurofsky to S. W. Jacobs, telegram, Oct. 6, 1925 (S. W. Jacobs Papers, Public Archives of Canada).

Louis Gurofsky to S. W. Jacobs, Oct. 30, 1925 (S. W. Jacobs Papers, Public Archives of Canada).

Joseph Singer to S. W. Jacobs, Oct. 30, 1925 (S. W. Jacobs Papers, Public Archives of Canada).

Dr. Abraham Brodey to S. W. Jacobs, Oct. 31, 1925 (S. W. Jacobs Papers, Public Archives of Canada).

S. W. Jacobs to Joseph Singer, Nov. 5, 1925 (S. W. Jacobs Papers, Public Archives of Canada).

James Simpson [Sec.-Treas. of the Labor Temple, Toronto] to Hon. Peter Heenan [Minister of Labour, Ottawa] Jan. 12, 1927.

Rabbi Y. L. Graubart to I. M. Korolnek, 1928 (Hebrew; Courtesy Mr. Harry Korolnek).

A. L. Jolliffe [Commissioner of Immigration] to Baltic American Line, New York City, Aug. 4, 1928 (Dept. of Immigration Papers RG 76, Vol. 54, File 2240, Public Archives of Canada).

Rabbi F. M. Isserman to H. M. Smith, Nov. 14, 1928 (Collection of Mrs. Evelyn Goodman, Toronto).

Max Clavir [President of *Journal* Press Ltd., Toronto] to S. W. Jacobs, Feb. 6, 1930 (S. W. Jacobs Papers, Public Archives of Canada).

Hebrew National Association (Folks Farein) Toronto, circular letter to executive, Feb. 2, 1931.

Rabbi Samuel Sachs, circular letter re: Talmud Torah Campaign, 1932 (Associated Hebrew Schools archives, Toronto).

Edmund Scheuer to Samuel Meir Shapiro, May 9, 1932 (Holy Blossom Temple Archives).

Judge John Tytler to Mayor Wm. J. Stewart, July 8, 1932 (City of Toronto Archives).

G. Tellson [Secretary of the McCaul St. Synagogue] to E. Pullan [President of the Kehillah of Toronto], Oct. 30, 1933 (Courtesy Mr. Samuel A. Kurtz, Toronto).

H. M. Caiserman [General Secretary of the Canadian Jewish Congress] to Hon. Wesley A. Gordon, Minister of Immigration, Feb. 12, 1934 (Dept. of Immigration Papers RG 76, File 541782, Public Archives of Canada).

Henry S. Rosenberg to Rabbi B. Treiger, March 1935 (Associated Hebrew Schools archives, Toronto).

Dr. A. Lipson [President, B'nai B'rith Toronto Lodge #836] to Board of Directors, Toronto Hebrew Free School, March 30, 1935 (Associated Hebrew Schools archives).

Rabbi Maurice Eisendrath, circular letter to obtain money to reopen Talmud Torah, May 10, 1935 (Associated Hebrew Schools archives).

Canada Permanent Mortgage Corp. to M[oses] Gelber, June 27, 1935 (Associated Hebrew Schools archives).

Circular letter inviting the public to a meeting forming the "Jewish Centre of Toronto," Oct. 1935 (Associated Hebrew Schools archives).

Martin M. Cohen [Exec. Director of the United Jewish Welfare Fund of Toronto] to Moses Gelber [Pres. of Toronto Hebrew Free School] Apr. 10, 1938 (Associated Hebrew Schools archives).

H. N. Sivitz to A. G. Volpe, Dec. 18, 1959 (Canadian Jewish Congress Archives, Montreal).

Aaron G. Volpe to B. G. Kayfetz, March 26, 1960 (Canadian Jewish Congress Archives, Montreal).

Rabbi J. J. Price to the author, Aug., 1971.

Rabbi J. J. Price to the author, Sept., 1971.
New York Public Library to the author, Nov. 16, 1971.
Mrs. F. M. Isserman to the author, Jan. 13, 1972.
Mr. Harry Aschkinasi, National Jewish Hospital & Research Center, Denver, Colo. to the author, Feb. 10, 1972.
Frank H. Levine [Exec. Director, Jews' College, London], to the author, Nov. 29, 1973.

OTHER UNPUBLISHED MATERIAL

Adath Israel Congregation, Toronto. *Pinkas di Ershte Yiddishe Congregation Adath Israel af Toronto [Minutes of the First Jewish Congregation Adath Israel (Anshei Roumania) of Toronto]*, 1903.
Anglo-Jewish Association, Toronto Branch. "Report for General Meeting held Sunday April 19, 1896" (Holy Blossom Temple Archives).
_____. "Minutes of Committee meeting, Sept. 22, 1921" (*Ibid.*)
"Agreement between Shochtim and Rabbis of Toronto Oct. 30, 1915" (Canadian Jewish Congress Archives, Montreal).
Associated Hebrew Charities, Toronto. "Minute Book containing the minutes of the several relief societies assembled in co-operation for the relief of the local poor and unfortunate at the Charities Building 218 Simcoe St." (Courtesy Mrs. Ida L. Siegel).
Associated Hebrew Schools, Toronto. "Historical Data Concerning Life Members" (typescript, undated, 2pp., Associated Hebrew Schools archives).
"Biographical Sketch of Rev. S.B. Rohold prepared for the Historical Committee of the Presbyterian Church in Canada 1918" (United Church Archives).
Brown, Alexander. "Half a Century of Jewish Educational Achievements" (typescript, 1957, 6pp., Associated Hebrew Schools archives).
Caiserman, H.M. "First Annual Report of the General Secretary Submitted to the Executive of the Canadian Jewish Congress for the Period of March 19, 1919 to March 19, 1920."
Canadian Jewish Congress. *Minute Book of the Central Division* 1937 (Canadian Jewish Congress Archives, Montreal).
The Christian Synagogue, Toronto. "Miss D. McDonald's Report of 1918" (United Church Archives).

_____. "Miss Elizabeth Brown's Report for the Year 1918" (United Church Archives).

_____. "Mrs. Rohold's Report for the Year 1918" (United Church Archives).

The Christian Synagogue, Toronto. "Statistical Report for 1919" (United Church Archives).

_____. Summer Home. "Statement of Expenditure and Income for 1918" (United Church Archives).

"The Development of the Social Services in the Toronto Jewish Community" (mimeograph, 14pp. *ca.* 1965, Canadian Jewish Congress Central Region Archives, Toronto).

Eisen, David. "My Life in Toronto" (typescript, 13pp., 1973, author's collection).

Godfrey, Sheldon Jay (comp.). "Documents relating to Canadian Jewish history prepared for the Canadian Jewish Congress 1963" (Canadian Jewish Congress Central Region Archives, Toronto).

[Toronto Hebrew Congregation] Goel Tzedec. "Annual Financial Report 5674 [1913/14] (Canadian Jewish Congress Archives, Montreal).

_____. "Balance Sheet for the year ending Oct. 31, 1921."

_____. "Financial Statement 1922-23" (Collection of Mrs. Evelyn Goodman, Toronto).

_____. *Minutes.* Oct. 1904-Oct. 1908; Oct. 1908-Sept. 1912; 1922-33; 1933-40.

Graff, Vicki W. "A Quantitative Historical Study of the Social Geography of an Urban Community: Kensington Market, 1901-1950" (unpublished paper, University of Toronto, 1972).

Graubart, Rabbi Y.L. Statement by Rabbi Graubart concerning an agreement with the Kehillah of Toronto, 1925. (MSS. Hebrew, courtesy Mr. Nachman Shemen).

Group "B" and The Jewish Centre of Educational and Communal Activities. "An outline of Plan Approved by Directors of Toronto Hebrew Free School, which endeavours to place the school on a sound financial Basis for future operations. Also: Proposals for the eventual Development of the school into a Jewish centre of Educational and communal activities, Toronto 1935" (mimeograph, Associated Hebrew Schools archives, Toronto).

Guillet, Edwin C. *Racial Discrimination* ["Famous Canadian Trials" vol. 33], 1945, (Typescript, Metropolitan Toronto Central Library).

Hayes, Saul. "The Jewish Community of Canada," paper delivered at a conference of world Jewish organizations, London, England, 1958 (typescript, 8 pp., Canadian Jewish Congress Central Region Archives, Toronto).

Hebrew National Association (Folks Farein), Toronto. *Minutes* 1925-1937.

_____. "Report for Month of May, 1929."

_____. "Report for Month of June 1929."

_____. "Report Jan. 1-20, 1930."

_____. "Financial Report Oct. 1930."

_____. "Report Nov. 1930."

[Toronto Hebrew Congregation] Holy Blossom. "By-laws of the Toronto Hebrew Congregation 'Holy Blossom'," 1889. (Canadian Jewish Congress Archives, Montreal.)

_____. "By-laws of the Toronto Hebrew Congregation 'Holy Blossom'," 1894 (Holy Blossom Temple Archives).

_____. "By-laws of 'The Holy Blossom' Toronto Hebrew Congregation," 1904 (Canadian Jewish Congress Archives, Montreal).

_____. Copying Book, 1891-1896 (Holy Blossom Temple Archives).

_____. Minutes, 1856-1938 (Holy Blossom Temple Archives).

_____. "President's Report," 1926 (Canadian Jewish Congress Archives, Montreal).

_____. "President's Report," 1927 (Canadian Jewish Congress Archives, Montreal).

_____. Registrar [Register] Toronto Hebrew Congregation, 1857-1902 (Holy Blossom Temple Archives).

_____. "Report for 1924-25" (Canadian Jewish Congress Archives, Montreal).

_____. "Report of the Committee in charge of the Special Services for Young People Held on Rosh Hashonah and Yom Kippur under the Auspices of the Congregation," 1925 (Canadian Jewish Congress Archives, Montreal).

_____. "Revised By-laws of the Toronto Hebrew Congregation 1871" (Holy Blossom Temple Archives).

Toronto Hebrew Free School. Minutes.

Hutner, Florence. "Address to 25th Annual Meeting: United Jewish Welfare Fund of Toronto, Dec. 4, 1962" (archives of United Jewish Welfare Fund, Toronto).

Jennison, M. (ed.). Material on the history of social settlements in Canada, (Baldwin Room, Metropolitan Toronto Central Library).

Kehillah of Toronto. Agreement between the Kehillah of Toronto and Khal Adath Israel concerning Rabbi Graubart's entry into the Kehillah, ca. 1925 (Mss. Yiddish, courtesy Mr. Harry Korolnek and Mr. Nachman Shemen).

_____. Agreement by shochtim to submit to the authority of the local rabbis, 1930 (Mss. Hebrew, courtesy Mr. Harry Korolnek and Mr. Nachman Shemen).

_____. "Report of the Kehillah of Toronto, Inc. for Year Ending August 31, 1931." (Associated Hebrew Schools archives.)

Khal Adath Israel. Agreement by a butcher to submit to the authority of the Khal Adath Israel and not to the Kehillah, March 1924. (MSS. Yiddish, courtesy Mr. Harry Korolnek and Mr. Nachman Shemen.)

"Meyer W. Gasner," (biography, 3pp., typescript, Associated Hebrew Schools archives.)

Newman, David. Address to the Toronto Jewish Historical Society, Nov. 18, 1970. (Manuscript at Society offices.)

Ostrovtzer Congregation [Bais Ha Knesseth Ha Godol Bikkur Cholim Tifereth Israel Anshei Ostrovtze], Toronto. *Minutes* 1932-36 (courtesy Mr. Israel Weinberg.)

Perelmutar, Hy. Article on Jewish immigration from Poland (typescript, 39pp., 1935, Dept. of Immigration Papers, RG 76, File 541782, Public Archives of Canada.)

"Preliminary Agreement to form a 'Charitable Society' July 9, 1877," (MSS., Holy Blossom Temple Archives.)

Presbyterian Church in Canada. "Minutes of the Committee on Jewish Work [Toronto] Apr. 27, 1908" (typescript, United Church Archives.)

_____. "Minutes of the Jewish Sub-Committee of the Foreign Missions Committee, June 19, 1908," (typescript, United Church Archives.)

_____. Toronto Mission to the Jews, *Minutes*, Feb. 12, 1912; Apr. 17, 1912. (*Ibid.*)

_____. "Work Amongst the Jews: Policy" (typescript, 7pp., 1920, *ibid.*)

Rockaway, Robert A. "From Americanization to Jewish Americanism: The Jews of Detroit, 1850-1914." Unpublished Ph.D. dissertation, Dept. of History, University of Michigan, 1970.

Rohold, Rev. S.B. "Brief Statement for the Committee," Oct. 2, 1919 (typescript, United Church Archives.)

Rosen, Ben. "Jewish Education – What Program Should the Jewish Community Support?" speech at the Jewish Education section of the Council of Jewish Federations and Welfare Funds, Philadelphia, Jan. 28, 1937. (typescript, 8pp., Associated Hebrew Schools.)

Rosenberg, Louis. "Jewish Mutual Benefit and Friendly Societies in Toronto. The First Fifty Years 1896-1945" (typescript, 63pp., *ca.,* 1947, Canadian Jewish Congress Central Region Archives.)

Sachs, Rabbi Samuel. "Congregation Goel Tzedec's Golden Anniversary" (typescript, 1933, courtesy Mr. Jack Orenstein, Beth Tzedec Congregation.)

Sadowski, Ben. "History of Jewish Social Welfare Development in Toronto," address delivered Sept., 1951 (typescript, United Jewish Welfare Fund of Toronto.)

Scheuer, Edmund. "Reminiscences of Canadian Jewry to be appended to Thesis of Arthur Brodey," Oct. 9, 1933 (MSS., American Jewish Archives, Cincinnati.)

Shemen, Nachman. "Orthodoxy in Toronto," Yiddish. Supplement for the Jubilee Edition of the *Hebrew Journal*, 1950. Printed but never distributed to the public. (Courtesy Mr. N. Shemen.)

Sons of Jacob Benevolent Society, Toronto. *Burial Ground Trustees Minute Book*, 1919-1958, Yiddish (Canadian Jewish Congress Central Region Archives, Toronto.)

Toronto Hebrew Benevolent Soc. [Holy Blossom]. *Minutes* 1878-1880 (Holy Blossom Temple Archives.)

Toronto Hebrew Free Loan Association. *Minutes*.

Toronto Hebrew Ladies' Aid Society. *Minutes* 1899-1908 (MSS., Yiddish, courtesy Mrs. Ida L. Siegel.)

Toronto Hebrew Ladies' Sick and Benevolent Society, "Chebra Gemilas Chesed." *Minute Book*, 1868-1877 (Holy Blossom Temple Archives.)

_____. "By-Laws and Regulations of the Chebre Gemilas Chesed or Toronto Hebrew Ladies' Sick and Benevolent Soc.," 1868 (Holy Blossom Temple Archives.)

Toronto Jewish Literary & Social Union. "Constitution and By-Laws of the Toronto Jewish Literary and Social Union," 1894 (Holy Blossom Temple Archives.)

Vaad HaKashruth, Toronto. Agreement of a wholesale butcher to submit to the authority of the Vaad HaKashruth organized by Rabbi Joseph Weinreb, 1918. MSS., Yiddish. (Courtesy Mr. Harry Korolnek and Mr. N. Shemen.)

Zionist Jewish Free School, Toronto. Registration Lists, 1908-1918 (MSS., Canadian Jewish Congress Archives, Montreal.)

DIRECTORIES
(in chronological order)

York Commercial Directory Street Guide and Register 1833-4. Compiled by George Walton. York: U.C.: Thomas Dalton, [1833].

Brown's Toronto City and Home District Directory 1846-7. Toronto: George Brown, 1846.

Rowsell's City of Toronto and County of York Directory for 1850-1. Toronto: Henry Rowsell, 1850.

Brown's Toronto General Directory. Toronto: W.R. Brown, 1856.

The Toronto City Directory for 1887. Toronto: R.L. Polk & Co., 1887.

The Toronto City Directory for 1888. Toronto: R.L. Polk & Co., 1888.

The Toronto City Directory for 1889. Toronto: R.L. Polk & Co., 1889.

The Toronto City Directory for 1890. Toronto: R.L. Polk & Co., 1890.

The Toronto City Directory, 1891-1930. Toronto: Might, 1891-1930.

PUBLISHED REPORTS AND PROCEEDINGS

Church of England. *Journal of the Incorporated Synod of The Church of England in Canada in the Diocese of Toronto.* 1909-1937. Toronto: Parker, 1909-1937 (Anglican Diocesan Archives, Toronto.)

The Federation of the Jewish Philanthropies of Toronto. *2nd Annual Report,* 1918-19.

Jewish Immigrant Aid Society of Canada. *Eighth Annual Report.* Montreal: 1928.

Mount Sinai Hospital, Toronto, Ladies' Auxiliary. *Calendar & Dues Book,* 1933-4.

Presbyterian Church in Canada. *The Acts and Proceedings of the General Assembly* 1907-1925. Toronto: Murray Printing Co., 1907-1925 (United Church Archives.)

United Jewish Welfare Fund of Toronto. *First Annual Report.* Toronto: 1938.

_____. *Second Annual Report 1938-39.* Toronto: 1939.

INTERVIEWS AND ORAL MATERIAL

Herschel Alt, personal interview, Aug. 22, 1977.

Hannah Arbus, interview, Jewish Oral History Project [J.O.H.P.], March 2, 1973.

Archie B. Bennett. "The Third and Fourth Eras in Canadian Jewish History," address to the Toronto Jewish Historical Society and discussion following, Oct. 27, 1971. (Tape in the author's collection.)

Archie B. Bennett, personal interview, Oct. 3, 1972.

Ida Berk, personal interview, Feb. 4, 1972.

David Biderman, interview, J.O.H.P., May 9, 1973.

Dr. Alexander Brown, interview, J.O.H.P., March 30, 1973.

Benjamin Brown, personal interview, Nov. 30, 1972.

Benjamin Brown, interview, J.O.H.P., March 13, 1973.

Arthur Cohen, personal interviews, Dec. 15, 1971; Dec. 20, 1971.

Bertha Draimin, personal interviews, Jan. 10, 1972; Feb. 15, 1972.

Dorothy Dworkin, personal interview, Feb. 8, 1972.

Dr. David Eisen, interview, J.O.H.P., May 3, 1973 and various personal interviews.

Max Federman, interview, J.O.H.P., March 13, 1973.

Paul Frumhartz, interview by Julius Hayman, March 17, 1957 for the Canadian Jewish Congress (transcript, Canadian Jewish Congress Archives, Montreal.)

Dr. Anna Gelber, personal interview, July 29, 1973.

Ben Geldsaler, personal interview, Sept. 28, 1972.

Joshua Gershman, interviews, J.O.H.P., Apr. 10, 1973; May 11, 1973.

John J. Glass, personal interview, Dec. 13, 1972.

Fanny Goldsmith, personal interview.

Morris [Maurice] Goldstick, interview by Julius Hayman, prob. 1957, for the Canadian Jewish Congress (transcript, Canadian Jewish Congress Archives, Montreal.)

Sue Goodman, personal interview, Jan. 12, 1972.

Wilferd Gordon, personal interview, Jan. 8, 1973.

David Green, interview, J.O.H.P., March 28, 1973 and personal interview Apr. 9, 1973.

Rose Heisel, interview, J.O.H.P., Feb. 28, 1973.

Dr. and Mrs. Samuel Hurwich, personal interview, July 2, 1974.

Florence Hutner, personal interview, Feb. 19, 1973.

Ben Zion Hyman, personal interview, Oct. 8, 1972.

Dr. Levi Jacober, interview, J.O.H.P., March 30, 1973.

B.G. Kayfetz, personal interview, May 11, 1967.

Harry Korolnek, personal interview, Dec. 26, 1972.

Samuel A. Kurtz, personal interview, Nov. 27, 1972 and J.O.H.P. interview, Apr. 5, 1973.

Mr. Lean, interview, J.O.H.P., March 5, 1973.

William Leibel, personal interview, Jan. 28, 1972.

Sinai Leichter, remarks during discussion at meeting of the Toronto Jewish Historical Society, Apr. 23, 1974.

Mrs. Levine, interview, J.O.H.P., May 8, 1973.

Judith McErvel, personal interview, Nov. 13, 1973.

David E. Newman, personal interview, Aug. 24, 1974.

Dr. Maurice A. Pollock, personal interview, March 15, 1973.

Harry Pullan, interviews, J.O.H.P., March 20, 1973; Apr. 11, 13, 1973.

Miss S. Rhinewine, personal interview, Feb. 9, 1972.

Dr. Henry S. Rosenberg, personal interview, May 4, 1973.

Dr. Mattie Rotenberg, personal interview, Jan. 25, 1972.

Rabbi Samuel Sachs, interview by Mr. Jack Provost, Research Project Associate, Jewish Federation Council of Greater Los Angeles at Santa Monica, Calif., Aug. 13, 1973 at the author's request.

Mrs. Herman Salb, personal interview, Dec. 28, 1972.

Joseph B. Salsberg, personal interview, Jan. 15, 1973, also J.O.H.P., Feb. 21, 1973.

William Samuel, personal interview, Oct. 9, 1973.

Julius Y. Seltzer, personal interview, Feb. 15, 1972.

Annie Shapiro, personal interview, Jan. 26, 1972.

Rosalyn Shaul, interview, J.O.H.P., May 8, 1973.

Nachman Shemen, personal interview, March 5, 1973.

Benjamin Sherman, interview, J.O.H.P., March, 1973.

Ida L. Siegel, personal interviews, July 29, 1971; Aug. 5, 1971; Aug. 12, 1971; Aug. 26, 1971; Sept. 2, 1971; Oct. 7, 1971; Oct. 28, 1971; Nov. 4, 1971; Nov. 25, 1971; Dec. 2, 1971; Dec. 9, 1971; Dec. 16, 1971; Dec. 23, 1971; Dec. 30, 1971; Jan. 6, 1972; Jan. 20, 1972; Jan. 27, 1972; Feb. 3, 1972; Feb. 17, 1972; March 2, 1972; March 9, 1972.

Moses Sigal, personal interview, Dec. 28, 1972.

Mrs. Saul Sigler, personal interview, Dec. 28, 1972.

Echiel Silverman, interview, J.O.H.P., March 29, 1973.

Mrs. E.F. Singer, personal telephone conversation, Oct. 16, 1974.

Alexander S. Socol, interview, J.O.H.P., March 29, 1973.

Nathan Strauss, interview, J.O.H.P., March 8, 1973.

Mrs. N. Sussman, personal interview.

H. Max Swartz, personal interview, May 24, 1973.

Esther Volpe, interview, J.O.H.P., March 16, 1973.

Dr. Fred Weinberg, personal interview, Jan., 1973.

Israel Weinberg, personal interview, Dec. 14, 1972.

Julius Weiner, interview, J.O.H.P., March 9, 1973.

Harry Wolfson, personal interview, July 29, 1973.

Annie Zeidman, interview, J.O.H.P., Apr. 25, 1973.

Louis J. Zuker, interview, J.O.H.P., Apr. 4, 1973.

MISCELLANEOUS SOURCES

Anglo-Jewish Association, Toronto Branch, File 1913-1930s, Canadian Jewish Congress Archives, Montreal.

Congregation "Bais Yehuda," Constitution, n.d. [ca. 1925], author's collection.

Canadian Jewish Congress 1919, Toronto Ballot, Canadian Jewish Congress Central Region Archives, Toronto.

Congregation "Eastern Children of Israel" n.d. [ca. 1918]. (constitution).

Eaton Company History, Scrapbook of Newspaper Clippings, 1900-1912, T. Eaton Co. Archives, Toronto.

Dr. Isidore Goldstick Papers, Jewish Public Library Archives, Montreal.

Rabbi Jacob Gordon Papers, Canadian Jewish Congress Archives, Montreal.

[Toronto Hebrew Congregation] Holy Blossom, Deed to the Bond St. Synagogue, 1894, Holy Blossom Temple Archives.

————. "Order of Service, Dedication of the new Synagogue, The Holy Blossom Congregation of Toronto Canada, Wed. Sept. 15, 1897/5657," Pamphlet, Holy Blossom Temple Archives.

"The Inside Story of Federation," handbill for 1934 campaign, Canadian Jewish Congress Central Region Archives, Toronto.

Samuel W. Jacobs Papers, Public Archives of Canada.

Kehillah of Toronto, Ballot for 1932, Canadian Jewish Congress Archives, Montreal.

Khal Adath Israel, leaflet *ca.* 1923-24, announcing that only butchers supervised by Rabbi Graubart should be patronized. Yiddish, Collection of Mr. Harry Korolnek, Toronto.

T.A. Reed Collection, Metropolitan Toronto Central Library.

John Ross Robertson Scrapbook, Robertson Collection, Metropolitan Toronto Central Library.

Edmund Scheuer File, Canadian Jewish Congress Archives, Montreal.

Edmund Scheuer Scrapbook, Holy Blossom Temple Archives.

United Church of Canada, Committee on Archives. "Finding Aid Relating to the Presbyterian Church in Canada. Mission to the Jews in Canada 1907-1925." United Church Archives, typescript.

United Jewish Welfare Fund (Toronto) File, Canadian Jewish Congress Archives, Montreal.

Zionist beginnings in Toronto, typescript resume, 5pp., n.d., author's collection.

INDEX

Note: The numbers given for each entry may refer to the first of several consecutive pages dealing with a particular entry.

Bund, The, 109
Bureau of Jewish Education, 312

Canadian Jewish Alliance, 268
Canadian Jewish Congress, 268,
  302, 331, 339
Canadian Jewish Review, 241
Canadian Order of Chosen
  Friends, 108
Caspar, Samuel, 13
Cemeteries, 16, 24, 112, 155
Central Butchers' Association,
  296
Charity Organization
  Movement, 156
Chebre Gemilas Chesed: See
  Ladies' Montefiore Hebrew
  Benevolent Society
Chesed Shel Emes: See Hebrew
  Free Burial Society
Child Care Services, 151, 267,
  274
Chona (Mosoff), 162
Christian attitudes towards
  Jews, 117, 122, 125
Christian Synagogue, The, 133
Christie Pits riots, 334
Church, Tommy, 252, 255
Cloakmakers' Union, 193
Cohen, Abraham, 261
Cohen, George W., 241
Cohen, Jacob (Butcher), 288, 302
Cohen, Magistrate Jacob, 191,
  193, 248, 249, 278, 322
Cohen, Mark G., 338
Communism – 1920s, 316
Community centre attempts,
  182, 184
Conference for Jewish War
  Sufferers, 269
Conference of Canadian Jews,
  269
Conservative Movement, 219,
  224

Cooper, Joseph, 174
Co-operative Relief Board, 158,
  264
Cosmopolitan Club: See
  Primrose Club
Court King David, 108

D'Arcy St. Talmud Torah: See
  Eitz Chaim Talmud Torah
Daughters of Zion, 181, 202
de Sola, Rabbi Abraham, 29
de Sola, Clarence I., 269
de Sola, Rabbi Meldola, 34, 53
Denison, Col. George Taylor,
  249
Depression – 1930s, 335
Dickman, Marcus, 280
Driscoll, Elizabeth, 19
Dunkelman, Rose, 242, 298
Dworkin, Dorothy Goldstick,
  151, 307
Dworkin, Henry, 191, 241, 257,
  262 f, 274 f
Dworkin's News Agency, 88,
  235

T. Eaton Company, 74, 192
Eaton's factory strike – 1912,
  193, 205
Edelstein, Hyman, 244
Education – ethnic divisions, 172
Education – Galician attempts,
  171
Education – secularist, 175
Education, Public – Religion In,
  64, 67, 320
Education, religious –
  nineteenth century, 60, 167
Education, religious – 1920s,
  310
Eisendrath, Rabbi Maurice N.,
  216, 242, 331
Eitz Chaim Talmud Torah, 174,
  312

378

Anshei Shidlof, 101
[Chevra Knesseth Israel]
  Anshei Slipia, 101
Anshei Stashov, 101
Beach Hebrew Institute
  (Beth Jacob), 114
Berkeley St. Shul (Bnai Israel
  Hamizrachim), 114
Beth Israel Anshei Minsk, 101,
  305
Beth Jacob (Poilisher Shul),
  304, 323
Beth Tzedec Congregation:
  See Goel Tzedec Congregation
  and McCaul St. Synagogue –
  separate entries
[Chevra] B'nai Avraham, 113
[Chevra] B'nai Israel (Shaw
  St.), 114
B'nai Sholom, 39
Chevra Techillim: See Beth
  Hamidrash Hagodol Chevra
  Tehillim – separate entry
Chevra Tomchei Shabbos,
  101, 104
Ezras Israel Anshei Apte, 101
Goel Tzedec: See separate
  entry
Hebrew Men of England, 101,
  304
Henry St. Synagogue:
  See Beth Jacob
Holy Blossom Congregation:
  See separate entry
Knesseth Israel (West Toronto
  Junction), 114
McCaul St. Synagogue: See
  Beth Hamidrash Hagodol
  Chevra Tehillim – separate
  entry
Machzikei HaDas (Teraulay
  St.), 101, 103, 247
Moldaver Congregation, 101
Narayever Congregation,

First, 101
Shaarei Tzedec (Russisher
  Shul), 113
Shomrai Shabboth:
  See separate entry
Synagogue – ethnic aspects, 102
Synagogue – role in communal
  life, 102, 104

Talmud Torah Association, 168
Tarbut Schools, 186
Taylor, Prof. W.R., 183
Theatre – Yiddish, 236, 238, 277
Toronto Hebrew Benevolent
  Association, 57, 107
Toronto Hebrew Congregation
  Pirchei Kodesh: See Holy
  Blossom Congregation
Toronto Hebrew Congregation
  Sons of Israel: See Holy
  Blossom Congregation
Toronto Hebrew Free School:
  See Brunswick Ave.
  Talmud Torah
Toronto Hebrew Ladies' Aid
  Society, 105, 146, 159
Toronto Hebrew Ladies' Sick
  and Benevolent Society:
  See Ladies' Montefiore
  Hebrew Benevolent Society
Toronto Hebrew Religion
  School: See Simcoe
  St. Talmud Torah
Toronto Hebrew Students'
  Association, 183
Toronto Jewish Congress, 342
Toronto Jewish Convalescent
  and Maternity Hospital:
  See Mount Sinai Hospital
Toronto Jewish Literary and
  Social Union, 59, 66
Toronto Jewish Weekly, 236
Toronto Public Library –